This book is dedicated to Ilona, Jessica and to the 'wee fella'

Contents

Preface

Introduction

The main reason for writing this book is to show how to apply object-oriented techniques to the solution of practical problems. In particular, the popular Object Modelling Technique (OMT) of Dr James Rumbaugh is applied and extended in such a way that it is possible to solve a problem by examining initial system requirements and producing a working system in some object-oriented language.

The emphasis in this book is on C++ because of its immense popularity, but the results presented here could be mapped to other object-oriented languages, such as Smalltalk, Eiffel and non-object-oriented languages, such as relational database systems and Visual Basic. This book will be of interest to practising software engineers, developers, programmers and project leaders who use OMT and who wish to follow the software life-cycle from concept to implementation. It is also aimed at university and technical college students. Numerous exercises and draft solutions are given for nearly every chapter and some of the exercises could serve as useful term projects.

Why this book?

Why should there be yet another book on C++? First of all, this book attempts to integrate all phases in the software life-cycle into a coherent whole. When I first started working with OOT in 1988 there were very few books on C++, let alone on analysis and design techniques. The situation has improved somewhat, but most books on C++ still tend to concentrate more on syntax and less on design issues, while books on OOA are too abstract and long-winded for many software practitioners. My main interest in software is in writing applications for computer-aided design, engineering and financial applications, and during the last few years we have discovered that the object-oriented paradigm is by no means a mature technology.

My main concern with many of the well-known methods (including OMT) is that there is little attention paid to cognitive issues, such as knowledge acquisition, and that there seems to be more emphasis on the more technical details, such as inheritance, state transitions, associations and the like. This book thus attempts to bridge the gap between the initial requirements phase (where the 'chaos' begins) and the analysis phase. Furthermore, we map the design deliverables to C++ and other languages.

Some of the examples in this book have been taken from the author's experience while working in the IT business during the last 15 years, and also from the in-house software development at Datasim, where our mission is to create reusable software components for the engineering and financial worlds. Many of our ideas are to be found in this book, and we are now embarking on second-generation OO development, having learned from our mistakes with prototypes in the early 1990s.

The future of OO

We are convinced of the usefulness of OOT. However, we are a bit worried about how it is being applied in the market-place. If you read the literature (especially commercial blurbs), you would think that successful application of this technology is very easy. Nothing could be further from the truth. It takes a lot of discipline, hard work and motivation to become a good OO designer or developer, and there are numerous pitfalls to be encountered and overcome. OO is not the 'silver bullet'; it is another step in the right direction.

The reasons why OO is better than classical approaches are usually not the ones that are promoted in the literature. In our opinion we see OO as a technology that enables us to implement good software practices, which have their roots in the 1970s, especially in the works of Parnas (information hiding) and Dijkstra (levels of abstraction). Nowadays, inheritance is seen as the 'wondermiddel' which will solve all our software ills and this assumption can lead in many cases to unreadable and unmaintainable code if applied incorrectly.

The future for OO looks good, but be careful. It is not enough to solve problems by writing C++ classes. A risk-driven software model in which rapid prototyping plays an essential role should be applied if we wish to avoid disappointments.

Acknowledgements

This book has developed over the last four years from the OOA/OOD courses that we gave throughout Europe. I wish to thank the many participants who helped to improve the quality of the material presented here. There are too many to mention, but I should like to thank especially the following: Mr Nahrwar from the Technical High School, Amsterdam, where the first OMT course was given, Gijs den Besten (DEC) for his valuable feedback, and my colleagues from Datasim. I also wish to thank the staff of McGraw-Hill for the patience they have shown me, especially in the early days when I was learning the ropes of becoming a professional writer.

Finally, I dedicate this book to my family, Ilona, Jessica and Brendan.

Dr Daniel Duffy
Keizersgracht 66
1015 CS Amsterdam
tel +31 20 6240055
fax +31 20 4200075
CompuServe 100116,475

Part 1

Object orientation

Chapter

1

Object-oriented fundamentals

1.1 Introduction and objectives

The main objective of this chapter is to explain what objects are. The approach taken will be independent of any object-oriented language and it is our intention to show how objects arise in the real world, how they can be categorized and how they interact with other objects.

There are many interpretations of how objects should be defined and explained. There is no universal standard definition of what an object is. However, the view taken in Booch (1991) that an object is defined by three characteristics will be described in Section 1.3. We consider this definition to be accurate and we adhere to it. We have also attempted to define as accurately as possible the most important concepts which arise in the object-oriented paradigm. It is hoped that this approach will help the beginner in understanding the real essentials of this technology.

This chapter avoids implementation details wherever possible. We adopt this approach because many books (especially those on object-oriented programming) pay little or no attention to the fundamentals which are essential for a smooth implementation. This chapter, therefore, attempts to make you aware of the difference between objects in a given application domain and how they are coded in a language such as Smalltalk or C++.

1.2 An introduction to objects

The object-oriented paradigm is more than 25 years old. The first object-oriented language was Simula 67, having been developed at the Norwegian Computing Centre (Pooley 1987). It did not become a commercial success but was instrumental in stimulating research and development in new languages. The most important language to arise in the 1970s and 1980s was Smalltalk (Goldberg and Robson 1983), and in the late 1980s the C++ language started gaining in prominence (Ellis and Stroustrup 1990). There are many commercial and academic object-oriented languages available at the moment of writing, but it is safe to say that C++ and Smalltalk are the two most popular and widespread, with C++ taking the lion's share of widespread acceptance in the industrial and business worlds.

Although object-oriented programming (OOP) techniques and compilers have been in existence for more than a quarter of a century it would be a mistake to believe that the whole phenomenon is new. Ancient philosophers, such as Plato and Aristotle, as well as modern philosophers like Immanuel Kant have been involved in explaining the meaning of existence in general and determining the essential characteristics of concepts and objects (Rand 1990). In more recent times Minsky has developed a theory of objects whose behaviour closely resembles processes which take place in the human mind (Minsky 1986). Finally, objects play an important role in education and cognitive science (Novak and Gowin 1984). In this case concepts are discovered by finding regularities in objects designated by some label. Concepts and concept mapping techniques play an important role in discovering the essential abstractions in a given problem domain and these techniques will be examined in Chapter 6.

What is an object? An object models a real-world or fake-world entity. Thus, anything we can think about, see, touch or quantify in some way is an object. We learn about objects in the real world by our ability to use the concept of quantity. Objects are 'real things' having crisp boundaries. Each object is unique. It is always possible to distinguish objects because each one has its own set of unique characteristics. Identifying objects is equivalent to looking for 'things':

> THING: Whatever we may see or touch, we represent the scene in terms of separate thing-objects. We do the same for representing processes and mental states. In languages, these object-symbols tend to correspond to nouns (Minsky 1986).

Objects are sometimes relatively easy to find, since they correspond to nouns in text, requirements documents and the spoken word. Finding the objects and their behaviour is the basic objective of object-oriented analysis and design. This topic will be more fully discussed in later chapters.

Examples of objects are: process number 1542, the point whose coordinates are (1,2), Tweedledum, Tweedledee, pump number 4, the personnel department, 'IBM System Journal' and C++. No two objects can be confused with each other. Even twins are distinguishable because each has his or her own identity. Determining identity for objects is context-sensitive and many human, physical and other factors play a role. For example, we can determine that one human being is not the same as another one by the use of sight. In C++ each object may be uniquely defined by its address in memory, while in object-oriented databases objects acquire permanent object identifiers (OIDs) which last for the lifetime of those objects. These identifiers can never be changed and only when the object goes out of existence will its identifier (or handle as it is sometimes called) be released.

To summarize:

- Objects have well-defined and crisp boundaries
- Objects are distinguishable: no two objects are the same

1.3 Defining the essential characteristics of objects

The discussion in Section 1.2 was very general in nature. In this section we treat objects using more precise terminology. Note that the following remarks and conclusions are applicable to objects from any application domain. In particular, the results can be mapped to 'software' objects. The advantage of an abstract approach is that implementation details are ignored, thus allowing us to concentrate on more relevant issues.

The essential characteristics of an object are (Booch 1991):

- Its state
- Its behaviour
- Its identity

We have already discussed the concept of object identity. Identity is the unique code which allows us to distinguish one object from any other object. Identity is implemented in software by a machine-readable ID; however, it can be more useful to use a human-understandable ID, such as a clock number or counter. The state of an object represents the set of data which holds information about that object. The state corresponds to an object's memory. In other words, the state holds the essential structure of the object and its current values. For example, the two-dimensional point in Cartesian space with coordinates (1,2) has a state whose structure consists of two numeric values, the first element of which represents the *x*-coordinate and having the current value 1, while the second element represents the *y*-coordinate and has the current value 2.

The behaviour of an object corresponds to the services that the object provides to so-called clients. Behaviour is roughly equivalent to how an object reacts to events from sources outside itself and how the object interacts with other objects. Determining behaviour is highly context-dependent. Clients view an object in different ways, and thus the object will behave according to the domain in which it is expected to function. In the above example for instance, the behaviour of a point in a computer-aided design (CAD) application will be different from its behaviour in some other application area where geometrical properties are less useful. In the former case, the behaviour of a point object could consist of the following operations:

- Finding the distance between the point and another point
- Transforming the point in some way (e.g. rotation)
- Returning the *x*- and *y*-coordinates of the point
- Giving the polar representation of the point

In fact, the behaviour of an object is similar to the set of so-called messages which can be sent to the object. We can think of a message as a request from a client to an object. The object in its turn provides services to clients. For example, objects representing line segments in two dimensions could use the services of points for request servicing. A typical example would be the message which is sent to a line segment to calculate its length. The length of a line is conceptually identical to calculating the distance between its end-points.

Note that arbitrary changes to the state of an object have no effect on its identity. In other words, the identity of an object is not determined by the values in the state. For example, it is possible to create two points having exactly the same coordinates. This does not mean that they are the same point!

It is possible to group objects which have similar behaviour. For example, all two-dimensional points react in the same way to outside events and messages. Rather than attempting to think of all possible points at the same time (which is impossible anyway!), we prefer to create a concept under which all such objects can be subsumed. This concept is called a class and it can be seen as a template for generating objects with similar structure and behaviour.

The Object Management Group (OMG) defines a class as follows:

> A class is an implementation that can be instantiated to create multiple objects with the same behaviour. An object is an instance of a class.

The distinction between a class and an object is not always obvious. A class is abstract, while an object is concrete. However, there are categories of classes (the so-called metaclasses) whose instances are not objects, but classes! This book assumes all class instances are objects unless otherwise stated. Examples of classes and instances are:

- Project (Apollo 9, Apollo 11, Desert Storm)
- Singer (Michael Jackson, Pavarotti, Bono)
- Journal (*IBM Systems Journal*, *C++ Report*, *Journal of Object-Oriented Programming*)

A server class is one which provides services to other classes. A client class is one which uses the services of some other class. A given class may be a server for a group of other classes, while at the same time it can be a client of others.

Examples of client and server classes are:

- A point is a server for a line segment
- A pump motor is a server for a pump
- A pump is a client of a pump motor
- A pump is a server for a pump assembly
- A histogram is a client of lines and points

We define the class interface as the complete implementation of the behaviour of the class. Thus, the interface corresponds to the methods which can be used by clients of the class. In some languages the term 'class protocol' is used instead of class interface. We tacitly speak of the public interface; however, it is possible to have operations which do not belong to this public interface but are hidden from clients. This could be called the private interface, and it is supported in C++ for example. It contains useful initialization operations which are only of relevance to the class in question.

1.4 Encapsulation and information hiding

We have seen that an object has state, behaviour and identity and these characteristics are sufficient to define it uniquely. State tends to be static, while behaviour is dynamic. We say that an object embodies an abstraction and that clients respect this abstraction. Clients have no direct access to the state of an object. This is called encapsulation. It is possible, however, to access the object's data indirectly via the services that it advertises to clients. For example, although it is not possible to access the x-coordinate of a point directly, a service could be created which allows clients to determine what the value is. The services which the object offers may, however, access the data directly (Figure 1.1). In this case we state that the state of an object is private to the object while its services are public.

The main advantage of encapsulation is that objects can be viewed as 'black' boxes. How an object organizes its internal data structure is not visible to clients. Furthermore, structural changes to the state should have no effect on clients. This means that we can change the implementation of an object without causing ripple effects in client objects. As an example, suppose that we wished to implement points in polar coordinates. In this new situation a point's state consists of data for representing the angle made with the x-axis and the point's distance from the origin. This change of representation has no impact on the object's services.

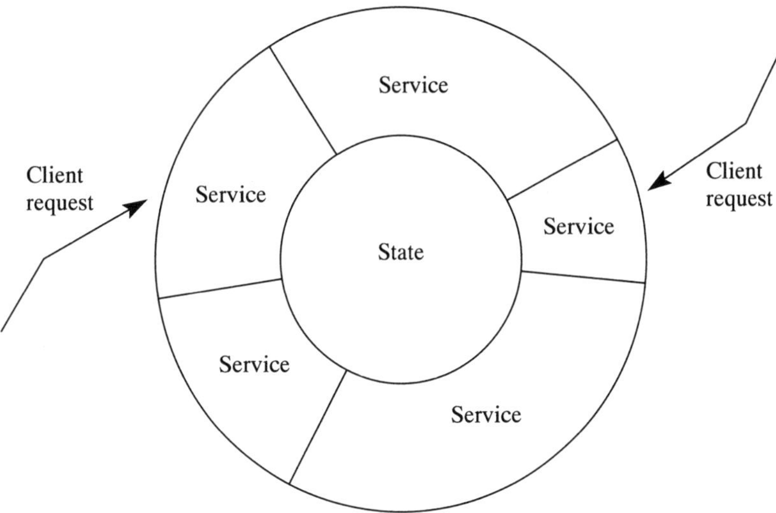

Figure 1.1 Encapsulation.

A generalization of encapsulation is called Information Hiding (Parnas 1972). Encapsulation applies specifically to objects, while information hiding is useful not only for objects but other software units, such as modules, systems and interfaces. We shall discuss this topic in more detail in later chapters.

1.5 Messages and methods

1.5.1 Categorizing messages and methods

An object's behaviour corresponds to the set of messages that can be sent to it. Messages are the same as the services which an object provides to its clients. Objects communicate by means of message passing. Methods, on the other hand are pieces of code (in a given object-oriented language) that implement messages. Corresponding to a given message there is a method which determines how a request is serviced. Methods may have direct access to the state of an object. It is useful to divide methods in groups according to what their influence is on the state of an object. The different types of methods are:

- *Constructors*
  These are methods which create new instances of a class. We say that 'an object is born' once a constructor method has been invoked. In object-oriented languages we say that a constructor converts raw memory into a structured object. It is possible to create new objects in different ways, hence many constructors can exist for a class.
- *Destructor*
  A destructor removes an object from memory. Some object-oriented languages (for example, Smalltalk) do not need destructors, since memory deallocation is automatically taken care of by a garbage collection mechanism, while other languages (for example, C++) do not have this facility so that the programmer must determine when an object should be removed from memory.

- *Selector*
  This is a method which does not change the state of an object. It can be seen as a 'read-only' operation. Selectors may involve objects from a number of classes.
  A selector method is sometimes called a preserver (Firesmith 1993).
- *Modifier*
  This is a method which changes the state of an object. It can be likened to a 'write' operation on the object data.

Constructors and destructors are special methods since the metaphor of sending messages to objects breaks down in these two cases. It is difficult to visualize a message being sent to an object in order to create or destroy another object. Rather, it is better to think of messages (so-called class methods) being sent to the class itself. Once an object has been created it then is possible to send messages directly to it.

We now give an example of a class which implements a counter abstraction in computer networks. A counter has a state consisting of a non-negative integer which monotonically increases to a given maximum value, from whence it wraps around and starts increasing again from zero.

We create a class COUNTER whose state contains some non-negative integer value. The syntax is loosely based on C++; for example the slashes '//' represent comments and the text representing functions is structured. It is more important at this stage to know what the class interface is in general terms than getting bogged down in the difficult syntax of C++ or some other language.

The methods which belong to this class are:

```
// Constructor
Create_default_counter(); // (maximum value = 256, for example)
Create_counter_with_a_given_maximum_value();

// Modifiers
increment();            // Increase the counter by 1
reset();                // Set the counter to 0

// Selectors
current();          // Give the current value of the counter
max_reached();      // Has the counter reached its maximum value?

// Destructor
// Remove object from memory
```

We see that it is possible to have more than one constructor for a given class. Note that the syntax for constructors and destructors is language-dependent, which is the reason that we have given only textual descriptions of what they do.

1.5.2 Instance and class properties (class descriptors)

It is possible to refine the concepts of object state and object methods. First, the state of an object is equivalent to its attributes and their corresponding values. Attributes come in two forms. Instance attributes are attributes whose values are specific to one particular object, while class attributes describe a value which is common to an entire object class. For example, suppose that the class HOURLY_EMPLOYEE represents employees who are paid on an hourly rate and that this rate is the same for all such personnel. Then an instance attribute would be the name of the employee (each employee has a name) while a class attribute would hold the value for the hourly wage rate and this would serve as a default value when creating new employee instances.

An instance method is a method which applies to one single object. This is the most usual situation in object-oriented programming. However, it is possible to 'send a message' to a class and the implementation of such a message is termed a class method (or sometimes, a class operation). A good example of a class method is the constructor method, as it applies to a class itself and not one of its instances.

1.6 Categorizing objects

Objects model different types of real-world (and virtual world) entities and concepts. For this reason we should be able to identify objects from various problem domains. Most objects can be allocated to one of the following categories (see Shlaer and Mellor (1988) for more information on these interesting categories):

- Tangibles
- Incidents (or events)
- Interactions
- Specifications
- Intangible objects
- Roles

These are the most important object categories, although it is possible to have more (Firesmith 1993).

Tangible objects are perhaps the easiest objects to identify in a given problem. These are objects which correspond to physical or real-world entities. They are labelled by a noun.

Examples of tangibles are:

- petrol pump, operating theatre, tank, vehicle, book

Incident or event objects model occurrences which happen at one moment in time. Such objects are very important since they model situations which arise in real or simulated worlds.

Examples of event objects are:

- accident, payment, appearance (of a journal), mouse click, flight, arrival

Incident objects play an important role in dynamic modelling, which will be discussed in Chapter 9.

Intangible objects model things which are not directly visible or tangible. They are what we could call 'conceptual entities'.

Examples are:

- street intersection, account, velocity, position

Interaction objects model interaction between other types of objects. They are 'glue' objects and they represent some type of contract between two or more autonomous objects.

Examples of interaction objects are:

- Circulation list (between a reader and issues of a journal)
- Enrolment (between student, course and grade)
- Any transaction between customer and vendor
- Reservation (at an airport)
- Operation (e.g. medical operation)
- Supervises (a professor supervises a student)

Interaction objects allow us to deal with structures as single things. In this way we treat an entire phrase as though it were a single word (Minsky 1986, p. 232). Furthermore, such objects will appear in later chapters when interaction objects are implemented by so-called associations in the object modelling technique (OMT).

Role objects can model persons in organizations. Examples of roles are:

- Customer, reader, employee, department, division, attendant, surgeon, nurse, patient

It is important to find roles when developing object-oriented software because a role can usually be defined in terms of a subclass of some primitive 'base' class. This leads to massive reusability benefits in the software process. Roles may be modelled in various ways.

Finally, specification objects define the quality of a standard or a definition. They correspond to metadata, which is data describing other data. In this sense they function as a blueprint or pattern for instances of things that meet the specification.

Examples of specification objects are:

- Car model, policy types, engineering drawing, catalogue

Exercises

1. We give a list of classes and a set of messages. Find the set of messages which can be naturally associated with each given class. In other words, enumerate those messages which can be sent to instances of each class.

   Classes: journal, issue of a journal, division (in a company), project, petrol pump, circulation list of a journal

   Messages:

   - Who is the publisher of 'C++ Report'?
   - Give start-date.
   - What is the name?
   - What is the duration?
   - When is the next issue of a journal due?
   - Initialize readings.
   - Allow a reader access to a journal.
   - List all the articles in an appearance of a journal.

2. A list of objects is given. Select the class to which each instance belongs.

Classes: set, array, sorted array, string, date

The objects are:

{1, 3, 8, –9, 10}

{1, 2, 7, 1, 9}

{1-1-1994, 2-7-1995, 5-8-1996}

{–23, 1, 3, 5, 8, 199}

{How, are, you}

{Hello, world}

{Bye, Bye}

All even numbers, that is {0, 2, –2, 4, –4, ...}

The world's capital cities

In some cases there may be more than one solution! For example, the collection {1, 200, 300, 989} can be simultaneously a set, an array or a sorted array.

3. An `EMPLOYEE` class has a structure consisting of a name, date-of-birth, salary and department and possibly other attributes. It provides the following services in its class interface:

   (a) Create a new employee

   (b) Give all details about an employee

   (c) Give a raise in salary

   (d) Move the employee to another department

   (e) Give the age of the employee

   (f) Which department does an employee work for?

   Find the constructors, selectors and modifiers in the above list of methods.

4. Find the structure and the corresponding methods for the following classes which can be used in three-dimensional computer graphics applications: point, line segment, circle, arc, polyline.

   Identify server and client classes.

5. Many business, scientific and engineering applications need to represent information in graphical form. In particular, line charts, histograms and pie charts are popular techniques for representing data. What are the server classes which would be needed if you had to write a system for displaying data in one of the above three forms?

6. Identify server and client classes in the following groups of classes. The answer depend in many cases on the context and most classes are either servers or clients. For example, an issue is a client of a journal because it is an appearance of a journal and thus 'knows' about it.

   - journal, issue, reader, article, topic
   - department, division, project, worker
   - time, day, date, month, minutes, hours, timestamp, duration

- Operating theatre, surgeon, senior surgeon, nurse, patient, ward

7. Propose at least two different ways of representing the state for instances of the following classes: dates, three-dimensional points, bank account.

8. Categorize the following classes according to the types which were treated in Section 1.6 (tangible, specification etc.):

   license, velocity, temperature, accident, flight, account, position, location (e.g. street intersection), project, petrol tank, delivery, circulation list, rectangle, direction, transaction, catalogue, architectural drawing, visit, enrolment, student, reader

9. It is possible to have different views of an object. An object will 'present' itself in different ways, depending on which aspects we deem to be important. To take an example we consider the case of a motor car. Which attributes and methods are of relevance to the following people and organizations:

   - The owner of the car
   - The garage which repairs the car
   - The bank which gave a loan for the purchase of the car
   - The tax and insurance policies on the car

10. Find a reasonable behaviour pattern for the following role objects: doctor, nurse, reader, worker, customer, petrol pump attendant, surgeon, senior surgeon. (Remark: there are different kinds of reader, e.g. at a college/university or a reader of a book.)

References

G. Booch (1991) *Object-Oriented Design: with Applications*, Benjamin Cummings, Menlo Park CA.

M. Ellis and B. Stroustrup (1990) *The C++ Annotated Reference Manual*, Addison-Wesley, Reading MA.

D. G. Firesmith (1993) *Object-Oriented Requirements Analysis and Logical Design*, John Wiley & Sons, New York.

A. Goldberg and D. Robson (1983) *Smalltalk-80, The Language and its Implementation*, Addison-Wesley, Reading MA.

M. Minsky (1986) *The Society of Mind*, Touchstone Books, New York.

J. D. Novak and D. B. Gowin (1984) *Learning How to Learn*, Cambridge University Press, Cambridge.

D. L. Parnas (1972) On the criteria to be used in decomposing systems, *Communications of the ACM*, **15**(12).

R. J. Pooley (1987) *An Introduction to Programming in Simula*, Blackwell Scientific Publications, Oxford.

A. Rand (1990) *Introduction to Objectivist Epistemology*, Meridian Books, New York.

S. Shlaer and S. J. Mellor (1988) *Object-Oriented Systems Analysis, Modelling the World in Data*, Yourdon Press, Englewood Cliffs NJ.

Chapter

2

Advanced object-oriented concepts

2.1 Introduction and objectives

This chapter introduces and examines the most important concepts which will be needed when analysing, designing and implementing systems using object-oriented techniques. Most of the concepts which are introduced here can be mapped onto C++. For this reason it is important to have a clear understanding before embarking on writing C++ code.

2.2 Abstract data types

2.2.1 Background to abstract data types

An abstract data type (or ADT for short) is an encapsulation of data and operations on that data. The study of ADTs has been used as the starting point for the development of a number of languages which support the class construct. Many object-oriented languages, such as Simula, Eiffel and C++ are based on implementation of ADTs (Meyer 1988; Pooley 1987; Ellis and Stroustrup 1990). Other non-object-oriented languages also implement ADTs. Modula-2, for example, used the module to this end, while Ada implements the feature using packages.

The advantages of studying ADTs are:

- They capture the essential properties of data types.
- They can be used as specifications for the construction of classes in C++.
- They promote the use of good software engineering practices.

When designing and implementing classes in a language such as C++, beginners tend to concentrate on low-level details such as how the states of objects are implemented and how the class interface should be created. This approach can lead to overspecification. It is better to treat the problem at a higher level of abstraction and to take the view of creating an ADT which can be later implemented in C++. In this way we ensure that software quality criteria, such as correctness and robustness, are carried through to implementation. An ADT is mathematically complete and correct.

Using ADTs to specify the behaviour of structures has a number of advantages for the software designer. First, the specification mechanism is declarative, which means that programming details and language dependencies can be ignored. Secondly, they are relatively easy to understand. Finally, they are sufficiently rigorous to permit a proof that a given implementation fulfils the specifications.

Classes in C++ can and should be considered as implementations of abstract data types.

2.2.2 Specification of an ADT

An ADT consists of two parts. The first part is a syntactic specification, while the second part consists of a set of so-called axioms. The syntactic specification contains information on the names, domains and ranges associated with the type, while the axioms define the meaning of the operations by stating the relationships between them.

In order to explain an ADT mathematically we first of all need to define a number of terms. Suppose that A and B are two arbitrary sets. The Cartesian product of two sets A and B is defined as a set of pairs of the form (a,b) with a in A and b in B. Formally this is represented as:

A×B = {(a,b): a in A, b in B}

The Cartesian product can be extended to any number of sets. The second concept that is needed for an understanding of ADTs is the mapping or function (Landin 1969). A mapping f is a relationship between elements of two sets A and B. The set A is called the domain of f while B is called the range of f. A mapping is a subset of A×B and the following are true:

domain(f) = {a: for some b in B, (a,b) is in f}
range(f) = {b: for some a in A, (a,b) is in f}

We sometimes denote a mapping between A and B in the form :

f: A → B

It is possible to combine functions. If f is a mapping from A to B and g is a mapping from B to C the combined mapping fg (apply f and then g) is a mapping from A to C. This notion is needed when we discuss the axiomatic part of an ADT. Axioms state the relationships between the functions of an ADT.

We consider the example of a Set ADT. A Set is a collection of unordered objects with no external keys. The elements in a Set are unique; this means that no duplicates are allowed. This definition would make the collection {1, 4, 7, 8} a Set, but not the collection {1, 4, 7, 8, 1}, since the value 1 is duplicated. We assume that the elements of the Set belong to a general date type T.

The syntactic specification is given by the following operations:

new:		→ Set
add:	Set × T	→ Set
remove:	Set × T	→ Set
empty:	Set	→ Boolean

The axioms for Set state the semantic relationships between the operations. For example:

(a)	empty(new)	== TRUE
(b)	empty(add(s, t))	== FALSE
(c)	add(remove(s, t), t)	== remove(add(s, t), t)

Axiom (a) states that a newly created Set is always empty while (b) states that a Set is never empty if an element has been added to it. In this case we assume that s is a Set instance and t is an element of T. Axiom (c) states that the order in which a new element is added to or removed from a Set is not important.

The main objective of using axioms is to create a consistent and sufficiently complete definition of an ADT. ADTs are later implemented by C++ classes, and the axioms can be used in order to make the code robust. There is no need to test the validity of axioms in the code since they are always true.

Associated with each ADT operation are zero or more related preconditions. A precondition is a constraint which must be satisfied if the operation is to function properly. For the Set ADT some preconditions are:

- Add an element: the element must not already be in the set.
- Remove an element: the element must be in the set.

Preconditions are very important and they have been implemented in a number of programming languages, notably Eiffel, where the notion of 'Programming by Contract' plays a central role (Meyer 1988). The contract is an agreement between two parties, the supplier and consumer. Each party has its own set of rights and responsibilities. In practice, the contract is usually broken by the consumer. For example, removing an element from a Set in which the element is not a member is seen as a violation of the precondition associated with the 'remove' function. If this situation occurs we can conclude that the contract has been broken. In practice an exception should be raised.

Preconditions and postconditions describe the properties of individual operations. There is a need to express global properties of ADT instances which must be preserved at all times. These are called ADT invariants. They can be implemented in object-oriented languages and in this case they are known as class invariants. Examples of invariants are:

- The number of employees in a department must be positive.
- A petrol tank must never go below 4% capacity.
- The number of elements in a set must always be non-negative.

2.2.3 Mapping ADTs to generic classes in C++

An ADT is, as its name implies, an abstract description of a set of values and the operations on those values. The internal state of an ADT is hidden from clients and no implementation details are used. In practice, we need to map an ADT to an implementation in C++. Since an ADT depends on a generic data type T we propose to implement it in C++ by a template. Templates are a new feature in C++ and a part of the proposed ANSI C++ standard, but not all compiler vendors support the feature at the time of writing. The rules for migrating from ADTs to C++ templates are:

(2.1)

- The ADT will be a C++ template with the same name.
- Choose a C++ data type to implement the other types which appear in the ADT.

- The operations in the ADT will become the C++ interface.
- The structure of the template class needs to be nailed down to specific data types.
- Preconditions will be implemented in the body of the member functions.
- Violations of preconditions and invariants should result in exceptions, which are to be processed by suitable handlers.

Since an ADT has no visible structure we need to design the state for its implementation. How to do this depends on the ADT. We shall see an example of this below. Furthermore, violations of preconditions can and should be considered as part of the C++ interface and the corresponding code should 'raise' or 'throw' an exception in this case. We shall treat exceptions and exception handling in a number of chapters in this book. Choosing to include exceptions as part of the software engineering process is important (Pyle 1985) and it has been used in class interface descriptions by a number of authors (Firesmith 1993). It is expected that the trend will be adopted by the C++ community now that exceptions are on the verge of becoming part of the C++ standard.

To take a simple example, we create an ADT representing a one-dimensional array whose values are from the generic type T. We give this ADT the name `ARRAY<T>`, where `<T>` denotes the fact that the underlying elements belong to the type `T`. Each operation (or function) associated with the ADT has a name, a set of input types (called the domain) and a possible return type (called the range). For example, the function for indexing in `ARRAY<T>` is denoted as follows:

(2.2)

index: ARRAY × Integer → T

This reads as: the function `index` has as domain a value from `ARRAY` and an `Integer` value. The range of the function is a value from type `T`. This is a mathematical way of stating something which is probably very familiar to C++ programmers; Equation (2.2) is an abstract way of declaring a member function in a template class representing arrays of objects. The implementation of Equation (2.2) could take a number of forms depending on how the ADT `Integer` is to be implemented in the language. One possible declaration is as follows:

(2.3)

T index(const ARRAY<T>& arr, size_t index);

Instead of using the `size_t` data type we could have used other built-in types for integers. Each choice results in a separate class implementation for `ARRAY`. We see from this example that a single ADT may be used to generate several implementations. In general the relationship between an ADT and its implementation in C++ is one-to-many.

The set of functions associated with `ARRAY<T>` are:

- new — create a new ARRAY of a given length
- count — count the number of elements in the array
- index — retrieve an object at a given position
- copy — make a copy of an array

The formal specification for these functions is as follows:

new:	Integer	→ ARRAY
count:	ARRAY	→ Integer

index:	ARRAY × Integer	→ T
copy:	ARRAY	→ ARRAY

There is one precondition associated with the function `index` which states that the `Integer` value used to access an element in the array must be between the upper and lower array limits. This condition must be checked in any implementation of `index` and an exception should be raised if the range is violated (this would be a so-called `RANGE_ERROR`).

Applying the rules in (2.1) to `ARRAY<T>` and choosing to implement the generic type `Integer` by the C++ built-in type `size_t` we arrive at the following template declaration in C++:

```
template <class T> class ARRAY
{

private:                     // Implementing the state of the array

  T* val;                    // A pointer to an element of T
  size_t size;               // The size of the array

public:                      // The public interface

// Constructors, implementations of 'new' in the ADT spec
ARRAY(size_t size);             // Array of a given size

// Selectors
size_t count() const;           // Number of elements in array
T index(size_t i) const;        // Indexing function
ARRAY copy() const;             // Copy of current element

// New selectors which are not in original ADT spec
size_t min_index() const;       // Start index of array
size_t max_index() const;       // End index of array

};  // End of template class declaration
```

In practice the definition (or body) for each of the above methods will need to be given in a separate file. We leave the details of this to Chapter 18, where a number of template classes will be designed and implemented.

Information on ADTs may be found in Guttag (1977), Guttag and Horning (1978), Guttag *et al.* (1978) and Liskov and Zilles (1975). Meyer (1988) implements ADTs in the Eiffel language and is worthwhile reading.

2.3 Classes and types

2.3.1 Are classes the same as types?

We have already discussed the class concept in Chapter 1. Classes are a means of grouping objects according to a common implementation. The concepts of type and class are very similar, but there are subtle differences between them. The notion of type is derived from languages which implement abstract data types. A type characterizes the behaviour of its instances by describing the operations that can manipulate those objects. Thus, types classify objects according to a common interface, while classes classify objects according to a common implementation. Types are sets of objects.

Examples of types are the set of all integers, a bank account and a window. Each type has a corresponding implementation which is usually a class with the same name. The type corresponds to an external view, while the implementation describes how the objects of that type are represented and how each operation is actually implemented in terms of that representation. For example, the type `POINT` represents a point in two-dimensional space. Operations exist for creating new points, finding the distance between two points and so on. However, how we represent the objects of the type is not given. This is the responsibility of the class which implements the type. We choose to represent each object by two numeric values; the interface for the class `POINT` is as follows (where we use C++ notation):

```
class POINT
{

private:
  double xcoord;              // First coordinate of point
  double ycoord;              // Second coordinate of point

public:
// Constructors
POINT();
POINT(double x, double y);

// Selectors
double dist() const;                      // Distance from origin
double dist(const POINT& p2) const;       // Distance from p2

// ... Other functions

};
```

The class interface usually contains more functions than the interface for the corresponding type. They are necessary in order to implement the external view of the type.

To summarize, type specifications represent the external view of a given type, which describes what is being represented, while the implementation of a type (namely, a class) is an internal view describing how objects of that type are represented and how the operations are actually implemented in terms of that representation.

2.3.2 Subtyping

It is possible to specify individual types without regard for other types. However, there are natural relationships between types. One of these is called subtyping. We say that a type `T1` is a subtype of type `T2` if every instance of `T1` is also an instance of `T2`. `T2` is sometimes called a supertype of `T1`. This definition implies that an instance of `T1` can be used whenever an operation of some other construct expects an instance of type `T2`. For example, the type `AUTOMOBILE` is a subtype of the type `VEHICLE` and the set of positive integers is a subtype of the set of all integers. Positive integers can be used in integer operations such as addition and multiplication.

The ability to use instances of subtypes in operations where instances of the supertype is expected is called substitutability.

The substitutability principle has far-reaching consequences for software development using object-oriented languages. In particular, the inheritance mechanism which is supported in languages such as C++ and Smalltalk allows classes to share states and operations based on relationships which are similar to the supertype–subtype relationship.

Since subtyping is defined in terms of behaviour, we view subtyping as a behavioural hierarchy. Classes, on the other hand implement types, and this can entail operations in the implementation of a supertype being implemented in a different way for the implementation of the subtype. To take an example, consider a project management environment for allocating, monitoring and updating resources. The supertype `PROJECT` has operations for calculating the status of a project, the resources needed to finish the project and what resources are available. The subtype `INTERNAL_PROJECT` represents the set of projects which are funded by a given organizational unit in a company. Each instance of `INTERNAL_PROJECT` behaves as if it is also an instance of `PROJECT`. However, the implementations of the above operations may be completely different for `PROJECT` and `INTERNAL_PROJECT`. This is why we say that types are classified according to a common behaviour, while the corresponding classes are classified according to a common implementation.

The process of subtyping is used to organize types in system development.

2.4 A closer look at object identity

Object identity can be a difficult topic to understand. However, it plays a vital role in object-oriented system development. For this reason we have devoted a section to explaining what it is and how it is implemented in various languages.

2.4.1 Why is object identity important?

We saw in Chapter 1 that one of the essential defining properties of an object was its identity. Every object is unique, and it is always possible to distinguish it from other objects. How this is done in practice depends on the context. In particular, different phases in the software life-cycle approach the problem of determining and saving object identity in different ways. Relational database systems, for example, use combinations of attribute values in order to make 'objects' unique. Object-oriented database systems (OODBMS) use object-identifiers which are immutable and which uniquely determine every object. Some object-oriented languages use memory addresses or variable names in order to define identity.

Identity is an intrinsic property and it should always remain internal to an object for the complete lifetime of that object.

The lifetime of an object determines whether it is transient or persistent. A transient object is one which does not survive the lifetime of the program or block in which the object is defined. A persistent object is one which does survive after the program in which it is defined has finished executing. The consequence is that the same object can be reused in future invocations of the program. Examples of transient objects are class instances in C++. These are transient because C++ does not support functionality for saving objects in permanent storage. It is possible to 'tack-on' extra functionality to C++ so that objects can be saved and retrieved in a transparent fashion. We speak of a persistent extension to C++, and it is usually delivered in the form of a persistent object database. Some examples of these systems will be discussed in Chapter 17. Finally, object-oriented database systems allow the programmer to combine programming techniques in C++ with database capabilities so that user-defined objects can be easily stored and retrieved for processing.

2.4.2 Object identity and independence

Object identity should be an intrinsic property of an object and it should not depend on any external entities or factors. To this end, we state a number of ideal states which we would like to have. It is not always possible to achieve these states in practice, although some systems do support them. They are:

- Location independence: an object's identity should be preserved under the changes in physical location. This means, for example, that disk addresses may not be used for implementing object identity.
- Structure independence: an object's identity should not depend on its structure. For instance, adding or removing an object attribute should not affect its identity. This rules out many relational database systems.

The above rule should hold for both persistent and transient data.

- Value independence: an object's identity should be preserved in the face of changes in attributes.

Most traditional programming languages and database systems fail to satisfy all three of the above ideals. Object-oriented database systems do, however, support them.

2.4.3 Implementing object identity

There are several ways of implementing object identifiers. Not all solutions are acceptable, because they can lead to situations which could leave a database in an inconsistent state. The most important techniques for implementing object identity are the following:

(2.4)

- By addresses
- By identifier keys
- By the use of so-called surrogates

We examine each of the techniques in (2.4) and we give examples of where they are used.

Identity using addresses This is the technique which is used in most programming languages, for example C++. An object's identity in C++ is determined by an address in memory. This implementation breaks the location independence rule since the mechanism does not allow us to move an object while still preserving its identity. Smalltalk implements objects rather differently than C++. Instead of virtual address space, each object has a pointer which is an entry in a so-called object table (this is called identity through indirection). The pointer is sometimes called 'oops' (an object-oriented pointer).

Identity using identifier keys This is the standard technique used in many database management systems. Identity is implemented by the use of unique keys. In relational database modelling an identifier key is formed from one or more attributes and this key is unique for all objects in the table. For example, a table representing a person has a key which is formed by the combination first name/last name. What happens if there are two people with the same first and last names?

The main disadvantages of using keys are:

(2.5)

- They cannot be changed without compromising integrity.
- The types representing keys are non-uniform.

The first condition in (2.5) can be violated in many situations. Think of a person who changes his or her name. This implies that all references to that name must be changed in the entire database. The second problem in (2.5) refers to the fact that different data types (such as integer, data and string) can be used as identifiers. This leads to non-uniformity in how different objects are accessed and manipulated.

Identity using surrogates Surrogates are system-generated and globally unique identifiers which are defined independently of an object's state or address. A surrogate is generated as soon as an object is born and it remains latched to the object for the lifetime of that object.

As in the Smalltalk approach, indirection is used in order to find the object based on its surrogate value. However, surrogates are unique throughout the system. They cannot be changed by users. In fact, users will not even be aware of their existence.

We can thus conclude that surrogates satisfy the location independence principle.

Object-oriented database management systems use surrogates to reference and identify objects. This topic is discussed in Chapter 17.

Good overviews of what object identity is and how it is implemented can be found in Kent (1991) and Khoshafian and Copeland (1986).

2.5 Specialization, generalization and inheritance

Inheritance, specialization and generalization are interrelated concepts which are much used in the literature on object-oriented development. The objective of this section is to define these as accurately as possible and to show when and how they can be used. A number of illustrative examples are given.

2.5.1 Specialization and generalization

Given a class B it is possible to create a so-called specialization D of it which has all the properties of B (state and operations), but which may have its own extra state and operations.

We say that there is an inheritance link between B and D; this link is often called an 'IS-A' or 'ISA' and we say that D is a specialization of B. This means that every instance of D behaves as if it were also an instance of B. The specialization process is usually one of invention; we start with a given class and we progressively produce more specialized versions of it. This is the practice which is used and advocated in many books on C++.

Examples of specialization are:

- An hourly employee ISA employee.
- A triangle ISA polygon.
- An internal project ISA project.

- A reader is a person.
- A camel is a kind of mammal.
- Clyde is an elephant.

Generalization is the opposite of specialization. We say that if D is a specialization of B then B is a generalization of D. In other words the so-called superclass B (or base class in C++) is a generalization of the subclass D (or derived class). The process of generalization is one of discovery; given a class it takes time to discover if there is a suitable superclass for it and what the properties of that class are.

Looking at the above list we might have the impression that there are many 'kinds' of ISA links. The main problem in this case is that ISA links have been used to represent a range of things, for example, sets, concepts, descriptions, propositions, individuals and prototypes. It is the objective here to show the different variations that are possible with ISA hierarchies. In general we have an ISA link between nodes. The question to be answered is what role the nodes play in the different scenarios which we ncw treat.

The ISA link can mean any one of the following:

- Subset/superset relations. In this case the nodes represent sets. Examples are: an internal project ISA project, a sophisticated pump ISA pump, a consultant ISA surgeon.
- Generalization/specialization. Generalization expresses a relation between predicates.
- AKO ('a kind of'). This is similar to generalization but it implies 'kind' status for the nodes that it connects. Examples of AKO relations are: a manager is AKO employee, a snake is AKO reptile, a nurse is AKO staff.

In many cases the generic type in AKO links is 'abstract' in the sense that no instances of that type can be created. For example, it is not possible to identify a specific reptile, only special cases, such as snake, lizard and iguana.

- Conceptual containment. This expresses the fact that one description includes another one. For example, the relation 'A rectangle is a polygon' is the same as 'A rectangle is a polygon with four sides'.
- Role value restriction. Examples are: a manager is an employee with a large salary, the trunk of an elephant is a cylinder 1.3 m long. This is not a taxonomic relationship, since there is no reference to supertype or subtype.

It is also possible to have generic/individual relations. This is called 'instantiation'. The possibilities are:

- Set inclusion. An individual belongs to a certain set. For example, Clyde is an elephant, 'IBM Systems Journal' is a journal.
- Predication. This is basically a predicate stating whether an individual is a member of the generic, for example, Journal('IBM Systems journal').
- Conceptual containment. This relates an individual node with its generic. An example is 'project' and 'Manhattan project', where the generic is used to construct the individual description. In this case 'project' is the generic node and 'Manhattan project' is the more specific node.
- Abstraction. This is a relation which goes from the individual to the generic. In this case the generic type is constructed. An example is 'the Division is responsible for

projects'. In this case the Division is the corresponding type. This situation arises frequently in natural language analysis of text in order to discover the main abstractions and concepts.

The above considerations play a major role when we wish to represent knowledge in semantic networks. We shall use some of the results developed when concept mapping techniques are discussed in Chapter 6.

2.5.2 Single and multiple inheritance

In general terms we can view inheritance as an implementation of generalization. The mechanism allows classes to share attributes and operations based on the generalization relationship. If class D is a specialization of class B we say that D inherits from B. In C++ we say that B is a base class and that D is a derived class. These terms will be used from now on in this chapter and the chapters which follow. Saying that D is a derived class of B means that an instance of D behaves as an instance of B. It is possible to add state and behaviour to D which is specific to the new situation.

There are two forms of inheritance that are supported in a number of object-oriented languages. They are:

- Single inheritance
- Multiple inheritance

Single inheritance occurs when a given class has only one base class. With multiple inheritance, on the other hand, a given class may have two or more base classes. Single inheritance is by far the most common form of inheritance, but multiple inheritance does find applications in the literature.

The literature on object-oriented techniques would tend to suggest that constructing inheritance hierarchies should be the main objective. C++ neophytes try to find classes which can be derived from other classes. Often the design is incorrect and a situation arises whereby the resulting code becomes unmanageable and difficult to understand. So, be careful using inheritance when writing applications! Using inheritance correctly in C++ will be discussed in Chapter 18, but we state the main guidelines and tips:

(2.6)

- Avoid deep inheritance hierarchies.
- Are you using inheritance correctly?
- Multiple inheritance is not necessary in 95% of cases.
- Inheritance is sometimes used to fix errors in design.
- Code using deep hierarchies can be difficult to understand.
- Inheritance increases coupling between classes.

A number of solutions and implementation strategies are given in this book which should help you to avoid many of the pitfalls which can result in an incorrect usage of inheritance in C++.

2.5.3 Inheritance scenarios

When deriving a new class D from an existing class B there are various strategies which can be chosen. In general, the derived class specializes and/or extends the base class. Instances of the derived class behave just like instances of the base class, but they have behaviour which is not shared with the parent. The different scenarios are:

(2.7)

- Extra state is added to D.
- New methods are added to D.
- Methods in B may need to be redefined for efficiency reasons.
- 'Default' methods in B can be accessed by instances of B.

We see from these scenarios that it is possible to extend classes in different ways. Which combination of scenarios in (2.7) to choose from depends on the design decisions that we have made and what functionality is needed. To take an example, consider the class `POLYGON`, which represents a general polygon with *n* sides. We assume that the state consists of an array of points and that the class offers the following general services:

- Finding the area of the polygon, method `area()`.
- Finding the total length of all sides of the polygon, method `length()`.

We wish to define a `TRIANGLE` class as a derived class of `POLYGON`. This is an example of the conceptual containment principle explained in Section 2.5.1 ('a triangle is a polygon with three sides'). It is known from the documentation (or from experience) that the algorithm for calculating the area of a general polygon is not very efficient and we would prefer to use a simpler formula when calculating the area of a triangle. Furthermore, we want to create a method in `TRIANGLE` for calculating the centre of gravity. Based on the above observations, we describe the interface of the new `TRIANGLE` class:

- No extra state is needed in `TRIANGLE`.
- The `area()` needs to be rewritten (overriding method).
- The default method `length()` is inherited from `POLYGON`.
- The new method `centre_gravity()` for calculating the centre of gravity needs to be created for `TRIANGLE`.

The relationship derived class – base class – is a special example of a client/server relationship. We thus see that a certain amount of coupling is introduced by deriving one class from another one. Carried to extremes, this process can lead to code that is difficult to understand, since we must always be 'looking up' to the base class to see which properties are inherited. This presents major problems, especially in very deep inheritance hierarchies.

2.6 Aggregation

Aggregation is the 'part–whole' relationship, and it states the relationship between an object and its constituent components. Aggregations can be discovered from English-language descriptions by words such as 'consists of', 'is part of' and 'has a'. We speak of an object (the so-called aggregate or composite) as consisting of a fixed or variable number of other objects (its so-called components).

An aggregate class is defined as a class whose structure consists of one or more 'simpler' objects. Examples of aggregate classes are:

(2.8)

- Polygons (a list of connected points)
- Dates (consist of a day, month and year)
- Timestamps (consist of a date and a time)
- Issues of journals (consist of articles)
- A company division (consist of departments)
- A binary tree (consists of other trees)

The aggregations which appear in (2.8) can be categorized. Three general classes of aggregates can be signalled (Rumbaugh *et al.* 1991):

- *Fixed aggregates*
  These are aggregates which consist of a fixed number of components. The structure is thus fixed. Examples of fixed aggregates are classes for dates, timestamps and petrol pump assemblies.
- *Variable aggregates*
  A variable aggregate consists of a finite number of components, but the actual number may vary. A good example of a variable aggregate is a class representing stacks. The total number of elements in a stack may vary because of pop and push operations. Other examples are queues, lists and a class representing an employee database. The number of employees in a company database varies depending on the workload and recruiting policy.
- *Recursive aggregates*
  The state of an aggregate object may have components of the same type. A good example of a recursive aggregate is that of a class which represents papers which are published in journals. A paper may refer to other papers. This type of reference appears in the structure of the class. In C++ the interface of a `PAPER` class would appear as follows:

```
class PAPER
{
private:

  PAPER* references;      // Papers which are referred to by
                          // the current paper
public:

  // ... Methods here

};
```

Another good example of a recursive data structure is the ubiquitous binary tree. Its structure in pseudo-C++ is:

```
class BINARYTREE
{ // Simple binary tree of integers
```

```
private:

  TNODE* node_info;

public:

  // Public interface to be specified

};
```

where the class TNODE has the structure

```
class TNODE
{ // 'Help' class for BINARYTREE

private:

  int val;       // The value at the given node
  TNODE* right;  // Pointer to right subtree
  TNODE* left;   // Pointer to left subtree

public:

  // To be specified

};
```

Just as there are many kinds of ISA relationships we have come to realize the same conclusion holds for the 'part–whole' relationship. There are different ways in which whole-part associations can be formed and we discuss what these are and what the pitfalls are so that 'real' aggregation is not confused with associations between independent entities.

The main kind of association are (Odell 1994; Winston *et al.* 1987):

- Component–integral object
- Material–object
- Portion–object
- Place–area
- Member–bunch
- Member–partnership

The component–integral aggregation defines a configuration of parts within a whole. This is a very common form of aggregation and it occurs in many applications. Examples are:

- A petrol pump consists of a display and a gun.
- A polyline consists of ordered lines.
- A cash-flow consists of dates and money amounts.
- A project consists of activities (sub-projects).

In all of the above cases we note that the parts have a functional or structural relationship to one another. For example, in the petrol pump example the petrol which flows through the nozzle of the gun component is registered in the display component. Each component is an object in its own right.

We say that the integral object representing the petrol pump is divided into its component parts.

The main properties of the component–integral aggregation are:

- Components bear a functional or structural relationship to one another and to the object that they are part of.
- Components can be removed from the integral part.

Material–object aggregation is similar to component–integral object aggregation except that in this case parts cannot be removed without destroying the integrity of the integral part. We say that the aggregation relationship defines an invariant configuration of parts within a whole. Examples are:

- An issue of a journal consists partly of articles.
- A car is partly iron.

Material–object relationships define what objects are made of. The integral object is in general different from its parts and the parts are also different from each other.

Portion–object aggregation relationships define an integral object in which the components are of the same type as the whole. Examples are:

- A sip of coffee is a part of coffee.
- A metre is part of a kilometre.

Note that each part or piece in a portion–object aggregation can be removed without destroying the integrity of the integral part.

Place–area aggregation is similar to the aggregation just presented, except in this case the pieces cannot be removed. Examples are:

- Amsterdam is part of Holland.
- A peak is part of a mountain.

Member–bunch aggregation relationships define a collection of parts which form a whole. There are no restrictions on the functional or structural relationships between the component parts. The only requirement is that the parts be members of some collection. In this sense member–bunch aggregations are similar to sets of parts. Examples are:

- A worker is part of a department.
- A department is part of a division.

Member–partnership aggregations are special member–bunch aggregations in which parts may not be removed. Examples are:

- Joe and Mary are married to each other.
- Lennon is part of Lennon and McCartney.

As noted in Odell (1994), aggregation can be confused with other kinds of relationships. This confusion is seen in all phases of the software life-cycle. In particular, many C++ classes are implemented on the assumption that they are aggregations.

The other types of relationships are:

- Topological inclusion
- Classification inclusion
- Attribution
- Attachment
- Ownership

These relationships are so-called associations, which will be discussed in Chapter 8 when the object modelling technique (OMT) is discussed. An aggregation is a special type of association. In other words, every aggregation is an association, but not every association is an aggregation.

Topological inclusion is a relationship between a temporal duration, container or spatial area and the object which is contained within it. Examples are:

- The petrol is in the petrol pump.
- November is in the autumn.
- A building is in an industrial estate.

Topological inclusion is often confused with place–area composition. For example, an issue is part of a journal, but the journal does not contain the issue.

Classification inclusion has already been discussed in Section 2.5 and is based on the idea that there is a common concept between two objects. It is similar to the member–bunch aggregation, but the latter concept is determined by spatial, temporal or social connection.

An object's attributes should not be confused with aggregation. For example, the colour and linestyle of a rectangle in a Windows environment can be considered as being part of the properties of the rectangle, but the properties are not part of the rectangle. There are in fact mappings from rectangles to other objects.

Attachment of one object to another object does not imply aggregation. Attachment is a special type of association in which one object is dependent in some way on another one. For example, toes are attached to feet but they are not part of feet.

Ownership relationships may be found by noting occurrences of 'has a'. Examples of ownership relationships are:

- A reader has an issue of a journal.
- An article has topics.
- Joe has a bicycle.

In Chapter 8 we shall pay attention to ensuring that the above relationships are analysed as associations and not as aggregations. In this way we shall avoid many painful and time-consuming changes during the design and implementation phases of the software life-cycles.

An important property is propagation (or triggering) of operations in aggregates (Rumbaugh *et al.* 1991, p. 60). For example, translation of a polygon implies the translation of each of its component points. Triggering is not only important in aggregates but for any network of objects in which dependencies are to be found. It is important to realize that propagation of an operation is correct only when the same kind of aggregation relationships exist. For example (Odell 1994), Bob works for the Maths department and Bob has four arms. Giving a 10% pay rise to the Maths department results in Bob getting a rise but does not imply that Bob's arms get the same pay rise!

2.7 Abstract and concrete classes

2.7.1 Abstract base classes (ABC)

An abstract class is one which has no direct instances. This type of class is usually created in order to be used as a base class for a range of other (as yet unspecified) classes. Since no instances of an abstract base class can be created it makes no sense to implement its methods. For this reason they are called abstract methods. Such methods act as a template for the same methods, which must be redefined in derived classes.

2.7.2 Discovering abstract classes

Finding ABCs during the object-oriented analysis and design phases of the software life-cycle is very important. ABCs are the generic types in AKO relations (Section 2.5.1) and discovering them means that a holder has been found for other classes which can be derived from them. Furthermore, instances of derived classes of an ABC can be used in argument lists of methods where an ABC instance is expected. This has far-reaching consequences for software development. For example, ABCs ensure that polymorphism can be supported in C++. How ABCs are implemented in C++ will be discussed in Chapter 3.

2.7.3 Concrete classes

A concrete class is one which has direct instances. A concrete base class is a concrete class from which new classes may be derived. An example of such a class is `POLYGON`, which has already been mentioned. It is possible to derive new classes from it which represent specific geometrical shapes in two dimensions, for example classes for triangles, rectangles and squares.

2.7.4 Examples of abstract and concrete classes

Statistics is the branch of mathematics which is concerned among other things with so-called distributions which can model processes in science, engineering and business. Distributions may model continuous or discrete events. An example of a discrete event is that of a queue in a supermarket: customers arrive at the cash desk and are serviced. The Poisson distribution models the arrival events, while an Exponential distribution models servicing.

The abstract classes which are needed here are for `Distribution`, `Continuous_Distribution` and `Discrete_Distribution`. We make these last two classes into derived classes of Distribution. This is the basic framework from which all concrete classes (such as Exponential and Poisson) can be derived.

Other examples of ABCs and some of their concrete derived classes are:

- Projects (`Internal_Project`, `External_Project`, ...)
- Matrix (`Full_Matrix`, `Symmetric_Matrix`, `Sparse_Matrix`, ...)
- Pump (`Normal_Pump`, `Sophisticated_Pump`, ...)
- Shape (`Line`, `Circle`, `Sphere`, `Polygon`, ...).

2.7.5 Combining abstract and concrete classes

One of the objectives of object-oriented design (OOD) is to create inheritance hierarchies which are extendible. The best way to ensure this is to find that ABC which is the base for all present and future abstract and concrete classes in the same 'family'. Both abstract and concrete classes may be derived from an ABC, but it is not usual to derive an abstract class from a concrete class.

2.8 Polymorphism

2.8.1 Introduction

The concept 'polymorphism' has its roots in programming language design and implementation (Harland 1984; Cardelli and Wegner 1985). A language is called monomorphic if functions, procedures and operands have a unique type. Examples of monomorphic languages are FORTRAN, C and Cobol. Being monomorphic means that it is not possible, for example, to define two subroutines in FORTRAN with the same name but differing number of parameters, as in:

- `SUBROUTINE draw(x1, y1, x2, y2)`
- `SUBROUTINE draw(x, y, r)`

This is not allowed because the procedure `draw` may only be declared once. The above subroutines are for drawing lines and circles, respectively. The solution to this problem in FORTRAN is to invent new names which bear some resemblance to the objects being drawn:

- `SUBROUTINE draw_line(x1, y1, x2, y2)`
- `SUBROUTINE draw_circle(x, y, r)`

Polymorphic languages support constructions whereby functions accept operands of different types. An example of a polymorphic language is POLY (Harland 1984). Polymorphism is supported in C++ to a certain degree. For example, in C++ the above subroutines could be declared as follows:

- `void draw(x1, y1, x2, y2);`
- `void draw(x, y, r);`
- `void draw(const LINE& lin);`
- `void draw(const CIRCLE& cir);`

In general, a polymorphic type is one whose operations are applicable to operands of more than one type.

2.8.2 Kinds of polymorphism

Several flavours of polymorphism are identified in Cardelli and Wegner (1985). It is important to discuss these because they are supported to a lesser or greater extent in C++. Knowing what polymorphism is and does will give us a better feeling for the language.

The different kinds of polymorphism are shown in Figure 2.1, together with how they are implemented in C++.

Parametric polymorphism occurs when a function can be applied uniformly on a range of types. Functions that manifest parametric polymorphic behaviour are sometimes called

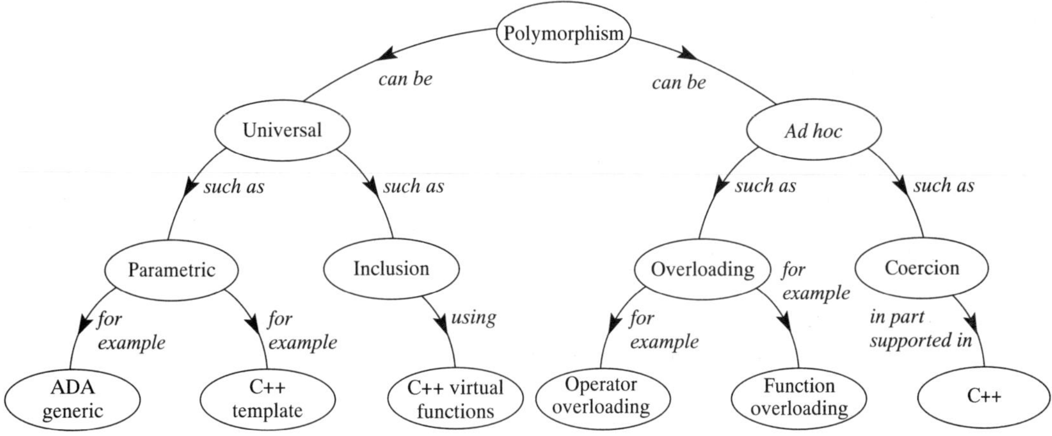

Figure 2.1 Kinds of polymorphism.

generic functions. An example is the function 'length' for calculating the size of a list whose elements are of an arbitrary data type. Thus, a generic function works for arguments of many types. Such functions can be found in Ada (generic functions) and in C++ in the form of template classes and functions.

Inclusion polymorphism was devised mainly to model subtypes and inheritance. In this case an object is viewed as belonging to a number of different classes. Some of these classes may not be distinct. For example, every `HOURLY_EMPLOYEE` instance is also an instance of `EMPLOYEE` and can thus be operated upon by all operations that are valid for `EMPLOYEE`.

Ad hoc polymorphism corresponds to a small set of monomorphic functions. Universal polymorphism, on the other hand, ensures us that functions which belong to that group will work on an infinite number of types.

The two types of *ad hoc* polymorphism are overloading and coercion. With overloading, the same variable name is used to denote different functions and the context is used to determine which function is denoted by a particular instance of the name.

For example, the following is an example of (function) overloading in C++:

```
double calculate_pay();
double calculate_pay(const DATE& d);
```

Coercion allows us to omit semantically necessary type conversions. This technique is useful, but it may lead to subtle errors. An example of coercion in C++ is the case of a function which expects a double as argument but which is called by supplying an integer value; the integer is 'coerced' or promoted into a double. For example:

```
void myfun(double d);
int val = 10;
myfun(10);
```

In this case the compiler sees that an integer value is given as input. The value 10 is first promoted to its double precision equivalent (namely 10.0).

2.9 Roles

No object is an island. If this were so the world would be a very uninteresting place. Objects typically depend on other objects for services (via message passing) and possibly for declarations of visible attribute type, class attributes and exceptions. Furthermore, objects may be components or parts of larger aggregate objects. There is a many-to-many correspondence between objects and roles. An object may play different roles while a role may be played by different objects. For example, a person in an engineering company may play the role of employee, project leader or manager. Conceptually, an object is at a higher level than role.

Relationships may exist between two or more entities (an entity may be an object, class or physical device, for example). A binary relationship is one between two entities, and such relationships are by far the most important ones in object-oriented software development. Directional relationships between two entities introduce so-called client and server roles. An entity that depends on (that is, sends messages to) another entity is said to have the client role, while the subservient entity plays the server role. It is possible that two entities are simultaneously client and server of each other, but this situation should be avoided as it does not promote understandability. It is possible to refine client and server roles into three categories. A master is the client of all other entities with which it is related but is the server of none. A servant is the server of all other entities with which it is related but is the client of none. Finally, an agent is a client of some entities and a server for other entities. Most roles fall into this category.

To take an example, consider a project management environment in which employees work on projects for various departments in the organization. Departments are grouped together to form divisions. In this case the entity 'project' is a master since it is a client of all the other entities, namely 'division', 'department' and 'employee'. The 'employee' is a servant since all other entities depend on it and it is not the client of any other entity. Both 'division' and 'department' are agent entities. For example, 'division' is a client of 'department' and a server for 'project'.

Exercises

1. An ADT for an unbounded stack has the following functions:

new:		→ Stack
empty:	Stack	→ Boolean
push:	Stack × T	→ Stack
pop:	Stack	→ Stack
top:	Stack	→ T

   Find the axioms and preconditions associated with `Stack`.

   Consider now the case of a bounded `Stack` ADT. A bounded `Stack` is a `Stack` which can hold a finite number of elements. Give the full ADT specification for this case.

2. Construct ADTs for the following types: singly linked list, queue, graph, undirected graph, binary tree and a doubly linked list. Determine the preconditions (if applicable) for each function in these ADTs (the above ADTs will be implemented in Chapter 18 using templates in C++).

3. The type PERSON has operations for creating new objects, and for retrieving information on the name, address, date-of-birth and age. Propose two possible class implementations for this type.

4. Determine the different types and subtypes in the following list: employee, postal worker, hourly employee, pump, special pump, external project, project, publication, internal publication, unpublished paper.

5. Discuss the relative merits of using employee numbers as identifier keys in relational tables. Would it be better to use social security numbers in order to achieve independence?

6. Identify the precise ISA relationship between the class of general rectangular matrices and the class of 4×4 transformation matrices in computer graphics.

7. Categorize the following ISA links in terms of the classification rules which were discussed in Section 2.5.

   - A surgeon is a kind of doctor.
   - An internal paper is a paper.
   - Pie charts are kinds of graphs.
   - The Poisson distribution is used in simulation experiments.
   - An external project is a project.
   - A sparse matrix is a matrix.
   - Men are humans.
   - Computers are a kind of hardware.
   - A histogram is a graph.
   - A customer is a person.
   - A square matrix is a matrix.
   - The *C++ Report* is a journal.
   - Henk is a robot.
   - Australia is a continent.

8. Apply the scenarios (2.7) (Section (2.5.3)) to the case of deriving a PASSENGER class (persons who travel a lot) from the class PERSON.

9. The following aggregations need to be categorized (fixed, variable or recursive):

   - A fixed array of double precision numbers
   - A cash flow class (an array of dates and payments)
   - A binary tree
   - A motor car
   - A line segment

10. Inheritance is often misapplied by newcomers to OO. Consider the possible alternatives for the following misuses of inheritance:

- `Circle` is derived from a `Point`.
- `Sales_Manager` is derived from `Sales_Person` and `Manager`.
- A `Stack` class is derived from a `List` class.

What are the consequences in terms of inherited state and operations?

11. Determine the types of aggregation to which the following relationships belong (use the terminology of Section 2.6):
    - The refrigerator is part of the kitchen.
    - The loaf is partly flour.
    - The engine is part of the car.
    - The piston is part of the engine.
    - Stan Laurel is part of Laurel and Hardy.
    - The attendant is in the office.
    - The ship is part of a fleet.
    - An Irish coffee is partly coffee.
12. Identify the roles played by persons in the following environments:
    - Engineering company
    - Petrol pump station
    - A hospital in which patients are cared for and operated upon

    Furthermore, find the attributes and operations of each role.
13. Identify masters, servants and agents for the following entities which are found in a petrol filling station:

    Attendant, customer, petrol pump, pump motor, tank, gun, petrol line, metering device, display
14. Determine the behaviour of the roles in a hospital environment. Typical role objects are nurse, patient, surgeon, senior surgeon and consultant.

References

L. Cardelli and P. Wegner (1985) On understanding types, data abstractions and polymorphism, *Computing Surveys*, **17**(4) December.

M. Ellis and B. Stroustrup (1990) *The C++ Annotated Reference Manual*, Addison-Wesley, Reading MA.

D. G. Firesmith (1993) *Object-Oriented Requirements Analysis and Logical Design*, John Wiley & Sons, New York.

J. Guttag (1977) Abstract data types and the development of data structures, *Communications of the ACM*, **20**(6) June.

J. V. Guttag and J. J. Horning (1978) The algebraic specifications of abstract data types, *Acta Informatica*, **10** 27–52.

J. Guttag, E. Horowitz and D. R. Musser (1978) Abstract data types and software validation, *Communications of the ACM*, **21**(12) December.

D. M. Harland (1984) *Polymorphic Programming Languages*, Ellis Horwood, New York.

W. Kent (1991) A rigorous model of object reference, identity and existence, *Journal of Object-Oriented Programming*, June.

S. N. Khoshafian and G. P. Copeland (1986) Object identity, *OOPSLA '86 Proceedings*, September.

J. Landin (1969) *An Introduction to Algebraic Structures*, Dover Publications, New York.

B. H. Liskov and S. N. Zilles (1975) Specification Techniques for Data Abstractions, *IEEE Transactions on Software Engineering*, **SE-1**(1) March.

B. Meyer (1988) *Object-Oriented Software Construction*, Prentice-Hall, Englewood Cliffs NJ.

J. J. Odell (1994) Six different kinds of composition, *C++ Report*, January.

R. J. Pooley (1987) *An Introduction to Programming in SIMULA*, Blackwell Scientific Publications, Oxford.

I. C. Pyle (1985) *The Ada Programming Language*, Prentice-Hall, Englewood Cliffs NJ.

J. Rumbaugh, M. Blaha, W. Premerlani, F. Eddy and W. Lorensen (1991) *Object-Oriented Modeling and Design*, Prentice-Hall, Englewood Cliffs NJ.

M. E. Winston, R. Chaffin and D. Herrmann (1987) A taxonomy of whole-part relationships, *Cognitive Science*, **11** 417–44.

Chapter

3

Mapping object-oriented concepts to C++

3.1 Introduction and objectives

The main objectives of this chapter are threefold. First, we show how the general object-oriented concepts which were developed in the first two chapters can be implemented in C++. Secondly, we give an overview of C++ and how it can be used effectively. Finally, we give a number of examples of C++ classes, some of which will be found in test cases and exercises.

This is not an introduction to C++ and we assume that the reader has a reasonably good working knowledge of the language.

3.2 Class structure and information hiding

3.2.1 Class header file and class code file

In order to implement a class in C++ it is necessary to create one or more source files which satisfy the rules of C++. In order to keep classes readable and maintainable we decide to split the functionality of a class into two source files. These are called the header file and code file, respectively. The header file contains the declarations of the attributes and member functions belonging to a class. It represents the class design. The code (or implementation) file is an ASCII file which contains the definition for each method that has been declared in the header file.

The advantage of using separate header and code files is that it is possible to use the header file as a working document for programmers who wish to use the class in order to create new classes and code. Another reason for providing separate files is that customers of a given class do not in general get access to the source code of the code file.

It is not strictly necessary to create a separate code file. Many books on C++ use this approach. Using header and code files ('separating the what from the how') promotes understandability, however.

The following two sections are meant as guidelines when writing C++ classes. This is especially important if you do not have access to a CASE tool and you need to document your classes.

3.2.2 Structuring a header file

Header files should be created in a structured and consistent fashion. This is important for other programmers who will use your classes. Choosing a consistent 'look and feel' means that it is relatively easy to read, understand and use your classes. The header file should contain the following information:

(3.1)

- The disk name of the file representing the class
- A description of what the class is intended to do
- The structure of the class (implemented in the private part)
- The class member functions divided into categories
- Tactical and strategic comments to document member functions and groups of member functions

The categories of member functions which are declared in the header file are those which have been discussed in Chapter 1. We implement selector functions in C++ by declaring them as `const`. Member functions should be documented in the header file by so-called tactical comments. These are 'one-liners' and formulating them properly can help new users of the class understand them. Strategic comments are used to document groups or blocks of related member functions. An example of a header file is given by the following simple class for representing an employee who is paid per hour:

```
// hourempl.hxx
//
// Class for all sorts of hourly paid employees.
//
// © Datasim BV, 1993 - 1994

#ifndef DSHOUREMPLOYEE_HXX
#define DSHOUREMPLOYEE_HXX
#include <iostream.h>
#include "employee.hxx"

class DSHOUREMPLOYEE : public DSEMPLOYEE
{
private:

   // Global values
   static double ghourly_rate;         // Rate for all hourly
                                       // employees
   static double govertime_rate;

   // Instance variables
```

```
    double hourly_rate;                 // The normal hour rate
    double overtime_rate;               // The overtime hour rate

  public:
    DSHOUREMPLOYEE(const DSDYNSTR& name);
    DSHOUREMPLOYEE(const DSDYNSTR& name, double hrate,
      double orate);
    ~DSHOUREMPLOYEE();

    // Selectors
    double calculate_pay(size_t number_hours) const;
    void print()  const;            // Print the object

    // Global (class wide) changes to rates globally
    void set_hrate(double h); // Set the global hourly rate
    void set_orate(double o); // Set the global overtime rate

    // Static member functions
    static double ret_ghrate() const;       // Return the global
                                            // hourly rate
    static double ret_gorate() const;       // Return the global
                                            // overtime rate
  };

  #endif   // DSHOUREMPLOYEE_HXX
```

3.2.3 Scope and the class code file

Each member function which is declared in the header file must have its implementation in the class code file. Furthermore, the code file is the place where the program modification details can be documented. The fully qualified name of the function must be used, and this is achieved by the use of the scope resolution operator '`::`'. It is also important to provide ample commentary to show how difficult and more obscure parts of the code work.

3.2.4 Function and operator overloading

C++ allows the programmer to define functions, all of which have the same name and return type but differing in the types or number of arguments. This is a form of *ad hoc* polymorphism and is called function overloading. Another form of *ad hoc* polymorphism which is allowed in C++ is called operator overloading. This feature enables operators to be defined for user-defined types. This property is extremely useful in scientific and engineering applications which have a heavy mathematical basis. For example, the class `FMATRIX` which represents general rectangular matrices has operators for addition, subtraction and multiplication. It is possible in this way to create a syntax which is very close to the mathematics of matrix algebra. The following code shows how matrices can be created, modified and used with other classes:

```
FMATRIX m1(10, 10);      // Constructor called
```

```
m1 = 3.14;                  // Overloading of operator '='

// Show how the operator '*' is overloaded
FMATRIX m2 = m1 * 0.5;
FMATRIX m3 = m2 * m1;

// Multiply a matrix and a vector
DLIST vec(10);
vec = 7.3;

DLIST result = m1 * vec;
```


Operator and function overloading can enhance the readability of code. It is important to remember, however, that indiscriminate use of this technique can lead to some very cryptic code (in the style of the APL language). One of the objectives in creating class interfaces is to make them understandable for other programmers. In order to achieve this we should use overloading only when the situation warrants it. With function overloading, we should choose names in such a way that they make sense for the problem domain that is being modelled. For example, writing a trigonometric class library for user-defined types such as radians and degrees entails overloading the functions which are defined in the standard library `<math.h>`. Using the same names means that programmers who already know the functions in `<math.h>` will have relatively little difficulty in moving to the new environment.

3.3 Single and multiple inheritance

C++ supports both single inheritance and multiple inheritance. Of the two, single inheritance is the more widely applied in C++ projects. Applying multiple inheritance is difficult and good examples which make use of this technique are lacking in the literature.

3.3.1 Putting inheritance into perspective

Using inheritance in C++ can help software productivity if properly applied. Knowing where to use inheritance is one of the deliverables of the analysis and design phases in the object-oriented software life-cycle. Unfortunately, the technique is often misused in application development. The main problems when attempting to use inheritance techniques in C++ are:

- Programmers tend to use it instead of delegation (Rumbaugh *et al.* 1991, p. 244).
- Deep inheritance hierarchies lead to maintenance problems (Linton and Calder 1987).
- Multiple inheritance is difficult to use and wastes development time.
- There are better approaches to multiple inheritance.

One of the objectives of inheritance is to share code among classes. This increases the reusability factor. However, the act of deriving a class D from another class B means that D inherits all the properties of B (state and member functions). Thus, every instance of D is also an instance of B. This may not be what we want, because B may have member functions which are not semantically correct for D. For example, consider a class which implements a singly linked list of characters. The member functions which are defined for this class are:

```
class LIST
{ // Simple linked list of characters

private:
// State (not important at the moment)

public:
  LIST();                     // Create an empty list
  void add(char c);           // Add an element to the list
  void remove(char c);        // Remove an element from list
  char first() const;         // Give the first element
  char  last() const;         // Give the last element

  // ...

};
```

The list class can be used to create new types of class with different semantics. For example, a class for a stack of objects is defined as a derived class as follows:

```
class STACK: public LIST
{ // Simple stack of characters

private:

  // No state necessary; it is inherited from LIST

public:
  STACK();

  void push(char c);          // Push element onto stack
  char pop();                 // Remove the top element

  // ...

};
```

So, what's wrong with this? The answer lies in the fact that `STACK` inherits a number of member functions which have nothing to do with stacks. The error which has been made here is that we made `STACK` as a specialized `LIST`. A `STACK` is not a special `LIST`. Rumbaugh *et al.* (1991) call this implementation inheritance, and its use can lead to major maintenance and understandability problems. The solution to this type of problem is to create the class `STACK` and allow it to selectively use the functionality from `LIST` on a need-be basis. For example, we could implement `STACK` by a `LIST` for the state. Furthermore, `STACK` is allowed to use the services of `LIST` in its code file. The new interface for `STACK` is now:

```
class STACK
{
private:

  LIST elements;     // A list of characters

public:
  STACK();

  void push(char c);
  char pop();

};
```

In this case we see that STACK is a client of LIST and only meaningful member functions from LIST are delegated to STACK.

We finish this section with some remarks on inheritance hierarchies. It is unwise in general to create deep hierarchies in the same way as has been done in languages such as Smalltalk. Experience with a number of commercial products has shown that such hierarchies lead to major maintenance problems. Furthermore, many classes in the hierarchy have little or no behaviour (the so-called 'tiny' classes). It is better in our view to create C++ class hierarchies for different application areas. This is the viewpoint taken by a number of C++ developers (Coggins 1990).

This is the 'Separation of Concerns' approach and a number of examples of this principle will be given in later chapters.

3.3.2 Access levels

The information hiding principle and encapsulation are both supported in C++. C++ implements these by the keywords 'private' and 'public'. Class members which are declared in the private area are visible only to the other instances and members of the class. All other objects ('the world') have no access. Class members which are declared in the public area can be accessed by any object or function. The public area is the implementation of the services that a given class offers to the world.

The private area is used mainly for state information about an object. It contains declarations of the data types which represent the attributes of an object. This area may also contain the declaration of member functions (private member functions) which are not to be used by clients.

A special case of the client/server paradigm is to be found in C++. This is the case of the relationship between a given class and its derived classes. It is possible to define a new so-called 'protected' area. Members of the protected area behave as public members to the derived class. We advise against the use of protected areas since they violate the information hiding principle. However, we give an example to show how the idea works:

```
class BASE
{
private:
  int a;
```

	Public member	Protected member	Private member
Member functions	Yes	Yes	Yes
Member functions of derived classes	Yes	Yes	No
Member functions of other clients	Yes	No	No

Figure 3.1 Access matrix for private, protected and public members.

```
protected:
  char c;

public:
  BASE();

  // Other member functions here ...

};

class DERIVED: public BASE
{

  // Interface ...

};
```

Instances of DERIVED have access to state variable c and also to the public interface of BASE. Other client classes have access to the public interface of BASE but they have no access to a or c.

Figure 3.1 gives the access matrix for the different types of inheritance relationships between base and derived classes. The rows represent the subject functions, while the columns represent the functions which may be accessed. An interesting case is 'private inheritance'; a class may be declared as follows:

```
class DERIVED_PRIVATE: private BASE
{ // BASE class already defined

  // Interface

};
```

Defining DERIVED_PRIVATE in this way has the consequence that no part of BASE is visible to instances of DERIVED_PRIVATE. Private inheritance is often used as an

	Public members	Protected members	Private members
Public inheritance	Public	Protected	Private
Protected inheritance	Protected	Protected	Private
Private inheritance	Private	Private	Private

Figure 3.2 Inheritance and visibility of members.

implementation workaround for problems that should have been solved in the analysis or design phases of the object-oriented software life-cycle.

The different scenarios showing the influence of inheritance on the visibility of members are shown in Figure 3.2.

We summarize this section by mentioning some of the guidelines which should be followed when applying inheritance:

- Is the relationship an ISA? If not, you might consider using delegation instead.
- Avoid deep hierarchies; they tend to contain tiny classes and are difficult to understand and maintain.
- Do not use the 'protected' keyword; it violates the information hiding principle.
- How to use multiple inheritance correctly is not well documented in the literature; C++ neophytes should not use it.

3.4 Composite objects

3.4.1 Implementing aggregate classes

C++ supports aggregation as part of the language. Aggregation is the 'part–whole' relationship. A so-called aggregate object is composed of simpler objects. Examples of aggregates are:

- A petrol pump
- A project
- A polyline
- An article in an issue of a journal

Aggregates are more than the sum of their parts. They can model real-world objects and they have behaviour which far outstrips that of their individual parts. Building aggregates in C++ is like bottom-up design; we first create low-level classes and then we combine these classes in some way to create more elaborate ones. This is achieved by choosing suitable member data to represent the new class. For example, the class `PROJECT` has the following state:

```
class PROJECT
{ // Simple class for projects
```

```
private:
  double budget;      // Total budget for project
  DATE   start;       // Start date
  DATE finish;        // When project ends
  char* desc;         // Description of project

public:
  // Interface

};
```

PROJECT is an example of a fixed aggregation (as explained in Section 2.6). It has a fixed number of components. Other examples of fixed aggregates are:

- DATE, TIME and TIMESTAMP classes
- JOURNAL
- EMPLOYEE
- POINT (points in two-dimensional space)

Variable aggregates can be implemented in C++ in a number of ways. The simplest approach is by using pointers. For example, a STACK can be implemented as an array as follows:

```
class STACK
{ // Stack of integers
private:
  int* arr; // Pointer to array
  int size; // Size of the array

public:

  // Interface

};
```

Other examples of variable aggregates are:

- CASH_FLOW (arrays of DATEs and MONEY)
- POLYLINE (an array of points)
- DIVISION (an array of DEPARTMENTs)

Recursive aggregates are perhaps the most difficult aggregates to understand and apply in C++. C++ allows the programmer to declare a class in which member data is a pointer to the class that is being defined:

```
class RECURSIVE
{
private:
  RECURSIVE* r;
```

```
public:

  // Interface

};
```

This is a useful feature since it allows us to create nonlinear data structures, such as trees. An example of a recursive aggregate is in the case of articles or papers which are published in issues of journals. A paper may refer to other papers, and the class interface is given by:

```
class PAPER
{
private:
  PAPER* reference;

public:

  // Interface

};
```

3.5 Virtual functions, abstract base classes and pure virtual functions

This section is devoted to discussing special types of functions. These are the so-called virtual functions and pure virtual functions. They are in most cases to be found in classes which serve as base classes.

3.5.1 What is a virtual function?

The `virtual` keyword specifier is used in a base class header file (not code file) in order to declare functions which define default behaviour for all derived classes of the base class. A virtual member function must have a body and this is defined in the class code file. This mechanism allows us to implement inclusion polymorphism (Section 2.8.2). The main advantage of using virtual functions can be seen at run-time: the system can determine the type of an object from which the correct member function will be called. To take an example, we consider the classic case of a hierarchy for two-dimensional shapes. The base class is called `SHAPE` and its interface is as follows:

```
class SHAPE
{
private:

  // ...

public:
  virtual void draw() const {}
};
```

Derived classes of SHAPE (such as POINT, LINE and CIRCLE) override draw( ) with their own implementation, while other derived classes (such as LAYER and COLOUR) for which draw( ) is irrelevant simply inherit it from SHAPE. If we now create a list of pointers to SHAPE we do not have to check the objects types as we loop through the list. For example,

```
// Create an array of pointers to shapes
SHAPE* figure[4];

figure[0] = new POINT();
figure[1] = new LINES();
figure[2] = new COLOUR();
figure[3] = new LAYER();

for (int j = 0; j < 4; j++)
  figure[j] -> draw();
```

Notice that the code works as long as a derived class has a draw( ) function defined in its interface. If the derived class has no such function the code still works since default behaviour is inherited from SHAPE::draw( ).

We give another example of a virtual member function. Consider the class EMPLOYEE which defines default functions for the name and date of birth for all derived classes of EMPLOYEE. The header file will then look something like:

```
class EMPLOYEE
{
private:
  char* nam;     // Full name of employee
  DATE  dob;     // Date of birth

public:

  // Constructors
  virtual char* name() const;
  virtual DATE date_of_birth() const;

};
```

Consider the class HOURLY_EMPLOYEE, which represents those employees who are paid on an hourly basis. It is not necessary to redefine the functions EMPLOYEE::name( ) or EMPLOYEE::date_of_birth( ) since they are inherited from EMPLOYEE.

The interface for HOURLY_EMPLOYEE is:

```
class HOURLY_EMPLOYEE: public EMPLOYEE
{
private:

  double h_rate;     // Hourly rate
public:
```

```
    // Constructor
    HOURLY_EMPLOYEE(char* c, const DATE& dob, double rate);

    double hourly_rate() const;    // What is rate?

};
```

The following code is now legitimate:

```
HOURLY_EMPLOYEE h("Daniel Duffy", DATE(29,8,1952), 100.0);
cout << h.name() << endl;
cout << h.date_of_birth() << endl;
cout << h.hourly_rate();
```

3.5.2 What is a pure virtual function?

A pure virtual function is a virtual function with no body. Pure virtual functions are declared in base classes. Deriving a class from a base class which contains pure virtual functions means that these functions must be declared and defined in the derived classes, otherwise a compiler error will occur. Using such functions is like saying that the base class has declared a certain common behaviour which must be implemented in all special cases. To take an example, consider the case of a base class `PROJECT` and its derived classes `INTERNAL_PROJECT` and `EXTERNAL_PROJECT`. The status of a given project cannot have a default value, and for this reason the use of 'normal' virtual functions is not allowed. We need something stronger in order to ensure that the clients (in this case the derived classes) implement the function. This is done as follows in the present case:

```
class PROJECT
{

    // ...

    int status() const = 0;

};
```

All derived classes must implement the `status()` function. Failing to do so will result in a compiler error. Writing pure virtual functions in base classes is equivalent to taking out an insurance policy; the base class knows that its clients (in this case its derived classes) must implement the function. Thus, clients are not able to compromise the integrity of the code.

3.5.3 Abstract base classes

An abstract base class (ABC) is a class which has at least one pure virtual member function. ABCs may not have instances. Thus, if `X` is an ABC the following code will result in a compiler error:

```
X my_variable;
```

It is, however, possible to declare variables as pointing to an ABC as in the following piece of code:

```
X* good_variable;
```

We should always try to find as many abstract classes as possible when designing software using object-oriented techniques. An ABC springs from a set of classes that share useful attributes and/or behaviour. If you discover behaviour which is shared among a number of classes, you should design an abstract superclass to capture the shared behaviour in one place.

For example, both internal projects and external projects have member functions for calculating the status of the project (on schedule, costs and so on). Since this function represents shared behaviour we create an ABC `PROJECT` from which the classes for the internal and external projects are derived. Another advantage of discovering ABCs is that they can be used as 'place-holders' from which other new derived classes can be created. In other words, having an arsenal of ABCs helps in the classification process because newly discovered classes should fit in as derived classes of at least one ABC for a given problem.

3.5.4 When to use ABCs or concrete classes

It is possible to derive classes from both abstract and concrete classes (CBCs). The correct combination of the two kinds will allow us to build good C++ class hierarchies.

The basic guidelines are:

- Choose one ABC to serve as a base class for all other classes (including other ABCs and CBCs). ABCs are designed to be inherited from.
- It is possible to create an ABC as a derived class from another ABC.
- Concrete classes are designed to be instantiated. CBCs should be derived from ABCs or from other CBCs.
- Never derive an ABC from a CBC.

A good example of the combination of abstract and concrete classes can be found in two-dimensional computer graphics applications, for example Microsoft Windows, Motif and computer-aided design (CAD). We are primarily interested in drawing simple and composite two-dimensional shapes on some graphical medium. Since everything is a shape, we discover that we can create an ABC (which we call `Shape`) from which other classes are derived. Concrete derived classes of `Shape` could be:

- `Polygon`, `LineSegment`, `Ellipse` and `Point`

It is possible to create ABCs under `Shape` to suit specific needs. For example, in X-Windows it is possible to edit line segments so that they meet in a certain way (Figure 3.3). All three ways of rounding the pair of line segments are special cases of a general rounding process. We decide to create an ABC called `Round` which will function as a base class for these (and possibly future) classes. Furthermore, common state and behaviour can be factored into this class. The class hierarchy for this case is shown in Figure 3.4.

3.6 Special metaclasses: templates

C++ supports the concept of templates, otherwise known as generic or parametrized classes. Although not supported by all compiler vendors at the moment of writing, the use and application of the template mechanism in C++ is becoming more widespread, as it allows

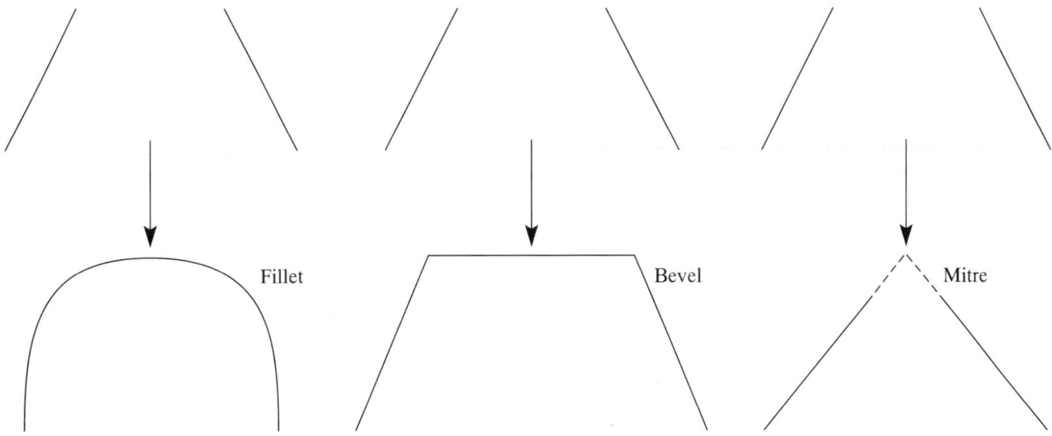

Figure 3.3 ABC representing how line segments are edited.

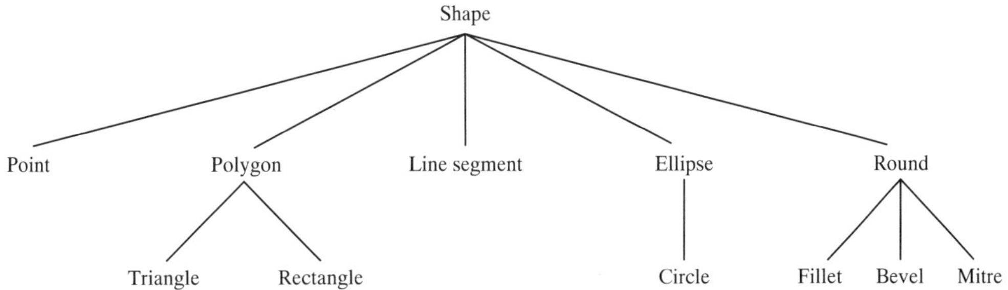

Figure 3.4 Simple class hierarchy showing combination of ABCs and CBCs.

the programmer to build families of classes which can be instantiated to suit different applications.

The template concept is not new. It has its roots in ADT theory and a number of languages support the concept in one form or another. For example, Eiffel (Meyer 1988) uses formal generic parameters in the class definition, Ada (Pyle 1985) has the package construction while Modula-2 (Koffman 1988) uses the `MODULE` construction.

Templates are similar to ADTs. In fact, they can be viewed as implementations of ADTs. Thus, a template has an interface and a body just like an ordinary C++ class, but the difference is that a template makes use of a formal parameter. For example, we could create a template class for arrays of arbitrary elements. In this case we say that the elements belong to the data type `T`. It is possible to create so-called specializations of a given template class by replacing the formal argument `T` by some specific data type. For example, the class `Array <T>` could have the following specializations, which are used in a number of applications:

- `Array <POINT>` is a polyline.
- `Array <DATE>` represents an array of cash flow dates.
- `Array <double>` represents a one-dimensional vector array.

- `Array <Array <double>>` is a two-dimensional matrix.

The advantages of using templates in C++ are:

- They only have to be written once; less code duplication.
- They can be specialized to give new ready-to-use classes.
- Combining inheritance with template specialization increases software productivity.

The main objective in this section is to show how templates can be declared, defined and applied in C++. Templates are still in an experimental stage in C++ and it is possible that the syntax may change when they become part of the official C++ standard.

3.6.1 Finding the correct terminology

Templates can be difficult to understand and master. This is partly due to the fact that they are metaclasses (an instance of a class template is also a class!) and that some programmers may not have been exposed to such ideas. In order to explain properly what templates are we propose giving a number of definitions (Ball 1993a,b; Ellis and Stroustrup 1990). To this end, we note that the definitions apply both to class templates and to function templates (yes, you can write generic functions!).

3.6.2 Template declarations

A template declaration announces the existence of a template without actually giving the contents or body of that template. Examples are:

```
// Class template declarations
template <class T> class Array;
template <class T> class Set;
template <class Key, class Value> class Dictionary;

// Function template declarations
template <class T> void swap(T& t1, T& t2); // Swap values t1
                                            // and t2
template <class T> void sort(T& t);         // Sort t
template <class T> T* save(const T& t); // Return a pointer
                                        // to a T after
                                        // saving data
```

Notice that it is possible to have more than one formal data type and it is advisable to choose names for these types which help the programmer in understanding what the template does. This is a form of 'syntactic sugaring'. For example, consider the associative matrix class which can be indexed by row and column from the data types `T1` and `T2`, respectively and which has values in `T3`. A legitimate declaration is:

```
template <class T1, class T2, class T3> class Matrix;
```

although the following declaration is easier to understand:

```
template <class Row, class Col, class Val> class Matrix;
```

Function template declarations are similar to normal function declarations except that formal parameters are used.

3.6.3 Template definitions

A template definition specifies either the members (data and functions) of a class template or the body of a function template. Examples are:

```
// Class template definition
template <class T> class Array
{
private:
  T* arr;    // Pointer to an instance of T
  int sz;    // The length of the array

public:
  // Constructors
  Array(int size);
  Array(const Array& arr2);
  // Destructor
  virtual ~Array();

  // Other functions
  Array& operator = (const Array& arr2);
  T& operator [] (int j);                  // Indexing

};

// Function template definition
void swap(T& t1, T& t2)
{
  T tmp = t1;
  t1 = t2;
  t2 = tmp;
}
```

Thus, the template definition for a class template is the same as its header file, while the template definition for a function template corresponds to the body of that function.

There is another type of function definition which must be discussed. This is the so-called template member function definition. All member functions which have been declared in the class template declaration should have corresponding template member function definitions. Examples in the case of the `Array` class are:

```
// Constructor
template <class T> Array <T>::Array(int size)
{
  sz = size;
  arr = new T[size];
}

// Destructor
template <class T> Array<T>::~Array()
```

```
{
  delete [] arr;
}

// Other functions
template <class T> T& Array<T>::operator [] (int j)
{ // Indexing (notice, no range checking)

  return arr[j];

}
```

3.6.4 Template specializations

A template specialization is created by providing a definition for a class or function with a particular set of parameters. Templates are useless unless they are specialized. Examples of template specializations are:

```
Array<double> arr(10);
Array<Date> date_arr(12);

Matrix<int, int, double> mathematical_matrix;
Matrix<char*, char*, double> assoc_matrix;

double d1 = 1.0;
double d2 = -34.4;
swap(d1, d2);

Array<Date> old(12);
Array<Date> new(12);
// ...
sort(old);
sort(new);
swap(old, new);
```

It is possible to use template specializations in code. For example, the following example creates an array of complex numbers:

```
typedef Array<Complex> ComplexArray;

ComplexArray carr(10);
for (int j = 0; j < 10; j++)
  carr[j] = Complex(double(j), double (j+1));
```

3.6.5 Template instantiation

The last topic which needs to be defined is template instantiation. This is the process of actually generating code which is needed to implement the particular template specialization that the programmer needs. This is a compiler-dependent process and should be transparent to the programmer.

3.6.6 Combining inheritance and templates

It is possible to create template specializations directly, as we have seen in Section 3.6.4. However, a more flexible way of working with template specializations is to combine them with the inheritance mechanism. This may also be necessary, since templates should not provide all the functionality which is needed in disparate domains. Thus, a template should provide minimal functionality. This has the advantage that clients do not pay for what they do not use. To take an example, assume that we would like to create a class for representing cash flows. A cash flow is an array of dates and money to be paid on those dates. A class representing cash flows should have member functions for the following messages:

- When is the next payment due and how much?
- What is the lifetime of the cash flow?
- How much has yet to be paid?

Obviously, the functions which should implement the above requirements are not to be found in any specialization of `Array`. They are thus specific to cash flows, from which we deduce that we should derive the cash flow class as a specialization of array. This is done as follows (where `Pair` is a template class representing pairs of objects from different classes):

```
class CashFlow : public Array<Pair<Date, Money> >
{
private:
  // No state needed, inherited from Array

public:
  CashFlow();

  // ...

  Date next_payment() const;
  Date lifetime() const;
  double shortfall() const;      // How much to be paid
};
```

Other examples are:

```
class Polyline : public Array <Point>
{

  // Add members specific to polylines

};

class QuickMatrix : public Array<Array<double> >
{

  // Add members specific to matrices
};
```

When using templates in conjunction with inheritance, the rules are:

- Make 'minimal' template classes.
- Create your own classes by deriving them from template specializations.
- Write your code carefully and get the syntax right.

3.6.7 Application areas for templates

Templates are new and not yet widely used in C++ applications. However, there are a number of commercial libraries which deliver templates. Most of these are of the building block type (foundation layer classes) and there are virtually no libraries available for business domains such as financial planning, MIS, CAD/CAM and project management.

Template classes have been created for the following abstractions:

- *Bags*. These are collections from some domain in which duplicates are allowed.
- *Sets*. Collections of items from some domain. Duplicates are not allowed.
- *Dequeues*. A sequence from which items can be added or deleted from either end.
- *Maps*. A collection forming a dictionary of domain/range pairs.
- *Queues*. A sequence to which items may be added from one end and removed from the opposite end.
- *Rings*. A sequence in which items may be added to and removed from the top of a circular structure.
- *Stacks*. A sequence in which items may be added to and removed from the same end.
- *Strings*. A sequence of zero or more items.
- *Graphs*. These are unrooted collections of nodes and arcs that may contain cycles and cross-references.
- *Lists*. A list is a sequence of zero or more items.
- *Trees*. These data types represent rooted collections of nodes and arcs that cannot contain cycles or cross-references.

Specializations of the above template classes should be used as building blocks when designing software. You can apply them as 'off-the-shelf' components in various applications. Chapter 18 will discuss the design and implementation of a number of these reusable data types.

We take an example to show how one of the above template classes can be created in C++. We consider the `Set` abstraction. The behaviour of instances of this class can be found by consulting any good book on set theory or algebra (see, for example, Landin (1969) or Stoll (1961). The behaviour is given by:

- // Set creation and population

  Create an empty set

  Add an element to the set

  Remove an element from the set

  Replace one element by another one in the set

Is a set empty?

Is an element in the set?

- // Interactions with other sets

Intersection, union and difference of two sets

Symmetric difference of two sets

Cartesian product of two sets

Do two sets intersect?

It is possible to write the interface for a generic set. It is given by:

```
template <class T> class Set
{
private:
  List<T> elements;      // Implement as a list
  int tally;             // Number of elements in set
  // (Redundant information)

public:
  // Constructors
  Set();                 // Empty set
  Set(const T& t);       // Set with one element

  // Modifiers
  void add(const T& t);
  void remove(const T& t);
  void replace(const T& old, const T& new);

  // Selectors
  Boolean empty() const;
  Boolean hasMember(const T& t) const;
  Set Intersection(const Set& set2);
  Set Union(const Set& set2);
  Set Difference(const Set& set2);
  Set SymmetricDifference(const Set& set2);
  Boolean intersect(const Set& set2);

  // Using operator overloading
  Set operator * (const Set& set2);     // Intersection
  Set operator + (const Set& set2);     // Union
  Set operator - (const Set& set2);     // Difference
  Set operator / (const Set& set2);     // Symmetric '-'

};
```

This template class has a high reusability factor. This means that specializations can be created and used in many different types of applications. For example, class `Set` could be used to build simple relational database systems.

3.7 Implementing exception handling in C++

In an ideal world, computer programs would never crash or stop functioning. However, situations can and do arise in which data and code become corrupted. We think of code as a contract between two parties: on the one hand the vendor (or supplier) of code and the consumer (or client) of the code. Both parties agree on a certain contract and each party must fulfil its part of the agreement. In other words, both parties have rights and responsibilities. If a party has satisfied its part of the bargain then the counterparty must ensure that the first party's rights are honoured. However, if the first party breaks the terms of the contract then the counterparty has no obligation to fulfil the bargain. This idea is the so-called 'programming by contract' metaphor, which is described in Meyer (1988). When a contract has been broken (for whatever reason) we speak of an error or exception being raised. Discovering exceptions and knowing how to handle them in C++ is the subject of this section.

Exceptions appear in many shapes and forms. In operating system design exceptions must be included as part of the overall system architecture. In this type of environment an exception is defined as an unusual condition that causes the processor to change the flow of control (Levy and Eckhouse 1980). Exceptions can also occur in C++ programs. Some examples are:

- Bad user input (range error, invalid input, ...)
- Numerical errors (overflow, underflow, division, ...)
- Storage errors (file access, ...)
- Process errors (process killed, stale, ...)
- Free store errors (memory allocation)

A number of languages, such as Ada and Eiffel, have support for exceptions built into the language. Exception handling in C++ is in the experimental phase. It is estimated that only 30% of all C++ compiler vendors support the feature at the moment of writing.

3.7.1 The elements of exception handling

An exception is an error event somewhere in a program. One of the objectives of good software engineering is the ability to discover exceptions and to deal with them in such a way that normal processing can continue. The design of exceptions involves two steps:

- Discovering and reporting exceptions
- Knowing how to handle exceptions

Working with exceptions promotes defensive and fault-tolerant programming. Conventional programming assumes that all data is correct, that there are enough resources available to carry out tasks and that things work as we would expect. Defensive programming, on the other hand builds 'firewalls' into the code so that unexpected and exceptional events can be handled in a uniform manner. Another objective is to ensure that the code can continue to run even after disastrous events occur. Some languages have predefined exceptions which are built into the language. For example, Ada supports range, access, index, numeric and storage error checking (Pyle 1985). C++ has no built-in support for exceptions. All exceptions must be defined and implemented by the programmer.

The act of indicating that an exceptional situation has arisen is called raising an exception. Once an exception has arisen further normal processing is impossible. In order to remedy

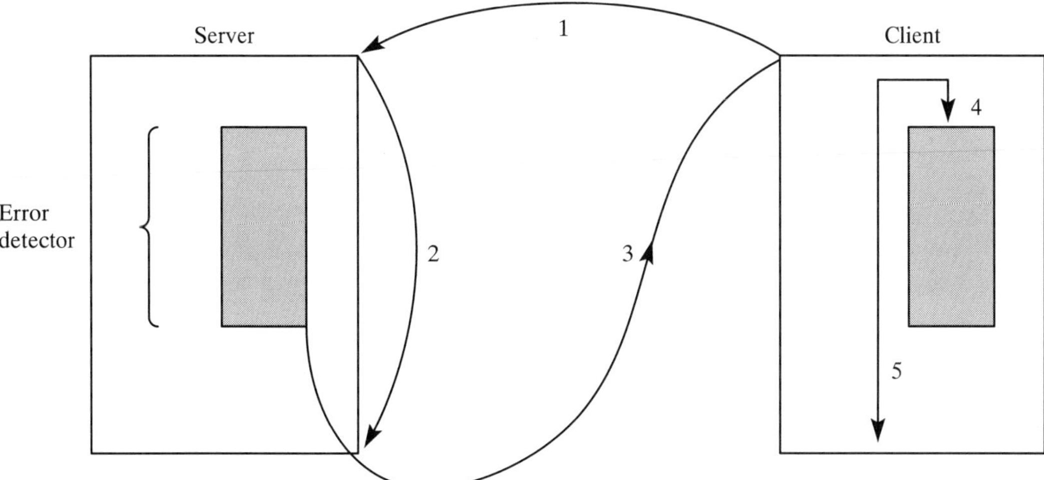

Figure 3.5 Events and responses in exception handling.

this situation we need to introduce software redundancy into the code. This redundancy allows us to specify the recovery action to be taken for the effective remainder of the code that was not successfully completed. Once an exception has been raised it needs to be handled in some way. To this end, the programmer must define handlers which carry out the recovery action and resume the normal sequence of execution.

Working with exceptions is very similar to the client/server metaphor: a block of code (the server) is called from code in another block (the client). The server knows how to detect errors but does not necessarily know what to do about them. The client, on the other hand, understands how to deal with errors but cannot always detect them.

The events and responses which take place when exception handling is used is shown in Figure 3.5. The steps are as follows:

- The client code calls the server (Step 1).
- Server code is executed.
- If no errors are detected, processing continues until the end of the block (Step 2).
- If an error is discovered, an exception is raised and 'thrown' (Step 3).
- The client uses a 'fishing net' to determine whether an exception has been thrown from the server.
- If an exception has been found, then execute the handler code (Step 4).
- If no exception has been found, then execute the normal-case body of the client code (step 5).

3.7.2 Implementing exception handling: syntax and guidelines

Both C and C++ have one built-in exception handler. This is the `assert()` function, which can be used for debugging programs. It is, however, unsuitable for large-scale problems, as it has no provisions which allow the programmer to carry on normal processing after an exceptional situation has occurred.

C++ implements the general ideas which were presented in Section 3.7.1. In particular, a number of new keywords have been added to the language; these are

```
throw          (server)
try            (client)
catch          (client)
```

Throwing an exception transfers control to a handler. When this happens, an object is passed and the type of the object determines which handlers can deal with it. In C++ we say that a handler catches an exception. Examples of throwing exceptions are:

```
throw "help!";    // For handler of type char*
throw -1;         // For handler of type int
```

It is possible to throw user-defined types. For example, the following statements represent valid C++ code:

```
throw OVERFLOW;
throw RANGE_ERROR;
throw STICKY_VALVE; // Application-based exception
```

The keywords `try` and `catch` are to be found in client code. A `try` block is a piece of code which calls the server code. Directly after the `try` block there should be a `catch` switch which has provisions for different types of exception. The `catch` switch represent the 'fishing net' in which all the different possible types of exception can be processed. As an example, consider a class `Array` for representing arrays of double precision numbers. We are interested in accessing the individual elements of the array by use of the overloaded indexing operator `[ ]`. We also wish to ensure that clients should not be able to access elements outside the limits of the array. If they do try this, a range error should be raised. How do we implement this in C++ and how do we detect range violations? First, the server code should produce code which actually raises the exception:

```
double& Array::operator [] (int j)
{
  // Precondition: j must be within limits of array
  if (j < 0 || j > = size)
    throw RangeErr();

  return arr[j];
}
```

In this case a `RangeErr` type is thrown if the index `j` is not within the limits of the array. Code which uses the services of `Array` can use `try` and `catch` to ascertain whether an error has occurred. An example is now given:

```
Array my_arr(10);                   // 10 elements in array
try
{
  double d1 = my_arr[2];            // OK
  double d2 = my_arr[2000];         // Range error
```

```
    // ...

}
catch (RangeErr& r)
{

    // ...
    cout << "Range error\n";

}
```

We finish this section with some tips on using the exception handling mechanism in C++:

- Describing exceptions should be an essential part of the interface of a class.
- Exceptions add to the correctness and robustness of classes, modules and systems.
- When designing C++ classes we should first pay attention to normal situations and add exceptions later to handle abnormal cases; in other words, separate normal-case and error-case processing.

3.7.3 Exception hierarchies

C++ classes can be created which reflect the types of exception which can occur in applications. For this reason it is useful to create exception hierarchies. This is really a design problem. For example, suppose that we are writing C++ classes which make use of file I/O (opening, reading, writing and closing files). The following errors are possible:

- Status error (file already in use)
- Name error (file does not exist)
- Use error (incorrect access mode)
- Device error (problems with underlying hardware or software system)
- Mode error (an operation is not possible (user problem))

Any one of these situations can occur, and to this end we create an exception class to handle each specific type of error. The hierarchy is shown in Figure 3.6. The notation used is from the well-known object modelling technique (OMT) which will be discussed in great detail in Chapter 8. The triangle-shaped object in this figure represents an

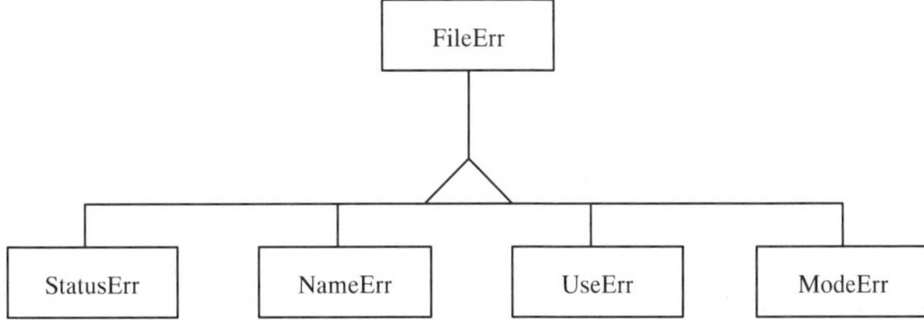

Figure 3.6 Exception handling for file I/O.

inheritance mechanism. These classes may be used in client code to catch one or more exceptions.

Suppose that client code is not sure which exception to catch. It is then possible to extend the number of options as follows:

```
void manipulate_file()
{
  try {
    // ...
  }
  catch(UseErr)  { // Do something }
  catch(ModeErr) { // Do something else }
  catch(NameErr) { // Do something else}

}
```

We shall come back to exceptions in later chapters, since they will play an essential role in the analysis, design and implementation of object-oriented systems.

3.8 Protection and violations in C++ of encapsulation

We have already discussed the access level 'protected', which can be defined in a C++ header file. Declaring member data as protected in a given class means that derived classes can directly access that data by name. This implies that objects in derived classes can access the data without having to use a public member function in the base class. However, if the protected data needs to be changed it entails that all the derived classes will need to change their code. This could become a maintenance nightmare. Instead of using protected variables we ensure that the base class has member functions for 'setting' and 'getting' the value of the member data. Thus instead of:

```
class BaseWrong
  {
private:
  // ...

protected:
  int color;

public:

  // ...

};
```

we create an interface with only private and public parts, as follows:

```
class BaseCorrect
{
private:
```

```
    // ...

    int color;

  public:
    // ...

    void colour(int new_colour);
    int colour() const;

  };
```

Using this approach derived classes have indirect access to the state via the public interface of `BaseCorrect`.

Rule: It is not necessary to use the 'protected' keyword. Place all member data in the private area and create public member functions for retrieving and updating the values of that member data.

3.9 Static member data and static member functions

Class attributes and class operations have already been discussed in Chapter 2. A class attribute is an attribute which serves as a default value for all instances of a class, while a class operation is one which is independent of any instance of the class. Discovering class attributes and class operations is part of the analysis and design stages in the object-oriented life-cycle. It is interesting to note that these can be implemented by static member data and static member functions, respectively. In order to show how they can be used we take the simple example of an employee class, in which static member data is used as the default hourly working rate. This member data has been made private and we have added a static member function which allows us to read its current value. The header file for the employee class is:

```
class Employee
{
private:
  static double h_rate; // Class attribute

  char* nam;

public:
  Employee(char* name);

  static double hourly_rate();    // Class operation
};
```

The code file for `Employee` is:

```
double Employee::h_rate = 178.00;

Employee::Employee(char* name)
```

```
{
  nam = new char[strlen(name) + 1];
  strcpy (nam,name);
}

double Employee::hourly_rate()
{
  return h_rate;
}
```

The following piece of code shows how the above static members can be used:

```
Employee dd("DD");
cout << "Current rate: " << Employee::hourly_rate() << endl;
```

It is possible to create static member data for both built-in data types (as above) and for user-defined types.

3.10 Software quality criteria

Writing software is sometimes more of an art form than a science. However, there are a number of metrics by which we can judge the quality of software (Meyer 1988; Carolan 1991). Such quality criteria attempt to highlight the shortcomings of the present state of the art in software development. The major problems in the software industry are:

- Systems often do not do what they are supposed to do.
- Programs are difficult to change.
- There is little use made of previous efforts.
- Systems do not work well together.
- They are not equipped to work under abnormal conditions.

Most of these problems are caused by a lack of languages, tools and development environments which promote the development of quality software. Object-oriented technology is a step in the right direction to eliminating some of the above shortcomings.

Key software qualities are (Meyer 1988):

- Correctness
- Robustness
- Extensibility
- Reusability
- Compatibility

We are interested in ensuring in the short term that C++ classes fulfil the above criteria. A class is said to be correct if it satisfies its specifications. Since a class is an implementation of an ADT we see that a class will be correct if its corresponding ADT has been properly specified. In particular, a class description should include preconditions, postconditions and class invariants. A class is said to be robust if it continues to function even under abnormal circumstances. Exception handling mechanisms promote the robustness of classes.

Extensibility is the extent to which classes can be customized to suit particular needs. C++ supports inheritance and templates and these allow clients to create derived classes and specializations. Reusability states how far classes can be used in many different types of application. Finally, compatibility (or interoperability) states how far classes from different vendors work together.

Finally, we deal with one final software quality criterion which deserves special mention. This is accessibility (Carolan 1991). This states how easy or difficult it is for new programmers to understand and use C++ classes. Creating classes which are easy to apply flattens the learning curve and ensures higher programmer productivity.

Exercises

1. How would the member functions `STACK::push()` and `STACK::pop()` which were discussed in Section 3.3.1 be implemented if delegation was chosen?

2. If we wished to create a class for a doubly linked list by using the services of a singly linked list, what would be the most efficient way of doing this (e.g. delegation, inheritance)?

3. Create classes for two-dimensional ellipses and circles for use in a simple drawing package. Which class would you create first? Investigate the possible use of inheritance to increase code reuse. Would you use delegation in this case?

4. Give at least two different ways to implement the state of the following classes:

   - `FMATRIX` (general rectangular matrices)
   - `SMATRIX` (sparse matrices, that is many zeros)
   - `HISTOGRAM` (a class for bar charts)
   - `DEPARTMENT` (a grouping of staff in a company)
   - `PURCHASE` (an interaction class)

5. Determine default behaviour (virtual functions) for the following base classes:

   - `PROJECT`
   - `MATRIX`
   - `PUMP`

   (*Hint*: What have all derived classes of the above base classes in common? Such commonality should be promoted to the base class and made virtual.)

6. Create template class declarations and definitions for the following abstractions:

   - Circular queue (ring buffer)
   - Stack

   Circular queues and stacks are often used in data structures in operating systems. For example, a ring buffer could be used to pass information between two or more routines. One routine is usually a producer, the other a consumer. The first routine feeds information to the list while the other routine removes and processes information. For more information, see Levy and Eckhouse (1980). (*Hint*: see Figure 3.7a.)

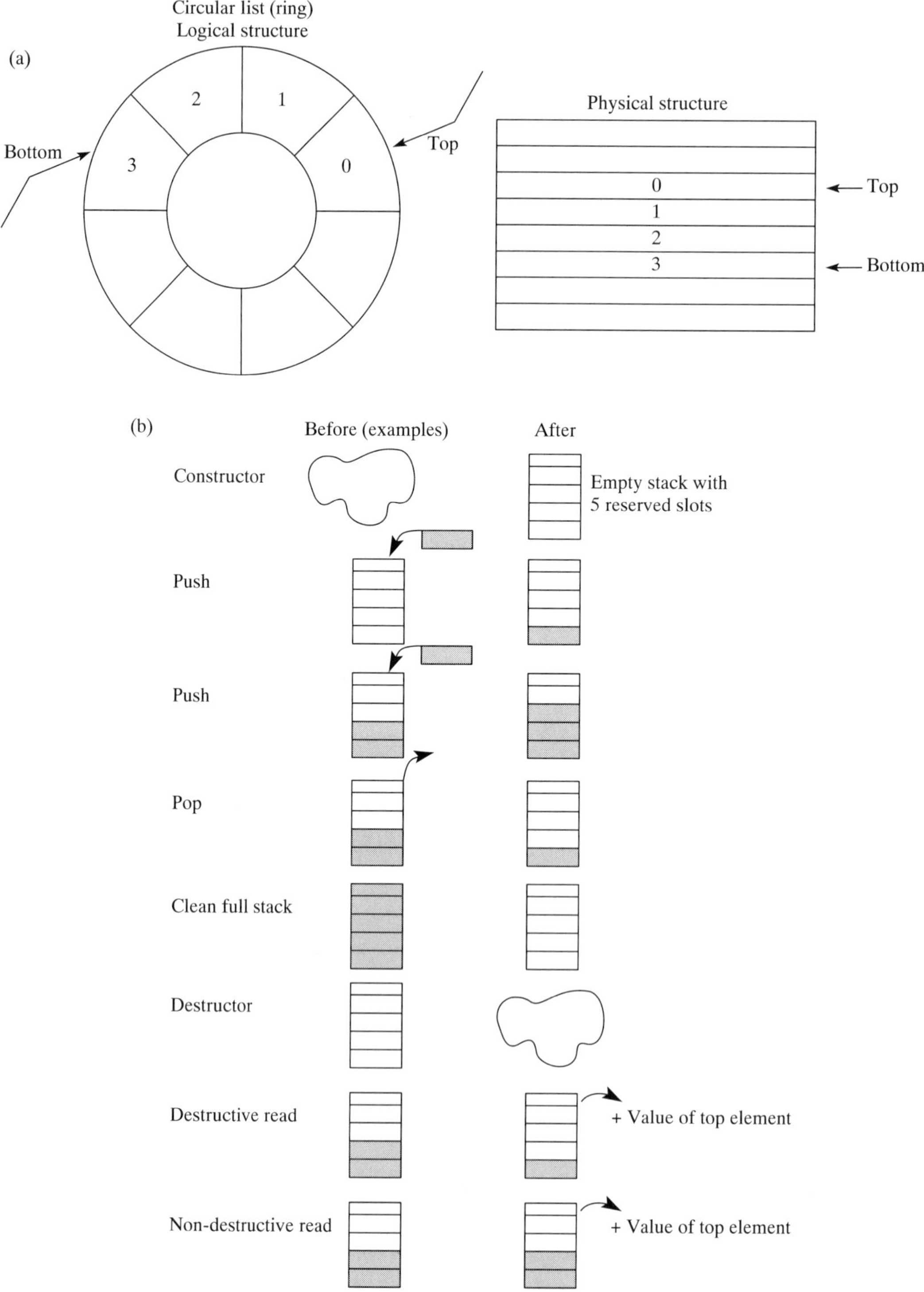

Figure 3.7 Rings and stacks.

7. Create a template class declaration for general numeric data types (integer, smallinteger, rational, double). Which specializations can be built based on it? (*Hint*: find the commonality among all numeric data types and create a template from it.) What are the advantages in terms of reusability, maintainability and efficiency?

8. What are the candidates for static members for the following classes?

   - Full-time employee
   - File access by users
   - Allocation of disk quotas to users

9. Give at least four different ways of making your C++ code more accessible for new and experienced C++ programmers.

References

M. Ball (1993a) What are these things called templates, *C++ Report*, February.

M. Ball (1993b) Implementing class templates, *C++ Report*, September.

J. Carolan (1991) *CommonView and Framework Design*, Glockenspiel Ltd, Dublin.

J. M. Coggins (1990) Designing C++ Libraries, *1990 USENIX C++ Conference*.

M. Ellis and B. Stroustrup (1990) *The Annotated C++ Reference Manual*, Addison-Wesley, Reading MA.

E. B. Koffman (1988) *Problem Solving and Structured Programming in Modula-2*, Addison-Wesley, Reading MA.

J. Landin (1969) *An Introduction to Algebraic Structures*, Dover, New York.

H. M. Levy and R. M. Eckhouse, Jr (1980) *Computer Programming and Architecture – The VAX*, Digital Press, Digital Equipment Corporation.

M. A. Linton and P. J. Calder (1987) The design and implementation of InterViews, *1987 USENIX C++ Conference*.

B. Meyer (1988) *Object-Oriented Software Construction*, Prentice-Hall, Englewood Cliffs NJ.

I. C. Pyle (1985) *The Ada Programming Language*, 2nd edn, Prentice-Hall, Englewood Cliffs NJ.

J. Rumbaugh, M. Blaha, W. Premerlani, F. Eddy and W. Lorensen (1991) *Object-Oriented Modeling and Design*, Prentice-Hall, Englewood Cliffs NJ.

R. R. Stoll (1961) *Sets, Logic and Axiomatic Theories*, W. H. Freeman, New York.

Chapter

4

Comparing C++ with other languages

4.1 Introduction and objectives

This chapter takes a look at a number of different programming paradigms and languages. C++ is compared with these languages and its advantages and shortcomings are enumerated. Languages are categorized according to how they support the different features in the object-oriented paradigm. Furthermore, a precise definition is given of what it means to say that a language is object-oriented.

A number of interesting extensions to C++ are discussed. These extensions have to do with objects with built-in support for concurrency and synchronization.

4.2 Object-based languages

Chapter 1 discussed what the essential characteristics of an object were. We recall that an object has state, behaviour and identity. Objects have 'memory', which resides in their state. Object operations are not the same as functions. A function is completely determined by its arguments and has no memory. Languages which do not support objects use global data in order to store information which survives function calls. The disadvantage of this approach is that global data can be accessed by any function in the system. This is seen as a violation of the information hiding principle. For example, FORTRAN uses common blocks to store global data, and the data in these blocks may be modified by any subroutine.

A language is called object-based if it supports objects as a language feature. This definition includes languages such as Ada, Modula-2, C++ and Smalltalk, but it excludes languages such as Cobol, FORTRAN and Pascal. Ada implements objects by packages. A package declaration is very similar to a C++ header file. Both the state and the operations are declared in the package. For example, a package for complex numbers in Ada is specified as follows:

```
package COMPLEX_NUMBERS is
  type COMPLEX is
    record
        RE: FLOAT := 0.0;
        IM: FLOAT := 0.0;
    end record;

  function "+" (X, Y: COMPLEX) return COMPLEX;
  function "*" (X, Y: COMPLEX) return COMPLEX;
  function "/" (X, Y: COMPLEX) return COMPLEX;
end COMPLEX_NUMBERS
```

The following example shows how the resources of this package can be used:

```
declare
  use COMPLEX_NUMBERS
  X,Y,Z: COMPLEX;
begin
  X := (1.5, 2.5);
  Y := X*X;
  Z := X/Y;
  Z := Z + X;
  Z.RE := 0.0;
  Z.IM := 0.0;
end;
```


Notice that the COMPLEX_NUMBERS package has been specified in such a way that it is possible to access the variables RE and IM directly. These variables are defined in the public part of COMPLEX_NUMBERS. It is possible to implement encapsulation in Ada by splitting the package specification into a public part and a private part, as follows:

```
package COMPLEX_NUMBERS
  type COMPLEX is private;
  function "+" (X,Y:COMPLEX) return COMPLEX;
  function "*" (X,Y:COMPLEX) return COMPLEX;
  function "/" (X,Y:COMPLEX) return COMPLEX;
private
  type COMPLEX is
    record
        RE: FLOAT := 0.0;
        IM: FLOAT := 0.0;
    end record
end COMPLEX_NUMBERS;
```

It is not possible for instances of COMPLEX to access the variables RE or IM directly because they are declared private.

Each package specification in Ada must have a corresponding package body. The body implements the resources which have been declared in the package specification. The body contains implementation-specific details which are hidden from client software. Furthermore, the body may access the private data area directly.

Let us suppose that we wish to create a package for pure imaginary numbers, that is complex numbers whose real part is zero. There is no way in standard Ada to create a package IMAGINARY_NUMBERS as a derivation of COMPLEX_NUMBERS. We must develop IMAGINARY_NUMBERS from first principles. This results in much code duplication, since most of the functionality is already in COMPLEX_NUMBERS! This is why we say that Ada is object-based and not object-oriented, since inheritance is not supported. The package specification for IMAGINARY_NUMBERS is:

```
package IMAGINARY_NUMBERS is
  type IMAGY is private;
    function "+" (X : IMAGY; Y:COMPLEX) return COMPLEX;
    function "*" (X : IMAGY; Y:COMPLEX) return COMPLEX;
    function "/" (X : IMAGY; Y:COMPLEX) return COMPLEX;

    function "+" (X : IMAGY; Y:IMAGY) return COMPLEX;
    function "*" (X : IMAGY; Y:IMAGY) return COMPLEX;
    function "/" (X : IMAGY; Y:IMAGY) return COMPLEX;
  private
    type IMAGY is
        record
            IM: FLOAT := 0.0;
    end record;
end IMAGINARY_NUMBERS;
```

Modula-2 implements objects as modules. A module is similar to an Ada package; it has a specification (the so-called definition module) and an body (the implementation module). Modula-2 does not support operator overloading as in Ada and C++, thus new function name equivalents must be devised for the operators +, * and /. The definition module for the complex numbers ADT in Modula-2 is:

```
DEFINITION MODULE COMPLEX_NUMBERS;
(*
  Specification of an ADT for complex numbers
*)

  EXPORT QUALIFIED
    COMPLEX
    CreateComplex, AddComplex, MultiplyComplex,
    DivideComplex;

  TYPE
    COMPLEX = RECORD
        RE, IM: REAL;
    END;
  PROCEDURE CreateComplex(VAR C: COMPLEX); (* C is output *);
```

```
  PROCEDURE ReadComplex(VAR X: COMPLEX);

  PROCEDURE AddComplex(X, Y : COMPLEX;
    VAR Z : COMPLEX);

  PROCEDURE MultiplyComplex(X, Y : COMPLEX;
    VAR Z : COMPLEX);

  PROCEDURE DivideComplex(X, Y : COMPLEX;
    VAR Z : COMPLEX);

END COMPLEX_NUMBERS.
```

The following code show how the module COMPLEX_NUMBERS is used to add, multiply and divide complex numbers:

```
MODULE TestComplex;

FROM COMPLEX_NUMBERS IMPORT
  COMPLEX,
  CreateComplex, AddComplex, MultiplyComplex,
  DivideComplex, ReadComplex;

VAR
  X, Y, Z : COMPLEX;

BEGIN
  CreateComplex(X);
  CreateComplex(Y);
  CreateComplex(Z);
  CreateComplex(ZZ);
  CreateComplex(ZZZ);

  ReadComplex(X);
  ReadComplex(Y);

  AddComplex(X,Y,Z);
  MultiplyComplex(X,Y,Z);
  DivideComplex(X,Y,ZZ);
  MultiplyComplex(X,Y,ZZZ);

END TestComplex.
```

4.3 Classless and class-based languages

Objects which are not required to have a class are called classless objects. An object-based language is called classless if its objects are classless. Classless languages are useful in experimental programming due to the relaxed approach taken to type checking. An example of a classless language is Ada. However, this is a language with strong type-checking features, and this can seen as one of its major strengths, which is on of the reasons why it is used in mission-critical applications.

Classless languages have a number of advantages when compared with languages whose objects belong to a given class. The main ones are:

- Class-independent operations. It does not always make sense to associate an operation with one specific class, because an operation may apply to several classes or it may change both the state and interface of objects. This functionality is not directly supported in C++ and it is the responsibility of the programmer to write suitable code if this is needed.
- Classes with a single element. In this case it is not sensible to talk about shared behaviour since there is only class instance. C++ allows the developer to create classes having only one element; these are the so-called static classes.

An object-based language is called class-based if every object has a class. We see that class-based languages are a proper subset of the set of object-based languages. An example of a class-based language is CLU, in which CLU's clusters are used as templates for generating objects. CLU's objects are 'first-class' objects in the sense that they can be assigned as variables, used as components of structures and passed as arguments in functions. Other examples of class-based languages are C++, Eiffel and Smalltalk, although these languages have more to offer than just the facility for creating objects.

4.4 Strong and weak typing

A language is called strongly typed if 'type compatibility of all variables and expressions which represent values can be determined from the static program representation at compile time' (Wegner 1987). Examples of strongly typed languages are C, C++, FORTRAN, Pascal and Ada. In other words, variables bind to values at compile time (early binding). A language is called weakly typed if the type of a variable is determined not at compile time, but at run-time (late binding). A good example of a weakly typed language is Smalltalk, in which weak typing is implemented in order to achieve dynamic binding. In Smalltalk variables may be assigned values of different types at different points of execution. This approach has advantages and disadvantages.

4.5 Object-oriented languages

Chapter 2 dealt with abstract data types (ADTs), but we repeat the definition of data abstraction here for completeness (Wegner 1987):

> A data abstraction is an object whose state is accessible only through its operations. The state is generally represented by instance variables. Instance variables of a data abstraction are hidden from its clients and are accessible only through the object's operations.

We now say that a language is object-oriented if it requires that all objects belong to classes and class hierarchies may be incrementally defined by an inheritance mechanism. This definition includes C++, Smalltalk and Eiffel, but excludes Ada and Modula-2.

A strongly typed object-oriented language is an object-oriented language which is strongly typed and which requires all objects to be data abstractions.

The above definition includes C++ and Eiffel, but excludes Smalltalk. In Smalltalk, variable names are used in expressions to refer to the objects whose pointers they contain. A variable may contain different object pointers at different times. The object pointer contained in a variable changes when an assignment expression is evaluated. An assignment makes a copy of a pointer to an object, not a copy of the object itself. This feature has disadvantages because it makes programs less predictable in their behaviour.

The following code is the declaration in C++ of the class of complex numbers. It is similar to the package specification in Ada for the same abstraction. The class interface is very simple and in practice it would have much more functionality so that it could be applied to problems in scientific and engineering computing:

```
// complex.hxx
//
// Class of complex number in two-dimensional space.
//
// © Datasim BV 1990 - 1994.

#ifndef DSCOMPLEX_HXX
#define DSCOMPLEX_HXX

class DSCOMPLEX
{
private:

  double x, y;

public:
  // Constructors
  DSCOMPLEX(double real, double imag);
  DSCOMPLEX(const DSCOMPLEX& p);

  // Member operator overloading
  DSCOMPLEX  operator +  (const DSCOMPLEX& c2) const;
  DSCOMPLEX  operator *  (const DSCOMPLEX& c2) const;
  DSCOMPLEX  operator /  (const DSCOMPLEX& c2) const;
};
#endif   // DSCOMPLEX_HXX
```

Since C++ supports inheritance it is possible to define the set of pure imaginary complex numbers as a derived class `DSIMAGINARY` of `DSCOMPLEX`. This implies code sharing because we do not have to redefine member functions which are common to `DSCOMPLEX` and `DSIMAGINARY`. Compared with the Ada solution this saves the programmer having to redefine the operators '+', '*' and '/'.

4.6 Delegation and prototypical objects

Inheritance is a mechanism for sharing behaviour between objects. Inheritance groups objects into classes, and these classes encode shared behaviour among a group of instances.

The class/instance distinction is not needed if prototype objects are used. A prototype is a default behaviour for a concept. It is possible for new objects to reuse part of the knowledge stored in the prototype by stating how the new object differs from the prototype. The prototype is the 'ancestor' of the newly created object, and we say that responsibility has been delegated to the prototype. Delegation is more intuitive than inheritance, since it is easier to think about specific objects rather than their corresponding classes. For example, suppose that Clyde is an elephant. Stating this fact conjures up ideas of what other elephants look like.

The official definition of delegation is as follows:

> Delegation is a mechanism that allows objects to delegate responsibility for performing an operation or finding a value from one or more designated ancestors.

Inheritance is a specialization of delegation in which the entities that inherit are classes; with delegation objects can be seen as inheriting from their ancestors. However, delegation is less familiar than inheritance and it is not used in commercially available compilers.

A delegation-based language is defined as an object-based language that supports classless objects and delegation.

Delegation and prototypical objects are discussed in Aksit *et al.* (1991), Lieberman (1986) and Stein (1987).

4.7 Actor-based languages

With the advent of parallel hardware systems and processors there is a growing need to build software compilers and applications which can take advantage of these new possibilities. For this reason we discuss some emerging ideas and concepts which will help to build the next generation of parallel compilers. Most of the ideas presented here are taken from the excellent monograph by Agha (1986). C++ does not support parallel processing and it is thus fitting to discuss how it can be implemented, at least on a conceptual level.

Concurrency is defined as the potential parallel execution of actions without a determinate predefined sequence of their actions. There is a need for a software environment in which processes can work together in a meaningful manner. (Time-sharing systems are not concurrent under this definition because processes in such systems have no influence on each other.) The processes can be distributed over a network of processors. Many applications are inherently parallel in nature (for example, genetic algorithms) and the actor paradigm is one attempt to lay the infrastructure for such applications.

An actor language is a low-level language which can be used to create more complex and sophisticated languages. Actor languages support objects, abstraction and concurrency, but not classes, inheritance or strong typing.

An actor is an object or computational agent which has a mail address (mailbox name) and a behaviour. The mailbox designates a buffer which can store an unbounded linear sequence of messages or 'communications'. An actor's behaviour is determined by its actions in response to a communication. It is worth mentioning that the only way that actors may affect each other is by communications. The identity of the actor is determined by its mailbox name.

Actors respond to communications by sending messages, creating new actors and creating replacements. This is shown in Figure 4.1. In this case an actor is associated with a mail queue and the actor has a sequence of incarnations in which $X(n)$ represents the incarnation

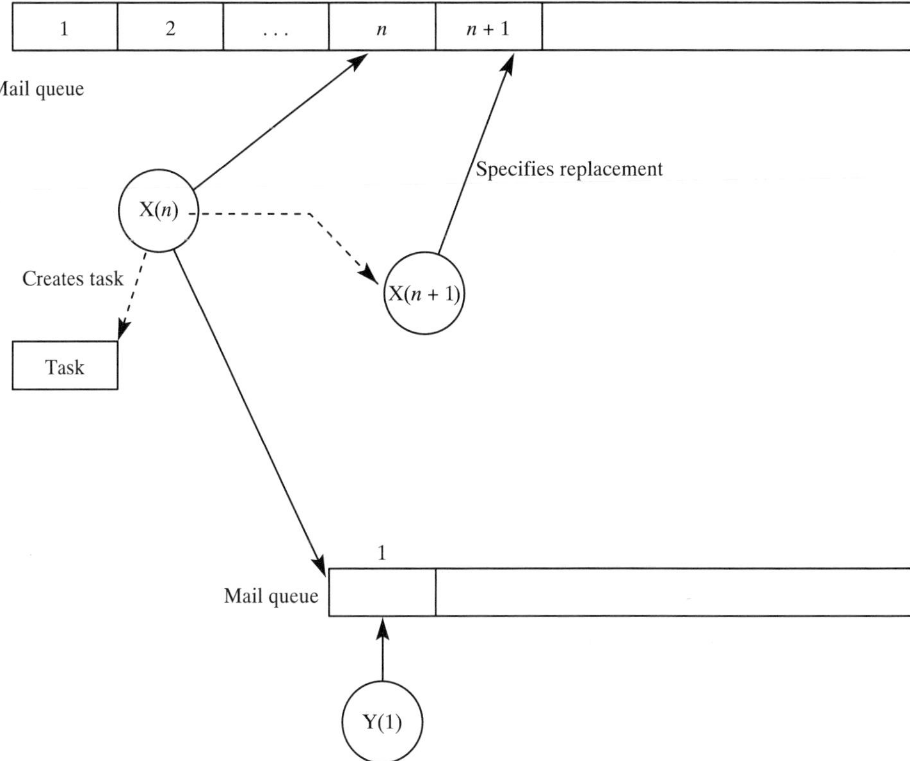

Figure 4.1 Actors.

that processes the nth communication. $X(n)$ must wait until its communication (in slot n of the queue) arrives. It then creates a replacement behaviour $X(n+1)$ which processes the $(n+1)$th communication. As can be seen from Figure 4.1, a new actor is also created.

A task is a 3-tuple consisting of the following:

- A tag or task ID, which uniquely distinguishes the from all other tasks in the system.
- A target, which is the mail address to which the communication is to be delivered.
- A communication which contains information which is made available to the actor at the target when that actor gains possessions of the given task.

Communications are contained in tasks. As computations proceed in an actor system new tasks and new actors are created as a result of processing tasks already in the system. Tasks that have already been processed and actors that are no longer needed may be removed from the system by a process of garbage collection. This will not affect subsequent behaviour.

Data structures and control structures can easily be created in actor systems. They obviate the need to use pointer types as is the case in C or C++. To give an example, we consider a stack type which is implemented as a linked list of actors. We needs some definitions. An actor 'a' is said to be an acquaintance of an actor 'b' if 'b' knows the mail address of 'a'. Getting back to the stack, we assume that the linked list is a collection of nodes with each node storing a value and which knows about the mail address of the next actor in the list.

The top of the stack is the only actor which can accept communications from outside the system, and for this reason it is called a receptionist. For a stack the number of receptionists is constant (namely one), but in general the set of receptionists in a general system evolves dynamically as we allow the mail address of actors are communicated to the outside world. When a 'pop' operation is executed the actor residing on the top of the stack becomes a forwarder to the next actor.

4.8 Object-based concurrency

Concurrent object-based languages model the world by the use of concurrently executable objects called processes. A process is used in the context of operating systems to mean a computation performed on a given processor. Informally, a sequential process is a program in execution. Thus, at any point in time at most one instruction is executed on behalf of the process. We say that a sequential process is a process with only one thread of control. A thread is a basic unit of CPU utilization. The environment in which a thread executes is called a task. Traditional (heavyweight) processes are tasks with one thread. A quasi-concurrent process is one that has at most one active thread of control. Finally, a concurrent process is one which may have multiple active threads of control.

C++ is the language of choice for many developers and many attempts have been made to add concurrency to the language (Buhr *et al.* 1992; Arjomandi *et al.* 1994). The main issues are:

- *Memory model*
  There are two forms of memory which are supported in concurrent languages. These are the distributed memory model and shared memory model. The distributed memory model assumes that processors have exclusive access to their own local memory and communicate via message passing. In the shared memory model all processors share a large global memory. Communication occurs via synchronized access to shared variables.
- *Object interaction*
  Objects communicate in C++ by sending messages to each other. The way that such communication takes place is either via asynchronous or synchronous message passing. Basically, an object sends a message to another object and does one of two things:
  - Proceeds with its own activity until the result of the request is needed.
  - The caller object 'blocks' until a reply is received from the object to which the message is sent.
- *Intra-object concurrency*
  An important question when modelling objects is to determine the level of concurrency within an object. An object-oriented language may support sequential, quasi-concurrent or completely concurrent objects.
- *Concurrency and inheritance*
  Concurrency and object-oriented features are not orthogonal. In particular, there is a conflict between inheritance and synchronization mechanisms. These mechanisms maintain object integrity by specifying under what conditions object methods may be invoked.

There are three categories of concurrent object-oriented languages based on C++. These are based on the following:

(4.1)

- Implicit concurrency
- Explicit concurrency
- Mixed concurrency

The first category in (4.1) may be subdivided into two classes. The first relates to concurrency created and controlled by active objects. An active object is one which encapsulates data structures, operations, communication and synchronization mechanisms. Languages with active objects lend themselves well to a distributed memory model of computation. Intra-object concurrency may be supported in the active object in a quasi-concurrent fashion or in a concurrent fashion by using multiple concurrent threads. An example of a language which supports active objects is ACT++. This uses a shared memory, actor-based paradigm. The basic version of the language does not support inheritance between active objects.

The second class of languages which have implicit concurrency are those which support concurrency at the class level. Objects are not active because they do not encapsulate communication or synchronization mechanisms. However, there is a strong integration of concurrency and object-oriented principles. Concurrency, synchronization and mutual exclusion are implicitly supported in the class definition. A passive object is one which does not have its own thread of control and which must rely on active objects for its integrity. The necessary threads are created at the time of method invocation.

With explicit concurrency, there is less integration of concurrency and the object-oriented paradigm. The programmer is confronted by two challenges, namely:

- Creating objects
- Creating concurrent units

Examples of languages incorporating the explicit concurrency paradigm are Concurrent C++ and Extended C++.

Finally, in the mixed concurrency paradigm, concurrency is achieved by the creation of active objects. In some languages new type constructs for co-routines, monitors, co-routine monitors and tasks are supported. An example of such a language is MC++.

4.9 Distributed processes

A distributed process is one with a separate address space. This means that it cannot directly access any resource outside its local address space and can communicate with the outside world only by message passing.

Combining the distributed process and object-oriented paradigms is difficult. Wegner (1987) claims that the two are incompatible. On the one hand, distribution increases the autonomy of processes, while on the other it makes it expensive to share nonlocal resources by mechanisms such as inheritance. This is basically because the goals of modularity and resource sharing (state or behaviour) are incompatible.

4.10 Object parallelism

Objects communicate by sending messages to each other. A number of research-oriented object-oriented languages offer services which mirror the functionality which exists in UNIX, TCP/IP and other network protocols in which entities send requests to and receive answers from other entities. In most cases, communication takes place at process level. Most communication concepts conform to the client/server metaphor in which a client process initiates a connection and requests services from a server process. The server process can react in one of two ways:

- Asynchronously
- Synchronously

An asynchronous request to a server process allows the client to carry out other duties while the server is executing the task. The client process does not have to wait for completion of the task. A synchronous request implies that the client process must wait until the server process has executed the request.

4.11 Concluding remarks

C++ is a strongly typed object-oriented language. It is a hybrid language because it allows procedural code written in C to be used in conjunction with its object-oriented extensions. It is superior to object-based and non-object-oriented languages because of its support for information hiding and inheritance. A number of extensions have been proposed for the language, such as support for concurrency and synchronization, and these extensions are important in distributed applications.

C++ is set to become one of the most important programming languages for the next decennium. It would be unwise however, to think that C++ is always the best language to use for all projects. If it is productivity that you are interested in, Smalltalk may be a more viable answer, because it is easy to produce a prototype solution to a given problem within days. It is less easy to make programming mistakes in Smalltalk than in C++; for example, memory management is automatic (via garbage collection), while the C++ programmer must take care of memory problems for each developed class. Furthermore, most Smalltalk implementations are delivered with a complete graphical environment containing user interfaces, class browsing tools and utility classes for developing new applications.

A number of large projects have been developed in both C++ and Smalltalk, and it is interesting to compare notes on how each was designed the way it was and how the choice of language affected the final solution. These and other issues are discussed in the interesting book by Tom Love (1993). This book is a must for managers, project leaders and other decision makers who have decided that their organization will make the move to the object-oriented paradigm.

References

G. Agha (1986) *ACTORS*, MIT Press, Cambridge MA.

M. Aksit, J. W. Dijkstra and A. Tripathi (1991) Atomic delegation: object-oriented transactions, *IEEE Software*, March.

E. Arjomandi, W. O'Farrell and I. Kalas (1994) Concurrency support for C++, an overview, *C++ Report*, January.

P. A. Buhr *et al.* (1992) MC++: concurrency in the object-oriented language C++, *Software Practice and Experience*, **22**(2) 137–72.

H. Lieberman (1986) Using prototypical objects to implement shared behaviour in object oriented systems, *OOPSLA '86 Proceedings*, September.

T. Love (1993) *Object Lessons*, SIGS Books Inc., New York.

L. A. Stein (1987) Delegation is inheritance, *OOPSLA '87 Proceedings*, 4–8 October.

P. Wegner (1987) Dimensions of object-oriented languages, *OOPSLA '87 Proceedings*, 4–8 October.

Part

2

The object-oriented software process

Chapter

5

General overview of the object-oriented life-cycle

5.1 Introduction and objectives

In Part 1 we gave a global introduction to the most important ideas and concepts which are the foundation for the object-oriented paradigm. It was implicitly assumed that we knew where to find the types and classes which would eventually be implemented in C++. Whereas it is relatively easy to find classes for small isolated problems, this is much more difficult for real-world applications. A process needs to be established which can be executed in steps or phases with the output from one phase functioning as input for the next phase. Eventually we arrive at a set of deliverables which can be used as input for a full implementation of the problem to be solved. In general terms, a requirements document is drawn up which describes what a software system should do. The final product is usually one or more executable images which fulfil the specifications in the requirements document. Between these two extremes there is a sequence of well-defined steps to be followed. The objective of this chapter is to explain what these steps are, what needs to be done in each step and how the different steps interface with each other.

This chapter lays the foundation for the other chapters in Part 2. It gives a helicopter view of the software life-cycle from initial requirements to implementation.

5.2 The phases in the object-oriented software process

The first step in the software life-cycle is defining and describing user needs. This is called requirements determination and it is the process of determining candidate needs. In other words, the requirements determination phase results in a set of needs which are later reconciled into a consistent set of requirements that form a viable system. This is the responsibility of the requirements analysis phase. Determining initial requirements is not an easy process. Its success depends on the people (designers, users, domain experts) taking

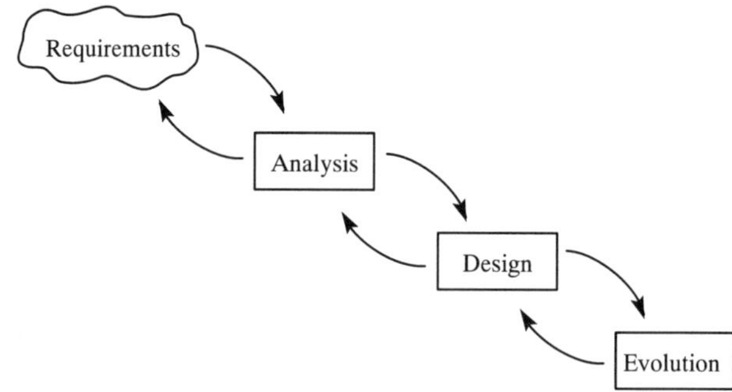

Figure 5.1 Object-oriented software life-cycle.

part in the project. In Chapter 6 we shall discuss concept mapping techniques which aid in this initial requirements phase of the software life-cycle.

There is a general agreement in the literature that the object-oriented or iterative software life-cycle has the form shown in Figure 5.1. Once the requirements for a system have been determined we can proceed to the analysis phase. The main responsibilities of this phase are finding the classes, attributes, relationships and inheritance hierarchies which arise for the given problem. This phase concerns itself with the 'what' and not the 'how'. The analysis phase produces a consistent set of requirements describing what the system should do. The main responsibilities of the design phase are in determining the overall hardware and software architecture, how object classes are to be designed and how the analysis model should be elaborated upon. It is in this phase that new classes are created which do not occur in the original problem domain. These are the so-called internal or software classes and they act as the 'glue' between the external or application classes. To summarize, the design phase produces a blueprint which can be used for an implementation.

The final phase of the object-oriented life-cycle is called 'evolution'. This is similar to the coding phase in classical software life-cycles, except in this case the product from the evolution phase is a prototype solution. There is no concept of 'the final product'. Prototypes go through a number of revisions before a definitive or production prototype is realized.

In an ideal world the sequence of steps from requirements to evolution should be in one direction only. However, it may prove necessary to 'backtrack' from one phase to another one 'further upstream'. For example, we may discover in the design phase that certain key abstractions from the problem domain have been left out or have not been discovered in the analysis or requirements phase (or both!). In this case we would need to go back and carry out these processes again. This can happen if we are working on a project whose full requirements are not fully specified when we embark on the analysis of the problem. This is common with highly complex and new applications. One cannot expect to get it right the first time and a certain amount of backtracking is unavoidable. This does not have to be a big problem, since different parts of a problem can be simultaneously worked on. For example, it is possible that some team members are working on the design of a problem while other members are simultaneously implementing a prototype solution.

An advantage of using the model in Figure 5.1 is that it is possible to work with the same conceptual tools in each phase of the life-cycle. This results in seamless interfaces between the different phases, and we thus avoid the 'impedance mismatch' problem which is seen

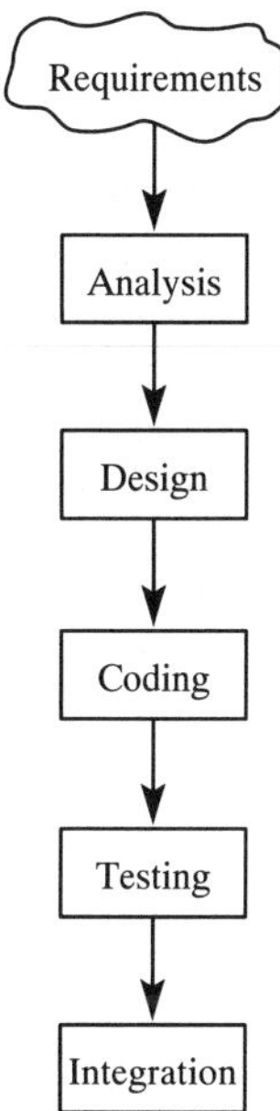

Figure 5.2 The waterfall software life-cycle.

with classical development methods. For example, a class which has been created in the analysis phase continues to be a class in both the design and implementation phases. Compare this with classical methods, in which real-world entities in the analysis phase are transformed to relational database tables or records in Cobol in the design phase. All semantic relevance has been lost when moving from analysis to design. We are unable to trace objects from one model to another. This makes it difficult to modify the system once design decisions have been made.

5.3 Classical development methods

The classical software life-cycle is represented in Figure 5.2. This is equivalent to the classical and outdated waterfall development method. The term 'waterfall' is used because the different steps are executed sequentially with no possibility of backtracking. This feature makes the waterfall method unsuitable for problems whose specifications are not well understood. It is difficult to backtrack without a lot of effort being spent in a new analysis and design of the problem. This is all the more difficult because the conceptual models used in the different phase of the software life-cycle are different. Analysts use entity relationship diagrams and functional decomposition techniques. Designers use data flow diagrams (DFDs), structure charts and action diagrams. Programmers and coders use Cobol, PL/1, C and FORTRAN.

Object-oriented techniques use the same conceptual model in all phases of the software life-cycle. Thus, object-oriented techniques tear down the conceptual walls between analysis, design and implementation (Martin and Odell 1992).

5.4 Risk-driven software life-cycle

One of the major disadvantages of the object-oriented software life-cycle approach is that it is not always clear when to stop designing and evolving a product and when to get the product out to the customers. We run the risk of endlessly looping in the analysis–design–evolution circle. Another shortcoming of this approach is that the waterfall method is well-suited for problems which are fully specified, and in these cases the iterative approach is less effective. In order to combine the best of both of these approaches the so-called spiral model has been devised (Boehm 1986, Boehm and Papaccio 1988). This is a risk-driven life-cycle model and it represents a more robust foundation for software development than the two previous models. The main features of this model are:

- It includes previous models as special cases.
- It provides guidance on how to combine the best fit of previous models.

The spiral model is shown in Figure 5.3. Software development is seen as a sequence of cycles. Each cycle has a start and a finish and a corresponding cost. The software process is represented in polar coordinate form in Figure 5.3. The radial dimension represents the

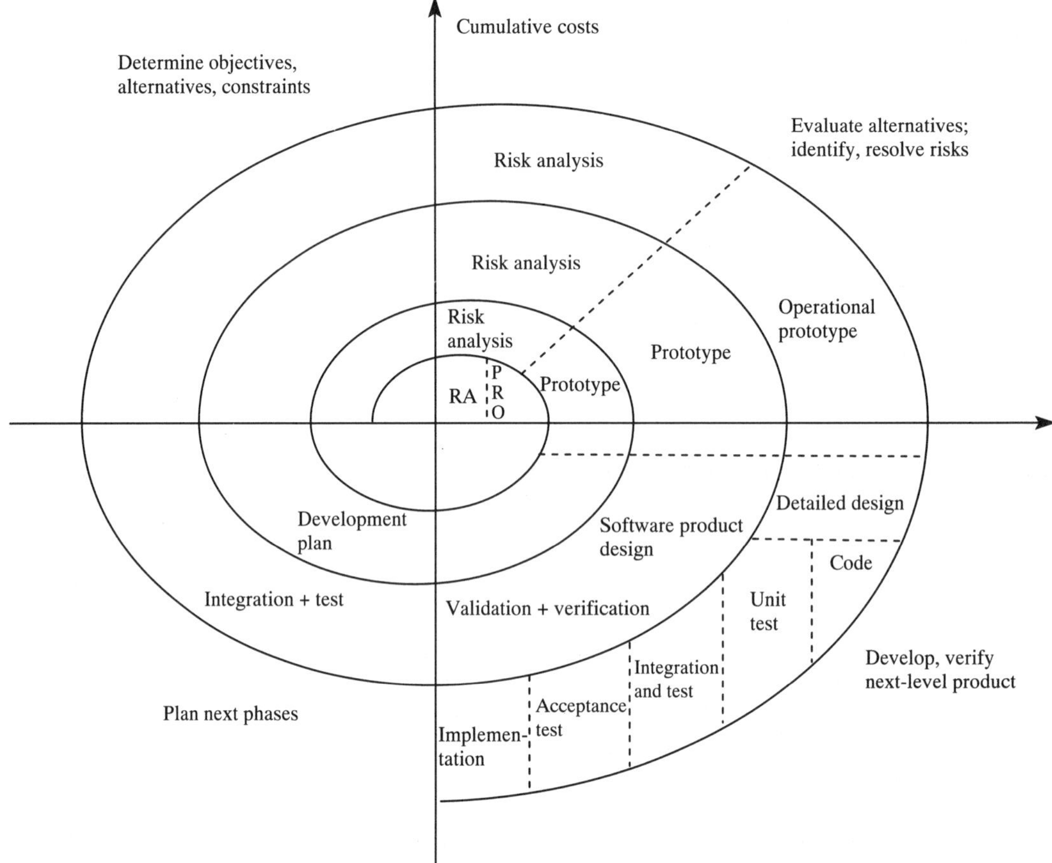

Figure 5.3 Risk-driven software life-cycle (Boehm 1986).

cumulative cost incurred in accomplishing the steps to date, while the angular dimension represents the progress made in completing each cycle of the spiral. All cycles have the same 'look and feel' in the sense that they all involve a progression through the same sequence of steps from an overall concept-of-operation document down to the coding of each individual program.

Before a cycle can begin, a number of steps need to be carried out:

- Identify the objectives of the portions of the product being elaborated, for example performance, functionality, ability to accommodate change.
- Examine the alternative means of implementing this portion of the product, for example choosing for design A, design B, reuse and purchase of software.
- Identify the constraints imposed on the application of the alternatives, for example cost, schedule and interfaces.

Having identified the objectives and constraints we now need to evaluate the alternatives with respect to these objectives and constraints. The main reason for this is to identify areas of uncertainty, which are a source of project risk. A cost-effective strategy for resolving this risk needs to be proposed. Possible solutions are:

- Prototyping
- Simulation
- Administering user questionnaires
- Analytic modelling

Each cycle in the spiral model is completed by a status review by those organizations and personnel involved with the product. The review should cover the following topics:

- The products developed during the previous cycle
- Plans for the next cycle
- Identification of resources which will be needed for the next cycle

The spiral model reduces to one of the other two models under certain conditions. For example, if a software product's requirements are very stable then the waterfall model should be employed. For example, if a number of prototypes of a software product have been developed we may decide to employ the waterfall method in order to create the final 'production prototype', including the classical steps of unit and integration testing, acceptance testing and final implementation. On the other hand, if a project has a low risk as far as losing budget or schedule predictability are concerned then the spiral model is driven into the equivalent of the object-oriented development method.

The advantages of using the spiral model are:

- It proposes strategies for developing program families.
- Reuse of existing software is encouraged.
- It accommodates life-cycle evolution, growth and changes to the software product.
- We can introduce checklists for software quality objectives at each round of the spiral.
- It focuses on eliminating errors and unattractive alternatives at an early stage of the software life-cycle.

- It accommodates iterations and early termination of non-viable software projects.
- It answers the question 'How much is enough'. For example, it gives guidelines on when to stop performing a requirements analysis or when testing software.

5.5 Object-oriented requirements determination

The first step in the object-oriented development method is to determine what the user of the system needs. A 'user' may be a person, organization, hardware or software. To this end, we need to carry out an object-oriented requirements determination (OORD). This is the process of determining candidate needs. How do we do this? Most books assume that the objects and classes which are part of a given problem domain are known in advance or can be easily found. For example, Meyer (1988) claims that objects are 'for the picking'. This may be true for simple problems or problems which are already well understood, but for new or complex it is less clear-cut.

This book uses a number of techniques which will help in determining candidate needs. These are:

- Concept maps (Novak and Gowin 1984)
- Event–response lists and storyboards (Umphress and March 1991)
- Use case models (Jacobson *et al.* 1992)

Concept maps have their foundations in education and cognitive theory. They are an effective visual tool for learning in the classroom and they have been used in schools throughout the USA. Their use allows schoolchildren to focus on key ideas, thereby externalizing their understanding of material and strengthening their ability to think in a logical fashion. The advantages of concept mapping techniques in the requirements determination phase of the software life-cycle is that they allow us to draw up a list of initial objects and the relationships between them. Concept mapping techniques are thus used as a conceptual front-end to bridge the semantic gap between user conceptualization of needs and developer realization of requirements. Concept maps will be discussed in Chapter 6, and they are used for all the test cases presented in this book.

Concept maps concentrate on the long-term structural relationships in a system. They are static in nature and thus do not show component behaviour when reacting to external stimuli. In order to complement concept maps, event–response lists and storyboards are constructed which describe dynamic behaviour and how the system reacts to external events. An event–response list is a triple of event, response and constraints. Events describe external stimuli. Examples of events are:

- User presses a button
- A timer expires
- A new issue of a journal appears
- A file is copied across a network

Responses describe reactions to events. Possible responses to the above events could be:

- Coffee is dispensed
- Object is removed from cache memory

- Interested readers are placed on a circulation list
- Another user gains access to the file

A given event may cause a number of responses. For example, when a petrol pump has been enabled by an attendant (the event) the following responses follow:

- The pump motor is started.
- The clutch is freed.
- The pump display counters are zeroed.

Constraints are optional and they describe non-functional characteristics of the event–response pair. Constraints can describe such things as the maximum or minimum amount of time that can occur between an event and its corresponding response. Examples of responses and their constraints are:

- Start pump motor
- Enough petrol in the petrol tank (constraint)

- Read project data from the mainframe database
- Data has not already been read (constraint 1)
- It must be the last day of the month (constraint 2)

- Place reader on a circulation list
- Reader must be approved by his department (constraint)

The main use of the event–response list is to enumerate as fully as possible the expectations of the user when interacting with the system. Only visible events should be described.

Storyboards tie together concept maps and event–response lists by describing in comic book fashion a frame-by-frame account of the system being defined. Its main use is to illustrate the user's concept of the completed system.

A storyboard depicts action for a single representative scenario. It should only show major functions that bridge understanding between the user and the designer; minor housekeeping details should not be included.

Jacobson *et al.* (1992) uses a number of techniques which are quite similar to event–response lists and storyboards. He introduces the notion of a requirements model in which all functionality that the system is to fulfil is defined. Central to his method is the 'use case' model, and this serves as the basis for both construction and testing processes. It controls a large part of system development.

The use case model makes use of actors and use cases. An actor represents an entity which interacts with the system, while use cases describe what should be performed by the system. They are useful concepts which aid our understanding of what happens in the system. Since actors are outside the scope of the system they are not described in detail. When a user uses a system he or she will perform a related sequence of transactions during a dialogue with the system. Such a sequence is called a use case. The set of all use cases in a system constitutes the functionality of the system as perceived by the user of the system. For a use case the

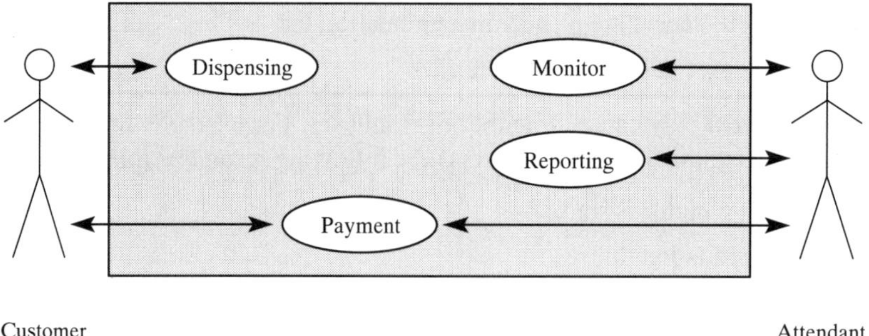

Figure 5.4 Use case model for petrol station.

Jacobson approach uses so-called detailed descriptions. These descriptions allow us to identify the actual objects in the system. Descriptions are equivalent to event–response lists.

In a petrol station system we can identify a number of use cases. The main actors are the attendant and the customer. Other actors could possibly play a role. For example, tanks can be refilled and equipment can be maintained by an oil company and by a service company, respectively. The main use cases are for the following scenarios:

- Dispensing of petrol
- Payment
- Tank level monitoring
- Reporting on customer usage

The use case model for this problem is shown in Figure 5.4.

Figure 5.5 is a concept map for the main ideas presented in this section and the relationships between them.

Concept maps, event–response lists, storyboards and use case models will be discussed in more detail in Chapters 6 and 7. Taken together these techniques result in an inexpensive prototype of the system to be built.

There are number of other informal techniques based on natural language which help in the determination of candidate classes (Abbott 1983; Saeki *et al.* (1989). The main conclusion in these articles is that nouns in requirements documents correspond to classes while verbs and verb phrases correspond to methods.

5.6 Object-oriented analysis (OOA)

The products from the requirements determination phase of the object-oriented life-cycle are a set of candidate needs in the form of concept maps, event–response lists and storyboards. The main purpose of the OOA phase is to reconcile these needs into a consistent set of requirements that form a viable system (Umphress and March 1991). Analysis is concerned with the 'what'; this means that we are interested in the abstractions, concepts, events and relationships which form part of the problem domain under discussion. Thus, implementation or design details should be absent from this part of the life-cycle. We should try to eliminate this type of irrelevant information as early as possible.

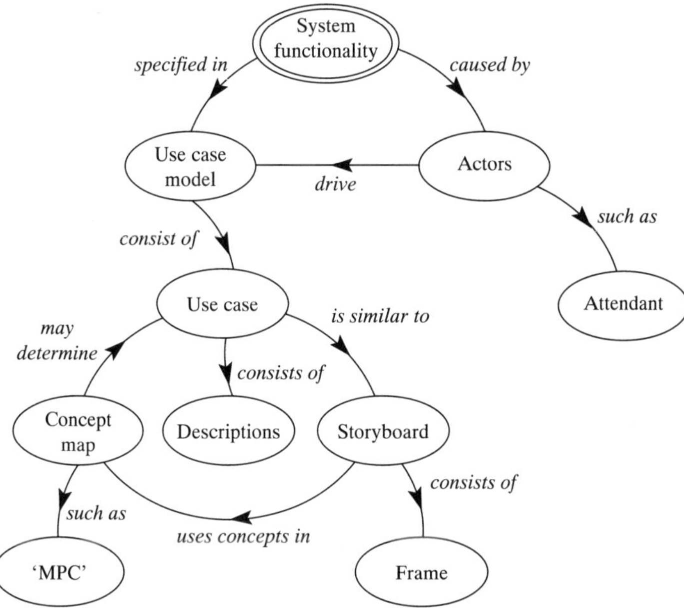

Figure 5.5 Concept map for concept maps, storyboards and use cases.

It is generally accepted in the literature on object-oriented analysis that the real world can be approximated by three different models. The first model is the structural or object model and this describes the objects in the system and the structural relationships between them. The second model is the state or dynamic model and is responsible for describing those aspects of the system which change in time. The last one is called the functional or process model, and this describes the data value transformations and calculations within a system. Each model can be studied independently of the other two models and the three models must be combined in order to produce a set of deliverables which will be used as input to the design phase.

There are a number of approaches to solving problems using an object-oriented approach. Some approaches advocate creating the object model, then the dynamic model (Rumbaugh *et al.* 1991) while others advocate a user-driven approach whereby the objects are discovered or invented at a later stage. To make matters more confusing many graphical techniques are used to represent the different models. The various techniques are:

- Object model: object diagrams, entity relationship diagrams and fern diagrams
- Dynamic model: state transition diagrams, Harel charts, event schemas
- Functional model: data flow diagrams, object flow diagrams

For more information on these and other techniques we refer to Rumbaugh *et al.* (1991), Martin and Odell (1992), Shlaer and Mellor (1988, 1992), Coad and Yourdon (1991), Coleman *et al.* (1994) and Firesmith (1993).

This book uses the object modelling technique (OMT). We provide a number of add-ons to this technique in order to make the method easier to understand and to use. In particular, we use concept mapping techniques as a front-end to object diagram creation in OMT. Furthermore, we use event–response lists and storyboards as input for the dynamic model.

The deliverables from each model are:

- Object model
  - Identifying object classes and their attributes
  - Identifying relationships (associations) between classes
  - Discovering generalization relationships
  - Creating a data dictionary
- Dynamic model
  - Temporal interactions between objects
  - Stimuli to objects and their responses
  - Events are mapped into object operations
- Functional model
  - Functional dependencies of values
  - Object computations
  - Each process is implemented by a method on some object

5.7 Object-oriented design (OOD)

Whereas analysis is concerned with the what, the main objective of the design phase is to create a blueprint or architectural framework for an eventual implementation. Thus, the design is the 'how'. The attention areas in OOD are:

- System design
- Object design

System design (Rumbaugh *et al.* 1991) is the phase in which the architecture for solving the problem is determined. The overall structure and style need to be determined at this stage. Since most problems are too complex or too big to solve in one attempt we usually decide to split the system into a number of independent or weakly coupled subsystems. Each subsystem should have narrow interfaces with other subsystems. Furthermore, a subsystem can be designed independently of the others.

The object design stage is an elaboration on the output of the object model. Full definitions of classes and associations need to be determined as well as nailing down attributes to specific data types. Algorithms which will implement object operations need be designed as well as constructing optimizing access paths to data. When this has been done we will be in a position to implement the solution.

5.8 Implementing the design

Having completed the design stage we are in a position to carry out an implementation. There are various alternatives, namely:

- Implement in hardware

- Implement a non-object-oriented language
- Implement in C++ or Smalltalk
- Implement using a relational database system

Our primary interest in this book is to show how C++ can be used in order to solve problems which have been analysed and designed using object-oriented techniques. C++ supports most object-oriented concepts; thus, the mapping from design to C++ is seamless. In some cases it may be necessary to store objects on disk for possible future use. Since C++ does not support persistence (all objects are transient) we have solved one test case using a software product which functions as a persistent extension to C++.

Since relational databases are so widely used and understood we include in one of the test cases (Supplier–Product problem) a solution in which relational database tables implement the design. This is discussed in Chapter 16. This is a useful example for newcomers to the object-oriented paradigm because the solution relates to concepts that are already known, and it also allows them to move to a 'higher plane' in which not only are there solutions using relational database tables but also C++ and even non-objected languages. This approach is related to the concept of subsumption in cognitive theory, which states that new information is often relatable to and subsumable under more general, more inclusive concepts (Novak and Gowin 1984). Some of the world's greatest scientists and thinkers got much of their inspiration by studying very simple problems. Sir Isaac Newton, for example, studied simple pendulums, weights, mirrors and prisms. From these simple examples emerged his famous theories of mechanics and optics. As Minsky (1986) puts it:

> In science, one can learn the most by studying what seems the least.

In music teaching we see similar trends. For example, the Suzuki approach to learning a musical instrument strongly emphasizes listening, practice and mastery of even the smallest details before progressing to the next level of study (Suzuki 1981). The same conclusions can be made for software engineering (Love 1993).

Exercises

1. Identify the main events in the following environments:

   - Coffee vending machine
   - VCR (video cassette recorder)
   - Activities at a petrol station

   (*Hint*: For a VCR a good place to start is by reading the user manual!)

2. Identify as many use cases and actors as possible for a hospital database system which administers wards, private rooms and operating theatres. Furthermore, information pertaining to nurses, surgeons and consultants needs to be maintained.

References

R. J. Abbott (1983) Program design by informal English descriptions, *Communications of the ACM*, **26**(11) November.

B. Boehm (1986) A spiral model of software development and enhancement, *ACM SIGSOFT Software Engineering Note*, **11**(4) August.

B. Boehm and P. N. Papaccio (1988) Understanding and controlling software costs, *IEEE Transactions on Software Engineering*, **14**(10) October.

P. Coad and E. Yourdon (1991) *Object-Oriented Analysis*, Prentice-Hall, Englewood Cliffs NJ.

D. Coleman *et al.* (1994) *Object-Oriented Development, The Fusion Method*, Prentice-Hall, Englewood Cliffs NJ.

D. G. Firesmith (1993) *Object-Oriented Requirements Analysis and Logical Design*, John Wiley & Sons, Chichester.

I. Jacobson *et al.* (1992) *Object-Oriented Software Engineering*, Addison-Wesley, Wokingham.

T. Love (1993) *Object Lessons*, SIGS Books Inc., New York.

J. Martin and J. J. Odell (1992) *Object-Oriented Analysis and Design*, Prentice-Hall, Englewood Cliffs NJ.

B. Meyer (1988) *Object-Oriented Software Construction*, Prentice-Hall, Englewood Cliffs NJ.

M. Minsky (1986) *The Society of Mind*, Simon & Schuster, New York.

J. D. Novak and D. B. Gowin (1984) *Learning How to Learn*, Cambridge University Press, Cambridge.

J. Rumbaugh, M. Blaha, W. Premerlani, F. Eddy and W. Lorensen (1991) *Object-Oriented Modeling and Design*, Prentice-Hall, Englewood Cliffs NJ.

M. Saeki, H. Horai and H. Enomoto (1989) Software development process from natural language specification, *11th International Conference on Software Engineering.*

S. Shlaer and S. J. Mellor (1988) *Object-Oriented Systems Analysis, Modeling the World in Data*, Yourdon Press, Englewood Cliffs NJ.

S. Shlaer and S. J. Mellor (1992) *Object Life Cycle: Modeling the World in States*, Yourdon Press, Englewood Cliffs NJ.

S. Suzuki (1981) *Ability Development from Age Zero*, Ability Development Associates, Athens OH.

D. A. Umphress and S. G. March (1991) Object-Oriented Requirements Analysis, *Journal of Object-Oriented Programming*, Focus on Analysis and Design, pp. 35–40.

Chapter

6

Concept maps and requirements determination

6.1 Introduction and objectives

There are a number of documented techniques for object-oriented analysis and design. Some are strong in analysis, while others have a well-developed strategy for system and object design. For example, OMT (Rumbaugh *et al.* 1991) proposes a thorough set of steps for analysing the classes which are found in a given problem domain. However, this method gives few guidelines on how to determine what the system requirements are. It is implicitly assumed that the classes are more or less known before the analysis process starts. Similarly, the fusion method (Coleman *et al.* 1994) treats a number of test cases, but assumes that the full requirements document has been drawn up. Martin and Odell (1992) pay some attention to modelling and discovering real-world entities as concepts, but no guidelines are given on how to find them. What is needed is a simple and effective medium in which domain experts, users and software designers can express themselves in ways that are understandable to others. To this end, we make use of a number of techniques which have their origins in education and cognitive theory (Novak and Gowin 1984). These are used by the US Air Force as an aid in requirements determination (Umphress and March 1991). The objective in this chapter is to deal with concept mapping techniques in some detail because they can be used to draw up a list of candidate classes and the relationships between these classes. The products from the concept mapping process will be used as input for the object modelling phase of the OMT method.

In order to show the usefulness of concepts maps we apply the technique to a number of test cases. A three-letter code name is used for each of the different cases in order to refer to them later: The test cases are:

- JRP (journal registration problem)
- MPC (manpower control problem)
- PPD (petrol pump delivery system) (Coleman *et al.* 1994)

We have been using concept mapping techniques for the last two years in our training and consultancy projects and we have seen that they provide a simple-to-understand and attractive means of finding the most important concepts and the relationships between them.

For a good introduction to concept mapping, we recommend the book by Novak and Gowin (1984).

This chapter describes how to discover the main abstractions in a given problem and the long-term structural relationships between concepts. Time-dependent behaviour is discussed in Chapter 7 when event–response lists, storyboards and use cases are defined.

6.2 Concepts, links and propositions

A concept is defined as a regularity in objects or events designated by some label (Novak and Gowin 1984). Each concept is a particular idea or understanding we have of the world. If we possess a concept we are in a position to apply it to things around us. For example, the concept 'car' is a label which is used to represent an object which has four wheels, an engine and a steering wheel. Similarly 'wind' is a label for an event that is involved with air which is in motion.

Martin and Odell take a slightly different viewpoint of concept. They define a concept as being 'an idea or notion we share that applies to certain objects in our awareness' (Martin and Odell 1992). Concepts can be used as so-called recognition devices; we can choose from different kinds of concepts, for example:

- Concrete: person, car, pump
- Intangible: period, project, payment, circulation list
- Judgements: high pay, productive employee
- Roles: nurse, attendant, customer, reader, author
- Relational: ownership, attachment, partnership
- Events: journal issue, pulse, monthly database update

Meaningful relationships can be created between concepts by connecting them together to form propositions. A proposition consists of two or more concepts which are linked together by words or word phrases to form a semantic unit. Examples of propositions are:

- A reader is interested in a journal.
- An internal project is a project.
- A Poisson distribution is a discrete statistical distribution.
- An article is published in an issue of a journal.
- The pump display is updated.
- A division consists of departments.

The 'glue' which connects concepts is usually a verb or a verb phrase, as can easily be seen from the examples above. These verbs and verb phrases are called links. In order to make propositions more explicit and easy to understand we employ a simple graphical technique in which concepts are represented by ellipses and links as arrows connecting the concepts. Some examples are given in Figure 6.1. A more complicated example of concepts and links is shown in Figure 6.2.

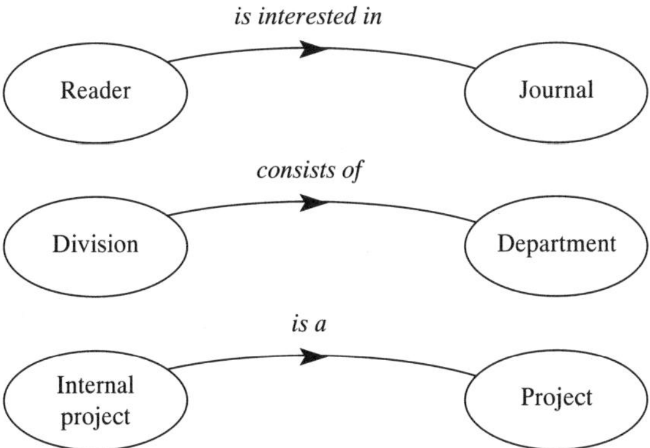

Figure 6.1 Some simple concepts and links.

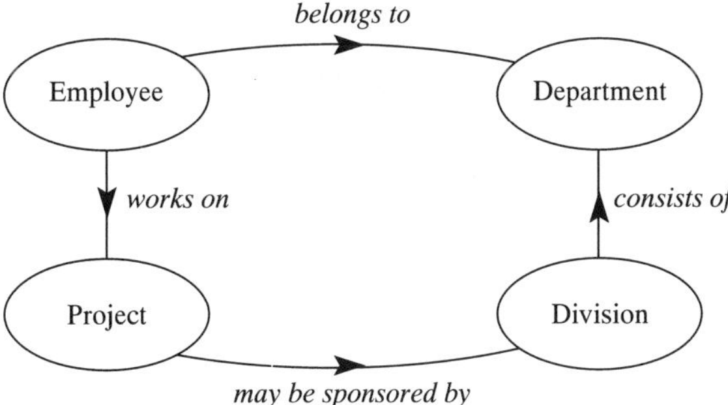

Figure 6.2 Concept map invoking several concepts.

6.3 Creating concept maps

A concept map consists of a number of concepts and links connecting these concepts. Concepts correspond to nouns in most cases, while links correspond to verbs or verb phrases. Figure 6.3 represents a concept map which was created by an eleven-year old child after hearing a lecture on the geography of Australia. Older children would probably produce more comprehensive and meaningful maps. We see from this simple example that a concept map is a simple graphical tool which allows us to represent concepts within a framework of propositions. A concept map is a road map which shows some of the routes that connect concepts in order to arrive at a meaningful semantic unit. We note that it is possible to create concept maps at any level of abstraction. For example, in order to produce a summary of the main concepts that were discussed in Chapter 1 and the propositions that they form we have produced the tentative concept map as shown in Figure 6.4. The map is tentative because it was the first attempt and it probably suffers from a number of deficiencies, such as:

- It is missing some important concepts.
- Not all links have been discovered.
- Certain concepts may be invalid or incorrect.
- Certain links may be incorrect or ambiguously formulated.

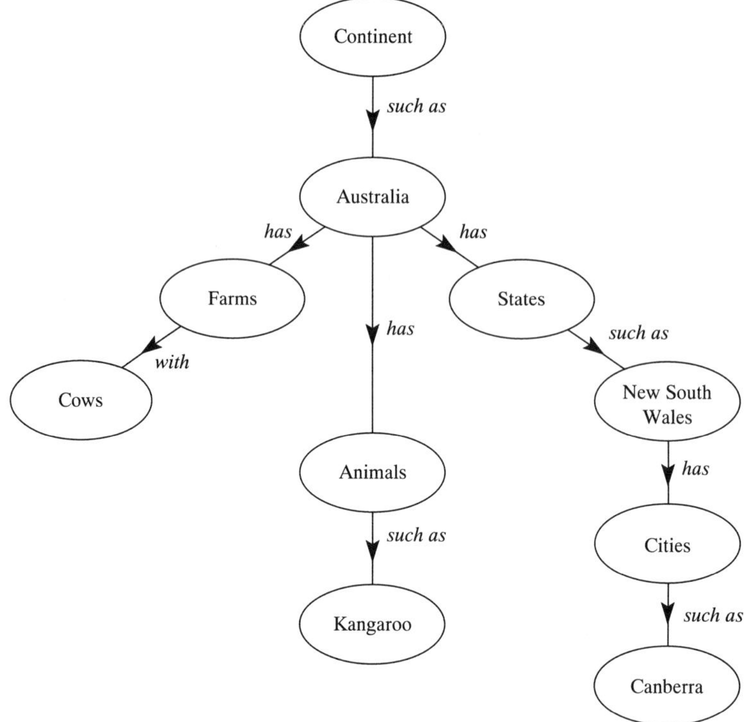

Figure 6.3 Concept map based on a geography lesson.

The way to remedy these problems is to read the text of Chapter 1 again and to create a second draft of the concept map. It is also advisable to show the map to colleagues so that they can give their opinions on it. Be prepared to 'defend' your map, because others may see things differently than you do. This should be seen as a constructive scenario, since questions should force you to focus on particular parts of the map. Your concept map should stabilize after five or six iterations, at which stage the map should be a reasonably accurate approximation of the world that you are trying to model.

6.4 Concept maps as an aid in requirements determination

Experience has shown that concept mapping techniques help in focusing user and designer attention on the essence of a problem. Such techniques are absolutely necessary if we wish to prepare the way for an object-oriented analysis. As already mentioned, most commercially available products pay little attention to requirements determination. They assume that the filtering of redundant and invalid classes, associations and attributes occurs somewhere in the analysis phase or even during the design. One of the main advantages of using concept maps is that both users and designers can agree on an inexpensive paper model of the system to be developed. Concept maps lead to discovery or meaningful learning, something which is difficult to achieve using object diagrams, for example.

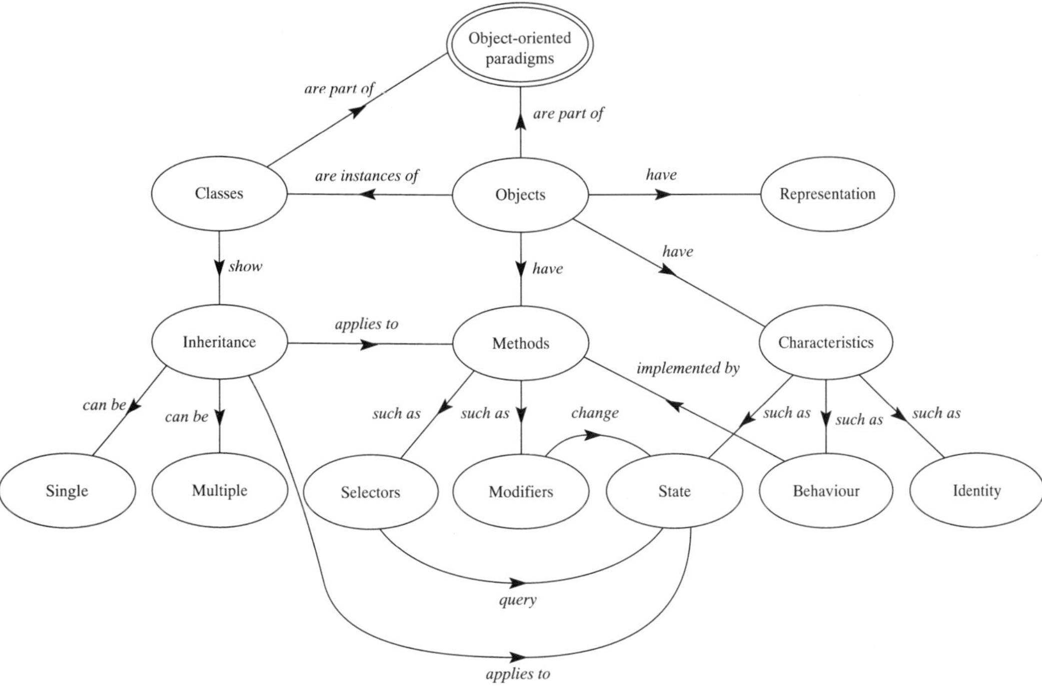

Figure 6.4 Concept map for topics from classes and objects (after Novak and Gowin (1984)).

The main advantages of using concept maps in the requirements determination phase are:

- Concepts correspond to classes.
- Links are implemented as associations in OMT.

If concept maps have been properly constructed (achieved by iterating the original map) we shall have eliminated the following shortcomings and problems which can arise later in the software life-cycle:

- Missing classes and associations
- Invalid and incorrect classes and associations
- Overspecified entities.
- Loss of valuable time due to 'analysis paralysis'

We conclude that concept mapping helps in validation and verification of the requirements document, that is 'we do it right and we do the right things'.

There are other advantages to using concept maps. The main ones are:

- They provide common ground for understanding between the designer and the user. Concept maps are a visual means of communication in which both groups can express themselves.

- They promote the free flow of ideas.
- They encourage so-called focus questions; different focus questions force us to concentrate on different concepts or links that we are observing.
- They provide concise and visual imagery, which is so important when we try to communicate our insights and observations to others.
- They promote the subsumption theory in which new ideas are related to existing ideas.
- We see relationships that we have never seen before.

6.5 Strategies for introducing concept mapping techniques

One of the most difficult steps in the object-oriented software life-cycle is finding the objects and the interactions between them. To this end, concept maps help us in finding the main concepts from the requirements description. They also help in discovering flaws in the requirements. Concept maps can be hierarchically structured and then used as a communication tool between user and designer.

This section develops the steps which should be developed in order to construct good concept maps.

6.5.1 Preparing for concept mapping

The first step in the process is to draw up a list of the nouns which appear in the requirements document. These nouns are candidates for concepts. To this end, we eliminate the following types of nouns:

(6.1)

- Attributes
- Concepts which are outside the scope of the problem
- Ambiguous and superfluous objects

Attributes are not concepts but properties of objects. They should not appear in this stage of the life-cycle since they are determined in the analysis phase. Furthermore, including them in a concept map tends to make the map less understandable. Concepts which fall outside the scope of the current problem should not be included. Finally, requirements documents may include information which is vague, ambiguous or overspecified in some way. The cause is due to the fact that the requirements are expressed in natural language, which tends to be imprecise. The main sources of confusion are (Meyer 1985):

(6.2)

- Noise (redundancy)
- Silence
- Overspecification
- Contradiction
- Ambiguity
- Forward references
- Roles

Any one of the above problems can arise in a requirements document. Eliminating them at this stage saves us time during the later stages of the software life-cycle. Noise occurs when there is information in the form of words and phrases which is not pertinent to the present situation. We say that there is redundant information in the document. In some cases noise can manifest itself in the form of design and implementation details, for example what type of hardware the system is to run on and the type of relational database to be used. Silence refers to the situation in which some essential element or feature in the problem domain does not appear in the document. Overspecification usually occurs when design details are present in the document. It is not the concern of the requirements phase to state how a problem should be solved, but it should be concerned with what has to be done. A contradiction occurs when a number of words or phrases in a document lead to an impossible solution. Ambiguities occur when there is a possibility that a statement can be interpreted in more than one way. For example, does the concept 'user' refer to an actor outside the system or does it refer to some other concept in the system, such as employee, customer or piece of software? Forward reference occurs when words or phrases are used which have not yet been defined. Roles abound in requirements document. A role is really a view of something. The 'something' is the real concept. Examples of roles are employee and customer. Each of these is a role for a person concept.

Most object-oriented methods have some provisions for removing invalid classes during the OO software process. OMT does this in the analysis phase while Wirfs-Brock *et al.* (1990) do this in the design phase. The advantage in our case is that both the user and the designer are involved in determining what is relevant to the current problem.

The products from this filtering operation are a set of nouns which are promoted to the status of concepts. The concepts are not yet hierarchically ordered nor are there any links between them.

Having determined what the main concepts are we then create a list of verbs. The verbs and verb phrases are linking words and are used in conjunction with concept words to form sentences.

To summarize, preparing for the concept mapping activities consists of four steps (Novak and Gowin 1984):

1. Make a list of words and objects appearing in the current problem domain.
2. Apply the filtering process by eliminating entities using (6.1) and (6.2).
3. Find the linking words (verbs, verb phrases).
4. Construct sentences using words from Steps 2 and 3.

6.5.2 Concept mapping activities

The concepts which have been found in Section 6.5.1 need to be arranged in a top-down fashion, with more general and inclusive concepts appearing at higher levels than less general concepts.

Good concept maps tend to be well-structured and easily understood. Each concept map should have as root one all-inclusive concept which is placed at level 0 of the concept hierarchy. Examples of key concepts are 'ManPowerControl System', 'Delivery System' and 'Hospital Database'. The other concepts should be placed under the key concept. Links connect the key concept with its supporting concepts and cross links connect concepts in

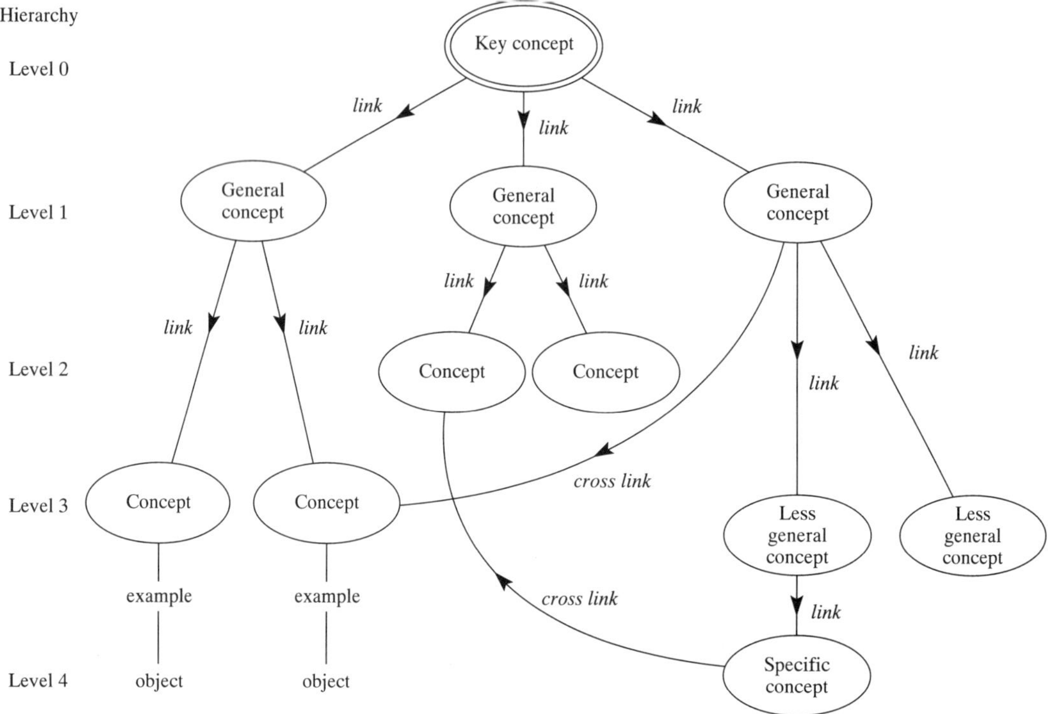

Figure 6.5 Structuring concept maps (after Novak and Gowin (1984)).

different parts of the concept hierarchy. The correct way of constructing concept maps is shown in Figure 6.5.

The steps in constructing a concept map are:

1. List the key concept.
2. List the supporting concepts at lower levels of abstraction.
3. Create the links between the main concept and its supporting concepts.
4. Create cross links between supporting concepts.
5. Iterate the steps 1–4 by applying them to the supporting concepts.

We see that the concept mapping process uses a top-down approach. It is possible, to create concept maps in a bottom-up manner if we do not have a complete overview of the current problem. Supporting concepts can be merged in this case to form larger and more general concepts.

An example of the steps 1–5 above is given in Figures 6.6, 6.7 and 6.8. This is a metamodel in which the foundations of the concept mapping principle are represented in two concept maps. Notice how the concepts 'verb' and 'noun' are viewed as supporting concepts in Figure 6.6, while in Figures 6.7 and 6.8, respectively, they are viewed as key concepts.

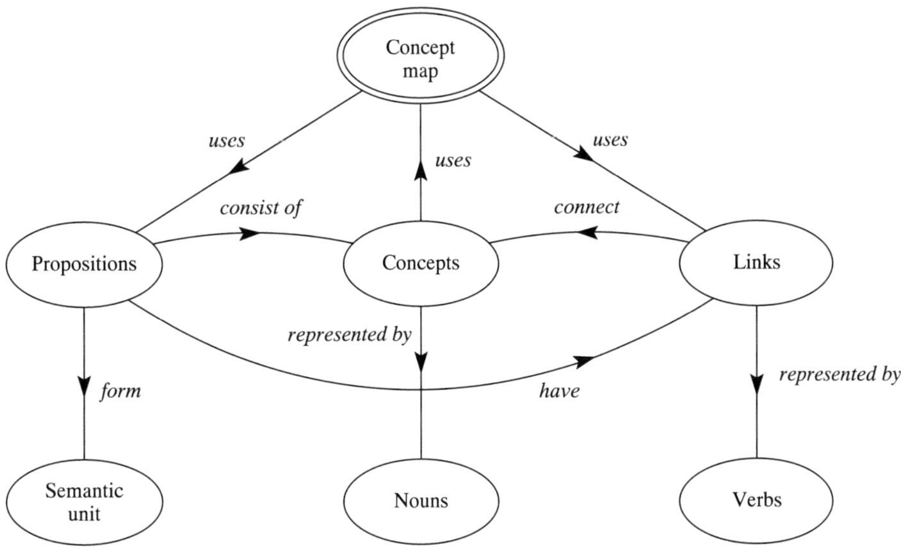

Figure 6.6 Structuring concept maps: the concept for the concept mapping process.

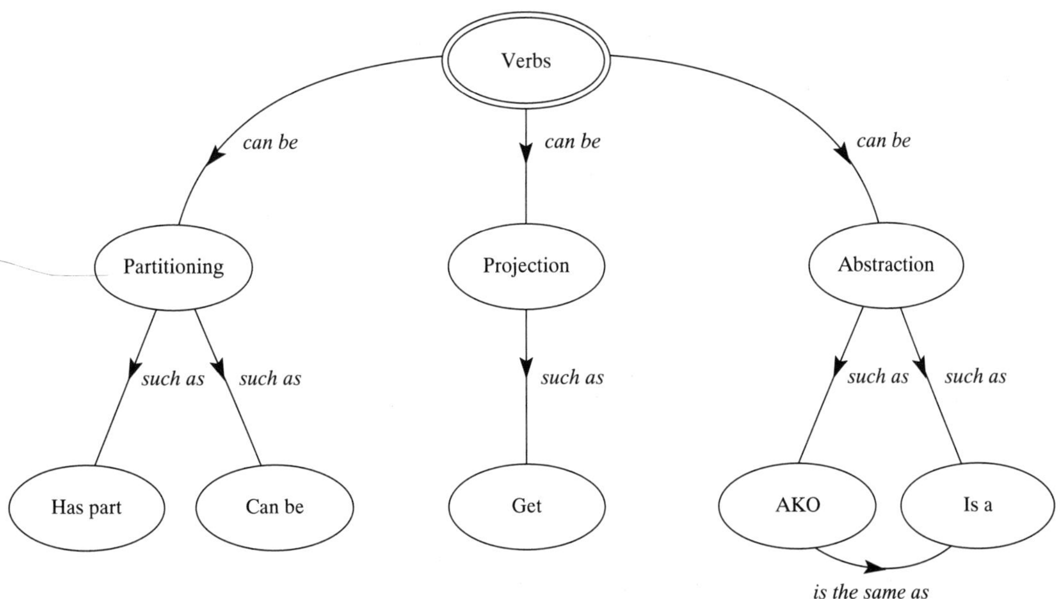

Figure 6.7 Concept map for verbs.

6.5.3 Example: hospital database

The problem that we have chosen to use in order to show how the process is executed is similar to the hospital database problem in Hughes (1991). The objective is to apply the steps developed in Sections 6.5.1 and 6.5.2 to the following requirements document:

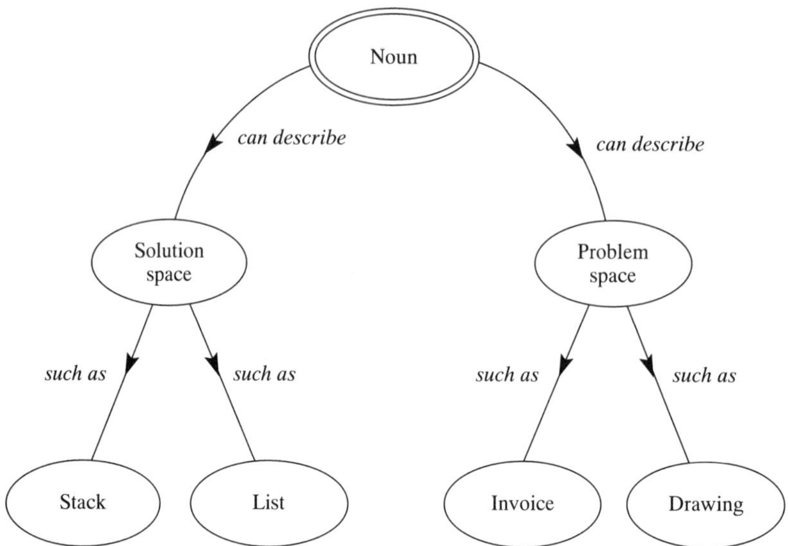

Figure 6.8 Concept map for nouns.

The EDP department of a medium-sized hospital wishes to create a system which will assist in the administration of its wards, operating theatres and private rooms. Furthermore, information relating to patients, surgeons and nurses needs to registered.

The following information should be present in the system:

1. Patients are assigned to a ward when admitted to the hospital unless they are private patients, in which case they will be assigned to a private room and they are treated by consultants. A consultant is a senior surgeon. Each room has a unique identification number. The attributes of a patient are patient name, number, address, sex, date of birth and blood group.

2. A nurse may or may not be assigned to a ward. However, a nurse may not be assigned to more than one ward. A ward may have many nurses assigned to it. Nurse attributes include name, address, phone number and grade. Ward attributes include unique identification number and its type (e.g. maternity, paediatric).

3. A patient may undergo a number of operations.

4. Only one surgeon may perform an operation, while other surgeons may assist at operations. Surgeons are coached by consultants who are experienced surgeons. A consultant may assist or perform at an operation. Surgeon attributes include name, address and phone number. Each consultant specializes in a certain area.

5. An operation is performed in only one theatre and a given theatre may be the venue for many operations. Theatre attributes include identifying number and some may be specially equipped for certain classes of operation.

6. A nurse may be assigned to an operating theatre. However, a nurse may not be assigned to more than one theatre. A theatre may have many nurses assigned to it.

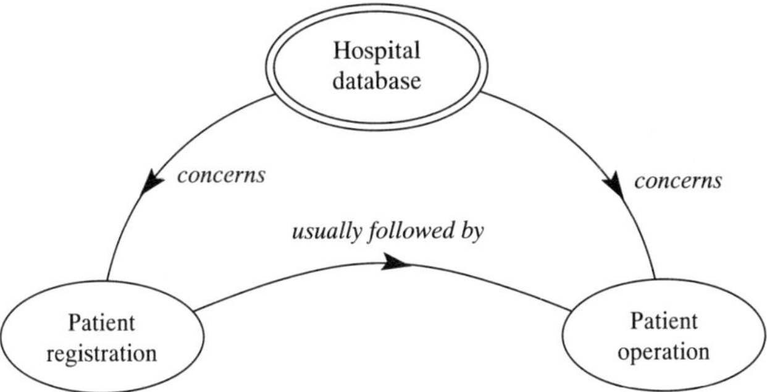

Figure 6.9 High-level concept map for Hospital Database Problem.

The top-level concept map for the Hospital Database Problem is shown in Figure 6.9. The use cases approach is taken because the functionality of the system can be directly found from the level 1 concepts 'Patient registration' and 'Patient operation'. Both of these concepts can be viewed as key concepts and these are shown in Figure 6.10.

The initial concept map for the Hospital Database Problem is shown in Figure 6.11. Notice that this map is less structured than the map in Figure 6.10. This is because the map in Figure 6.11 attempts to represent two sets of independent scenarios.

6.6 Using concept maps as a front-end to OOA

The deliverables from the concept mapping phase are concepts and links. Concepts are embryonic classes, while links describe the types of relationships between concepts. There are three types of link possible. These are:

- Projection links
- Abstraction links
- Partitioning links

Projection links describe interactions between concepts and they tend to be action-based. Examples are 'get', 'display' and 'move'. Abstraction links are related to class hierarchies and they tend to have instances such as 'is a', 'can be' and 'such as'. Partitioning links describe a concept in terms of its constituent parts. Examples are 'consists of', 'has' and 'is part of'.

Discovering concepts and links give us some insight into how they are to be implemented in the analysis phase. The rules are:

- Concepts suggest objects and events.
- Projection links suggest object operations.
- Abstraction links suggest inheritance relationships.
- Partitioning links suggest aggregation relationships.

It is important to remember that a concept map is only as good as the effort that is put into making it. Choosing good names for links and concepts should be chosen as carefully as possible so that they do not mislead or convey the wrong meaning.

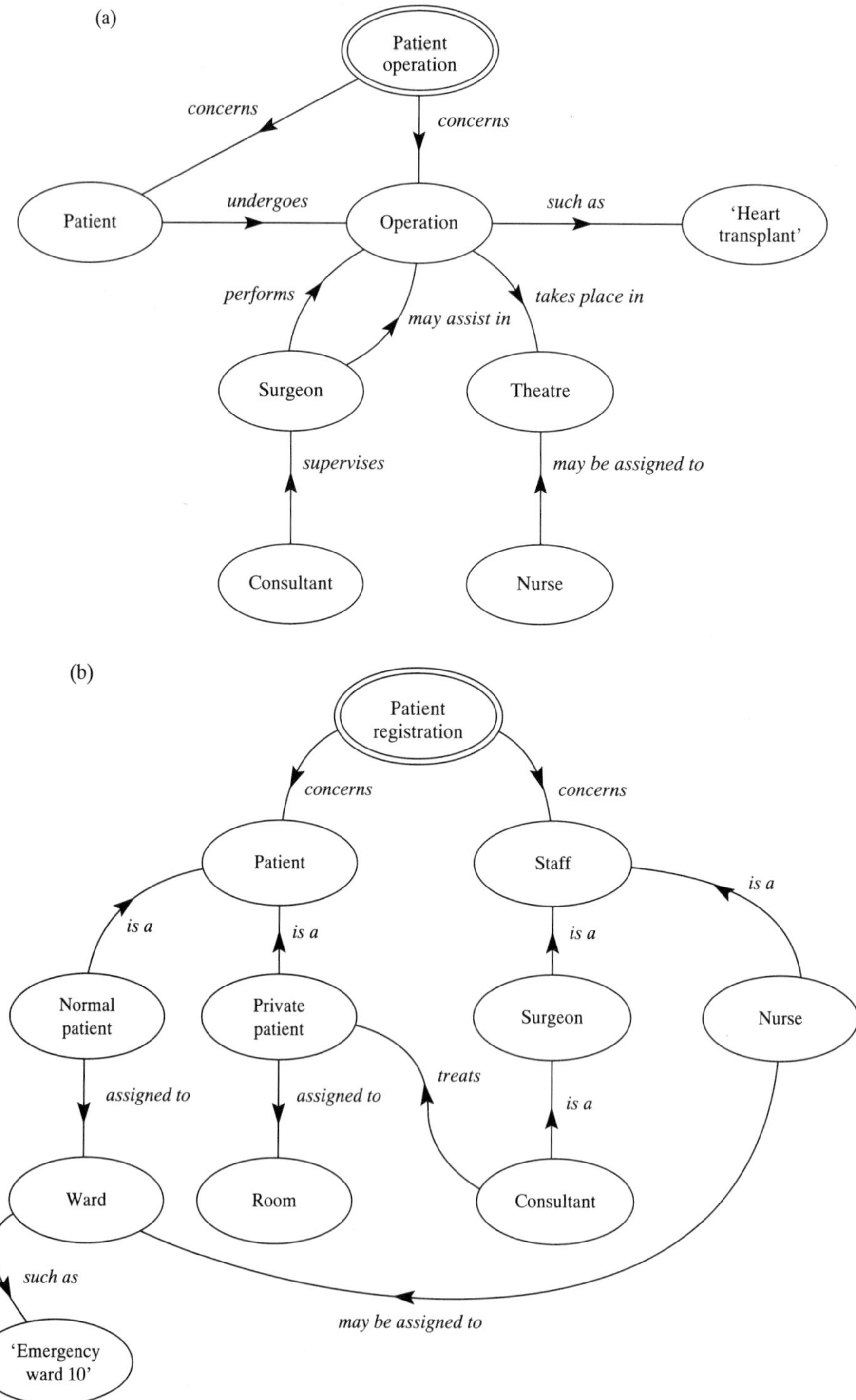

Figure 6.10 Concept maps for (a) patient operation subproblem and (b) patient registration subproblem.

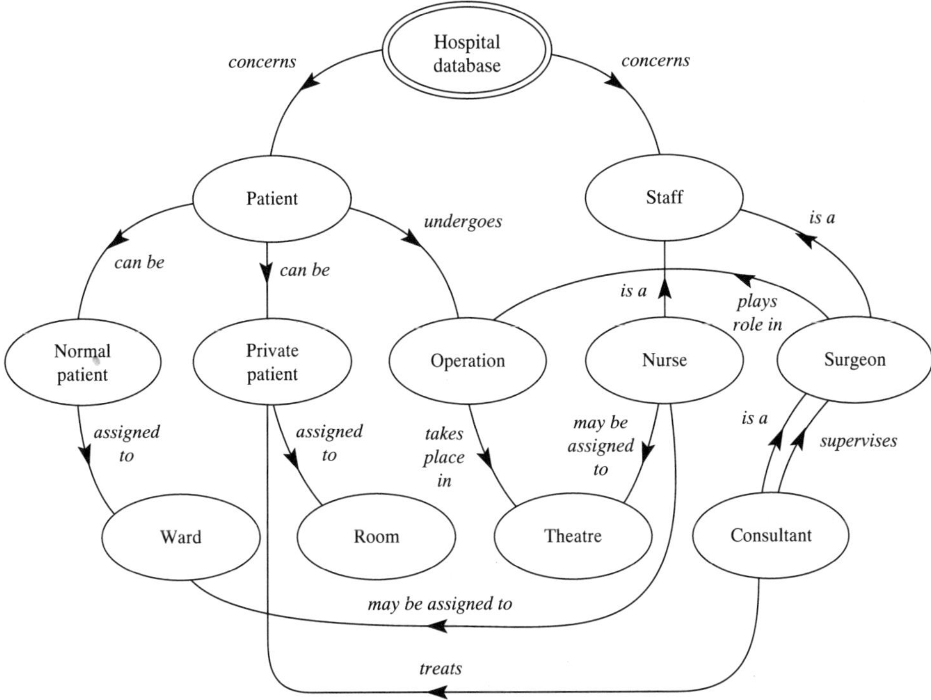

Figure 6.11 Initial concept map for Hospital Database Problem.

6.7 Test case: journal registration problem

6.7.1 Journal registration problem (code name JRP)

The personnel department of a large research institute is responsible for the purchase and dissemination of journals to readers in other departments in the organization. Readers may be interested in certain specific topics relating to their research interests, while it is also possible to be placed on a circulation list. Usually, readers get access to an issue of a journal for a fixed period of time, typically two weeks. It is possible to have access to an issue for a longer period of time, but permission must be granted from the personnel department.

Journals appear on a regular basis and each journal contains information on the publisher, language and frequency of publication.

The system should keep readers informed of the topics that are of interest to them and which appear in the different journals. Furthermore, it should be possible for readers to find articles which deal with topics that they are interested in.

6.7.2 Concept mapping for JRP

The nouns which appear in the requirements document are:

(6.3)

- Personnel department
- Company
- Journal

- Reader
- Department
- Circulation list
- Article
- Keyword
- Topic
- Title
- Author
- Publisher
- Frequency
- Language

Not all nouns in (6.3) will be valid concepts. In particular, we need to filter entities which are attributes; these are:

keyword	title	publisher
frequency	author	language

Sources of noise are eliminated because they are not part of the problem. They are:

- personnel department
- department
- circulation list (this is a derivative concept)

Having carried out the filtering process we are left with a list of candidate concepts:

(6.4)

- Journal
- Issue
- Reader
- Topic
- Article

The relationships between the concepts in (6.4) are:

- An issue is an appearance of a journal.
- A reader is interested in a journal.
- A reader is interested in a topic.
- An issue contains articles.
- An topic may be found in an article.

The next step is to arrange the different concepts in such a way that the resulting concept map is easy to understand and well-structured. You will find that this is the most difficult part of the concept mapping process and you should discuss your results with others so that they can give their views on your work. In most cases a concept map will undergo a number

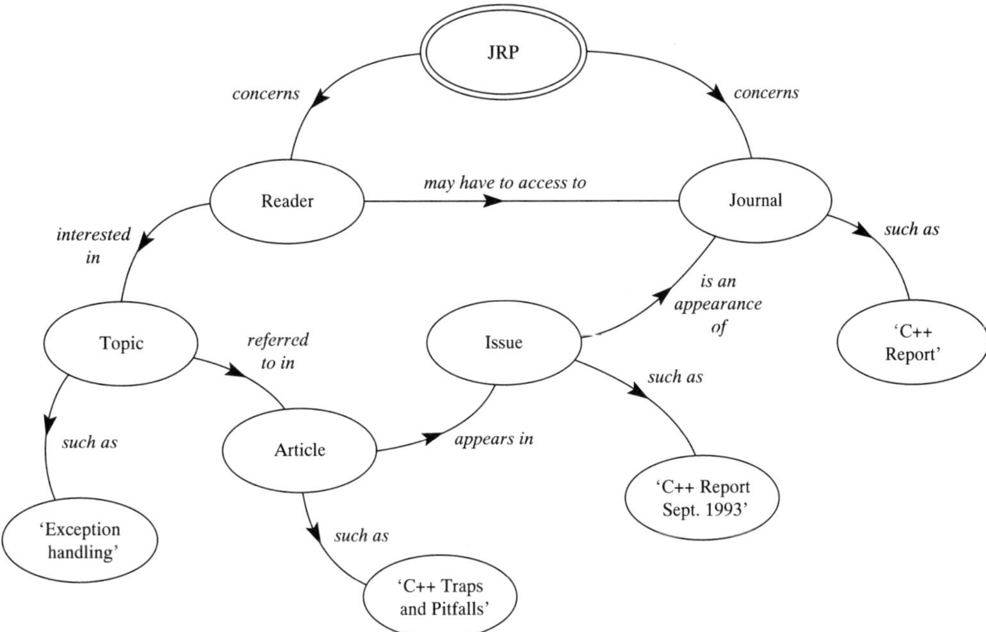

Figure 6.12 Concept map for JRP problem.

of revisions; don't be disappointed if seven or eight iterations are needed before a decent map is arrived at! It is all part of the process of understanding the essence of a given problem.

The concept map for JRP is shown in Figure 6.12. This is a straightforward solution. We note that the concept 'Circulation List' does not appear in the map. This is because we have not approached the problem from a 'use case' perspective. Furthermore, there is no provision for informing readers on information which is of interest to them. The two most important use cases are:

- Creating circulation lists
- Creating attention lists

The modified concept map for JRP is shown in Figure 6.13. This map implements user requirements as a central feature. Each supporting concept can then be separately analysed, allowing us to separate problems into different areas of concern. Furthermore, new user requirements (such as setting up special interest groups) may be implemented by creating supporting concepts at the correct level of abstraction. It might even be possible to reuse some of the concepts that have been developed in other use cases.

6.8 Test case: manpower control system

6.8.1 General background

Many engineering companies work as contractors for external customers in order to construct nuclear power stations, roads, railways and software systems. Many projects can last for several years, and much expertise may be needed in order to complete the project. For

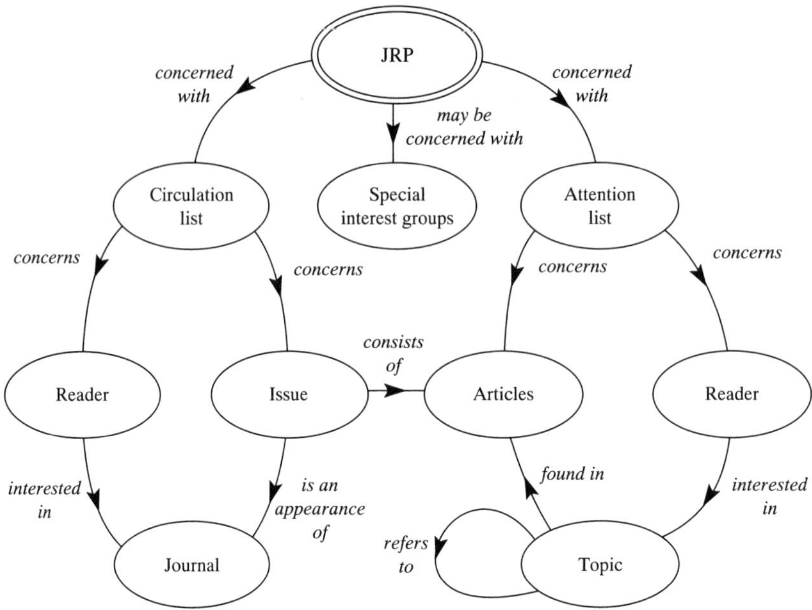

Figure 6.13 Use case-driven concept map for JRP.

example, in order to construct a nuclear power plant many disciplines, such as mechanical, process and civil engineering, may need to work at different times on the project. Employees typically spend time on different projects, and this time must be registered and aggregated on a departmental basis for later invoicing to the customer. Some projects, such as support activities (e.g. the EDP department), are not sponsored by external clients and are seen as overheads. Such projects are typically sponsored by a division or some other decision-making body.

Since a company may be involved in many projects at any given moment it is necessary to be able to have decision-support systems (DSS) in order to monitor the progress. Progress is determined in many cases by comparing used resources with the resources which were allocated at the beginning of the project. In general, each employee is allocated a certain number of hours per project and the employee must ensure that he finishes his part of the project before the allocated hours run out. It is the responsibility of the employee to ensure that the hours used on a project are registered on a regular basis, usually once per month.

6.8.2 Manpower control system (code name MPC)

An engineering company works on projects for external and internal customers. Projects have a start date and an end date and a fixed amount of hours in which the project should be completed. Employees in the company are organized into departments. A department is a centre of expertise in one particular area, for example piping design, acoustics and steel design. Each department is responsible for one or more activities in the project. Departments are grouped into divisions, for example mechanical engineering, process and piping. A division may sponsor internal projects. Resources (in this case hours) are allocated in the same way for external and internal projects. The resources for external projects are divided among the departments which can play a role in the successful execution of the project. It is

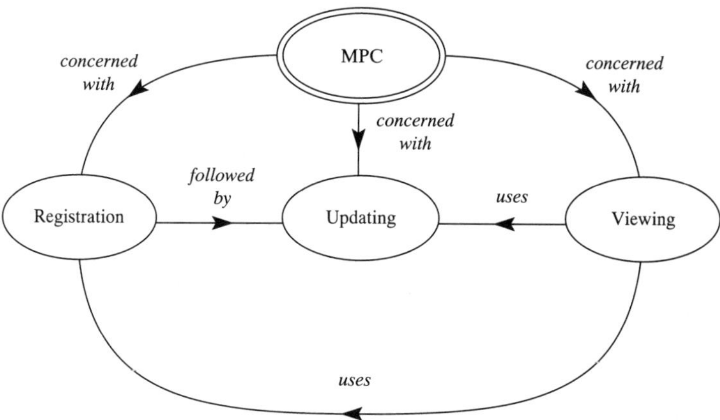

Figure 6.14 High-level concept map for the MPC problem.

then the responsibility of each department to allocate resources to employees in the department.

An employee belongs to one department and an employee will work on a project for his 'home' department. However, there may be some slackening of work in some departments and an employee may be seconded to another department

We wish to create a (database) system in which project resources can be registered, validated and monitored on a regular basis. In particular, we assume the following:

- The used hours per project are updated per month and are based on employee, project and department.
- An employee may work for at most one department on any given project.
- There is no distinction made between the different types of employee who are involved on a project.

It should be possible to visualize the progress of a project by displaying scheduled hours against used hours in the form of line charts, histograms and similar charts. Progress can be displayed on department, division and project levels.

This problem will be analysed in Chapter 12. The most important use cases for MPC are:

- Initial registration of project infrastructure
- Periodic updating of project data
- Viewing project data

The first two use cases from the core of MPC, while the third use case uses the products of the first two. It is essentially a derived use case and its main function is to present data in graphical and textual form.

The high-level concept map for the MPC problem is shown in Figure 6.14.

6.9 Test case: petrol pump delivery system (PPD)

The following problem is based on the problem statement in Coleman *et al.* (1994) where it is solved using the Hewlett-Packard Fusion method.

6.9.1 Statement of the problem

A computer-based system using object-oriented techniques needs to be built. This system should be responsible for the dispensing of petrol, customer payments and the monitoring of tank levels. The system is based on a self-service regime. There are several pumps in the station and before a pump can be used by a customer it must first be enabled by the station attendant. Enabling a pump entails the motor being started and the pump clutch being freed. If the pump is already started no action takes place in the motor. If the customer presses the trigger in the pump a micro switch is closed, the pump becomes enabled and the clutch is freed. However, when the trigger is released the clutch becomes free. The pump gun is kept in a special holster and this holster has a switch which prevents petrol being pumped until the gun is taken out of the holster. Replacing the gun in the holster has the effect of stopping the delivery. The pump becomes disabled at this stage. The delivery is deemed to be complete and further depressions of the trigger have no effect on petrol delivery. The pump motor is not turned off immediately but there is a short stand-by period in which the motor remains so that a new customer can use the pump without having to start the motor again.

A petrol line connects the pump and a number of tanks and it contains a metering device which sends a pulse to the pump for each 0.01 litres of petrol dispensed. The pump display shows how much petrol has been dispensed and its cost.

Transactions concerning the delivery are stored until the customer pays. A receipt may be requested and a token will be given for every 5 money units spent. It is possible that dishonest customers leave without paying and annotation should be made, for example their car registration number.

The monitoring of the system is an important part of this system. A given pump gets its supply from one of a number of tanks. No tank may drop to less than 4% of its full capacity. If a customer is dispensing from a tank that reaches this critical value the delivery will be completed for that customer, the pump will be disabled and a message is sent to the operator's terminal.

This problem will be analysed in Chapter 13. The two most important use cases are:

- Delivery of petrol
- Payment transaction

6.10 Concept maps and scalability

Concept mapping techniques are extremely useful for nailing down requirements. However, they break down for very large problems if used without prior planning. The main problems are:

- A large number of classes may appear in the map.
- There are many links in the map.

The net result is a concept map which is too difficult to understand. The problem is solved by viewing a requirements document as a set of weakly coupled use cases. Each use case is implemented as a separate key concept which can then be independently studied by applying the procedures developed in this chapter. In this way we can solve both small and large problems.

Exercises

1. Read Chapter 1 again and review the validity of the concept map in Figure 6.4. Concentrate on the following aspects in turn: missing concepts, incorrect concepts, missing links, incorrect links and finally labels represent concepts and links which cause confusion.

2. Create a concept map from the following textual description of the requirements for a dictionary class in Smalltalk (Digitalk 1992): 'A dictionary is a collection of key-word/value pairs of objects. The keys in the dictionary are unique, whereas values may be duplicated. A dictionary may be searched either by key or by value. Key searches use hashing for efficiency. Elements may be entered into and extracted from a dictionary either as a pair of objects or as association.'

3. Create a concept map for an automated teller machine (ATM) system (Wirfs-Brock *et al.* 1990). Apply the filtering process as described in Section 6.5.1. The requirements specification is as follows.

   An ATM is used by customers of banks in order to perform certain financial transactions. It is not possible to carry out a given transaction if an account is frozen or there is not enough money in the source account. In particular, we wish to carry out the following:

   1. **Withdraw money from an account**
      Two accounts are necessary, the source account and the beneficiary account. Furthermore, customers must tell how much money should be withdrawn. If successful, customers will get their money through the cash dispenser.

   2. **Deposit money in an account**
      An account number is needed as well as an envelope which should contain money and which is entered into the ATM via the deposit drawer.

   3. **Transfer money between two accounts**
      It is possible to transfer money between two different accounts.

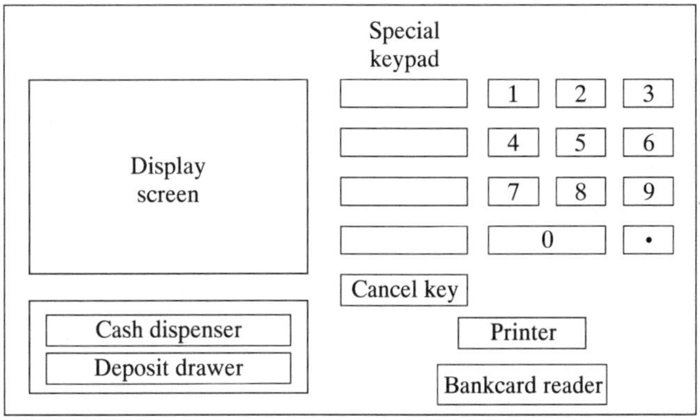

Figure 6.15 An automated teller machine.

4. **Query the balance of an account**
   It is possible to see how much money there is in a given account.

The ATM machine has provisions so that a customer can carry out each of these transactions. The physical layout is given in Figure 6.15.

For a more thorough treatment of this problem, see Wirfs-Brock *et al.* (1990).

4. Carry out a filtering process on the following imprecise and faulty requirements document for a simple text-processing system (Meyer 1985). The original problem is: Given a text consisting of words separated by BLANKS or by NL (new line) characters, convert it to a line-by-line form in accordance with the following:

   - Line breaks must be made only where the given text has BLANK or NL.
   - Each line is filled as far as possible as long as no line will contain more than MAXPOS characters.

   Filter the following specifications based on the ideas which were discussed in Section 6.5.1:

   The program's input is a stream of characters whose end is signalled with a special end-of-text character, ET. There is exactly one ET character in each input stream. Characters are classified as:

   - break characters: BL (blank) and NL (new line)
   - nonbreak characters: all others except ET.
   - end-of-text indicator: ET

   A word is a non-empty sequence of non-break characters. A break is a sequence of one or more break characters. Thus, the input can be viewed as a sequence of words separated by breaks, with possibly leading and trailing breaks, and ending with ET.

   The program's output should be the same sequence of words as in the input, with the exception that an oversize word (i.e. a word containing more than MAXPOS characters, where MAXPOS is a positive integer) should cause an error exit from the program (i.e. a variable Alarm should have the value TRUE). Up to the point of an error, the program's output should have the following properties:

   - A new line should start only between words and at the beginning of the output text, if any.
   - A break in the input is reduced to a single break character in the output.
   - As many words as possible should be placed on each line (i.e. between successive NL characters).
   - No line may contain more than MAXPOS characters (words and NL).

5. Find the projection links, abstraction links and partitioning links for the problems JRP, MPC and PPD. Furthermore, determine in which of the following object categories the different concepts belong: tangibles, interaction objects, intangibles, roles, incidents, specifications.

6. Create a concept map for Exercise 3.

References

D. Coleman *et al.* (1994) *Object-Oriented Development, the Fusion Method*, Prentice-Hall, Englewood Cliffs NJ.

Digitalk (1992) *Smalltalk/V Windows Manual*, Digitalk Inc., Los Angeles CA.

J. G. Hughes (1991) *Object-Oriented Databases*, Prentice-Hall Englewood Cliffs NJ.

J. Martin and J. J. Odell (1992) *Object-Oriented Analysis and Design*, Prentice-Hall, Englewood Cliffs NJ.

B. Meyer (1985) On Formalism in Specifications, *IEEE Software*, January.

J. D. Novak and D. B. Gowin (1984) *Learning How to Learn*, Cambridge University Press, Cambridge.

J. Rumbaugh, M. Blaha, W. Premerlani, F. Eddy and W. Lorensen (1991) *Object-Oriented Modeling and Design*, Prentice-Hall, Englewood Cliffs NJ.

D. A. Umphress and S. G. March (1991) Object-Oriented Requirements Analysis, *Journal of Object-Oriented Programming*, Focus on Analysis and Design, pp. 35–40.

R. Wirfs-Brock, B. Wilkerson and L. Wiener (1990) *Designing Object-Oriented Software*, Addison-Wesley, Reading MA.

Chapter

7

Events, storyboards and use cases

7.1 Introduction and objectives

Concept mapping techniques are useful in finding the concepts and the links between those concepts in a given problem domain. They show the static structure of the system. They do not give us any insight into how a system will behave when events occur in a system. Concept maps fail when it comes to showing component behaviour when reacting to external stimuli. Furthermore, they need to be complemented by other techniques if we are to be able to communicate with the user of the system. Concept maps are not 'live' and we need some way of simulating the final system before we actually start analysing and designing the problem. To this end, we create storyboards and use cases.

Event–response lists and storyboards are used as input to the dynamic modelling view in the object-oriented analysis phase of the software life-cycle. Dynamic modelling techniques are described in Chapters 9 and 10.

This chapter is an introduction to the subject of object-oriented requirements determination (OORD) whose main objectives are to generate specifications that describe system behaviour unambiguously, consistently and completely. In particular, we shall show how the practical techniques developed here can be integrated with state-of-the-art results in this field which, when applied to real problems will pave the way for OOA.

7.2 Event–response lists

Events describes external stimuli. In the MPC problem an external stimulus would represent the transfer of used hours per employee at the end of each month. In PPD the following external stimuli are identified:

- The attendant enables the petrol pump.
- The customer removes the gun from the holster.
- The customer replaces the gun in the holster.

- The metering device sends a pulse to the pump display.

A response describes the reaction to an event. For example, when the attendant enables the pump the following responses occur:

- The pump motor is started.
- The pump clutch is free.

Constraints describe non-functional characteristics of the event–response pair. Constraints describe the following things:

- Maximum or minimum amount of time between an event and its response
- The range of values an entity can take on
- Probability of the occurrence of a response to an event
- Rate of occurrence of events

The main purpose of the event–response list is to enumerate as fully as possible the expectations of the user when interacting with the system. A given event–response list should only describe those events and responses that are visible to the user. It is possible to verify each event or response by observing the system.

Not all event–response lists have constraints. An event may cause multiple responses and multiple events may have to occur before a response can take place.

Event–response lists are useful for verification and validation. Verification is a formal activity and it lets us define completeness aspects of the system, for example by formally stating in the requirements document that all output variables have been defined or that all events have been included. Verification is concerned with the question 'Are we doing it right?'. Validation is concerned with the question 'Are we building the right system?'. Validation is aimed at establishing the system's operational correctness, safety and completeness. It is an informal process, addressed through human judgement (Williams 1994). Event–response lists can help in verification and validation.

Some rules concerning event–response lists are (Umphress and March 1991):

- Event–response lists are general; they do not refer to any particular scenario.
- Event–response lists should describe visible or verifiable events and responses.
- Constraints on event–response lists should be real, validated items.
- Event–response lists should be tailored to the audience. Different types of user are interested in particular views of the system.

To take an example, we consider JRP. The main events have to do with new journals, issues and the creation of circulation lists.

Typical event–response lists and their optional constraints are:

E1: A new journal is announced.

R11: Certain readers will get access to all issues of the journal.

E2: An issue of a journal appears.

R21: A circulation list is created.

C21: There must be at least one reader on the list.

Figure 7.1 Storyboard layout using frames.

E3: A journal goes out of circulation.

R31: All issues must be sent back to the personnel department.

E4: A reader seeks information on a certain topic.

R41: A list of articles is created which refers to that topic.

To summarize, we note that event–response list describe the overall dynamic behaviour of the system. Each event–response list serves as a functional description of how one or more objects behave. Events translate into preconditions while responses translate into postconditions. We shall see that responses are implemented by member functions of some class while the events represent the preconditions which when satisfied will result in the rest of the body of the member function being executed. If a precondition is not satisfied an error or exceptional condition arises and it should be handled by the system.

7.3 Scenarios and storyboards

The third component in the requirements determination phase is the so-called storyboard. This ties the concept map and event–response list techniques in order to refine the interaction characteristics by describing, possibly in comic book fashion a frame-by-frame portrayal of the system being defined. It illustrates the user's concept of the completed system.

Storyboards depict system actions for a single representative scenario or a small set of scenarios. Storyboards should only show the major functions in order to promote understanding between the user and developer.

A storyboard is a narrative consisting of a number of snapshots or frames. A frame consists of narrative and symbols explaining the system at a given point in time. Other frames describe the system at future points in time (Figure 7.1).

It is possible to combine concept maps and event–response lists using frames. Major concepts from the already constructed concept maps can be shown pictorially in the picture portion of the frame. The narrative potion may contain elements which are not obvious in the picture portion. The event–response list is used to describe the behaviour from one frame to the next one. Each element of the frame should be linked to the concept map; each action should be traceable to the event–response list.

Some rules for working with storyboards are:

- Each symbol in the storyboard should correspond to a concept in the concept map.
- Ensure that the transition between storyboard frames is small enough to be understood yet large enough not to show implementation details.
- Demonstrate major functions in storyboards; exclude minor housekeeping details.
- Transitions from frame to frame should be linked to event–response lists.

- Storyboards can be merged in a bottom-up fashion to form larger and more comprehensive storyboards.

Scenarios are used in dynamic modelling in the OMT method. The results developed in this chapter will serve as a front-end for Chapter 9.

For each system responsibility a storyboard should be constructed. In JRP for example, the main responsibilities are:

- Informing readers of new journals and issues
- Browsing for information on topics

The relationship between responsibility and storyboard is one-to-many and thus it is necessary to break each responsibility into one or more storyboards. For example, the first responsibility above can be split into the following scenarios:

- Register a new journal.
- Make a circulation list for a journal issue.
- Inform readers of interesting articles in an issue.
- Take a journal and all its issues out of circulation.

In general, the set of all storyboards for a given problem will comprise the complete functionality of a system. Thus, determining all storyboards implies that we have determined the full functional requirements.

7.3.1 Example: journal registration problem (JRP)

We take the following storyboards:

(7.1)

- Register a journal
- Handling new journal issues
- Reader browsing of available articles and issues
- Removing a journal from circulation

The first of these will now be discussed in detail while the others will be left as an exercise. Thus, the storyboard for registering a journal has the following steps:

(7.2)

1. A new journal appears on the market.
2. We find out which readers are interested.
3. A circulation list of readers is created. These readers will get access to all future issues of the journal. All readers get the same period of time in which to read an issue, but this default period may be overridden if permitted by the personnel department.
4. A mailing list is made of those readers who are interested in the topics to be treated in the journal.

The products in (7.2) are used in order to find operations on object classes. This is the topic of Chapters 9 and 10.

7.4 Jacobson's use cases

We include a discussion of the use case model due to Jacobson *et al.* (1992) for a number of reasons. First, it is very close in spirit to the storyboard idea and secondly it can be used to solve some of the shortcomings in the OMT model. The major problems with OMT lie in the difficulty with which the dynamic and functional models can be integrated into the object model. Specifically, the following conclusions can be drawn:

- The integration of the object, dynamic and functional models is not clear; furthermore, it is difficult to check for consistency.
- OMT assumes a very simple mapping of events and states to class interface operations.
- Many design decisions are not taken care of, for example exceptional situations.
- The object model does not support levelling or layering. It is difficult to take different views of the system due to the difficulty of choosing different levels of granularity (D'Souza 1993).

Most of the above shortcomings can be solved by concept maps, storyboards and use cases. In particular, use cases offer a solution to the weak coupling between the different models in OMT by viewing system functionality as a set of use cases. Each use case is a behaviourally related sequence of transactions in a dialogue with the system. Each use case model uses actors and use cases. These are two concepts for defining what exists outside the system (the actors) and what should be performed by the system (use cases). Actors are not described in detail since they do not belong in the system. The actors in the PPD problem are customer and attendant. In an ATM application actors are customers. In a telephone exchange system actors are subscribers.

In order to support use cases Jacobson assumes that a suitable domain object model is available. This object model contains all the problem domain objects and serves as a support for the development of the requirements model. Concept mapping techniques are one way to generate an object domain model. The requirements model is regarded as formulating the functional requirement specification based on the needs of the system users.

The use case model is developed in cooperation with the domain object model and it may be expressed in terms of domain objects.

The main steps involved in the use case model are:

- Determine what is outside the system (actors).
- Define the functionality inside the system (use cases).

A given use case is described by the use of so-called descriptions. These descriptions are the sources for the identification of the objects in the system.

During a use case we can identify three types of objects, namely:

(7.3)

- Entity objects
- Interface objects
- Control objects

Entity objects model information about the system which survives for longer periods of time. Such information survives cases. Most entity objects are found at an early stage and are usually easy to find. Examples of entity objects are:

- Reader, journal, article (JRP)
- Employee, project, department (MPC)
- Tank, pump, switch (PPD)

Interface objects implement use cases which are directly dependent on the system environment. It is through these objects that actors communicate with the system. The main function is to translate the actor's actions into events in the system. They can also translate system responses into a form that is understandable to the actors. Thus, interface objects describe bidirectional communication between the system and its users.

To take an example, consider the MPC problem. A use case corresponds to the scenario whereby the used hours are transferred from a possibly remote mainframe computer to the machine where the system runs. In this case the actor is the mainframe, while an interface object for communicating with the actor is one which can read the necessary data, possibly in ASCII form (for example, a comma-delimited file).

Simple use cases can be described by entity and interface objects. In these cases we can delegate behaviour to one of these object types. For more complex use cases it is possible to find behaviour which does not belong to either of these two. This behaviour is placed in so-called control objects. They act as glue or cushions in order to unite the remaining objects so that they form one use case. The behaviour which remains after both entity and interface objects have been provided for will be placed in the control objects.

7.5 Where do event–response lists, use cases and storyboards fit into OORD?

Most OO methodologies pay only lip service to determining system requirements. They tacitly assume that the specifications have already been found before they start on the analysis phase. Furthermore, the role of the user is either neglected or not considered. This chapter is an attempt to find what the external behaviour of a system should be before effort is spent on analysing, designing and implementing a solution which probably does not satisfy the needs of its users. To this end, we give a discussion of the topic of scenario analysis as expounded in Hsia *et al.* (1994). There the authors consider the problem of applying formal techniques to scenario analysis. The products of the scenario analysis process are a set of scenarios (or user views of the system) which are consistent, complete and unambiguous. By consistent, we mean that no set of requirements is in conflict with any other set. Completeness means that everything the software is supposed to do is included in the specification and unambiguous refers to the fact that each requirement has only one interpretation.

A user view consists of scenarios. A given scenario is initiated by an agent (typically external users, external stimuli or even objects). Scenarios consist of events. An event type is a set of event sharing the same attributes. A scenario schema is defined as a sequence of event types that accomplishes some functional requirement. A scenario instance is an instantiation of a scenario schema. It has a specific user with specific interactions between the user and the system. An example of a scenario schema in PPD would be 'Customer tanks an amount of a certain grade of petrol' while an example of a scenario instance would be 'Fred tanks 30 litres of Euro-98 lead-free petrol'.

The steps in Hsia *et al.* (1994) are:

- *Scenario elicitation*

  In this phase the requirements analyst elicits the system's expected inputs (events) and responses. The user of the system is heavily involved in this phase. A so-called scenario tree is constructed which describes and represents all the scenarios for a particular user view. A user view in this context is a set of specific scenarios as seen by a certain user group. All users in this group use the system in a similar manner. This tree is similar to ER lists and storyboards; the nodes of the tree correspond to object states in which the edges correspond to events or responses. However, the tree is not necessarily object-oriented, while a storyboard is.

The user groups in the MPC (Manpower Control) problem are MIS staff, project leaders and data operators, and each group has its own particular set of views of the system. The user groups in the PPD (Petrol Pump Delivery) problem are attendants and customers. At a later stage it may become necessary to introduce new groups, such as service operators, oil company representatives and car-wash staff.

- *Scenario formalization*
  In this stage the analyst models the input and responses from the first stage in order to create a representation of the system's expected behaviour. In particular, each scenario tree is converted into an equivalent regular grammar. The details of how this is done are beyond the scope of this book and we refer the reader to Hsia *et al.* (1994). The model is in its turn used to construct a conceptual state machine. We see opportunities for creating Harel charts which would tie in more closely with the OMT method (this could be a research topic for a Ph.D. student in Computer Science). User involvement decreases somewhat in this stage.
- *Scenario verification*
  We verify the scenarios by manually checking the abstract model from the previous phase for possible errors in expected behaviour. User assistance may be needed in order to help the analyst verify all steps.
- *Scenario generation*
  The analyst generates scenarios from the conceptual state machine. This is done with little or no user help.
- *Prototype generation*
  The analyst uses rapid prototyping to produce a POC (proof-of-concept) for the expected system based on the generated scenarios. This prototype should be generated as quickly as possible. There are a number of dedicated languages (such as Gist and Paisley; see Balzer *et al.* (1982) and Bruns (1986)) which are suitable for specifying real-time and distributed systems, but most mortals will probably opt for a third-generation language such as Ada, Smalltalk or C++. C++ is less suitable than Smalltalk because it is a compiler and it does not have the wealth of reusable components and classes that we see in Smalltalk. The general guideline is: make the prototype in Smalltalk and then write the 'real' application in C++ once the user is satisfied.
- *Scenario validation*
  This is the phase in which the analyst uses the prototype to validate the scenarios and demonstrate their validity to the user. It is conceivable that invalid scenarios will be discovered, in which case the analyst must return to the elicitation phase and the process is started again.

Scenario analysis is completed when both the users and analyst agree that the scenarios are valid. The product of scenario analysis is a set of scenarios which is complete, consistent and unambiguous.

An interesting approach to requirements determination is taken in Potts *et al.* (1994). This article takes an inquiry-based approach and it emphasizes where and when information needs occur. The steps in the process are:

- Requirements documentation
- Requirements discussion
- Requirements evolution

Requirements documentation is the first phase of this inquiry-based process and it usually starts with a review of an existing requirements document. If no document exists we start from scratch in order to write down requirements which may be based on interviews, technical documentation and other sources of information. A good way to capture requirements is by using scenario analysis, which we have already discussed in this chapter. It is important to note that scenarios are not the same as specifications; a scenario describes system behaviour in one specific situation, while specifications describe what a system does in all situations.

Requirements discussion is the phase in which questions are asked about the system. It starts with a question by one of the project parties. An answer describes a solution to a problem and can cause refinements or revisions to questions. There are different kinds of questions which can be posed:

- *What-if questions*
  These are useful in cases when an action could go wrong or that preconditions are not satisfied. The main advantage of what-if questions is their ability to give us insight into apparently unrelated issues.
  An example of a what-if question is:

  What happens if there are too many readers on a circulation list?

  The conclusion to this question may be that a second set of issues needs to be ordered via the procurements department.
- *Follow-on questions*
  This type of question is similar to the Ausubel subsumption theory in which one question generalizes another one. Discovering the more general case may force us to modify the requirements. An example from JRP could be:

  Can we create a circulation list with zero readers?"

  This could be generalized to produce:

  What are the preconditions for creating a circulation list?
- *What-is questions*
  These questions solicit more information about a given requirement. It is similar to the question 'What do you mean by ...?'. It is surprising how often this is forgotten in practice.
  An example of such a question in MPC could be:

  What is an external customer?

- *How-to questions*
  These questions ask how a given requirement is to be carried out.
  All questions tend to be very focused and they force us to think hard about parts of the system. These questions could effectively be used when studying concept maps.
  An example from MPC would be:

  How is monthly data brought into the MPC system?

- *Who questions*
  These questions ask for confirmation of the agents which are responsible for certain actions. These agents can usually be found from storyboards and to a lesser extent from concept maps.
  For example, the following questions are typical:

  Who is responsible for the operating theatres?

  Who keeps the MPC data up to date?

  Who's responsible for filling the petrol tanks?

- *What-kinds-of questions*
  These questions request further refinement of a concept. For example, we could ask the following questions:

  What kinds of project are there?

  How many different types of nurses are there?

  Asking such questions leads to abstractions which can be implemented as class hierarchies during OOA.

- *When questions*
  These questions ask about timing constraints on some event or group of events. By asking this question we discover holes in the requirements.
  Examples of such questions are:

  When is MPC data loaded?

  When does the customer pay?

- *Relationship questions*
  These questions ask about how one requirement is related to another one.

The last phase in the inquiry-based model is devoted to requirements evolution. In this stage we either freeze or modify a requirement. A change request can be traced back to a discussion which took place at an earlier stage. Both evolution and discussion phases may occur gradually and informally or in discrete bursts, in which cases formal review and approval procedures are followed. Changes to requirements can take one of three forms, namely:

- Mutation
- Restriction
- Editorial

A mutation is a request to change the requirements themselves. It is also possible that new requirements are added. A restriction request calls for a change in the requirements document. This usually corresponds to a clarification and the main objective is to remove ambiguities. The original specification remains intact, however. Finally, an editorial request results in the rewriting of a requirement. Its main objective is to remove grammatical or spelling errors and to foster consistent terminology.

We finish this section with a summary description of a transaction-based problem in a local area network environment. The problem is posed in a very generic way and it is more a statement of achievable goals than a complete specification. The objective now is to use the inquiry technique to capture more requirements.

A Supervisor Override function is a mechanism whereby an operator can get authority to perform a certain transaction. Operators are grouped according to the transaction that they are allowed to execute. Conditions determine whether a transaction may or may not be performed. Examples of transactions are (in special cases):

- Pay 1000 dollars to a bank account.
- Commit a record on a remote database engine.
- Open a foreign currency account for a customer.

All successful and unsuccessful transactions should be logged.

Examples of conditions are:

- Operator is authorized to pay up to 2500 dollars.
- Operator has read-only privilege to security database.
- It is not possible to open a foreign account in North Korea.

If an operator is not authorized to execute a transaction the supervisor must be notified. (The supervisor is in principle authorized to execute any bank transaction; however, supervisors may be grouped just as operators are.) In this case a copy of the transaction (the so-called transaction data) is sent to the supervisor, who then decides what should be done. If the request is accepted the transaction can be executed by the operator and the modified transaction data is returned to the operator's terminal. If the transaction is rejected by the supervisor a message is sent to the operator to this effect with an explanation of why the request was rejected.

It is possible to change authorization levels for operators. Similarly, it should be possible to create and modify groups.

The above statement of goals is not yet in a form that can be used as input to the OMT method. We ask some questions concerning the text in the hope that they will lead us to more concrete requirements. We apply the different types of questions which have just been discussed to this problem.

- What-if
  - What happens if an operator asks clearance for a transaction which he is already entitled to execute?
  - What if all supervisors are busy?

  (These questions are resolved by answers about the system.)
- What-is
  - Define what you mean by a transaction.
  - Define precisely what 'transaction data' is.

  (These questions are resolved by defining the terms.)

- How-to
  - How is an operator authorized to execute a transaction?

  (This question is resolved by scenario analysis.)
- Who
  - Who grants permission to an operator to execute a transaction?
  - Who owns transaction data?
- What-kinds-of
  - Refine the concepts operator, supervisor, transaction and condition.

  (These correspond to things not stated and usually refer to abstract base classes.)
- When
  - When is a transaction committed/aborted?
  - When does transaction data become the property of the supervisor?

  (This is resolved by a possible mutation in the requirements.)
- Relationships
  - What is the relationship between conditions and the granting of authority?

Follow-on question pairs:

(a) Is there an overlap between supervisors and operators?

(b) Which groups do these agents fit into?

(a) What happens to a transaction after it is committed?

(b) What are the facilities for storing historical and 'back-office' transaction information?

(a) Is transaction data the same as a message?

(b) Can we set up the system in terms of message handling?

7.6 Deliverables

Storyboards help the designer to decide which objects induce stimuli and which objects subsequently react to external stimuli. Objects which induce stimuli are called agents and the reacting objects are called servers. An agent is thus a client of a server. This is equivalent to identifying the sender and receiver of each event. Storyboards provide valuable insight into object communication. Furthermore, the designer assigns event–response pairs to specific objects. Finally, the storyboard technique is also useful in determining the different states an object can find itself in.

Exercises

1. Draw up the list of events, responses and possible constraints for the ATM problem which was given as an exercise in Chapter 6.

2. Identify the following situations in the MPC problem:

   - Events causing multiple responses
   - Responses which occur only if multiple events take place
   - Events having constraints

3. Identify events, responses and constraints for the following problem which is taken from Williams (1994). Create storyboards for this problem.

   We wish to create a computerized system for water-level monitoring system (WLMS) that is to be used in the safety system of a steam-generation application, for example a power plant. The WLMS consists of two vessels or tanks. One tank acts as a reservoir, while the other acts as a steam-generation vessel or drum. Water is pumped from the reservoir to the drum from which the water evaporates. The ultimate fate of the steam is not a concern of WLMS; only the drum's water level is important (Figure 7.2). Pump P2 pumps water from the reservoir to the drum, and is normally regulated by the control system. Pump P1 pumps water from the drum to the reservoir and mimics loss of water to the drum due to steam generation. The control system normally regulates the rate of steam generation. The WLMS monitors and displays the drum's water level. When the level is too high or too low WLMS issues an audible alarm and shuts down the pumps. The pumps are also shut down if the WLMS itself fails, which it may do if an external device like the water-level detector or system clock fails or the control unit itself fails because of a memory or CPU failure. WLMS detects any failure of an external device or memory. An external watchdog timer, which periodically receives a timer from the WLMS detects any CPU failure. If the signal is not received, the watchdog timer shuts down the pumps.

   In both cases the WLMS shuts the system down by turning off the power to both pumps, which it does through a single output signal.

   WLMS has two push buttons. The SelfTest button lets the operator check the WLMS output hardware while the system is shut down. The Reset button returns the system to normal operation after a shutdown or test, provided that the water level is within safe limits.

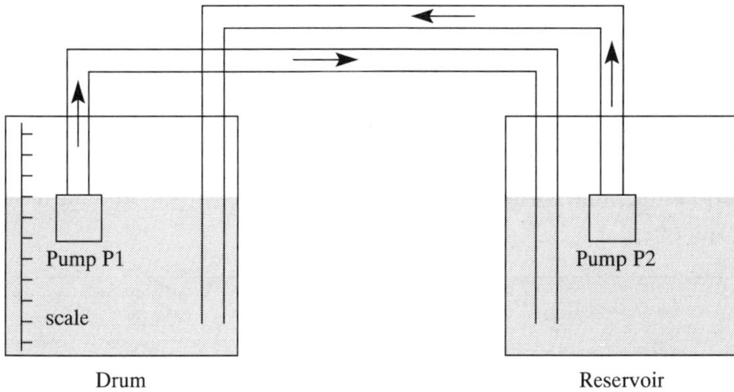

Figure 7.2 WLMS tank and pump configuration.

4. Draw up storyboards for the Hospital Database problem whose concept map was developed in Chapter 6.

5. Give a list of the storyboards for MPC and PPD based on their high-level system responsibilities.

6. Create storyboard narrative for the storyboard descriptions in (7.1) (for JRP), (7.2) (for MPC) and (7.3) (for PPD).

7. Create event–response lists for the problem described in Exercise 3 above.

8. Find the agent objects and server objects for all events in JRP, MPC and PPD.

9. Construct concept maps, event–response lists and storyboards for the following problem.

   A simple digital watch has a display and two buttons to set it (A and B buttons). The watch has two modes of operation, namely display time and set time. In display time mode hours and minutes are displayed, separated by a flashing colon. The set time mode has two submodes, namely set hours and set minutes. The A button is used to select modes. Each time it is pressed the mode advances in sequence, namely from display to set hours to set minutes to display etc. Within the submodes, the B button is used to advance the hours or minutes once each time that it is pressed. Buttons must be released before they can generate another event.

10. Prepare use cases for the following problem (Jackson 1983).

    A building with six floors has one elevator. The elevator cabin contains six buttons, each button corresponding to a different floor. Each floor (except the first floor and the sixth floor) contains two buttons next to the elevator doors, the so-called up and down buttons. The first floor has no down button, while the sixth floor has no up button.

    The elevator moves continuously between the first floor and the sixth floor, irrespective of whether a request has been issued or not. After reaching the sixth or first floors the elevator changes direction, momentarily opening and closing the elevator door. The elevator stops at a given floor under two conditions. First, the person in the elevator may press a button corresponding to a given floor. The response is to stop at the given floor and is independent of the elevator's current direction. Secondly, the button on the wall of each floor which corresponds to the elevator's current direction can be pressed. Once stopped, the elevator opens its door and the request that was made is serviced. When the elevator leaves the floor the button that was pressed is released and is available for pressing again.

    How would you generalize this problem to the case of an *n* elevator system which is to be installed in a building with *m* floors (Saeki *et al.* 1989)?

11. Identify entity, interface and control objects for the problem JRP. Use the results achieved in Chapter 6.

References

R. Balzer *et al.* (1982) Operation Specifications as the Basis for Rapid Prototyping, *Software Engineering Notes*, December, pp. 3–6.

G. Bruns (1986) Technology Assessment: PAISLEY, *Technical report STP-296-86*, Microelectronics and Computer Technology Corp., Austin TX.

D. D'Souza (1993) Working with OMT, *Journal of Object-Oriented Programming*, October.

I. Jacobson (1987) Object Oriented Development in an Industrial Environment, *SIGPLAN Notices*, **22**(12).

I Jacobson *et al.* (1992) *Object-Oriented Software Engineering*, Addison-Wesley, Wokingham.

M. Jackson (1983) *System Development*, Prentice-Hall, Englewood Cliffs NJ.

P. Hsia *et al.* (1994) Formal approach to scenario analysis, *IEEE Software*, March.

C. Potts *et al.* (1994) Inquiry-based requirements analysis, *IEEE Software*, March.

M. Saeki, H. Horai and H. Enomoto (1989) Software development process from natural language specification, *11th International Conference on Software Engineering*.

D. A. Umphress and S. G. March (1991) Object-oriented requirements analysis, *Journal of Object-Oriented Programming*, Focus on Analysis and Design, pp. 35–40.

L. G. Williams (1994) Assessment of safety-critical specifications, *IEEE Software*, January (Special Issue on Safety-Critical Systems).

Chapter

8

The object model

8.1 Introduction and objectives

This chapter is based on the object modelling techniques developed in Rumbaugh *et al.* (1991). In particular, we are interested in creating object diagrams from concept maps. The products from the concept mapping phase are concepts and links. Use is made of concept maps in order to create a so-called object model. However, the object model needs more information than is delivered by concept mapping techniques alone. The end-result of the object modelling phase is a number of object diagrams. Each object diagram contains the following information:

(8.1)

- A list of object classes from the problem domain
- Object attribute names
- The associations between classes
- Generalization relationships

The steps in (8.1) will be discussed in this chapter and a test given to show how the process works.

8.2 Links and associations

OMT has its own notation for representing classes and associations. A class is represented by a rectangle which is divided into two parts, the upper part for the name of the class and the lower part for its attributes. Examples of classes and their attributes are shown in Figure 8.1. In OMT, attributes should be simple data types, such as numerical, string or date types.

A class is similar to a concept except that it has attributes. We state this as an equation:

class = concept + attributes

Figure 8.1 Graphical notation for classes in OMT.

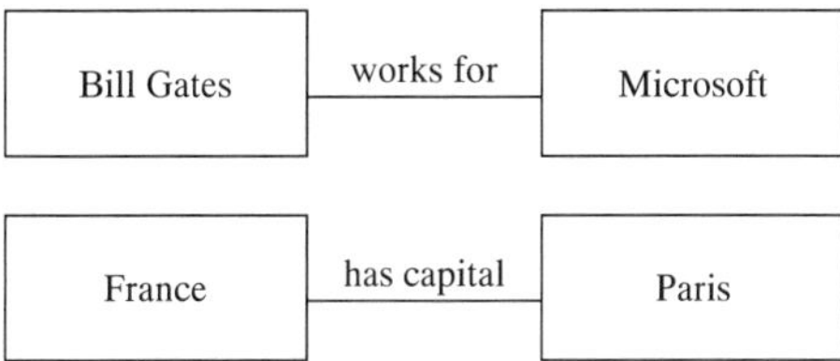

Figure 8.2 Examples of links in OMT.

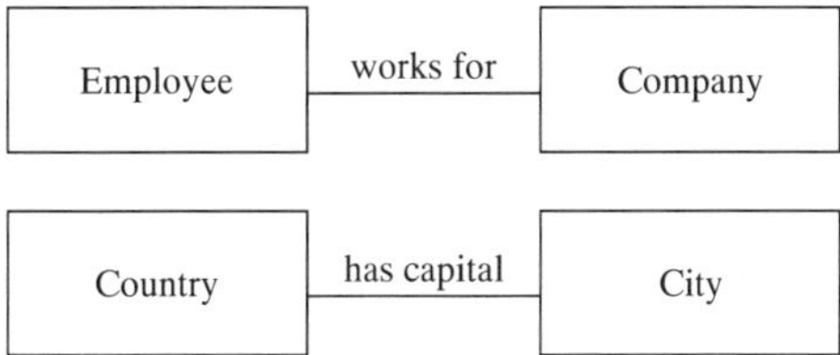

Figure 8.3 Associations between classes.

Concepts are connected by links in order to form semantic units. In the same way classes are related by so-called associations. In order to define what an association is we must first define what a link is in OMT (not to be confused with a link in concept mapping). A link is a conceptual or physical connection between objects. An association describes a group of links which have common structure or common semantics. We can thus view a link as an instance of an association. The associations corresponding to the links in Figure 8.2 are shown in Figure 8.3.

An association in OMT is an implementation of a link from a concept map. Associations can be discovered by finding verbs and verb phrases which connect classes.

The multiplicity of an association is that property which specifies how many instances of one class may relate to a single instance of an associated class. The possibilities are:

(8.2)

- One-to-one (1:1)
- One-to-many (1:*N*)
- Many-to-many (*N*:*M*)

Examples are given in Figure 8.4. The association 'pump contains display' is one-to-one because a pump contains one display while one display is contained in one pump. The association 'employee works for company' is many-to-one since a company employs many

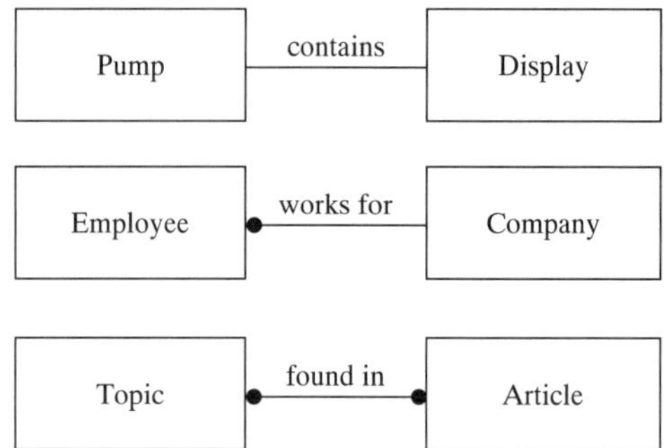

Figure 8.4 Multiplicity and associations.

employees while an employee works for only one company. In some circumstances the association could be many-to-many if we allowed an employee to work for several companies. Finally, the association 'topic found in articles' is many-to-many because a given topic is discussed in many articles while an article may deal with many topics.

Multiplicity depends on assumptions on how the boundaries of a problem are defined. This is context-sensitive. The most general approach is to make all associations many-to-many in the object modelling phase. This may reduce to a one-to-many or even one-to-one as our knowledge of the problem becomes more complete. It is important not to lose too much time pining about the exact multiplicity during analysis because this may change during design and implementation. A safe bet is to use many-to-many associations in the short term.

It is possible to define zero-to-one, or optional, associations. An optional association may represent the possible absence of the relationship between one class and another one. For example, in an environment where projects are worked on it may be possible that an employee is seconded to some other department. This is optional. An employee may be seconded to a new department for the duration of a given project. Otherwise, the employee carries out duties for the 'home' department. Similarly, in the political arena the association between a 'cabinet minister' and 'portfolio' is optional; a minister may or may not have a portfolio, while one portfolio is the responsibility of one minister. Examples of optional associations are shown in Figure 8.5.

It is possible to define recursive associations. A recursive association is an implementation of a recursive link in concept mapping and it represents a relationship between some object and other instances of the same class. Examples of recursive associations are:

- A published article refers to other articles.
- A window may be a parent of another window.

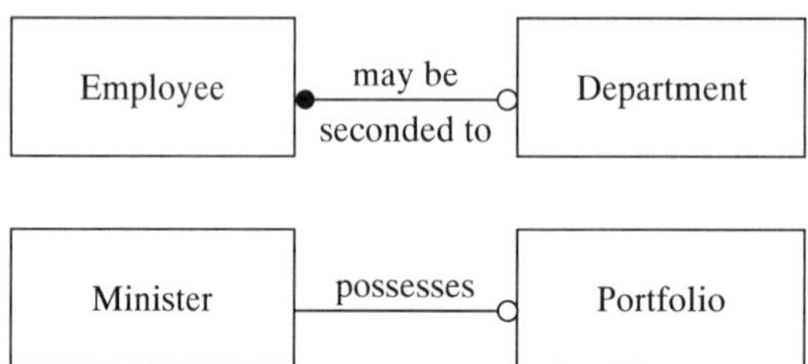

Figure 8.5 Optional associations.

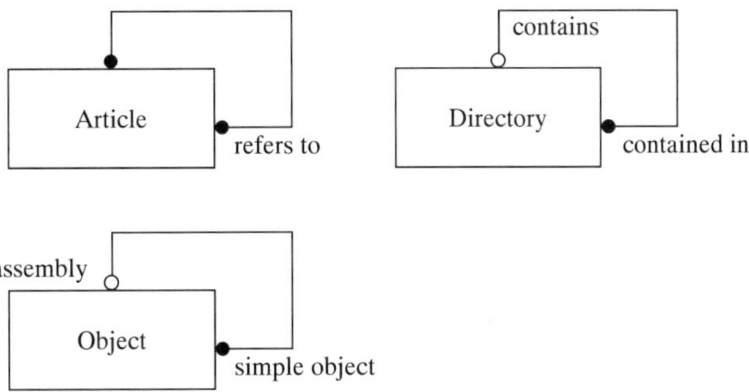

Figure 8.6 Examples of recursive associations and roles.

- A project may be composed of projects.

Figure 8.6 shows how recursive associations are represented in OMT.

There are different kinds of association. The most common is the binary association. This is a relationship between two classes. A ternary association is one which defines a relationship between three objects. Examples of ternary associations are:

(8.3)

- An employee works on a project for a department.
- A student takes a course from a professor.
- A nurse assists a surgeon in the operating theatre.
- An employee is assigned a desk on a given day of the week.
- A vendor sells products to a customer.

Associations can be extended beyond binary and ternary (or trinary, as they are sometimes called) associations to produce n-ary or n-place associations. Associations are objects and such objects are called n-tuples or simply tuples. It is convenient to create names for such complex objects. For example, the association 'a vendor sells products to a customer' is the same as the ternary association 'Contract'.

We shall not discuss ternary or n-ary associations in this book. They are difficult to understand and they can be decomposed into simpler binary associations. For example, the ternary association 'cashier enters transaction for account' can be decomposed into the pair of binary associations 'cashier enters transaction' and 'transaction concerns account'.

Binary associations are closer in spirit to concept mapping techniques than ternary or n-ary associations.

8.3 Roles and qualified associations

A role is one end of an association. Binary associations have two roles, one for each class. Consider the classes Person and Company. There are many associations possible between these in which instances of these classes will play different roles. Possible roles for Person and Company are:

(8.4)

- For Person
  - Employee
  - Manager
  - Security officer
  - Programmer
  - Director
  - Trade unionist
- For Company
  - Employer
  - Consortium member
  - Producer of consumer products
  - Cost centre
  - Profit centre

It is important to find roles during the object modelling phase. Roles are not the 'real things', but can be seen as views of other objects. In practice, role classes may be specializations of basic classes. For example, the role Employee is a specialization of Person. However, role objects can be implemented in other ways. An instance of Employee behaves just like an instance of Person but it has extra state and behaviour. In this case an Employee instance has a given grade and salary (something that an instance of Person does not have). Typical behaviour corresponding to Employee is:

- How much does the employee earn per year?
- Which department does the employee work for?
- What skills does the employee possess?

In order to communicate the fact that we are working with roles, OMT suggests using the name of the original object in object diagrams and placing the label for the role name played by the class near the end of the association. Examples in Figure 8.7 show how to do this.

The multiplicity between a 'real' object and its possible roles is many-to-many. An object may assume a number of roles, while a role may be relevant for many objects. Objects are at a higher conceptual level than roles. Similarly, there is a many-to-many correspondence between roles and behaviour.

A number of approaches to object-oriented analysis and design use so-called role modelling as a core aspect (Wirfs-Brock and Johnson 1990). The concept Role is introduced, which

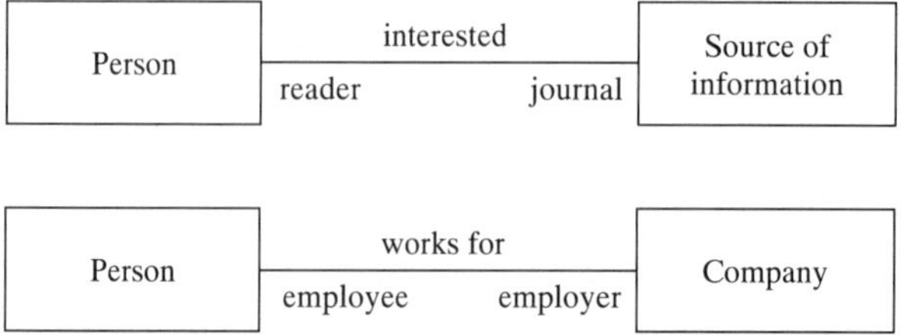

Figure 8.7 Roles and association.

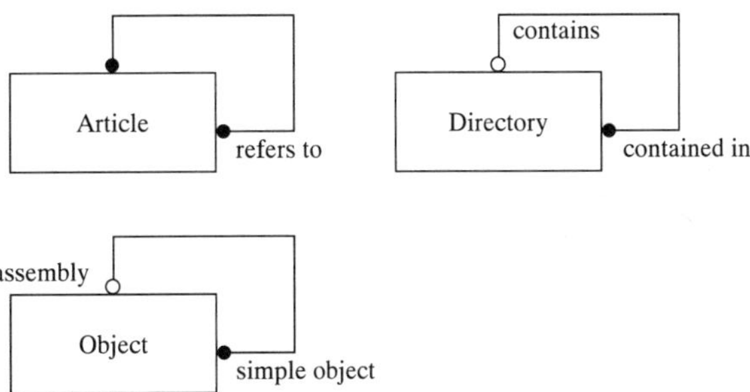

Figure 8.8 Roles in recursive associations.

corresponds to the 'why' of an object, and the Role represents the task of an object within an organized structure of objects. We speak of a Role Model in which a given problem domain is separated into a number of areas of concern. Each area is modelled as a structure of interacting objects and each object is abstracted into a Role according to its purpose in the Role Model structure.

The advantage of using Role Model lies in reusability. New problems can be analysed and designed by identifying the classes and asking ourselves the question 'is this a role for some other class?'.

Roles are optional in binary associations but they must be included in recursive associations. Examples are given in Figures 8.6 and 8.8.

Role modelling is not discussed at length in OMT. We feel that it deserves more attention since it promotes reusability, because the classes which implement roles usually turn out to be specializations of classes which have been found in previous projects.

A qualified association relates two classes and a qualifier. The qualifier is a special attribute which reduces the multiplicity of the association. This has advantages when navigating in object diagrams. Furthermore, qualified associations may be designed and implemented by reusable classes for hash tables, dictionaries of key/value pairs and even by indexes in relational database systems. A qualifier is like a unique attribute key. For example, in a DOS directory each filename is unique.

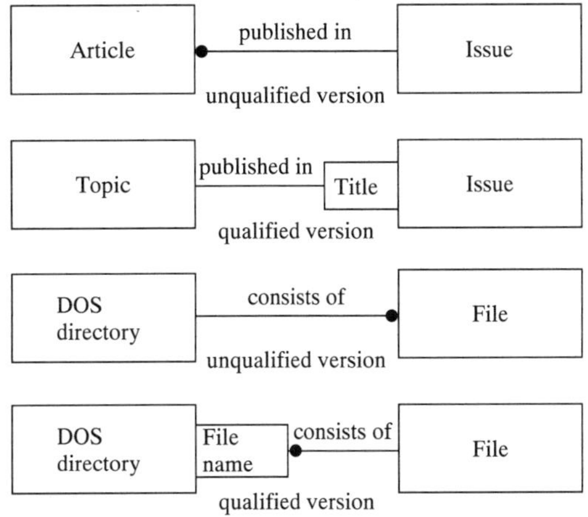

Figure 8.9 Using qualified associations.

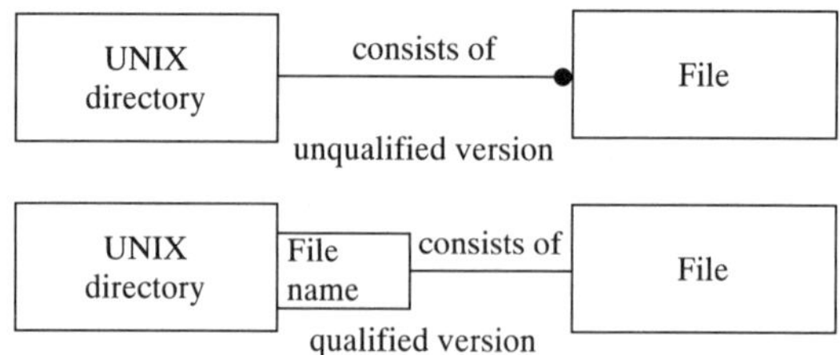

Figure 8.10 Example of many-to-one qualified association.

Qualification occurs in practice when we wish to supply names. Examples of this are given in Figure 8.9. Here we see that one-to-many associations are reduced to one-to-one associations by the introduction of the qualifier. This is not always the case. For example, in a UNIX file system the combination of directory name and filename is not sufficient to characterize a file uniquely. This is shown in Figure 8.10.

8.4 Aggregations

We have already discussed aggregations in Chapter 2. The kinds of aggregation appearing in OMT are:

- Fixed aggregates
- Variable aggregates
- Recursive aggregates

Fixed aggregates have a fixed number of components. OMT uses a diamond-shaped symbol to show that a class is an aggregation. See Figure 8.11 for examples of fixed aggregates.

A variable aggregate consists of a finite number of components, but the actual number may vary. Examples of variable aggregates are given in Figure 8.12. Such aggregates are implemented in C++ as lists and arrays.

A recursive aggregation is a special case of a recursive association. Examples of recursive aggregations are:

- A binary tree consists of other binary trees
- A project consists of projects

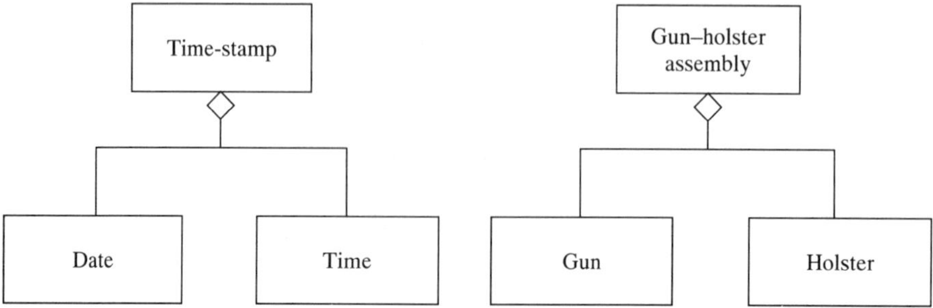

Figure 8.11 Fixed aggregates.

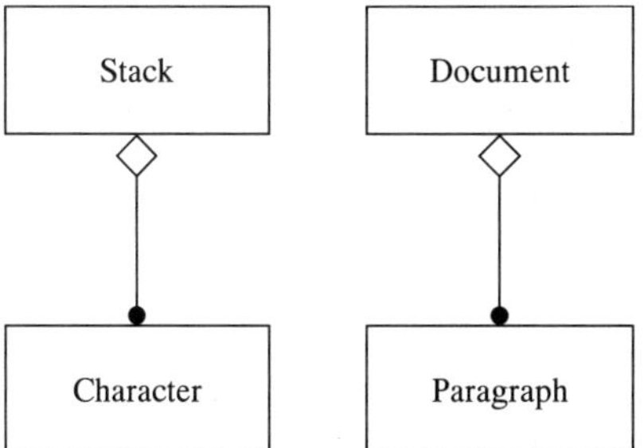

Figure 8.12 Variable aggregates.

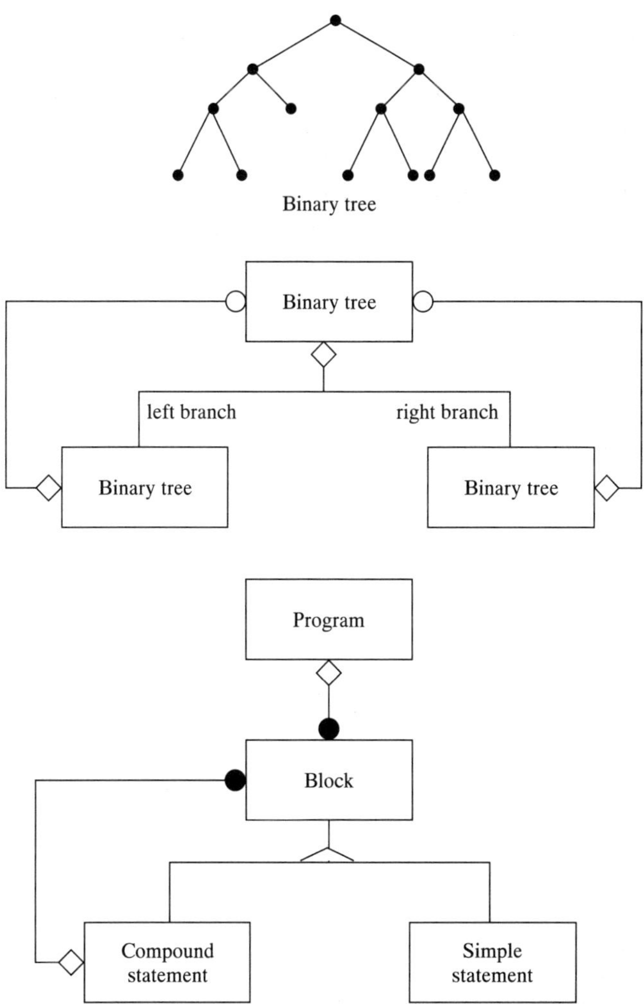

Figure 8.13 Recursive aggregates.

- A directory contains directories

Figure 8.13 shows some examples of displaying recursive aggregations using the OMT notation.

8.5 Inheritance

OMT uses a triangle-shaped drawing symbol to show that a given class is a specialization of another class. The triangle is hollow if specializations have no overlap, either in state or behaviour. If there is overlapping membership the triangle is filled in. We do not discuss this case as the former case is much more common.

There are no special symbols for showing the differences between abstract classes, concrete classes or generic classes in OMT. This is a shortcoming and the 'type' (abstract, concrete or generic) of a class should be documented.

Examples of inheritance hierarchies are given in Figure 8.14. The first example is taken from the MPC problem, while the second is taken from the world of financial investment. An option is a contract which confers the right but not the obligation to buy or sell an asset on a given date (the so-called exercise or maturity date) at a predefined (exercise) price (Gemmill 1993). Options can be taken out on almost any type of asset, for example gold, silver, grain, the value of a company and so on. There are options to buy assets. These are known as call options. Put options grant some party the right to sell the assets. Call options are more common than put options and also easier to understand. One buys a call option in

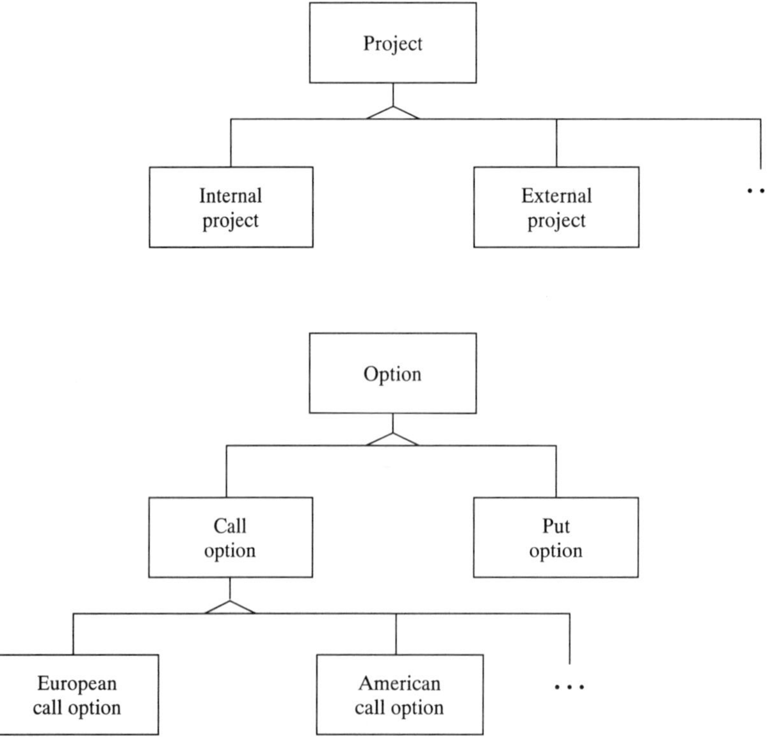

Figure 8.14 Inheritance hierarchies in OMT.

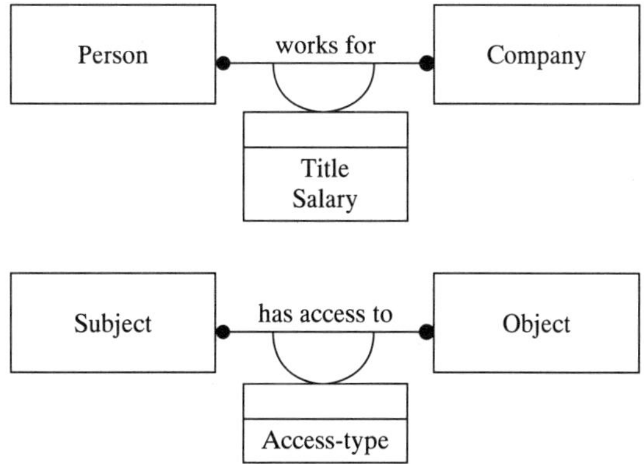

Figure 8.15 Link attributes.

the hope that the price of the asset will increase in time. Some options give a buyer an additional right. The option may not only be exercised at the maturity date, but also on any date before then. These are known as American options. Options that do not allow such early exercise are known as European options. Most options that are traded on exchanges are American, but many of the off-exchange ('over-the-counter') deals are for European options.

8.6 Link attributes

Link attributes occur when interaction objects crop up in concept maps and object diagrams. A link attribute is a property of the links in an association. A link attribute is a property of the link and thus it cannot be attached to either object.

For example, the link 'Borland sells C++ compilers' could have the following link attributes:

- The quantity shipped
- The version number of the compiler
- The intended OS platform in which the compiler operates

Some examples of link attributes and how they are represented in OMT are shown in Figure 8.15.

8.7 The steps involved in object modelling

The object modelling phase in OMT is executed as a number of steps which are described in Rumbaugh *et al.* (1991, p. 152). We adopt the same scenario, with the following additions:

- Concept maps as a front-end; this means that invalid classes and associations are filtered prior to entering the object modelling phase. OMT does this processing during the analysis phase.
- More emphasis is placed on discovering abstract and concrete classes. Finding generic classes is also important since they are a useful alternative to inheritance and they can be implemented in C++ as templates.

- OMT object diagrams are 'flat'. Since we see object diagrams as implementations of concept maps, our object diagrams are hierarchical. This provides levelling mechanisms which are not possible in 'classical' OMT.
- Roles. Discovering roles during object modelling means that less work needs to be done later because roles are specializations of classes that have already been found in previous projects.

Some recent extensions to and experiences with OMT are discussed in D'Souza (1993, 1994) and Gilliam (1994). Gilliam suggests modifying OMT by splitting a system into subsystems and analysing each subsystem independently of the other subsystems. We doubt whether such an approach is the correct way of doing things. The main problem is in determining how to group objects. To solve this problem Champeaux (1991) suggests working with ensembles. An ensemble is a cluster or bundle of less abstract entities which are either objects or lower level ensembles. These entities only act among each other or with the encompassing ensemble. The ensemble acts as a gateway between the components and the ensemble's context. An ensemble is an entity with internal parallelism and it conforms to the information hiding principle. Ensembles have state and behaviour.

Examples of ensembles are:

- A pump assembly in a petrol station
- The loan department in a bank (loan officers work in parallel)
- A fleet of ships

In the last example we can think of each ship in the fleet as having a direction; the fleet itself can also have a direction (an attribute) which is the direction in which all the ships are travelling at a given moment in time.

Each key concept map will be mapped to an object diagram. In the Hospital Database Problem, whose concept maps were created in Chapter 6, we have two main concepts, namely:

- Patient Registration
- Patient Operation

Each of these concept maps has been created in a top-down fashion. The corresponding object diagrams will also reflect this structure.

To summarize, the lack of layering techniques in OMT has been solved by applying concept mapping techniques as a front-end to the object modelling phase.

- OMT assumes that objects operate in an ideal world. There are no provisions for exception handling although constraints are discussed. Furthermore, exceptions can be seen as objects and no provision is made for these in OMT. Some authors (for example Firesmith (1993)) use exceptions as part of their class descriptions. Such support is vital for safety-critical applications.
- OMT treats the class as the basic building block. This is not always a good approach. The 'use cases' approach (Jacobson *et al.* 1992) is preferable because it focuses initially on the functionality of the system and then on the objects. We advocate creating a concept map for each use case and implementing this as an object diagram. We then apply the 'classical' OMT approach.

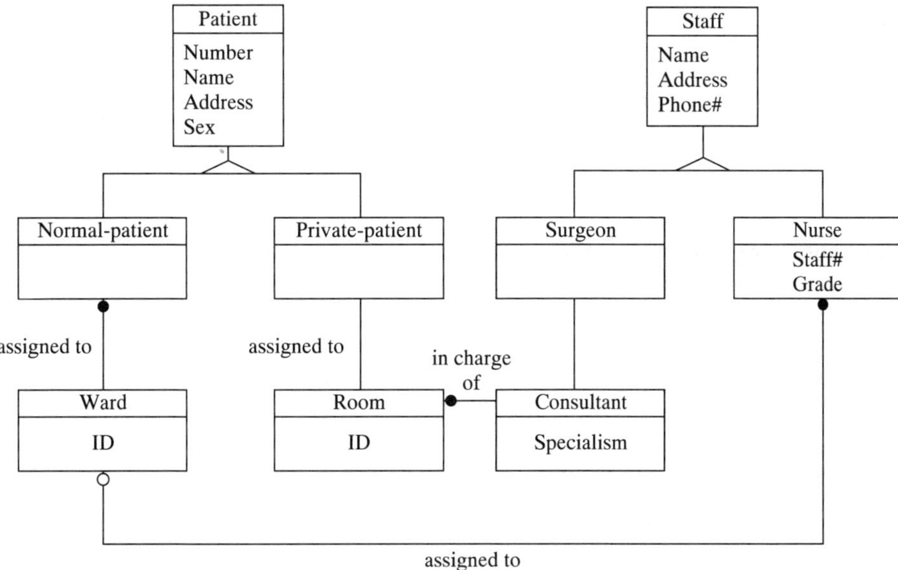

Figure 8.16 Object diagram for Patient Registration.

To give an example of an object diagram, let us consider the Hospital Database Problem again; in particular, we are interested in creating an object diagram from the concept map for 'Patient Registration'. The steps are:

(8.5)

- Use the requirements document as input!
- Concepts are promoted into classes.
- Attributes are added to the classes.
- Links are implemented as associations (roles, qualified associations).
- Implement abstraction links as inheritance relationships.
- Implement partitioning links as aggregation relationships.
- Implement projection links as object operations.

The resulting object diagram in this case is given in Figure 8.16. The steps in the object modelling phase are:

(8.6)

- Identify objects and classes.
- Create a preliminary data dictionary.
- Identify associations and aggregations.
- Identify object and link attributes.
- Group similar classes into inheritance hierarchies.
- Determine likely queries and navigation paths.

- Iterate and refine the model.
- Group classes into modules.

We describe how each of these steps is carried out, with the exception of the last one. This is not absolutely necessary in our present situation because of the way that we have created object diagrams.

8.7.1 Test case: journal registration problem (JRP)

We show how the steps in (8.6) are applied to creating the object diagram for JRP, whose concept map was constructed in Chapter 6.

A: Identifying classes Identifying classes is relatively easy because the concepts which have been found in the concept mapping phase evolve into classes in the analysis phase.

B: Creating a data dictionary The purpose of the Data Dictionary is to give:

- A precise description of each class
- The scope of the class within the current problem
- Assumptions and restrictions
- A description of the associations, attributes and operations

In this case we devote attention to determining the function of each class in the current problem.

Reader

A person who is interested in a certain topic. A reader can also be somebody who gets access to certain issues of a journal on a regular basis. The operations are:

- Creating new instances of Reader.
- A reader wishes to be placed on the circulation list of a journal.
- A reader becomes interested in a topic.
- A reader ceases to be interested in a topic.
- A reader wishes to know whether a certain topic is treated in a given issue and which articles deal with that topic.

Journal

This is an abstract concept. A journal is a set of issues with the same name, for example *BYTE* or *IBM System Journal.*

- A new journal becomes available.
- When is the next issue of a journal due?

Issue

An appearance of a journal. An issue contains articles which in turn concern topics.

- Create an instance of an Issue (including a list of associated articles).
- Give information on articles in a given issue.
- Topic information on articles in an issue.

Article

A piece of text which is published in an issue of a journal. An article is written by one or more authors, has a title and is concerned with one or more topics.

- Create an Article.
- Is a certain topic mentioned in article?
- Find all topics pertaining to a particular article.

Topic

A topic represents a keyword which can be used as a search key. This is a borderline class as it has very little behaviour.

C: Finding associations We see associations between classes in JRP as implementations of the links found in the concept mapping phase. In this phase we include multiplicity. The multiplicity should ideally be specified in the Requirements Document; in this case we decide in the analysis phase to do this.

The associations and their multiplicities are:

- A Reader is interested in a Topic
  This is a many-to-many association; a Reader is interested in a number of Topics while a given Topic is of interest to a number of Readers.
- An Issue of a Journal contains Articles
  A given Issue consists of a number of Articles while a given Article is published in only one Issue. This is therefore a one-to-many association.
  It is possible to qualify this aggregation by noting that the title of an Article in an Issue is enough to specify it uniquely.
- A Reader may get access to a Journal
  This is a many-to-many association. A Reader may have access to a number of Journals, while a given Journal may be accessed by a number of Readers. One of the link attributes is a class attribute `$default_duration`, which represents the default value for the length of time that issues of a Journal may be in the possession of a Reader.
- An Issue is an appearance of a Journal
  This is a one-to-many association. A Journal has many Issues, while a given Issue appears only once in a Journal. It is possible to qualify the association by noting that an Issue is uniquely defined if we give its volume number and year of publication.
- A Topic is found in an Article
  This is a many-to-many association. A Topic may be mentioned in many Articles while an Article is concerned with a number of Topics.

D: Determining object attributes The following is a preliminary list of object attributes.

- Reader:
  - Name
  - Department
- Journal:
  - Name

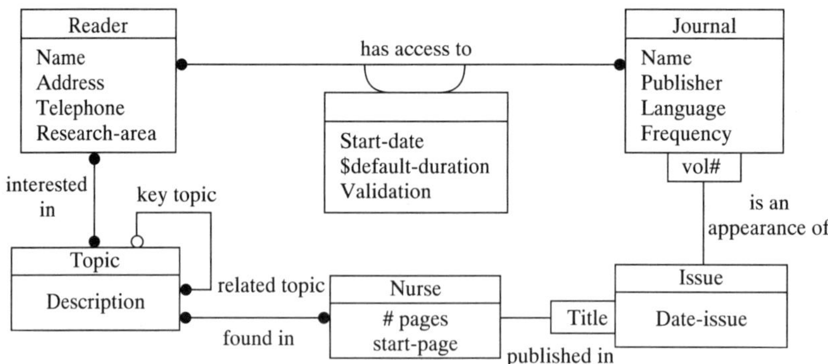

Figure 8.17 Object diagram for JRP.

Publisher

Frequency of publication (so many times per year)

Language used (English, French, ...)

- Issue:

  Journal

  Volume number

  Year of publication

- Article:

  Title

  Author (assuming that there is only one)

  Issue (in which issue it was published)

  Topics

- Topic:

  Description of topic

  Other related topics (role association)

It is important not to spend too much time looking for attributes, as new ones will be discovered during dynamic and functional modelling.

E: Classification process This is straightforward for JRP. No generalization relationships have been found.

The completed object diagram for JRP is given in Figure 8.17.

8.8 The products of the object modelling phase

The object modelling phase produces the following entities, which can be used in the dynamic and functional modelling phases as well as in the object design phase:

- The classes in the application domain
- Object attributes

- Relationships between classes (associations)
- Classes with similar behaviour grouped into an inheritance hierarchy

8.9 Object diagrams and scalability

Object diagrams are essentially generalized entity relationship (ER) diagrams. They are easy to create and maintain for small to medium-sized problems but for larger problems they become unmanageable and difficult to understand. The same can be said of concept maps. However, if we adopt the policy of creating object diagrams based on use cases the complexity of the resulting object diagrams will be minimized.

Exercises

1. Determine the circumstances under which the following associations have one-to-one, one-to-many or many-to-many multiplicity:
   - An issue is an appearance of a journal.
   - An operation takes place in an operating theatre.
   - A payment produces a receipt.
   - A gun has a trigger.
   - An employee works on a project.
   - An employee belongs to a department.
   - An article is published in a journal issue.

2. Implement the ternary associations in (8.3) as simpler binary associations.

3. Give the state and behaviour of the roles in (8.4).

4. On a stock exchange floor we identify the following roles: trader, senior trader, market maker, asset, swap, bond, option, call option, Dow Jones average, counterparty, buyer, fool (there must be a fool!). What are the objects corresponding to these roles? Can you find other roles?

5. Find the objects and roles in the following list: table, arch, road, bridge, tunnel, reservoir, drum, tank, vessel, arcade, shelves, road.

6. Qualify the following associations (i.e. find the qualifier attribute):
   - An issue is an appearance of a journal.
   - An article is published in a issue.
   - A reader is interested in a journal.
   - A division consists of departments.

7. A candidate key is the minimal set of attributes that uniquely identifies an object or a link. Identify the candidate keys for JRP.

8. A circulation list can be seen as an instance of the association between a Reader and a Journal. Find the attributes and behaviour of such a circulation list.

9. Create an object diagram for the concept Patient Operation of the Hospital Database Problem. Use the steps in (8.5).

References

D. de Champeaux (1991) Object-oriented analysis and top-down software development, in *European Conference on Object-Oriented Programming 1991*, Lecture Notes in Computer Science (ed. P. America), Springer, Berlin.

D. D'Souza (1993) Working with OMT, *Journal of Object-Oriented Programming*, October.

D. D'Souza (1994) Working with OMT, part 2, *Journal of Object-Oriented Programming*, February.

F. J. Fabozzi (1993) *Bond Markets: Analysis and Strategies* (2nd edn), Prentice-Hall, Englewood Cliffs NJ.

D. G. Firesmith (1993) *Object-Oriented Requirements Analysis and Logical Design*, John Wiley & Sons, Chichester.

G. Gemmill (1993) *Options Pricing, An International Perspective*, McGraw-Hill, London.

C. Gilliam (1994) An approach for using OMT in the development of large systems, *Journal of Object-Oriented Programming*, February.

I. Jacobson *et al.* (1992) *Object-Oriented Software Engineering*, Addison-Wesley, Wokingham.

J. Rumbaugh, M. Blaha, W. Premerlani, F. Eddy and W. Lorensen (1991) *Object-Oriented Modeling and Design*, Prentice-Hall, Englewood Cliffs NJ.

R. Wirfs-Brock and R. E. Johnson (1990) Surveying current research in object-oriented design, *Communications of the ACM*, **33**(9) September.

Chapter

9

An introduction to dynamic modelling

9.1 Introduction and objectives

Objects interact by sending messages to each other. An object has both state and behaviour. State is static, as it relates to how objects are laid out in space. This static information is represented by the object model. Behaviour refers to the way in which object state changes over time within the boundaries of their defined structures. The state of objects may change over time as well as the relationships between objects. Those aspects of a system which change with time constitute the dynamic model.

This chapter describes the major concepts dealing with interactions, flows of control and sequencing of operations in systems of concurrently active objects. The products from this stage of analysis will be appended to the object model. In particular, we shall show how events from the dynamic model are represented as operations in the object model.

9.2 Overview of techniques for capturing dynamic behaviour

Temporal relationships are difficult to understand. This is because changes in object state can be caused by a multitude of external stimuli, and such changes can trigger other objects to change state. It is necessary to represent the dynamic behaviour in a system in a way that is easy to understand and which is amenable to verification and validation procedures. This is no easy task, and a number of techniques have been proposed (Davis 1988). Most approaches use some form of state transition diagramming techniques. A state transition diagram (STD) is a directed graph in which the nodes represent object states while the directed arcs represent transitions from one state to another state. Variations on this basic theme have been proposed, such as:

(9.1)

- Petri nets (Peterson 1977)
- Finite state machines (FSMs)
- State transition diagrams and state transition matrices

- Extensions to structured analysis, real-time (Hatley and Pirbhai 1988).

The main objective in general is to find errors in documents which describe in detail the expected external behaviour of a system. Such documents are called software requirements specifications (SRS) documents. Simple examples of SRSs were discussed in Chapter 7. These were the so-called event–response lists and storyboards. These work reasonably well for small problems like the simple digital watch example, but they break down for larger problems. The main sources of error in SRSs in general are:

- Incorrect facts
- Omissions
- Inconsistencies
- Ambiguities

The reason for these errors is that specifications are written in natural language, which is imprecise and ambiguous. Formal methods need to be developed to specify a system's external behaviour so that the number of errors in SRSs can be reduced and to alert software designers of omissions in the specifications.

OMT uses modified state transition diagrams in order to analyse object behaviour. The method used the structured state diagrams originally proposed by Harel (1988) and Harel *et al.* (1988) (see also Harel *et al.* 1987) and will be discussed in Sections 9.5 and 9.6. They are an improvement on classical state transition diagrams and can be integrated with the object model. In particular, there are commercial CASE tools supporting the OMT approach which combine the object and dynamic models into one integrated environment.

9.3 Main concepts in dynamic modelling

9.3.1 Events and states

A system in which nothing happens does not occur very often in practice. Things happen in expected or unexpected ways and the system should be able to react to stimuli in an appropriate fashion. Changes in system behaviour are caused by events. An event is something which happens at one moment in time. An event has no duration, at least in theory. In practice it takes a finite (albeit small) amount of time before an event has completed.

Events may be related or unrelated. Chapter 7 discussed some examples of causally related events when event–response lists were defined. The responses are causally related to their events because the effect of an event is to trigger a sequence of one or more responses. Each response is also an event and can in its turn trigger a sequence of responses somewhere else in the system. It is possible that two events are causally unrelated and in this case we say that the events are concurrent. Thus the fact that one event occurs has no effect on the other event. Concurrent events cannot influence each other. These events typically occur in distributed applications where there are several areas of control. For example, in the JRP problem a reader can query a new issue for interesting articles while a member of the personnel department can create new circulation lists.

A pair of objects communicate by exchanging messages. An event is the carrier of information between such objects. The information flow is in one direction only. We speak of a sending object and a receiving object. The sending object may expect a reply, but the reply is itself a separate event which is under the control of the receiving object, which may

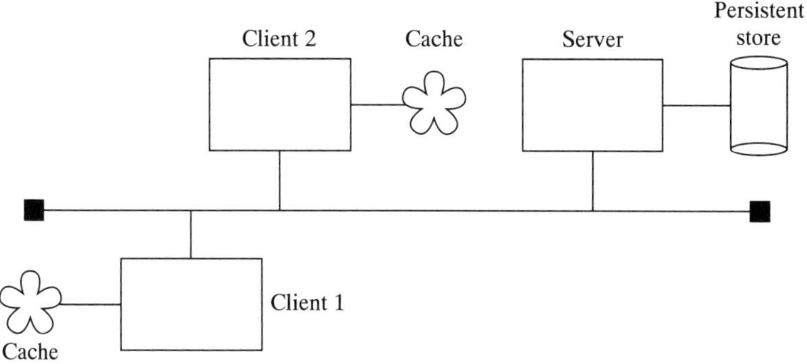

Figure 9.1 Communicating objects in a distributed client/server environment.

or may not choose to send it. A good example of message passing in combination with events can be found in object-oriented databases which operate in a networked environment (Object Design 1992). Figure 9.1 shows a distributed database environment. The server object contains the definitive database information. Client objects may access the data which is present in the server's persistent store. In order to reduce network overhead it may be more efficient for a client to copy part of the database into its own cache area for local processing. When the client has finished processing the updated cache data can be transferred to the server. We can identify a number of events in this example. First, the event 'request database information' is an event in which a client is the sending object and the server is the receiving object. Similarly, the event 'send data to client' has the server as sending object while the client is the receiving object.

A receiving object may or may not respond to an event from a sending object. For example, the server in Figure 9.1 will not send data to a client if it realizes that the same data is in use by another client. The process by which this can be administered by the server is called lock management. The server keeps track of which objects are in the cache of which clients. When client 1 in Figure 9.1 requests an object from the server the server can do one of two things. First, if the object is not in use by another client the object will be copied to the client's cache. If the server notices that the object is in the cache of another client it checks to see whether the access modes conflict. If they do, the server will send a message to the client holding the lock (client 2) asking it to remove the object from its cache. This is a so-called 'callback' message, since it is a request from a server to a client, which is not the usual direction in such matters. When client 2 receives the callback it may do one of two things. First, it may ignore the request, in which case the server forces the requesting client 1 to wait until client 2 is finished with the transaction. The second alternative is that client 2 does not have a lock on the object, in which case it relinquishes the lock immediately, thus allowing the server to copy the object to client 1.

Events can be grouped into so-called event classes. An event class is given a name in order to indicate common structure and behaviour. Event classes can be classified in the same way that object classes are. Some classes of event are simple signals which state that something has happened, while others carry information or data from one object to another object. The conveyed data carried by an event are its attributes. Examples of event classes and their attributes are:

- `request_object(client, server, object_name)`
- `copy_object(server, client, object_data)`
- `enable_pump(pump#)`
- `register_journal(Journal)`

The attribute values held by an object are called its state. An object has a definite state at any given moment in time. This state can only be changed by modifier member functions. External events may cause changes in object state because they trigger an object's member functions. The response to an event by an object depends on its present state and it can include a change of state, or an event can be triggered in the form of another event to the sending object or to a third object. Thus, the pattern of events, states and state transitions is usually represented in the form of so-called state transition diagrams (or STDs for short).

9.3.2 Transitions and conditions

When an object receives an event the next state depends on the current state as well as the event. The change of state caused by an event is called a transition. We say that the transition fires when the object enters the state at the target end of the transition. For example, a telephone can be in the state 'idle'. The event 'off-hook' causes a transition to the 'dial tone' state. Similarly, the event 'on-hook' causes a transition from any state to the 'idle' state. This is shown in a simple state transition diagram in Figure 9.2, where states are represented as roundangles and transitions are represented as arrows from the receiving state to the target state.

A condition is a boolean function of object values. Conditions are used as guards on transitions. A guard is similar to a constraint in event–response lists. A transition will fire if its guard condition is true. For example, a petrol line in a petrol station is enabled for operation only if there is sufficient petrol in the tank supplying it. This is the guard condition under which the transition will fire. The graphical representation for guard conditions is shown in Figure 9.3, where the conditions are surrounded by square brackets.

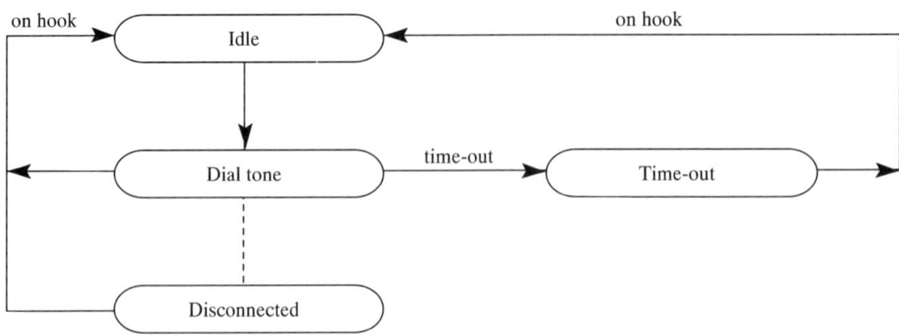

Figure 9.2 Simple state transition diagram for a telephone.

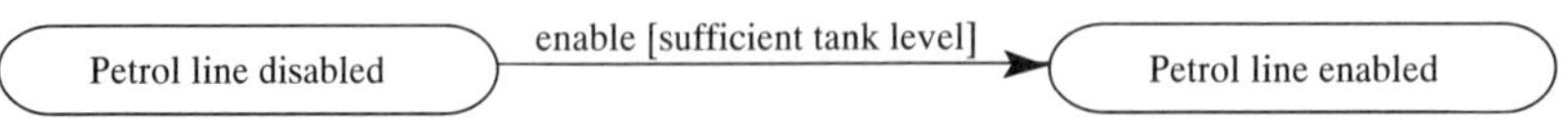

Figure 9.3 STDs with guarded conditions.

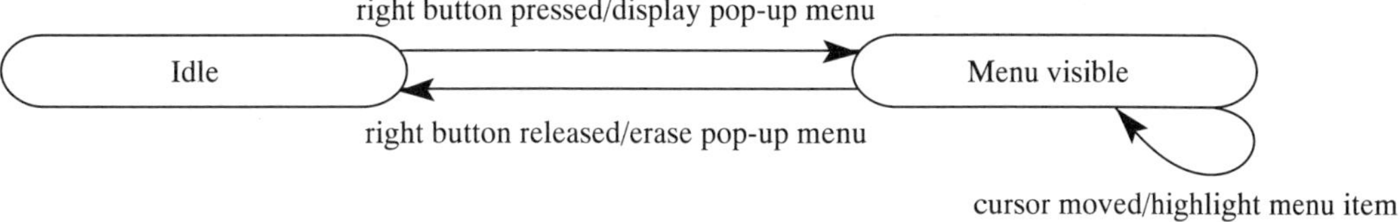

Figure 9.4 Actions in state diagrams (pop-up menu).

9.3.3 Operations

Operations are performed in response to the corresponding transitions. There are two main types of operation, namely actions and activities. An action is an instantaneous operation. It is associated with an event and has no duration, or its duration is insignificant relative to the other events in the state diagram. For example, the process of enabling a pump in a petrol station is an action. OMT uses a slash ('/') when representing actions. An example is given in Figure 9.4. This is the case of a pop-up menu on a workstation running some GUI interface software. There are two states, the first of which corresponds to the case in which a pop-up menu is not visible (Idle) and the other in which the menu is visible. Pressing the right button of the pointing device will result in the menu being displayed; releasing the right button will result in erasure of the pop-up menu. If the cursor is moved while in the 'Menu visible' state the item whose bounding box contains the cursor will be highlighted.

An activity is an operation which takes a finite amount of time to complete. Unlike actions which are associated with events, an activity is associated with a state. Activities correspond to:

- Continuous operations
- Sequential operations that terminate themselves after a period of time

A state can control a continuous activity. The activity lasts as long as the state in which it is activated has not been left. Any event which causes the state to be exited will also cause the activity to be terminated. Examples of activities are:

- Dispensing petrol from a pump to a car
- Ringing a telephone bell
- Performing an operation in a hospital

An activity may last for a fixed period of time or it may be prematurely broken off. This may be caused by an event which causes the corresponding state to be exited. For example, the activity of pumping petrol may be prematurely terminated if the supply tank's level reaches a critical capacity level.

The notation 'do: A' in a state box indicates that activity A starts on entry to the box and stops on exit. An example is shown in Figure 9.5.

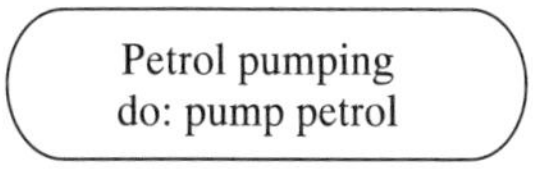

Petrol pumping
do: pump petrol

Figure 9.5 Activities in a petrol pump environment.

9.3.4 Scenarios and event traces

A scenario is a sequence of events which occurs during one execution of a system. A scenario is similar to the storyboard concept. Scenarios may contain all events in the system or some subset thereof. For example, it is possible to create scenarios for all relevant events pertaining to one object.

A scenario for a the case of a pump in a petrol station system is given as follows:

- Attendant enables pump
- Pump motor started and display cleared
- Customer removes gun from holster
- Customer presses trigger
- Petrol is pumped
- Customer releases trigger
- Delivery is complete

Events transmit information between objects. One object is called the sender, while the other object is called the receiver. It is necessary to identify senders and receivers of events in scenarios. This is achieved by the use of event traces. Objects are shown as vertical lines, while events are represented as horizontal arrows from the sender object to the receiver object.

9.4 Classical state transition diagrams

9.4.1 Introduction

One of the main challenges in system development is to devise a notation and methodology for the specification and design of large and complex reactive systems. A reactive system is one which is characterized by its event-driven nature. Such systems have to react to both internal and external stimuli. Examples of reactive systems occur in the following application areas:

- Telecommunications
- Embedded systems
- Machine interfaces
- Many software applications

Various solutions have been proposed to specify requirements in an unambiguous way. An overview of some methods is given in Davis (1988). One of the most widespread and popular approaches is to use state transition diagrams which are visual representations of finite state machines (FSMs). An example of a state transition diagram for a simple digital watch is given in Figure 9.6. There are three states, namely Display, Set hours and Set minutes. Pressing button A allows us to move between the three different modes, while pressing button B causes a counter (which is context-sensitive) to be incremented.

9.4.2 Shortcomings of classical STDs

The state transition diagram shown in Figure 9.6 is understandable because it describes a very simple situation. It would be difficult to extend this diagram to real watches, which have

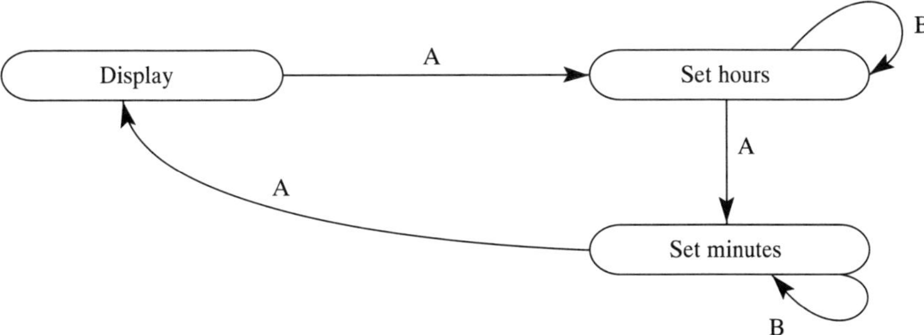

Figure 9.6 STD for a simple digital watch.

functionality for dates, times, alarms and stopwatch capabilities. We would have to create a new STD from scratch. The main shortcomings of the classical approach may be summed up as follows:

- STDs are 'flat'. There is no notion of depth, hierarchy or modularity. For example, Figure 9.6 has two Set states which are independent of each other. Furthermore, STDs do not support top-down or bottom-up development. Again, it is not possible in Figure 9.6 to define an abstract state Set from which Set hours and Set minutes are defined as substates.
- STDs are inherently sequential in nature. There is no support for the notion of concurrency.
- They do not scale well. Linear growth in the size of a system implies exponential growth in the number of states in the STD.
- STDs are uneconomical in the use of transitions. An event that causes the same transition from a large number of states must be attached to each of them separately. This results in a multitude of arrows.

Many of these limitations are solved by the structured state diagrams proposed by Harel (1988).

9.4.3 Example of a classical STD

Before we leave classical state diagrams it is useful to give an example of how they can be used for simple problems. The example taken represents a class for a UNIX-like process and the objective is to determine the states of such a process and the events which cause the corresponding transitions to fire. The concept of process is fundamental to operating system design. For a good introduction, see Silberschatz *et al.* (1991).

It is possible to create classes in object-oriented languages that simulate processes. A process is a sequence of computations which are carried out by objects and which send messages to other objects and wait for an answer. The state of a class Process consists of a name and a priority. A process can find itself in one of several states. These are shown in Figure 9.7. It is possible for a Process object to make transition from one state to another state. We have numbered the transitions in Figure 9.7.

We now give an explanation of each of these transitions:

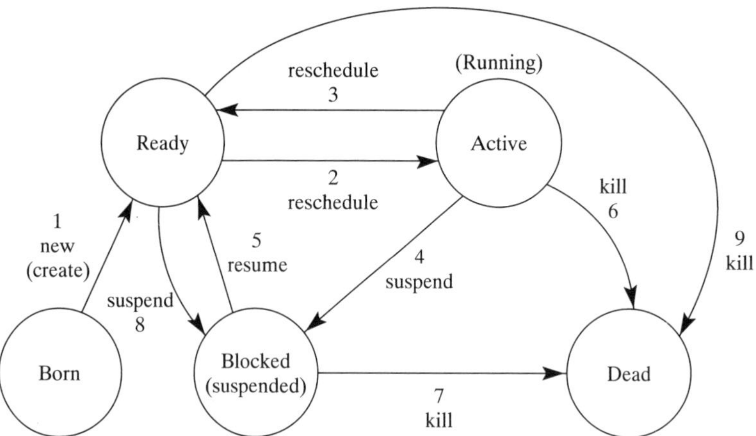

Figure 9.7 State transition diagram for class process.

1. A new process is created and enters the ready state.
2. A ready process becomes active (is running) if it is the longest waiting at its priority and there are no higher priority ready processes and (a) the current active process becomes dead or is blocked, (b) the ready process has higher priority than the active process, or (c) the ready process has the same priority as the active process current process goes into another state.
3. An active (running) process becomes rescheduled when it is replaced by a ready process under the conditions described for transition 2.
4. An active process becomes blocked when a message wait is sent to a semaphore which has no excess signals.
5. A blocked process becomes ready when it is the first in the waiting queue of a semaphore and the message signal is sent to the semaphore.
6. An active process becomes dead.

9.5 An introduction to higraphs

Graphs have many uses in applications but they do suffer from a number of drawbacks. There is a need to have edges which connect a set of nodes rather than just two nodes. This can be achieved by the use of so-called hypergraphs, but it is difficult to represent them graphically. There is also a need to present information in visual form, which allows us to combine both the functionality of hypergraphs and the visual convenience of Venn diagrams. These conditions are satisfied by the higraph technique due to Harel (1988). Higraphs are used in a number of situations in order to represent different kinds of information, for example:

- They are a viable alternative to ER diagrams.
- They solve many of the shortcomings of classical state transition diagrams.

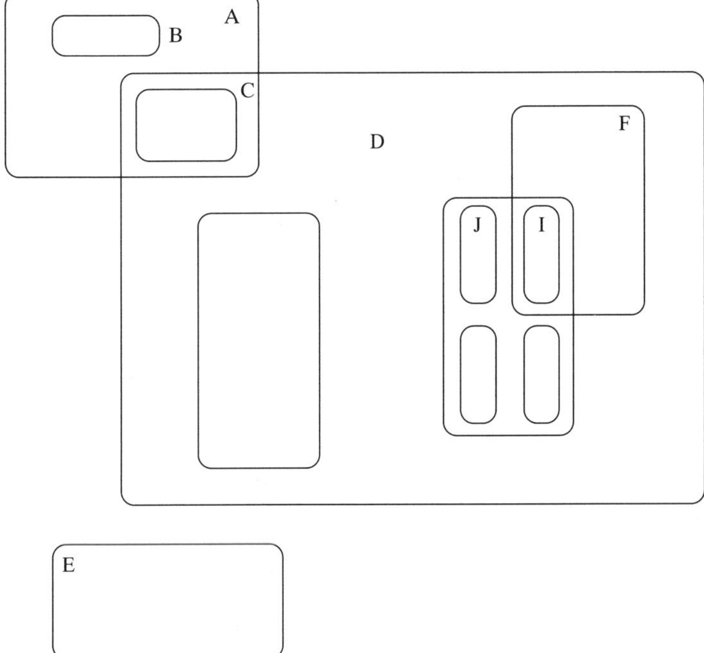

Figure 9.8 Blobs.

- They are a useful technique for representing knowledge.
- They can be used for representing data flow diagrams (Harel 1988).

A higraph is represented by a rounded rectangle object, sometimes called a blob. Blobs are used to implement set-theoretic principles such as union, intersection and difference of two sets. Furthermore, it is possible to implement the so-called Cartesian product of two sets. An example of using blobs is given in Figure 9.8. The blobs D and A have intersection C while the blob B represents the difference A–D. If we had left B out of the figure we could not refer to the difference A–D at all.

In order to show how the Cartesian product of two blobs works, consider Figure 9.9. In this case we say that the blob J is decomposed into its orthogonal components W and X, where W is the union of K and N and X is the union of I, L and M. The set J is the set of pairs (a, b) when a is in W and b is in X.

Having discussed what blobs are, we now turn our attention to annotating the relations that exist between them. This leads to a situation in which simple higraphs can be constructed. For example, in Figure 9.10 a higraph edge connects two blobs A and B. A higraph edge is fundamentally different from a graph edge because the higraphs connect sets while edges connect instances of sets. Thus, all subsets of blobs A and B are included in the relationship. This has the advantage that we can use one label which applies to many sets.

Higraphs are used as a structured alternative to data flow diagrams. The higraph-based versions of such diagrams are called activity charts. In these charts the blobs represent activities (or processes), while the edges represent the possible flow of data. The subset

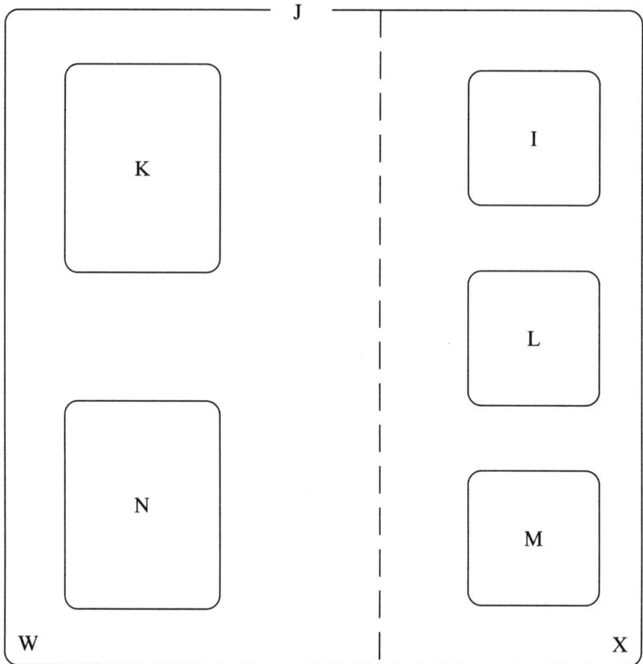

Figure 9.9 Cartesian product of blobs.

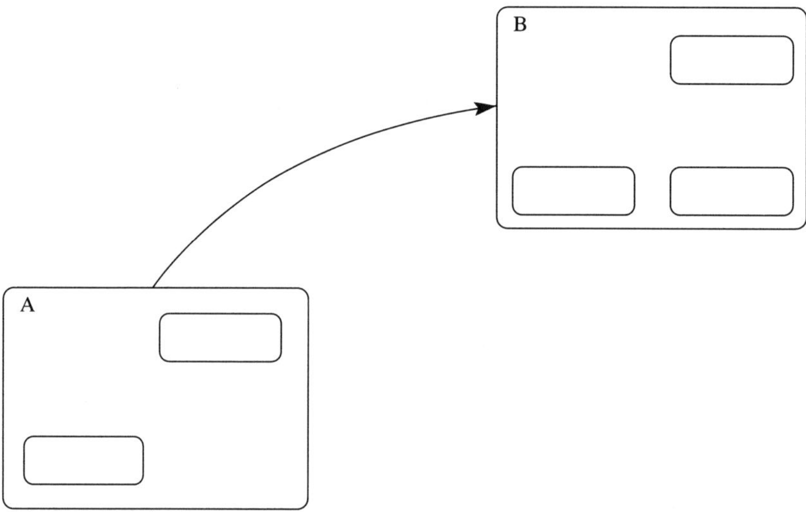

Figure 9.10 A simple higraph.

relationship now represents the subprocess relationship. An example of an activity chart is shown in Figure 9.11.

It would seem that the object flow diagram (OFD) technique of Martin and Odell (1992) is based on the Harel activity chart concept.

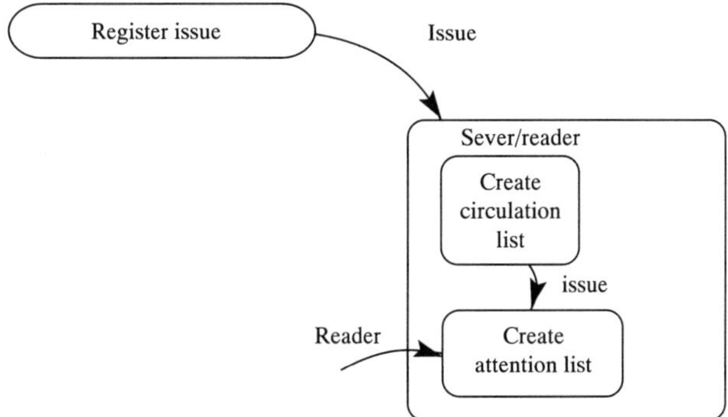

Figure 9.11 A simple activity chart.

9.6 Applying higraphs to dynamic modelling techniques

Higraphs are employed in the specification of complex reactive systems. Harel uses the term statechart to denote the application of higraphs to classical state transition diagrams. Statecharts use blobs to represent states while edges represent transitions between states. The subset relationship between blobs is now replaced by the concept of a nested state. In particular, we can think of a state being a superstate which is used to aggregate sets of states with common transitions

To take an example, consider the case in Figure 9.12, in which two states S1 and S2 both may cause a transition to state S3 upon the stimulus a. If we used class state transition diagrams we would need two edges from S1 and S2 to S3. The statechart approach is more compact as it reduces the number of edges by one in this case.

The state S4 is said to be decomposed into its subordinate states S1 and S2 in Figure 9.12. The semantics in this case imply an OR function; this means that if we are in state S4 at a higher level of abstraction we are either in state S1 or in state S2. It is also possible to have AND decomposition. This is represented by using dashed lines. An example is shown in Figure 9.13. If we are in state S then we are in states S1 and S2. This is even more meaningful if S1 and S2 are further refined. The term orthogonal is used in this case to denote the fact that states S1 and S2 are independent of each other.

Harel introduced the concept of default entry state, and it is always defined relative to a superstate. The default entry state of a superstate is the subordinate state that the finite state machine enters when no other subordinate state is specified as the next state. Default entry states are represented as in Figure 9.13. State S12 is the default entry state for S1, while state S22 is the default entry state for S2.

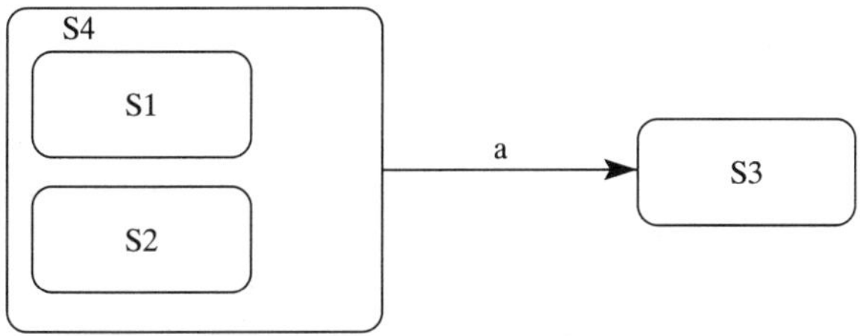

Figure 9.12 Aggregate state in a statechart.

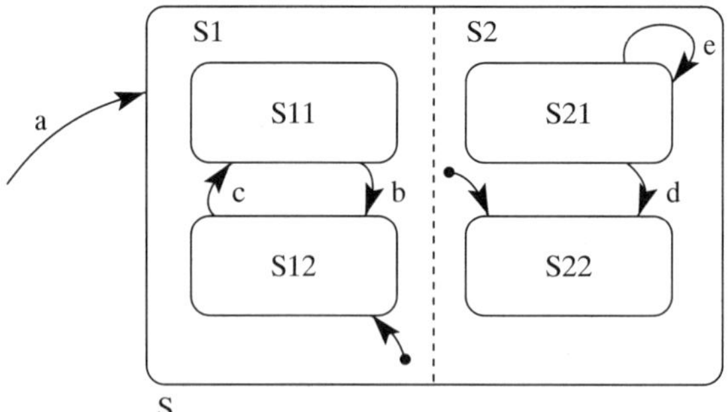

Figure 9.13 Orthogonal states in a statechart.

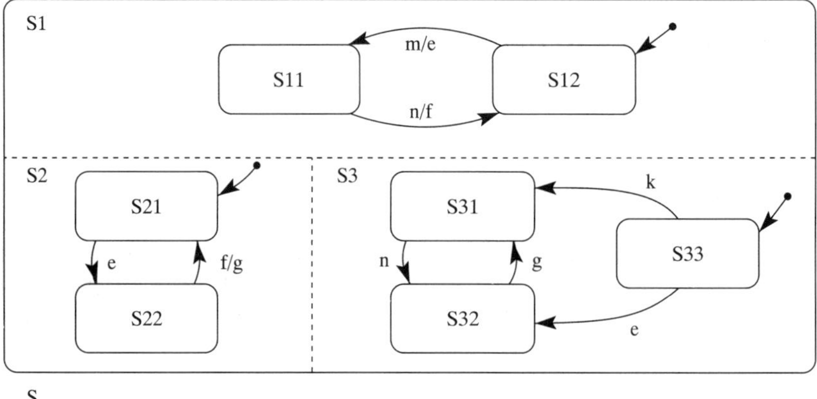

Figure 9.14 Chain reactions.

Statecharts support the concept of chain reactions. These arise in the cases when certain events give rise to actions which themselves cause other actions to trigger. An example is shown in Figure 9.14. The state S is decomposed into three orthogonal states S1, S2 and S3. Assume that the initial state is (S21, S33, S12). After the external event m has occurred the next configuration will be (S22, S32, S11). This is because event m triggers event e which itself causes a number of transitions. This is a chain reaction of length 2, since two transitions are generated from event m.

9.7 Aggregation concurrency

An important situation in which orthogonal states arise is in the case of object assemblies. There is a one-to-one correspondence between the assembly and a given superstate, while at the same time there is a similar correspondence between its components and their own independent states. The aggregate state corresponds to the states of all the component diagrams. Figure 9.15 shows an example in which a petrol environment consists of a pump assembly, a tank and a petrol line. In this case the states 'Flow line' and 'Tank' interact. The transition occurs when the tank level reaches 4% of its total capacity (as represented by event

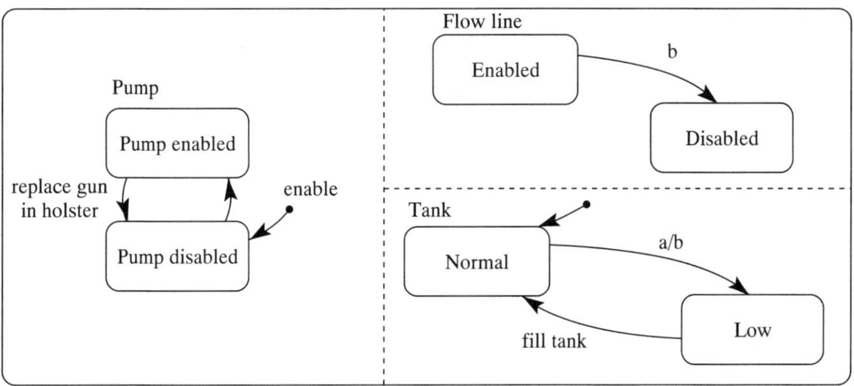

Figure 9.15 Aggregation concurrency.

'a'), whereby a chain reaction of length 1 is created; specifically, the flow line is disabled and no more petrol can be dispensed.

9.8 Using event–response lists as a front end to dynamic modelling

Statecharts are not easy to learn or to use. However, event–response lists can aid in creating statecharts for a given problem. Some mapping rules are:

- Events map to transitions.
- Responses map to actions.
- Constraints map to guard conditions on transitions.

Event–response lists have no explicit support for states; however, states can usually be deduced from constraints. For example, the following event–response list determines a state for the simple digital watch:

E0: 'A' button pressed
R01: Watch goes into set mode
C01: Watch must be in display mode

From this constraint we deduce that a watch can be in a display mode. Event–response lists place more emphasis on the behaviour of a system rather than on state. This is in keeping with the object-oriented philosophy, in which it is more important to know what an object is responsible for than to know how an object implements such responsibility.

The state of an object is implemented as an attribute. Thus, new attributes are discovered in the dynamic modelling phase. They can be implemented as enumerated types which contain all possible states of an object. In the case of the simple digital watch the state is implemented in C++ as follows:

```
enum WatchState {DisplayMode, SetHoursMode,
SetMinutesMode};
```

9.9 Example: simple digital watch

We consider the case of a simple digital watch (codename SDW). The example is taken from Rumbaugh *et al.* (1991). We adapt it to include more functionality and interesting behaviour.

A simple digital watch has a display and two buttons (A and B). The watch has two modes of operation, namely the display mode and the set mode. Furthermore, the set mode has two sub-modes called set hours mode and set minutes mode. The A button is used to select modes. Each time it is pressed the mode advances in the sequence:

display → set hours → set minutes → display

Within sub-modes, the B button is used to advance the hours or minutes by one unit each time it is pressed. In particular, the set minutes mode can influence the set hours mode when the number of minutes reaches 60 (the so-called 'wraparound' value).

The concept map for SDW is given in Figure 9.16. We are interested in finding the behaviour of SDW. To this end, we shall use ER lists and storyboards.

We now give the event–response lists for the simple digital watch. The following shorthand is used: H=Hours, M=Minutes. Note that only discernible and external events are given.

E0: 'A' button pressed
R01: Watch goes into set mode
C01: Watch must be in display mode

E1: 'A' button pressed
R11: Watch goes into M mode
C11: Watch must be in H mode

E2: 'A' button pressed
R12: Watch goes into display mode
C12: Watch must be in M mode

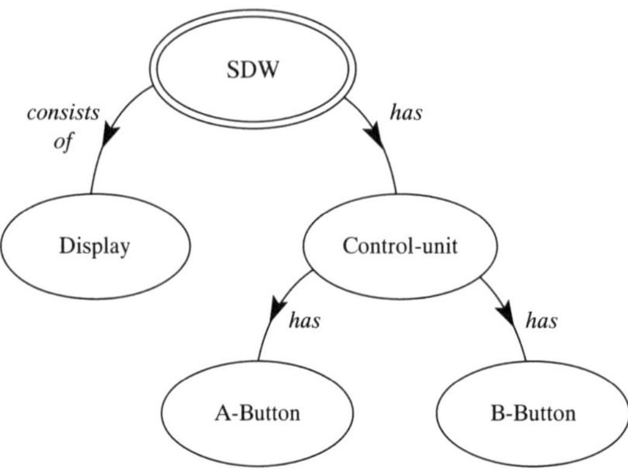

Figure 9.16 Concept map for SDW.

E3: 'B' button pressed
R31: Hour counter raised
C31: Watch must be in H mode

E4: 'B' button pressed
R41: Minute counter raised
C41: Watch must be in M mode

There are a number of so-called internal events in SDW which must be taken into account. These have to do with the effects of changes to the watch display. In order to take care of wraparound effects we need to add two more entries to the above list. They are for the cases when the current values of hours or minutes reach their maximum values (24 and 60, respectively)

E5: Minutes counter reaches its maximum value
R51: Hours counter is increment by one hour unit
R52: Minutes counter is set to 0

E6: Hours counter reaches its maximum value
R61: Hours counter set to 0

9.9.1 Simple storyboard in SDW

We consider the problem of configuring the watch to display a given time. For example, we may wish to set the watch to 18:00 hours. The storyboard uses the concepts and event–response lists from SDW to produce a viable solution as follows:

Frame 1:

Watch is in display mode
Hours and minutes displayed
User presses A button

Frame 2:

Watch is in set hours mode
Hours value is blinking
User presses B button

Frame 3:

Compare hours value with expected value
If values are different goto frame 2
else press A button

Frame 4:

Watch is in set minutes mode
User presses B button

Frame 5:

Compare minutes value with expected value

If values are different goto frame 2
    else press A button

Frame 6:

Watch is back in display mode

The storyboard depicted in this example could correspond to a member function of the Watch device.

Exercises

1. Create event–response lists and storyboards for the distributed lock management problem in Section 9.3.1 (see also Figure 9.1). Find the corresponding event classes and their attributes.
2. A new version of the simple digital watch has been designed. The new design has a display showing hours, minutes and second. A C button on the watch allows the user to set the seconds part of the display. Analyse this problem (object model, dynamic model).
3. Modify the SDW problem so that there are buttons for both incrementing and decrementing hours, minutes and seconds.
4. Draw the classical state transition diagram for the statechart in Figure 9.13.
5. Determine the length of the chain reaction when event n occurs in Figure 9.14.
6. Find superstates, subordinate states, actions, activities and default entry states in Figure 9.15.
7. Find the event–response lists and storyboards for the following problem:

    A large company wishes to automate the functions of the Help Desk in a computer installation. At present the main duties of the Help Desk are in registering user problems and assigning these problems to the appropriate specialists, who should then solve the problems as soon as possible. The present situation is not very satisfactory and something needs to be done in order to solve user dissatisfaction with the way in which problems get solved. It has been decided to automate the logging of user calls at the Help Desk. The following should be included in the system:

    All logged calls are registered and given a priority level stating the maximum amount of time within which the problem should be solved. If the problem is not solved within the allowed time frame it is escalated and notice is given to a contact person.

    All calls should be logged because management can review the frequency of types of problem. Some problems may be solved by the Help Desk personnel, while more difficult problems may need to be assigned to a specialist group (for example, the DBA or system management).

Users and user groups should be able to query the status of their calls so that they can be kept informed about the actions taken to solve the problem.

References

A. M. Davis (1988) A comparison of techniques for the specification of external system behaviour, *Communications of the ACM*, **33**(9) September.

D. Harel (1988) On visual formalisms, *Communications of the ACM*, **31**(5) May.

D. Harel *et al.* (1987) On the formal semantics of statecharts, *Proceedings of Symposium on Logic in Computer Science*.

D. Harel *et al.* (1988) STATEMATE: a working environment for the development of complex reactive systems, *10th International Conference on Software Engineering*.

D. J. Hatley and I. A. Pirbhai (1988) *Strategies for Real-Time System Specification*, Dorset House Publishing, New York.

J. Martin and J. J. Odell (1992) *Object-Oriented Analysis and Design*, Prentice-Hall, Englewood Cliffs NJ.

Object Design (1992) *ObjectStore Technical Overview*, Object Design, Inc., Burlington MA.

J. Peterson (1977) Petri Nets, *ACM Computing Surveys*, **9**(3) September.

J. Rumbaugh, M. Blaha, W. Premerlani, F. Eddy and W. Lorensen (1991) *Object-Oriented Modeling and Design*, Prentice-Hall, Englewood Cliffs NJ.

A. Silberschatz, J. Peterson and P. Galvin (1991) *Operating System Concepts*, Addison-Wesley, Reading MA.

Chapter

10

The steps in dynamic modelling

10.1 Introduction and objectives

The main objective of this chapter is to assemble the steps that are needed in order to perform a dynamic analysis of a given problem. The technique is applied to a simple problem to show how it works.

A short discussion on object behaviour analysis (OBA) from Martin and Odell (1992) and the Fusion method from Coleman *et al.* (1994) is given and comparisons with the approaches here are given.

10.2 The model problem

We use the codename 'MCS' for the following problem description, which is more fully explained in Rumbaugh *et al.* (1991). We concentrate on those parts that are important for this chapter. The requirements are rephrased here because the original version is too informal.

A system is to be built which models a certain type of motor controller. This is a device which determines when a motor should be on, and the former continuously asserts 'on' when the motor is indeed running.

When the 'on' condition is asserted, the motor control starts and the motor runs. To start a motor, power must be applied to both of its component windings, which we call the 'start' and 'run' windings. A special sensor (called a starting relay) determines when the motor has started, and at this point the start winding is turned off while the run winding remains powered on. If the 'on' condition is not asserted, both windings are shut off. The system can fail to start if the motor overheats. In order to prevent damage in such a case the motor control is fitted with a special sensor (called an over-temperature sensor) which knows when the motor overheats. If such a situation should arise the motor control removes power from both windings and all 'on' assertions are ignored until the manual reset button has been pressed and the motor has cooled off.

An analysis of this problem can be made, starting from concept maps and progressing to an object model. We do not do so here because the problem is very easy. The classes in MCS are `MotorControl`, `Motor`, `StartingRelay` (a sensor) and `OtSensor` (over-temperature sensor). `Motor` is an aggregate class which contains two types of `Winding` (start and run) while `MotorControl` is also an aggregate class containing an over-temperature sensor and a starting relay.

10.3 Preparing scenarios

A scenario in OMT is a sequence of events which occurs during one execution of the system. The set of possible scenarios constitutes all interactions between the external world and the system. A scenario is the same as a storyboard. Therefore, in order to construct a scenario we need to create event–response lists and couple them with concepts.

Scenarios are made for the following types of situation which arise in practice:

(10.1)

- Normal functioning of the system

  Special scenarios

  Scenarios arising from abnormal behaviour in the system

Most scenarios simulate interactions with the system, and these represent the bulk of cases. Special scenarios correspond to situations which should not occur but do, for example maximum or minimum or repetition values being reached. Finally, some scenarios correspond to abnormal or exceptional conditions. Examples of abnormal scenarios are:

- Invalid input values
- Power failure
- An assembly starts to malfunction in some way
- Resources become depleted
- Communication lines break down

It is important to deal with normal scenarios first during the dynamic modelling phase because they account for 90% of the dynamics in the system. The other 10%, representing special and exceptional conditions, should be dealt with once the basic infrastructure has been set up.

The scenarios in MCS correspond to the following situations:

(10.2)

- Motor is running normally (an activity)
- Motor powers up via an 'on' assertion
- Motor overheats
- Motor is reset

These scenarios are built up from event–response lists.

E0: Assert 'on'

R01: Start motor control

R02: Run motor
C01: Motor control is enabled (assert is 'off')

E1: Motor overheats
R11: Wind motor control down
R12: Start cool-down timer

E2: Motor is reset
R21: Assert 'on' (enabled)
C21: Overheat timeout period has expired

E0, E1 and E2 are the major external events occurring in MCS. The responses in this list can also be seen as events which in turn have responses and corresponding constraints.

E3: Start motor control (R01)
R31: Apply power to motor start winding
R32: Apply power to motor run winding
R33: Start timer in starting relay sensor

E4: Start timer in starting relay sensor (R33)
R41: Turn off motor start winding

E5: Wind motor control down (R11)
R51: Remove power from motor start winding
R52: Remove power from motor run winding
R53: Motor control is disabled

10.4 Identifying external events in scenarios

Once the scenarios have been created the next step is to identify the sender and receiver objects of each event. OMT recommends creating event trace diagrams. Other approaches are discussed at the end of the chapter. The sender object is called the client, while the receiving object is called the server or collaborator. In this case the client sends a message to its server. In OO terms the event will correspond to a method which belongs to the receiver class.

To take an example of how the above client/server approach works we consider the interactions which take place between `MotorControl`, `Motor`, `OtSensor` and `StartingRelay`. `MotorControl` is the client for most events, while `Motor`, `OtSensor` and `StartingRelay` are its collaborators. Furthermore, `OtSensor` and `StartingRelay` are clients of `Motor`. `OtSensor` knows when `Motor` has overheated, while `StartingRelay` knows when `Motor` has started.

As illustration, we show the interactions which take place between `MotorControl` and `Motor`. These are derived from the corresponding event–response lists. `MotorControl` sends the following messages to `Motor`:

```
start();    // Start the motor
run();  // Run the motor
```

The operation `Motor::start()` causes the following messages to be executed:

```
powerup(WindingType);
```

where `WindingType` is an enumeration for 'start' winding and 'run' winding. Similarly, `MotorControl` can power down (or shutdown) a motor:

```
shutdown();
```

Once a `Motor` instance receives a `start()` or `shutdown()` message from the `MotorControl` it sends appropriate messages to its windings:

```
powerup(WindingType);
powerdown(WindingType);
```

`MotorControl` contains an `OtSensor` instance whose function is to monitor the temperature in the `Motor`. Thus, this sensor should continuously send a message to `Motor` to determine what the current temperature is. Only the `Motor` can answer this question. This leads to a new method in `MotorControl`:

```
Temperature temperature();
```

The class `Temperature` is an abstract class; its specializations represent `Fahrenheit` and `Celsius` units, for example.

`StartingRelay` determines whether a `Motor` has been started; in order to determine whether this is true we need to have an operation in `Motor`:

```
Boolean started();
```

The above analysis gives an indication of the preliminary operations which belong to `Motor`. In other words, the responsibilities of `Motor` have been determined. This leads us to defining the class interface for `Motor`:

```
class Motor
{
private:

  Winding sta;        // Start winding
  Winding run;        // Run winding

  // Possible extra state

public:
  // ...

  // Main operations
  void start();
  void run();
  void shutdown();
  Boolean started();
```

```
  // Auxiliary operations
  void powerup();
  void powerup(WindingType);
  void powerdown();
  void powerdown(WindingType);
};
```

The class interface for `MotorControl` is:

```
class MotorControl
{
private:

  Motor mot;                  // The Motor being monitored
  OtSensor ots;               // The temperature-sensing device
  StartingRelay srl;          // Starting relay sensor

public:
  // ...
  assert_on();                // Assert is now "on"
  assert_off();               // Assert is now "off"

  Status assertion();                 // On or Off
  Boolean overheated();               // Is Motor cooling off?
  Temperature temperature();          // Temperature of motor
  void reset(); // Back into assert on mode

  // More operations in the design phase

};
```

Both `Motor` and `MotorControl` have a number of operations with the same names: `start()`, `shutdown()` and `run()`. However, `Motor` has no knowledge of constraints, and all checking should take place in `MotorControl` (it is after all the controller!). We show the differences between `start()` for these two classes:

```
void Motor::start()
{
  powerup(StartupWinding);
  powerup(RunWinding);
}

void MotorControl::start()
{

/*  E3: Start motor control (R01)
  R31: Apply power to start winding
  R32: Apply power to run winding
  R33: Start timer in starting relay sensor
```

```
*/

    mot.start();   // Includes responses R31 and R32
    srl.start_timer();     // Timer started in starting relay
}
```

The last operation that we show is one which asserts that the motor control should start and run the motor:

```
void MotorControl::assert_on()
{

/*  E0: Assert "on"
    R01: Start motor control
    R02: Run motor
    C01: Motor control is enabled (assert is "off")
*/

    // Precondition: control must not be in cool-off period
    if (enabled() == TRUE)
    {
      start();
      run();
    }

    // An exception could be raised here; it depends on the
    // context
}
```

One of the most difficult activities during design is to decide which objects are responsible for which operations. In most cases one object will be a client while one or more other objects will be servers. We may not get it completely right during the analysis phase, and modifications to class interfaces may be necessary during design.

10.4.1 Summary of class responsibilities

The classes in this test case have the following responsibilities:

`Motor` (primitive server class)

- start the motor
- run the motor
- shutdown motor
- power up and power down motor windings

`OtSensor` (client of `Motor`, component of `MotorControl`)

- Give temperature of `Motor`
- Has `Motor` overheated?

`StartingRelay` (client of `Motor`, component of `MotorControl`)

Time that `Motor` was started

MotorControl

`Assert_on`

Press reset button

What is current status of assert?

Is `Motor` in cooling off mode?

What is the temperature of `Motor`?

Functionality of `OtSensor` and `StartingRelay`

10.4.2 Client/server relationships in JRP

The basic classes in JRP are `Journal`, `Issue`, `Reader`, `Topic` and `Article`. Furthermore, the classes `CirculationList` and `AttentionList` were discovered by applying the 'use cases' approach to concept mapping. Some classes use the services of other classes, either in the form of including them in their state or in their class interfaces. The client/server relationships in JRP are thus:

- `Journal` and `Topic` are servants because they are servers of other classes and clients of none.
- `Issue` is a client of `Journal`.
- `Article` is a client of `Topic`.
- `Issue` is a client of `Article`.
- `CirculationList` is a client of `Reader` and `Issue`.
- `AttentionList` is a client of `Reader` and `Article`.

Classes `Issue` and `Article` are called agents because they are servers of some classes and clients of others. `CirculationList` and `AttentionList` are called masters because they are clients of all other classes with which they are related but server for none (Firesmith 1993).

10.5 Building state diagrams

The next stage in the dynamic modelling phase is to create a state diagram for each active class in the system. An active class is one which interacts directly with external agents. Classes with trivial dynamic behaviour should be ignored. The state diagram for `MotorControl` is shown

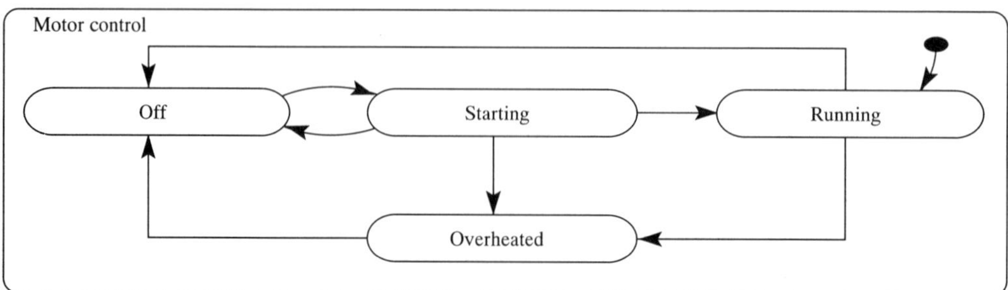

Figure 10.1 Minimal state diagram for motor control.

in Figure 10.1. A more thorough treatment of state transitions is given in Rumbaugh (1991).

10.6 Verifying and testing collaborative behaviour

The approach taken in this chapter is informal. The success of the process depends on how precisely the requirements have been written. In order to avoid shortcomings in the method we should checklist the following:

- List all events which are shared between classes.
- Ensure that all messages are received by some object.
- Verify the signatures of shared events.
- Generate new scenarios and test their applicability in the current system.

For small problems this approach can be done manually. For moderately sized applications this method is unworkable and CASE tools are needed. A popular tool for this is OMTool, which is marketed by the Advanced Concepts Center of Martin Marietta.

One way to control complexity during the dynamic modelling phase is to divide a system into loosely coupled subsystems and then to apply the ideas in this chapter to each subsystem. Chapter 14 discusses the problem of how to split a system into subsystems.

Formal methods can be applied to system design, but there are very few object-oriented methods which use them. One important formal approach is described in Jones (1990).

10.7 Comparisons with other approaches

OMT can be described as a first-generation technology, since it has been around for some time and new developments have in some ways added to the basic functionality of the method or even replaced it. In this section we discuss how some other well-known and important approaches handle object interactions. Attention is paid to the weak and strong points of these methods.

10.7.1 Object behaviour analysis

Object behaviour analysis (OBA) is described in Martin and Odell (1992) and it is concerned with showing events, the sequence in which they occur and how events change the state of objects. Its objectives are similar as those presented here. The basic unit of functionality in OBA is the event schema. An event schema is a network in which operations are the nodes and the directed arcs are operations which are triggered as a result of invoking the events. Event schemas relate the corresponding object schema (similar to the object model in OMT) and state transition diagrams. CASE tools should enable users to build object schemas and event schemas and to maintain a close relationship between the two types of representation. This is a powerful feature of the Martin and Odell approach and we see it as an improvement on classical OMT.

It would seem that the Harel approach has influenced the development of OBA. For this reason there are a number of similarities between it and OMT.

Another advantage of OBA is that changes in object state are performed during the analysis phase of the software life-cycle. Other methods deal with changes in object state during the design phase.

Scaling to large systems is possible with OBA, especially when used in combinations with object flow diagrams (OFDs).

10.7.2 Wirfs-Brock

Object interaction in the Wirfs-Brock approach is tackled during the design phase of the object-oriented life-cycle. Use is made of so-called collaboration graphs in order to represent and visualize object interactions. Objects interact with one another by means of a contract. A contract is defined as a list of requests that a client can make of a server. Both must fulfil the contract, the client by making only those requests that the contract specifies and the server by responding appropriately to those requests. Collaborations between classes are represented by an arrow from the client to the server. Clients and server may be individual classes or they may be systems of classes. The main disadvantage of collaboration graphs is that they become complex and difficult to understand even for moderately sized applications.

Scaling to large systems is difficult to realize with the Wirfs-Brock approach.

10.7.3 Fusion

Fusion is described as a second-generation OO method (Coleman *et al.* 1994). The method uses so-called object interaction graphs. Objects in Fusion represent high-level design components which may undergo further decomposition. An object is a black box with respect to input and output behaviour. The approach in this method is a high-level variation of the Wirfs-Brock *et al.* (1990) approach and it avoids some of its shortcomings. An object sends messages to other objects and there is a graphical notation for displaying message sequencing. The correct sequence of messages can be deduced from event–response lists, however.

The main disadvantage of object interaction graphs is that they are executed in the design phase. This precludes walkthroughs with users and domain experts because of the terminology used. Graphical animations and storyboards would be more effective.

A review of the Fusion method, including its strengths and weaknesses is given in Gossain (1994).

10.8 Summary of steps in the dynamic modelling process

- Create normal, special and exceptional scenarios.
- Identify senders and receivers of each event.
- Make state charts for each active class.
- Verify and test collaborative behaviour.

10.9 Scalability issues

The test case in this chapter was a very simple one. It consisted of a number of devices such as `Motor`, `OTSensor`, `StartingRelay` and `MotorControl`. We were able to find the client/server relationships among these devices as well as determining which devices were responsible for which operations. `Motor` is an example of a simple device because its interface does not include other devices. `MotorControl` is a so-called composite device because it is an aggregation of `StartingRelay`, `OtSensor` and `Motor`. Each device can be seen as a black box at its own level of abstraction. The approach taken here can be applied to interacting objects and systems of any kind of complexity. We shall show how this is done for a non-trivial problem in Chapter 13.

The approach proposed in this chapter can be applied in a bottom-up fashion. Simpler devices are analysed and their interface constructed before moving on to more sophisticated assemblies of devices.

Exercises

1. Categorize the scenarios in (10.2) according to the types in (10.1).
2. Determine the interactions between (a) `OtSensor` and `Motor` and (b) `StartingRelay` and `Motor`. Find clients and collaborators.
3. Give the body of the operations for the class interface in `Motor` (Section 10.4). (*Hint*: a new state may need to be defined in the private part of the interface; do not forget to include the effects of overheating and cool-off periods.)

References

D. Coleman *et al.* (1994) *Object-Oriented Development: The Fusion Method*, Prentice-Hall, Englewood Cliffs NJ.

D. G. Firesmith (1993) *Object-Oriented Requirements Analysis and Logical Design*, John Wiley & Sons, New York.

S. Gossain (1994) Object-oriented development: the Fusion method (book review), *Journal of Object-Oriented Programming*, March/April.

C. B. Jones (1990) *Systematic Software Development using VDM*, Prentice-Hall, Hemel Hempstead.

J. Martin and J. J. Odell (1992) *Object-Oriented Analysis and Design*, Prentice-Hall, Englewood Cliffs NJ.

J. Rumbaugh, M. Blaha, W. Premerlani, F. Eddy and W. Lorensen (1991) *Object-Oriented Modeling and Design*, Prentice-Hall, Englewood Cliffs NJ.

R. Wirfs-Brock, B. Wilkerson and L. Wiener (1990) *Designing Object-Oriented Software*, Addison-Wesley, Reading MA.

Chapter

11

Functional modelling

11.1 Introduction and objectives

The functional model (or process model, as it is sometimes called) describes the computations and which occur in a system. The functional model tells us what happens in the system. OMT uses classical data flow diagrams as the basic tool for implementing the functional model. The approach is similar to how functional modelling is done by other authors (Hatley and Pirbhai 1988; Yourdon 1979). Readers with experience of such techniques should find this chapter easy reading.

OMT uses classical DFDs in the functional modelling stage of the software life-cycle. This approach is based on a particular style of data flow diagrams and is not well suited to designing systems of interacting objects. This has been the experience in our own work and similar problems have been experienced by others (D'Souza 1993). Furthermore, integrating the functional model with the object model can be difficult to actualize. The developers of OMT have only loose guidelines on how to do this. For example, they state that processes are a clue to finding the methods in classes.

In order to solve some of the shortcomings of OMT we use a flow technique which is based on object flow diagrams (OFDs) (Martin and Odell 1992). OFDs are high-level functional views of a system and are closer in spirit to the object-oriented paradigm than the DFD approach taken in OMT. Furthermore, OFDs can be used as a tool in strategic planning and system integration, tasks which are almost impossible to execute using classical data flow diagrams.

It is our intention in this and later chapters to show how both DFDs and OFDs can be integrated with the object model. Advantages and disadvantages of each approach will be discussed by using a number of test cases.

OMT is not the only object-oriented method which uses DFDs; for example, there is the Shlaer–Mellor approach (Shlaer and Mellor 1988), where DFDs are used to create the process model. New results by the author on process modelling can be found in Duffy (1995).

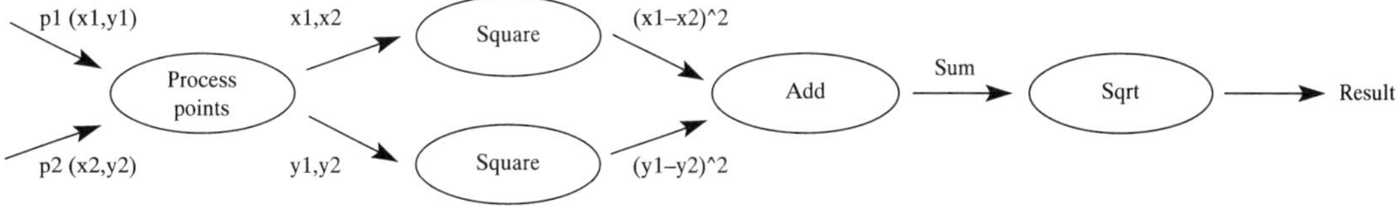

Figure 11.1 DFD for the JRP problem.

11.2 Data flow diagrams (DFDs)

This section introduces the most important concepts and the graphical notation which is needed when working with OMT. Our objective is to explain enough so that we can carry out a functional modelling analysis on JRP, MPC and PPD.

11.2.1 What do data flow diagrams do?

A data flow diagram (DFD) is a directed graph in which the nodes represent processes or operations and the directed arcs (the data flows) represent data flowing from one process to another one. DFDs show the functional relationships of the values computed by a system, including input and output values, as well as internal data stores which contain data for possible later use. Processes are usually represented as ellipses in OMT, while data flows are represented by straight line segments between the processes. An example of a simple DFD is given in Figure 11.1. This DFD shows the transformations involved in calculating the distance between two points in the plane.

Each process in a DFD may have zero or more input data flows and may produce zero or more data flows as output. For example the process 'Process points' expects two points as input, while it has two output data flows.

Data flow diagrams are concerned with data transformations and calculations within a system. They differ from the techniques which are employed in the dynamic modelling phase. Whereas dynamic modelling concentrates on the object state and the conditions under which such state changes, data flow diagrams do not give us any information on issues such as:

(11.1)

- Whether data flows between processes.
- When or how often data flows between processes.
- Whether the flow is initiated by the source process or by the sink process.

Answers to the questions raised in (11.1) should be given during the dynamic modelling phase.

11.2.2 Data context diagrams

We have said that a system's functional model can be described by a DFD. For each system there is exactly one data context diagram (DCD). A DCD is a top-level data flow diagram and it establishes the control boundary between the system and the environment and the entities in the environment with which the system communicates.

The essential elements of a DCD are:

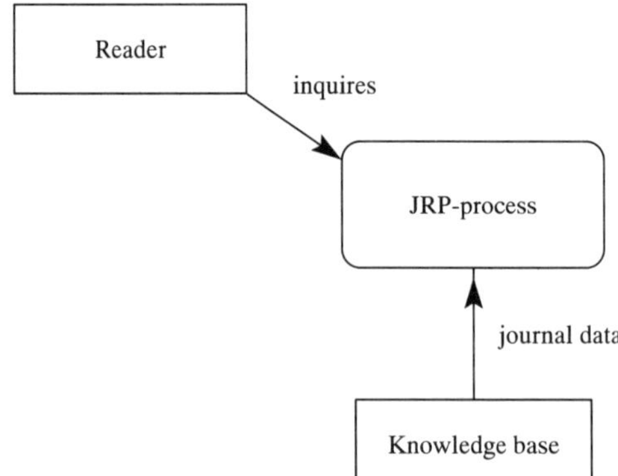

Figure 11.2 DCD for the JRP problem.

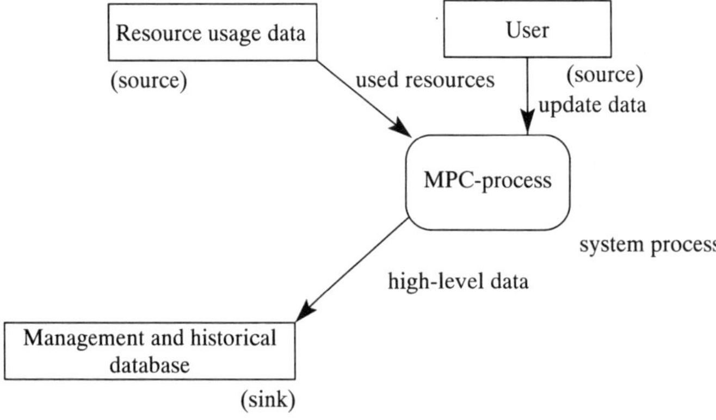

Figure 11.3 DCD for the MPC problem.

- One process which represents the functionality of the DCD
- Terminators
- Data flows between the terminators and the DCD process

A terminator represents any entity outside the context of the system. A terminator can be a transmitter of data (source) or a receiver of system data (sink).

Examples of DCDs for the problems JRP, MPC and PPD are given in Figures 11.2, 11.3 and 11.4.

OMT uses the term top-level context diagram instead of the term DCD.

11.2.3 Processes and data flows

A process transforms data. It is used to produce outputs from its inputs according to the action implied by its name. Processes can be described at both high levels and low levels of abstraction. The lowest level processes are pure functions without side effects. The process 'Square' in Figure 11.1 is an example of such a low-level process. It expects one input value (in this case a numeric value) and it produces one output value (namely, the square of the input). Higher level processes may produce more than one output value. Process names should be represented by verbs acting on a specific object.

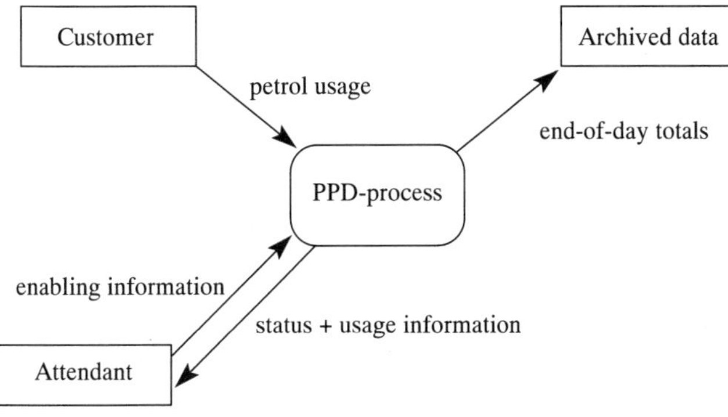

Figure 11.4 DCD for the PPD problem.

A data flow connects the output of an object or process with the input of another object or process. It can be seen as a pipeline through which data of known composition flows. A data flow may consist of a single element or a group of elements. Data flows should be named by using nouns or adjectives.

Processes are implemented as methods on object classes. We shall see how this is done in Chapter 12. For more information, see Duffy (1995).

11.2.4 Stores

A data or control store is data which is frozen in time. It is a passive object in a given DFD and its main use is to store useful data for later access. Stores represent persistent data in the DFD, while data flows represent values which change or which are not permanently stored.

Stores are represented graphically as solid parallel lines with the name of the store placed between them.

An example of a DFD which has a source store and a sink store is shown in Figure 11.5. In this case an issue of a journal is registered in an issue store (sink) while information from a journal store (source) is an input data flow. The output flow from the process 'Register_issue' is a group of articles which can then be used by other processes.

Data stores are objects which are implemented as flat files, relational database tables or persistent objects.

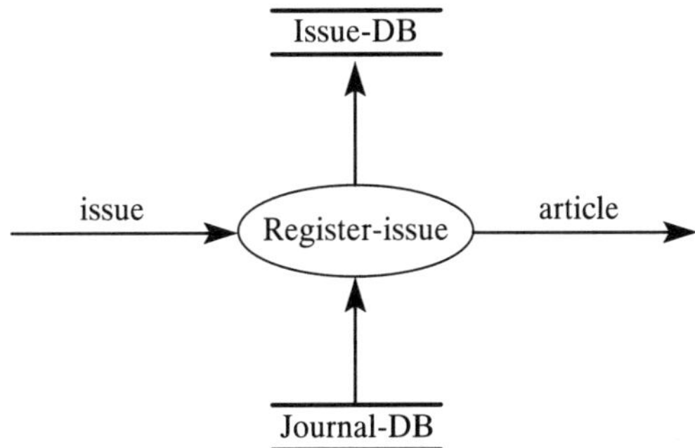

Figure 11.5 DFD with stores.

11.2.5 Terminators

A terminator is an entity which may either produce or consume data. OMT uses the term actor for the same concept. Terminators lie on the boundary of the data flow graph. In Figure 11.3 there are three actors, namely:

- Resource usage data: this is the source containing information on resource usage per employee in a given period.
- User: this is the person or persons responsible for managing and monitoring projects in MPC. This is a source.
- Management and historical database: this is a sink which contains high-level data about projects.

11.2.6 Levelling

Data flow diagrams are useful for showing the high-level functionality of a system. Processes appearing in a DFD can be broken down into simpler DFDs. This decomposition of DFDs into increasingly detailed diagrams is called levelling. For example the DCD for MPC could be decomposed into its first-level diagram as shown in Figure 11.6. In this case the main DCD process (level 0 process) is broken down into two simpler processes for processing data (per employee) and generating high-level data (for departments and divisions). It is possible to pursue the levelling process by further decomposition of the level 1 processes. This decomposition is continued until we arrive at a situation in which processes can be implemented in pseudocode, natural language or in some other way.

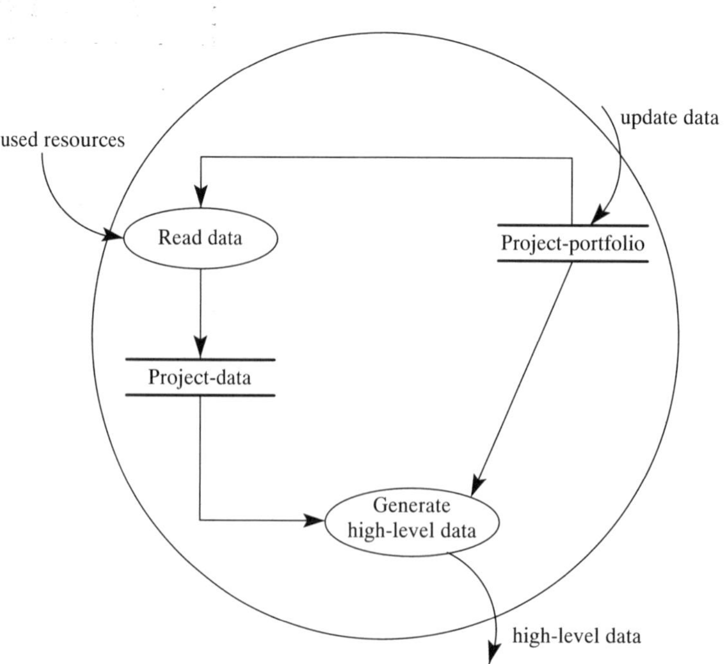

Figure 11.6 Level 1 DFD for MPC.

11.2.7 Control flows

A control flow is a pipeline through which control information of known composition flows. It may consist of a single element or a group of elements. Nouns and adjectives are used to denote control flows.

A control flow is a boolean value that affects whether a process is evaluated. It is not an input value to the process itself. A control flow is shown as a dotted line from a process producing a boolean value to the process being controlled. For example, in a login validation scenario a user may have to enter a password. If the password is correct it is then possible to carry on updating activities in a database application. The DFD together with the corresponding control flow is shown in Figure 11.7.

11.2.8 Example

We take the Journal Registration Problem (JRP) in order to show how DFDs work. The main responsibilities of JRP are first to create circulation lists when new issues of a journal arrive in the personnel department and secondly to create so-called attention lists. An attention list is made for each reader in the system and consists of a summary of those articles which contain information about which a given reader is interested.

The top-level DFD for JRP is shown in Figure 11.8. We consider that part of the DCD in which an issue enters the system. In particular, we are interested in producing attention lists for a given issue. There are three processes. The first, 'Register issue' has an issue as input and produces an output flow consisting of those articles which are published in the

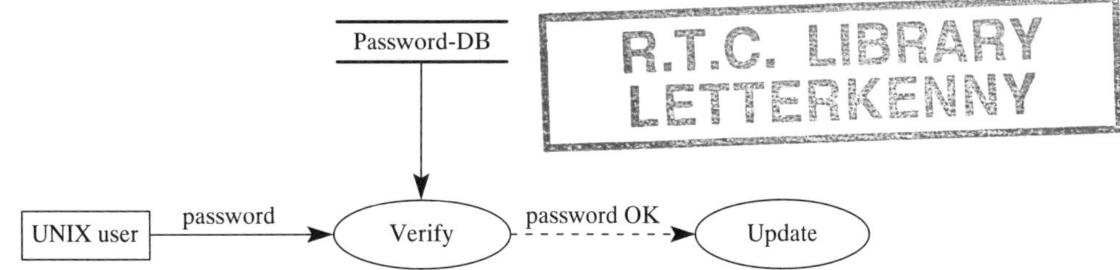

Figure 11.7 Use of control flows in DFDs.

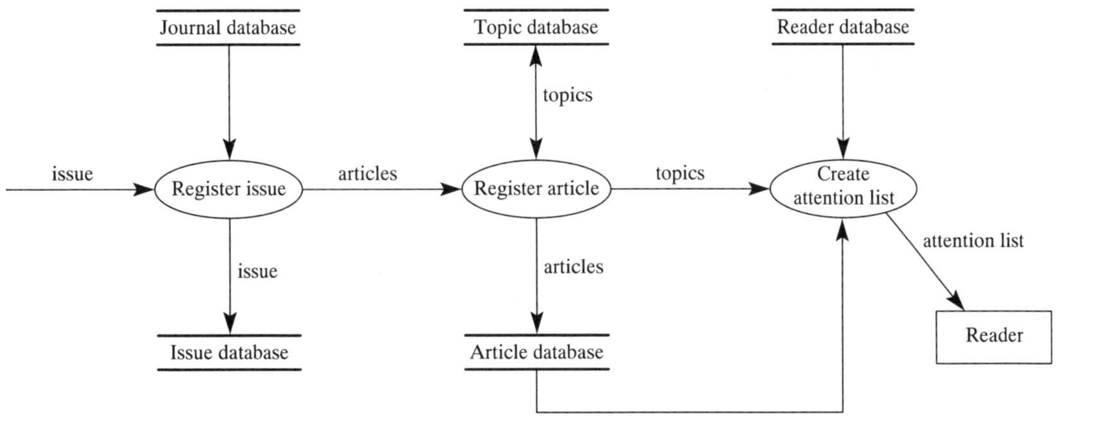

Figure 11.8 DFD for attention lists in JRP.

issue. The data stores 'Journal database' and 'Issue database' are involved. The latter is updated during the process. The process 'Register articles' stores the new articles in the article database while adding possible new topics and keywords to the topic database. Finally, 'Create attention list' produces a list of articles in which a given reader may be interested in.

11.3 Relating the functional model to the object and dynamic models

The functional model is the third part of the OMT analysis triad. It tells us what has to be done by the system. Each process in the functional model must eventually be implemented as operations on objects. Usually, the lowest level processes will correspond to operations. These operations are similar in structure to ADT functions, which were discussed in Chapter 2. In other words, each operation should contain the following information:

- The name of the operation
- Its return type (output data flow)
- The arguments in the argument list (input parameters).

There are different types of operation. The main ones are:

(11.2)

- Access operations
- Query operations
- Actions
- Activities

Access operations are those which read or write object or link attributes. They are the 'set/get' methods relative to the state of an object or a link. They may be listed in the object modelling phase, but this is a trivial matter. Access operations are derived directly from the attributes and associations of classes in the object model. Examples in JRP are:

- Give the publisher of a journal.
- How long does a reader have access to a circulation list?
- When is the appearance of an issue?

A query is an operation that has no side effects on the externally visible state of an object. It can be considered as a pure function and corresponds to a selector method. A query with no input parameters is called a derived attribute. A derived attribute is similar in form to one or more attributes in the state of an object but having different implementations. For example, the class Employee may have the following state:

- Employee name
- Employee date of birth

Queries and actions have no duration in time. They occur instantaneously.

An example of a derived attribute is an operation for the age of an employee; in this case the operation would be implemented by finding the difference between the system date (today) and the employee's data of birth.

An action is an operation that produces side effects, either on the target object or other objects in the system that are reachable from the target object. Actions may be specified in the form of algorithms or English language, for example. Thus the operation 'Create attention list' could be implemented as follows:

(11.3)

- Function: Create attention list
- Inputs: A list of topics, articles in issue, reader
- Outputs: A list of articles in which reader is interested

Transformation:

1. Create a set of those topics from the input topic set in which the reader is interested (the current topic set). Do this by ANDing the two topic sets.
2. Make a selection from the articles in the issue of those articles which deal with topics in which the reader is interested.

This is an operation which belongs to the join class representing attention lists. Its collaborators are classes Reader, Topic and Article.

Describing operations using the above approach is common in analysis (see, for example, Hatley and Pirbhai (1988)).

Finally, an activity in OMT is defined as an operation that has a duration in time. Activities only make sense for actors, the external agents that generate operations of their own accord. An example of an activity in JRP is when a new issue or journal is brought into the system. As we can see from Figure 11.8 such an activity produces side effects because of its extension in time.

The relationship between processes in the functional modelling phase and operations is many-to-many in general. For example, a high-level process may correspond to a number of operations, while an operation may be implemented by a number of possibly low-level processes. Data flows may model pure values or 'normal' objects. For example, in Figure 11.8 the input data flow to 'Register issue' is an instance of class Issue.

11.4 Disadvantages of DFDs in object-oriented development

We have devoted some time to describing what DFDs are and how they can be used in order to find the methods for object classes. The use of DFDs stems from the pre-object-oriented era and it is important to ask the question whether their use is correct when working in an object-oriented development environment. A number of authors have had problems, especially when integrating the functional model with the object model:

> The functional model, based on a particular style of using data flow diagrams, is not well suited to designing systems of interacting objects (D'Souza 1993).

The purpose of this section is to highlight some of the main problems with DFDs. A solution to these problems is developed in Section 11.5, where we employ the object flow diagram method of Martin and Odell.

11.4.1 Harmonizing data flows with objects

There is no uniform treatment of data flows in OMT. Data flows may represent values or objects. This imposes an extra burden on the software analyst. The ideal situation would be to treat every data flow as an instance of some object class in the problem domain.

Another weakness is that aggregate data flows can be split into their constituent values. For example, an address value may be split into simpler data flows for street address, city, state and postal code. The DFD which results from such a process becomes almost unreadable (and even unmaintainable) and is not in keeping with the object-oriented principle of encapsulation.

11.4.2 Weak support for interface objects

Interface objects represent those entities which directly depend on the system environment. An example of an interface object in MPC is the class which is responsible for reading the monthly data from the remote DB2 or Oracle database and importing them into the system proper. The interface object contains information for resource usage based on employee, used resources, project and the department for which the employee works during a certain interval of time.

OMT has provisions for so-called internal objects in the object design phase of the software life-cycle, but no distinction is made between classes that are products which are part of the design process (like list, sets and arrays) and classes that are strictly speaking application- or domain-based and those which are needed in order to tie the different use cases. The Objectory method from Ivar Jacobson (Jacobson *et al.* 1992) distinguishes between application objects and interface objects.

11.4.3 How data stores confuse matters

Data stores are objects or fragments of objects (for example, attributes) in OMT. Flows from a data store are queries (selectors) while flows into a data store are updates (modifiers). This dual role can be confusing, as it is not exactly certain whether we are working with objects or their attributes. We would prefer to operate at a higher level of granularity in which data stores and their corresponding data flows could be replaced by a single entity. A workaround to this problem is to demand that each store be owned by one object. This is the approach taken by Shlaer and Mellor and it could be applied to OMT and its DFDs; we should ensure that each data store is tied into a corresponding domain or interface object.

11.4.4 Problems with levelling

It is difficult to perform levelling in OMT. The main difficulty lies in the granularity of the data flows which are used at the different process levels. It is extremely difficult to carry out the levelling process because of the mass of detail. Furthermore, the classical DFD levelling approach has no object-oriented support. It is not possible to consider processes as having 'derived' processes. Similarly, data flows are simple objects and values and we cannot implement 'abstract' objects flowing from one process to another process. This lack of functionality and of abstraction makes it difficult to extend the system.

11.4.5 Supporting business modelling

A DFD represents a snapshot of one view of a system. In general we can say that DFDs are not created with reusability in mind.

It is difficult to level up or level down, thus making the job of merging and specializing flow diagrams almost impossible. It is also difficult to use DFDs as a tool for explaining to management or knowledge officers what they actually do and how they fit in the enterprise data model. The main reasons for this are:

- It is difficult to define good interface objects between DFDs.
- There is no facility for generalization or specialization.

For example, it is not possible in Figure 11.8 to add a new process for creating a special interest group (SIG) of those readers who are interested in a given topic without changing the topology of the graph. This is mainly due to the fact that DFDs cannot be nested in the sense that the Harel higraphs can be, although the DFD 'bubbles' can be levelled; however, my own experience in these matters is that it is very easy to become confused, especially with the way that data flows are implemented.

11.4.6 Concurrent engineering and systems integration problems

We mentioned that DFDs do not support interface objects well. This is a major drawback, especially in environments where different groups work on different parts of a problem. Furthermore, the big challenge in modern software systems development is in integrating products from different sources (Martin and Odell 1992).

11.5 Object flow diagrams

An object flow diagram (OFD) is a directed graph in which the nodes may be either activities or products and the directed arcs represent productions or consumptions. An activity is similar to a process, but it differs in a number of ways. First, an activity produces a product and its product is consumed by one or more other activities. A product is defined as the end result that fulfils the purpose of an activity. Thus, an activity is a generalized process while a product is a generalized data flow.

A simple example of an OFD is given in Figure 11.9. The notation used is taken from Martin and Odell (1992). There are two activities ('Petrol pump activity', 'Process deliveries'), two products ('Deliveries', 'Transactions') and two so-called external agents ('Customer' and 'Attendant'). This OFD is very similar to a DCD but with the following differences:

- The activities and products can be generic.
- The flow between activities and products are objects.

Whereas with data flow diagrams we speak about processes, data flows, stores and data exchange, with OFDs we speak exclusively about products, activities and object exchange.

11.5.1 Activities and products

Activities and products cooperate to form a supplier/consumer duo. An activity can have a product as either a so-called production or as a consumption. The general situation and an example are given in Figure 11.10. We see that high-level data is produced by one activity and consumed by another activity.

An activity may have zero or more productions and consumptions. An example is given in Figure 11.11 which contains two productions and two consumptions.

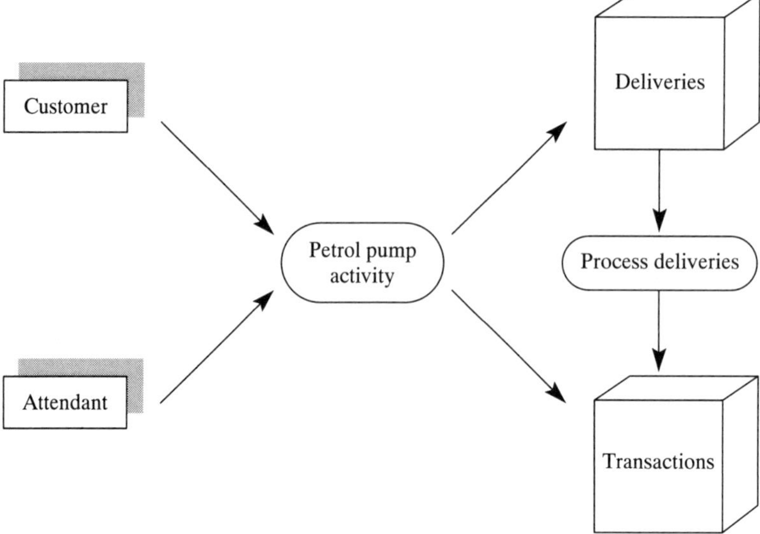

Figure 11.9 Simple OFD for the PPD problem.

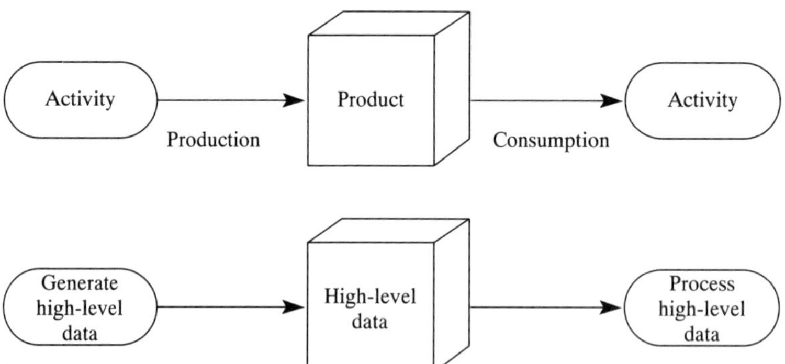

Figure 11.10 Activities and products.

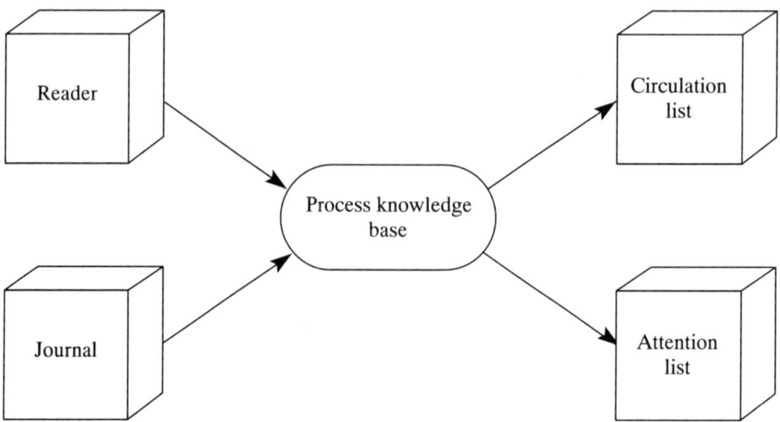

Figure 11.11 Multiple consumptions and productions.

11.5.2 Products and activities as types

A major advantage of using OFDs is that we can develop them in either a top-down or a bottom-up fashion. This is enabled by the fact that both products and activities can be seen as objects. In particular, generic activities and products can be included in OFDs from which concrete or more specialized versions can be created without disrupting the structure of the OFD. This has consequences for the traceability during software enhancements.

A product can be a subtype or a supertype. Examples of supertypes are `Used_Resources`, `Transactions` and `Interest_Information`. Subtype examples are `Used_hours`, `Payments` and `CirculationLists`. An activity can be a subtype or a supertype. This is because an activity can be seen as an object. Some examples of supertype activities and their subtypes are:

- Create reader interest list

  Create circulation list

  Create attention list

  Create SIG list
- Create transaction

  Create payment information

  Create bank account information

Having constructed OFDs using supertypes it is possible to extend the OFD by defining new subtypes. It should also be possible to generate code based on the new OFD.

11.5.3 Activity and product levelling

It is advisable to include the most general activities in an OFD. This allows us to level down and would correspond to a top-down approach in OFD design. It is also possible to level up using a bottom-up approach, whereby smaller products and activities can be merged which model new, more complex and subtle qualities that are created at every step in the enterprise.

Examples of levelling in products and activities are given in Figures 11.12, 11.13 and 11.14.

The OFD for the creation of attention lists is shown in Figure 11.14. This is equivalent to the DFD which is given in Figure 11.8

11.6 Products of the functional modelling phase

We have discussed the functional modelling phase of OMT in this chapter. Its shortcomings in relation to object-oriented development were mentioned and extensions and improvements were proposed. These will be applied to the solution of MPC in Chapter 12.

The following steps should be followed to execute the functional model in OMT:

- Build a DCD for the given problem.
- For problems of a reactive nature (i.e. those with a non-trivial dynamic model) collect the operations from the dynamic model. These operations can be discovered from event–response lists, for example.
- For problems with a trivial dynamic model, create a system DFD.
- Describe each process in the system DFD in the form (11.3).

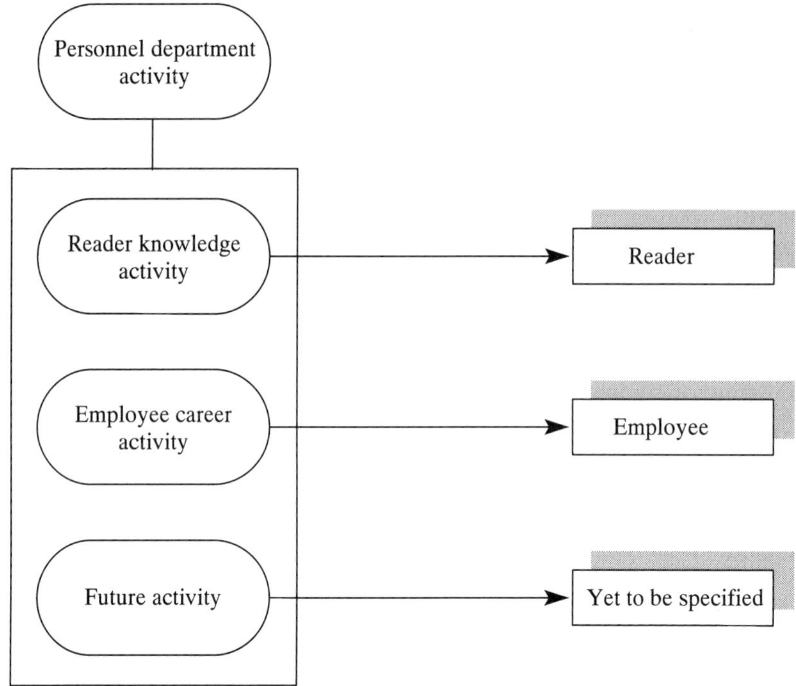

Figure 11.12 Activities levelling in OFDs.

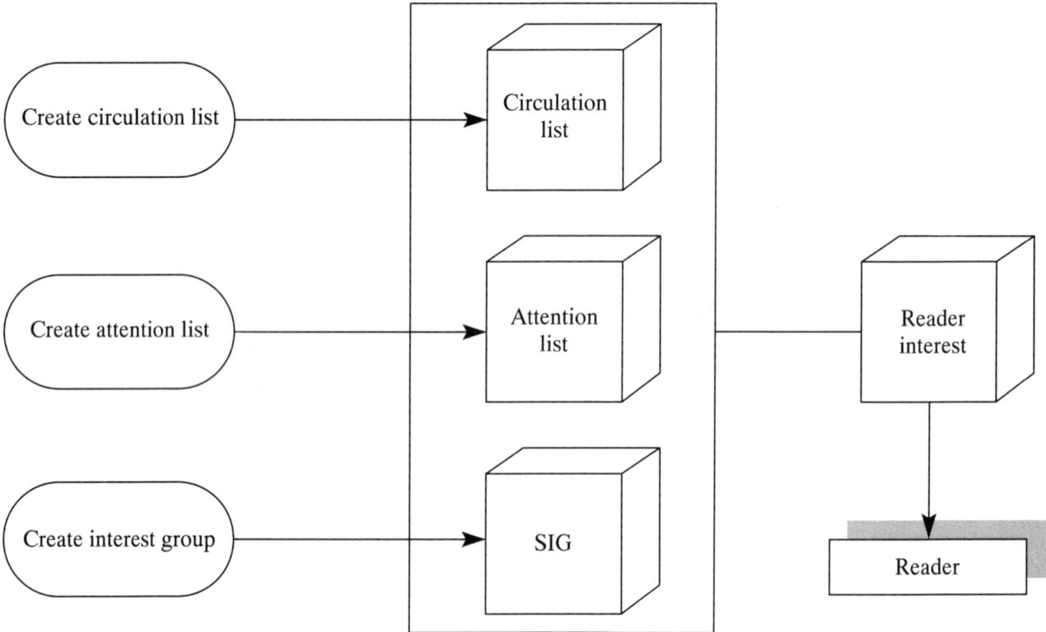

Figure 11.13 Product levelling in OFDs.

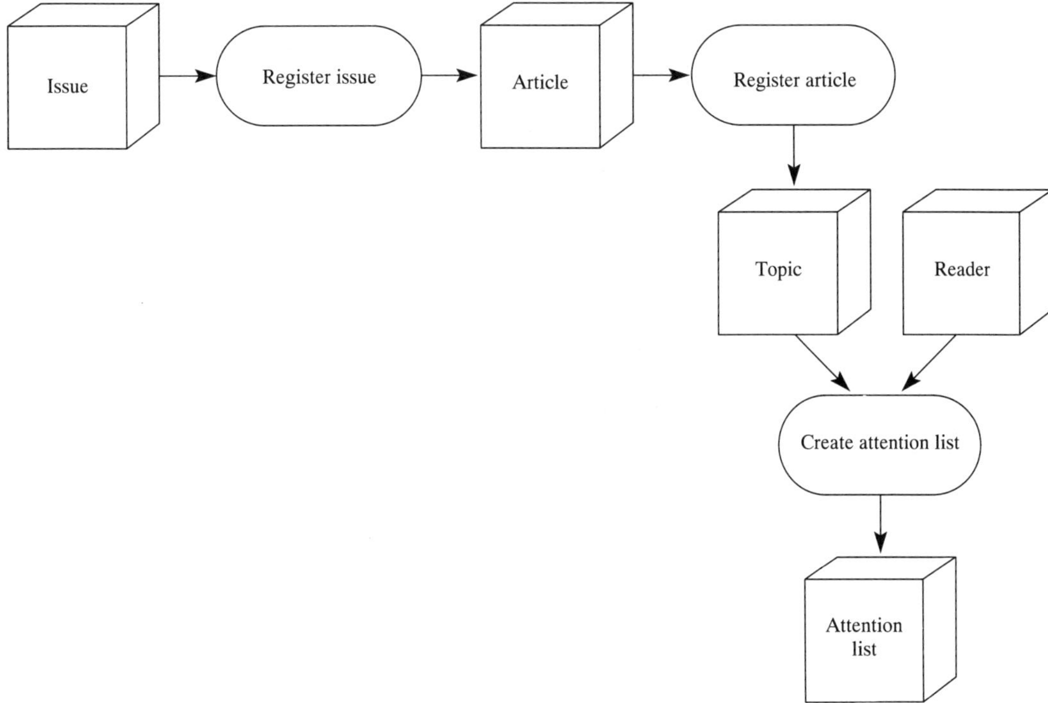

Figure 11.14 OFD for attention list in JRP.

- Expand complicated processes and processes with side effects.
- Execute storyboards to verify the system.

The deliverables are:

- Relative to the object model

The processes determine operations on classes and the signature of each operation.

- Relative to the dynamic model

The functional model shows the definitions of leaf actions (responses) and activities that are undefined in the dynamic model.

Exercises

1. Specify the JRP processes 'Register issue' and 'Register articles' according to the strategy in (11.3).
2. Modify the DFD in Figure 11.8 so that it can create special interest groups (SIGs) of readers who are interested in a given topic and who would like to contact each other in order to form workgroups and seminars.

3. Create DCDs for the hospital database problem.

References

D. D'Souza (1993) Working with OMT, *Journal of Object-Oriented Programming*, October.

D. J. Duffy (1995) 'Object-Oriented Requirements Analysis: Process Modelling and Scalability Issues', *AOAD*, May/June.

D. J. Hatley and I. Pirbhai (1988) *Strategies for Real-Time System Specification*, Dorset House Publishing, New York.

I. Jacobson *et al.* (1992) *Object-Oriented Software Engineering*, Addison-Wesley, Wokingham.

J. Martin and J. J. Odell (1992) *Object-Oriented Analysis and Design*, Prentice-Hall. Englewood Cliffs NJ.

S. Shlaer and S. J. Mellor (1988) *Object-Oriented Systems Analysis*, Prentice-Hall, Englewood Cliffs NJ.

E. Yourdon (1979) *Structured Design*, Prentice-Hall, Englewood Cliffs NJ.

Chapter

12

Object-oriented analysis of MPC

12.1 Introduction and objectives

This chapter analyses a class of problems which occur in many business and industrial processes. The problem is one of resource allocation and control. Many companies are interested in management information systems (MIS) and decision support systems (DSS) so that they can adapt to changing situations. Typical examples are:

- Controlling cash flow
- Monitoring the progress of projects
- Capital budgeting
- Allocation and control of industrial resources
- Monitoring disk usage in a network of computers
- Monitoring computer network traffic

Many of these areas have much in common. It is not our intention to solve the most general resource allocation problem, but we choose instead to solve a specific problem and later draw conclusions on how to generalize it to other interesting situations. The problem chosen is one of a company which contracts out to other companies. The main objective is to register and monitor the number of hours that employees spend on a given project during its lifespan. Each project has a budget with which it can play, and management is interested in how that budget is consumed. We choose to monitor used hours for a given project; the more general case is when a company would like to monitor other resources (e.g. hardware, software, expenditure) for a given project. Instances of resources (like hours, jelly beans, car rental agency and file systems) are tangible. We have introduced the concept of resource in order to emphasis the point that this problem could be formulated in a more abstract way. The advantage of this approach is that program families can be created from which the subproblem of used hours allocation would be a special case. In this way we could use the results achieved here in future projects. Typical examples are:

- Disk space management in a computer network
- Renting cars from a car rental company

The resources used in MPC (hours) are examples of fixed, consumable resources. This is because the system begins with a given quantity of hours. Objects (in this case workers) consume hours as time goes on and they ultimately use up all the hours that were originally allocated to them. New objects needing the resource either terminate without successfully completing their tasks or are delayed and wait for a resource that will never be provided. In the case of MPC such a situation occurs when a project overruns its budget.

Smalltalk has a number of classes which allow us to simulate real-world situations, and if the MPC were to be implemented in this language it would be a good idea to investigate the possibilities of applying these classes to the current problem before creating them ourselves.

12.2 Statement of problem and assumptions

Many engineering companies work as contractors for external customers in order to construct nuclear power stations, roads, railways and software systems. Many projects can last for several years and much expertise may be needed in order to complete the project. For example, in order to construct a nuclear power plant many disciplines, such as mechanical, process and civil engineering, may need to work at different times on the project. Employees typically spend time on different projects and this time must be registered and aggregated on a departmental basis for later invoicing to the customer. Some projects, such as support activities (e.g. the EDP department) are not sponsored by external clients and are seen as overhead. Such projects are typically sponsored by a division or some other decision-making body.

Since a company may be involved in many projects at any given moment it is necessary to be able to have decision support systems (DSS) in order to monitor the progress. Progress is determined in many cases by comparing used resources with the resources which were allocated at the beginning of the project. In general, each employee is allocated a certain number of hours per project and the employee must ensure that his or her part of the project is finished before the allocated hours run out. It is the responsibility of the employee to ensure that the hours used on a project are registered on a regular basis, usually once per month.

The requirements for the following problem have already been described in Section 6.8.2, but we repeat them here for completeness so that this chapter is as self-contained as possible.

12.2.1 Manpower control system (code name MPC)

An engineering company works on projects for external and internal customers. Projects have a start date and an end date and a fixed amount of hours in which the project should be completed. Employees in the company are organized into departments. A department is a centre of expertise in one particular area, for example piping design, acoustics or steel design. Each department is responsible for one or more activities in the project. Departments are grouped into divisions, for example mechanical engineering, process and piping. A division may sponsor internal projects. Resources (in this case hours) are allocated in the same way for external and internal projects. The resources for external projects are divided among the departments which can play a role in the successful execution of the project. It is then the responsibility of each department to allocate resources to employees in the department.

An employee belongs to one department and employees will work on projects for their 'home' departments. However, there may be some slackening of work in some departments and employees may be seconded to other departments.

We wish to create a (database) system in which project resources can be registered, validated and monitored on a regular basis. In particular, we assume the following:

- The used hours per project are updated once per month and are based on employee, project and department.
- An employee may work for at most one department on any given project.
- There is no distinction made between the different types of employee who are involved on a project.

It should be possible to visualize the progress of a project by displaying scheduled hours against used hours in the form of line charts, histograms and similar charts. Progress can be displayed on department, division and project levels.

The most important use cases for MPC are:

(12.1)

- Initial registration of project infrastructure
- Periodic updating of project data
- Viewing project data

The first two use cases form the core of MPC, while the third use case uses the products of the first two. It is essentially a derived use case and its main function is to present data in graphical and textual form.

We shall concentrate on the first two use cases in (12.1) in this chapter. The third case is easy to design, since many spreadsheet and database systems have capabilities for displaying data in a variety of forms. In this case we would choose to buy a system which could be easily integrated with MPC.

12.3 Concept mapping

The main objective in this section is to determine what the main concepts in the problem domain are. It is important to note that the present requirements document is incomplete and that further discussions with users and domain experts are needed in practice. In our case we shall make some simplifying assumptions, some of which are noted in this document.

At this stage in the modelling phase we wish to concentrate on those concepts which will form the kernel for a solution using object-oriented techniques. In particular, we see a number of sources of noise (or redundancy), for example:

- Reports and graphical output (representation problem)
- Used and scheduled hours
- Histograms and line charts

These concepts will not be considered in the concept mapping phase.

We have decided on the following concepts which will participate in an initial approximation to a solution of the MPC problem; the concepts are ordered in such a way that the more important concepts appear before the less important ones:

- Project
- Worker (same concept as Employee)
- Resource (this is a hazy concept at the moment)
- Department
- External project
- Internal project
- Division

The links between these concepts are:

- A worker is involved with a project.
- A worker consumes resources.
- A project may contain other projects (subprojects or activities).
- An internal project is a project (a project can be an internal project).
- A project can be an external project.
- A worker belongs to a department.
- A resource is allocated on the basis of department.
- A division consists of departments (a department forms part of a division).
- An internal project is sponsored by a number of divisions.

The concept map for the use case 'Initial project registration' is shown in Figure 12.1. This concept map contains the case in which a worker is seconded to another department in order to participate on a project. Thus, at any given instant in time individual workers may have relationships with several departments; first, their 'default' or 'home' departments and a number of departments with which they are involved due to the fact that other departments can avail themselves of their services.

We can now examine the above links which suggest object-oriented structure. These are:

- Abstraction links: can be, is a (generalization)
- Partitioning links: consists of, forms part of (aggregation)
- Projection links: involved with, consumes, allocated, sponsored by

These links will suggest associations which we create in the object model.

12.4 Object modelling

We give details of the steps that need to be taken in the object model for use case IPR. The deliverables from this phase are:

- A complete description of the classes arising in the problem domain (including their attributes and a tentative list of operations).
- The associations between the classes.
- Classes classified according to generalization relationships.

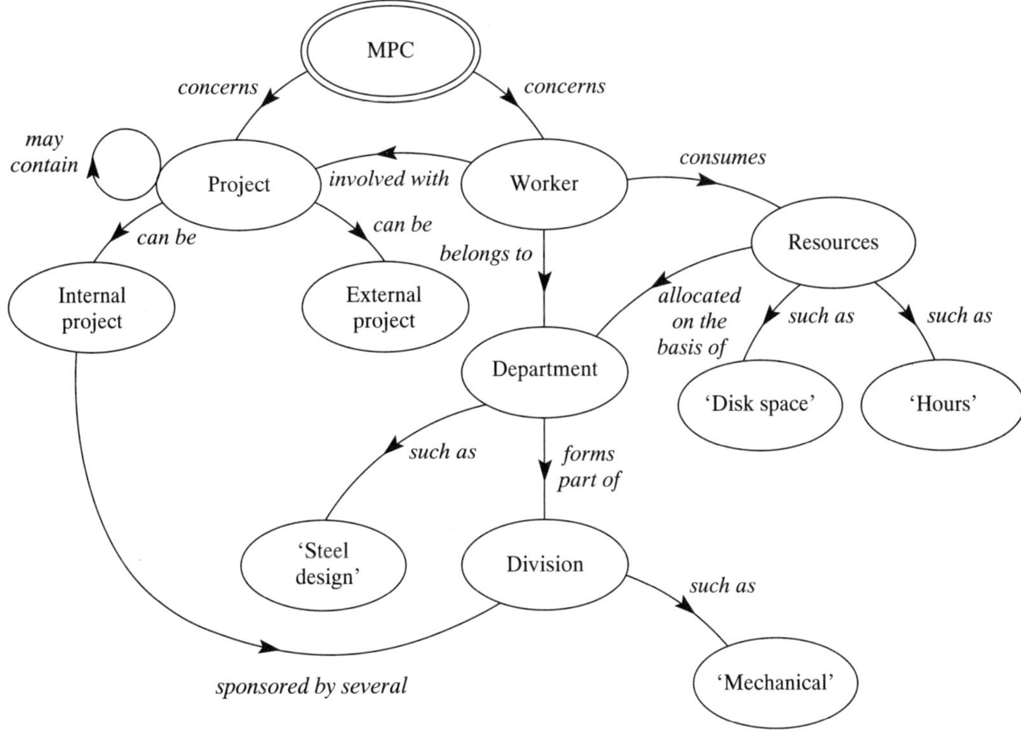

Figure 12.1 Concept map for MPC.

12.4.1 Identification of classes

The most important classes can be easily deduced from the concept mapping phase. Although we feel that not all classes have been discovered we prefer to proceed. In particular, the concept map in Figure 12.1 does not contain any information pertaining to ongoing project status, such as resource usage per employee, department and division (this will be dealt with during functional modelling). Classes which have been overlooked will be discovered in the functional modelling phase.

The most important classes at this stage are:

- Project (includes both internal and external projects)
- Worker
- Department
- Division

We have not implemented the concept 'Resource' as a separate class because we have chosen to treat the simpler problem of monitoring the used hours for a given project. In this case the concept reduces to an attribute (Rumbaugh *et al.* 1991, p. 155) because it primarily describes individual objects and it does not have its own independent existence. If we had chosen to solve the more general problem in which other resources, such as hardware, software, slush funds and out-of-pocket costs, were important we would create a class 'Resource' in order to model these cases.

Data dictionary The purpose of the data dictionary is to describe as accurately as possible the role of each class in the problem domain. This is necessary in order to minimize misunderstanding between the domain experts and the designers of the system. Furthermore, the information contained in the data dictionary can be placed in a company-wide repository so that other designer groups can use some of the ideas, classes and experiences that have been created in this project.

Project This is a description of a set of activities which when taken together achieve certain objectives. There are two basic types of project; first, internal projects which are sponsored within the company itself and secondly, external projects which are sponsored by external customers.

Projects have a start date and a duration. The duration is divided into a number of so-called periods. A period can correspond to any arbitrary interval of time, such as a week, month or year. In most cases a period is the same as a calendar month, but some companies base their planning schedules on a 13-month year.

Project data is read from an external computer at the start of each period. Data is given per worker for each project in which that worker is involved. This is the 'raw' data which MPC processes.

There are two specializations of Project. These are external and internal projects, respectively. An internal project is sponsored directly by a number of divisions within the company, while external projects are sponsored by outside companies. We have chosen not to include these outside companies as classes in MPC. This may need to be revised if we need more up-to-date information, such as the companies' cash flow data and assets. In this latter case we create an association between the class 'External-project' and a class representing a company.

Worker An employee who is engaged on different projects within a company. Workers may be assigned to different departments for various projects depending on their skills.

Each worker belongs to one 'home' department. Most projects are sponsored by this department but a worker may be 'seconded' to other departments which need the worker's skills for a particular project.

A worker is assigned a certain amount of resources (hours) at the start of a project. It is up to the worker to ensure that the used resources do not exceed the scheduled resources. The system, however, will check for overrun at the beginning of every period.

Department An organizational unit for the purposes of a project. Examples of departments are piping drafting, computer operations and mechanical drafting.

Each department is allocated a number of hours at the start of a given project. It is then necessary to schedule these hours for each period during the lifetime of the project. It is not possible to change those scheduled hours once the periods in which they are defined have expired.

Division A high-level organizational unit containing one or more departments. Examples of divisions are mechanical engineering, electrical engineering, process engineering and information processing.

A division has the power to start new internal projects and a number of divisions can agree to sponsor such projects.

Both Division and Department are examples of role objects.

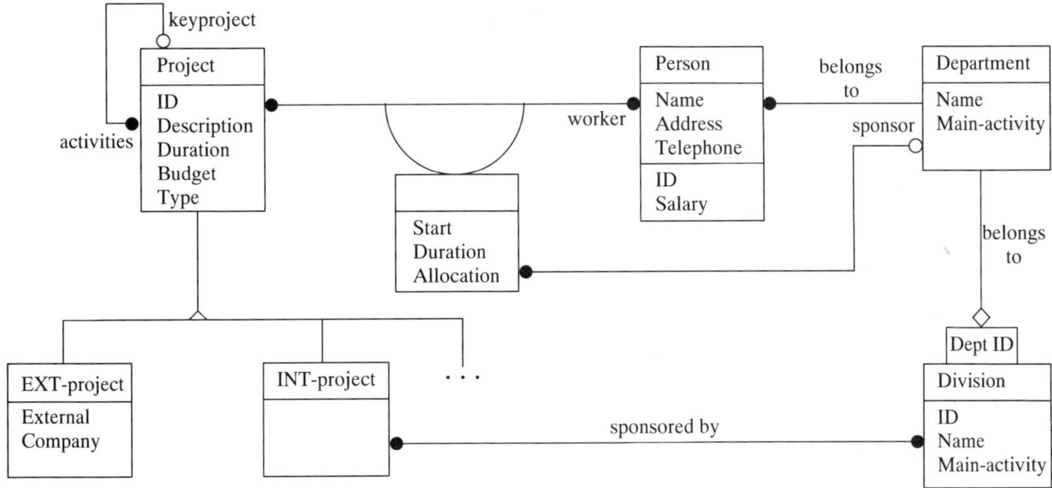

Figure 12.2 Object model for the MPC problem.

These are the most important classes arising in this problem. We shall see in the next section that new classes are discovered as soon as we start to examine the associations.

12.4.2 Identification of associations

Figure 12.2 shows the initial object model for MPC. We see a number of associations, namely:

- Recursive aggregation: a project may contain other projects.
- Variable aggregation: a division consists of departments.
- Generalization: a project is an internal project or an external project.
- Binary association: a worker is involved with a project, a worker consumes resources, resources are allocated on a department-wide basis, an internal project is sponsored by a number of divisions, a worker belongs to a department.

12.4.3 Object attributes

We now give the informal descriptions (no explicit data types given) of the attributes of the classes arising in the problem domain.

Project Project identification (ID)

- Project description
- Duration of project (start and end dates)
- Total number of hours budgeted
- When the last update of used resources took place
- Type of project (lump sum, ...)

An internal project has at this stage the same attributes as a standard project. This situation can change in the future but we have created an infrastructure in which extensions to the system can be made. Furthermore, new types of project can be included in the hierarchy without any disruption to the model.

External project Sponsoring company

Main topic: Worker

- ID
- Name
- Address
- Telephone
- Scale (a number between 1 and 10 which corresponds to the hourly rate of the worker). This is equivalent to salary.

Department Department ID

- Department name
- Main activity

Division Division ID

- Division name
- Main activity

Note that the ID attributes in the above classes correspond to domain-related information. They are unrelated to database or design-related attributes.

We now give a description of the object model for MPC (see Figure 12.2). We see that the class Worker is represented as a role for class Person. In fact we design Worker as a subclass of Person. Class Project contains attributes which are common to both external and internal projects. It has two subclasses which we call ExternalProject and InternalProject. There is an *N:M* association between project and Worker and its link attributes are shown. The class corresponding to the association will be called 'Resource' in the design phase. A qualified association is created between Division and Department. Finally, there is an *N:M* association between InternalProject and Division.

12.4.4 The classification process

We see from Figure 12.2 that there is one example of generalization, namely a project can be an internal project or an external project. The only difference between these two subclasses is that an external project contains information pertaining to the company which sponsors the project. The main advantage of the generalization relationship in this problem is that new types of project can be accommodated in the future by creating subclasses of Project and adding specific attributes and operations.

12.5 Dynamic modelling

The single main event in MPC is when the end of a given period is reached. When this occurs resource usage data must be read into MPC. This triggers a series of events resulting in an up-to-date version of the database.

Event–response lists and storyboards allow us to construct a simple prototype of the completed system. They can also be used as an effective communication tool between the user (domain expert) and the designer of the system.

MPC is a problem in which the dynamic model plays a minor role. The main event occurs at the start of each period when project data is read into the system.

The events discussed here will eventually correspond to class operations.

E0: A project has been approved.

R01: Determine which departments are involved and what resources are allocated to them.

E1: A new period starts.

R11: The used hours per (worker, project, department) are inserted into the project database.

R12: Hours per (department, project) are updated.

R13: Hours per (division, project) are updated.

C11: It is only possible to read hours more than once per period.

C12: All data (departments, projects) must be valid.

The main storyboards correspond to the responsibilities and high level behaviour. Storyboards can be seen as 'walkthroughs' and they can help us in determining suitable access paths in the system. Furthermore, they are meaningful to the users of the system as they allow them to follow a sequence of events in the system.

Storyboard 1: Updating the MPC database for a given project per period

1.1 Used hours are read for all workers involved in the project.

1.2 Update the used hours for the departments involved.

1.3 Determine the divisions corresponding to each department.

1.4 Update the used hours for each division.

In practice used hours are read based on worker, project and department. It may be more efficient to have this input data sorted on project, department and worker. In this case we can apply Storyboard 1 to all projects.

Storyboard 2: Determining project status for a department

The objective here is to determine the relationship between the used and scheduled hours for a given project and department. Furthermore, the project leader wishes to determine whether there is an (impending) overrun. It should be possible to calculate values between two arbitrary periods in the lifetime of the project.

2.1 Determine project and department (user input).

2.2 For each period determine the difference between used and scheduled hours for each period in the given range.

2.3 Sum the differences for all users in a given department.

2.4 Output the value.

Storyboard 3: Making Reports (Cumulative Line Graphs)

This storyboard is concerned with the problem of creating a cumulative line graph between two periods in the lifetime of a given project for one department.

3.1 Determine project and department (user input).

3.2 Loop from the start to end period.

3.3 The current cumulative hours are determined by adding the hours for the current period to the cumulative hours from the previous period.

3.4 Output the values in the form of a line chart.

Storyboard 3 can also be used in order to create cumulative line charts for a given division.

From these storyboards we can extract a list of preliminary operations for the classes from the application domain. The most important classes are project, department and division (it is possible to ask questions at the worker level, but this does not directly concern us here).

Department

- Input/modify scheduled hours for a given project (usually at the start of a project).
- Input/modify the hours to complete for a given department.
- Input scheduled hours as percentages of the total budget.
- Determine project status.
- How many internal/external projects is the department involved in?

Division

- What are the departments in a division.
- Determine resource allocation for a given project.
- How many internal/external projects is the division involved in?

Project

- Read resource data (per period).
- Determine resource allocation.
- Does a project contain subprojects?
- Is a project part of another project?

12.6 The functional model

We are interested in the data transformations which take place in MPC. The functional model plays an important role in MPC because many computations take place in the system. Examples are:

- Data is read from an external database (once per period).
- Data is collated for each user.
- Department-level data is aggregated.
- Department-level data is aggregated to division level.

- Division-level data is aggregated to project level.
- Multi-project level data needs to be calculated for high-level management software.
- Cumulative data per period is needed at department, division and project level.

We are not concerned with how, when or why these operations are carried out. The dynamic model controls which operations are performed and in which order. Which sequences of operations are carried out can easily be deduced from the event–response lists and the corresponding storyboards.

The following steps are carried out in MPC and in the given order:

(12.2)

- Per period related information

    Read in data per employee per period

    Check the validity of the periodic data

    Aggregate user data into department data

    Aggregate division data from department data

- Cumulative data

    Calculate data per employee

    Cumulative data for each department

    Cumulative data for each division

From (12.2) we see that six new classes need to be created which hold periodic and cumulative data for each type of organizational unit (employee, department and division) in MPC. We use the following names for these classes:

(12.3)

- Periodic data

    `PerEmployee`

    `PerDepartment`

    `PerDivision`

- Cumulative data

    `CumEmployee`

    `CumDepartment`

    `CumDivision`

These classes could have been discovered in the concept mapping phase of MPC had we chosen to view the problem from a 'use case' standpoint. All the classes are project-based, by which we mean that each contains a project ID as attribute. Furthermore, in order to populate these classes we need to use project information, such as which departments an employee works for on a given project and which departments are contained in a division.

The MPC system stores hours per period/worker/project and the corresponding attributes of `PerEmployee` are:

```
proj#
dept#
```

```
worker#
period_number
used_hours
scheduled_hours
```

The attributes of `PerDepartment` are:

```
proj#
dept#
period_number
used_hours
scheduled_hours
```

The attributes of `PerDivision` are:

```
proj#
division#
period_number
used_hours
scheduled_hours
```

The attributes of `CumDepartment` are:

```
proj#
dept#
period_number
cum_hours
```

The attributes of `CumDivision` are:

```
proj#
division#
period_number
cum_hours
```

We could have made a class `CumEmployee` which registers the cumulative hours used by an employee; if this level of detail is deemed for this problem we can define the attributes of this class as follows:

```
dept#
worker#
period_number
cum_hours
```

In this case we have stored the total used hours up until a certain period for a given employee.

The DCD (data context diagram) for MPC has three terminators, two of which are sources ('Resource usage data' and 'User') and one of which is a sink ('Management and historical database'). These are considered as being outside the MPC system and are not directly included in the analysis. It is important to understand that 'User' is responsible for updates to the scheduling data in MPC and has no relationship with the Worker class which was found in the concept map for MPC. The data context diagram for MPC is shown in Figure 12.3.

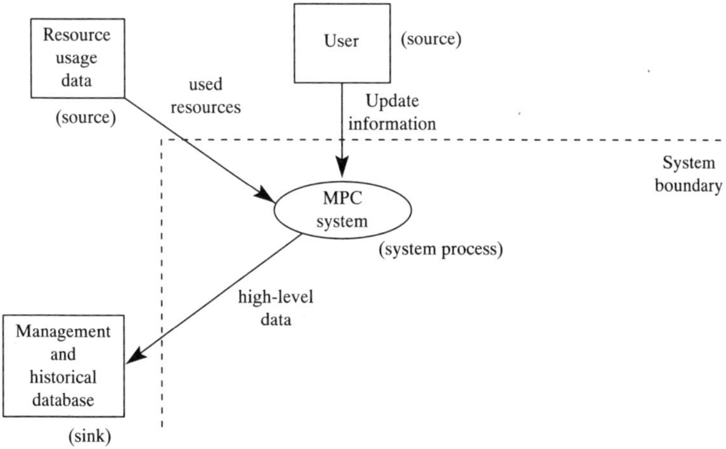

Figure 12.3 Data context diagram for the MPC system.

For MPC it is not necessary to carry through the functional modelling process as advocated by the classical OMT, as it is possible to achieve the same results using pseudocode.

12.6.1 Finding object methods from the functional model

In the object analysis phase it was not our objective to find the methods or operations which are part of objects. However, the functional model allows us to find them. The basic rule is:

Each process is implemented by a method on some object.

We must expand the functional model to the stage where each process is 'atomic' in the sense that it can be directly implemented as operations on objects. Rumbaugh et al. (1991, p. 130) give a discussion of the possibilities. We can choose for example, to write the solution in some type of pseudocode, C++ or in structured English.

As an example, we wish to reduce the process 'Generate division data' to the stage where it can be implemented in structured English. To this end, we need to calculate both the hours per period and the cumulative hours. We need both current data and knowledge about the organization if we want to achieve this. The processes can be implemented as structured text.

The process which populates the class `PerDivision` is given in pseudo-C++ form as follows:

(12.4)

```
for the current period do
{
  for each division in organization
  {
    division.used_hours := 0;
    for each department in the current division
    {
        divisions.used_hours += department.used_hours;
        next department;
    }
```

```
        // Store the current division in repository;
        next division;
      }
  }
```

The process which populates the class `CumDivision` is implemented as follows:

(12.5)

```
  for the current period do
  {
    for each division in organization
    {
      division.cum_hours :=
      division_previous.cum_hours + division.used_hours;

    // Store the current division data in repository;
    next division;
    }
  }
```

The pseudocode in (12.4) and (12.5) is in a form which can be implemented in C++. In these cases the processes map to member functions in `PerDivision` and `Cumdivision`.

The following methods are discovered after having completed the functional modelling phase:

Department

- Find all workers who are involved in a given project for this department.
- Does a worker belong to this department for this project?
- Give hours for department for one or all periods for a given project.
- Update hours up to the present period.
- Update cumulative hours up to the present period.

Division

- Find all departments in this division.
- Is a department part of this division?
- Update hours up to the present period.
- Update cumulative hours up to the present period.

Exercises

1. For the class `Worker` find the methods which come from the functional modelling phase. Do the same for class `Project`.

2. Constraints, preconditions and postconditions are part of the functional model, but have not been discussed here. An example of a constraint in MPC is that hours cannot be updated if the present period is in the past relative to existing periods in the 'Project data'

store. For example, if the project is living in period 10 it is not possible to update MPC with data which pertains to period 9. Find other constraints in MPC.

3. Most projects are so complex that they need to be divided into so-called activities. An activity portrays the actual operations or activities in a project and thus consumes time and resources. It is desired to introduce uncertainty estimates into MPC. This is done in the activity class by the use of three parameters:

   a = most optimistic (shortest) time

   m = most likely (modal) time

   b = most pessimistic (longest) time

   Activities are dependent on each other in the sense that some activities cannot start until others finish.

   Questions are:

   (a) Create a class `ACTIVITY`; what are its attributes and operations?

   (b) What is the relationship between `ACTIVITY` and the other classes in MPC?

   (c) How would you design and analyse dependencies between activities?

4. Write the pseudocode equivalent of (12.4) and (12.5) for the classes `PerDepartment` and `CumDepartment`. Identify the corresponding operations.

Reference

J. Rumbaugh, M. Blaha, W. Premerlani, F. Eddy and W. Lorensen (1991) *Object-Oriented Modeling and Design*, Prentice-Hall, Englewood Cliffs NJ.

Chapter

13

Object-oriented analysis of PPD

13.1 Introduction and objectives

This chapter applies the modified OMT model to the solution of a problem that was originally proposed in Coleman *et al.* (1994) and which has been solved there by the use of the Fusion method.

We carry out a reasonably thorough analysis of the PPD problem. The deliverables will be used as input to the system and object design phases, which are discussed in later chapters.

The PPD problem statement as specified in Coleman *et al.* (1994, p. 145) is less than one page long and it is difficult to see how we should proceed with an analysis. The problem is difficult to understand in one chunk and we found it necessary to divide it into a number of subproblems, with each subproblem having its own area of concern. The object model is important because of the abundance of tangible objects in the system, such as tank, pump and petrol line. The system has an event-driven subplot and thus dynamic modelling will play an important role. Finally, data transformations take place in the system when delivery data is converted into payments and transaction data.

We have used the following techniques, which produce an understandable solution:

- Concept maps
- Object diagrams
- Event–response lists to determine behaviour

13.2 Statement of problem and concept map

The problem is the same as that described in Section 6.9.1. For convenience, the requirements document is repeated below.

13.2.1 Requirements document for PPD

A computer-based system using object-oriented techniques needs to be built. This system should be responsible for the dispensing of petrol, customer payments and the monitoring of tank levels. The system is based on a self-service regime. There are several pumps in the station and before a pump can be used by a customer it must first be enabled by the station attendant. Enabling a pump entails the motor being started and the pump clutch being freed. If the pump is already started no action takes place in the motor. If the customer presses the trigger in the pump a micro switch is closed, the pump becomes enabled and the clutch is freed. However, when the trigger is released the clutch becomes free. The pump gun is kept in a special holster and this holster has a switch which prevents petrol being pumped until the gun is taken out of the holster. Replacing the gun in the holster has the effect of stopping the delivery. The pump becomes disabled at this stage. The delivery is deemed to be complete and further depressions of the trigger have no effect on petrol delivery. The pump motor is not turned off immediately but there is a short stand-by period in which the motor remains so that a new customer can use the pump without having to start the motor again.

A petrol line connects the pump and a number of tanks and it contains a metering device which sends a pulse to the pump for each 0.01 litres petrol dispensed. The pump display shows how much petrol has been dispensed and its cost.

Transactions concerning the delivery are stored until the customer pays. A receipt may be requested and a token will be given for every 5 money units spent. It is possible that dishonest customers leave without paying and annotation should be made, for example their car registration number.

The monitoring of the system is an important part of this system. A given pump gets its supply from one of a number of tanks. No tank may drop to less than 4% of its full capacity. If a customer is dispensing from a tank that reaches this critical value the delivery will be completed for that customer, the pump will be disabled and a message is sent to the operator's terminal.

13.2.2 Creating concept maps

The above requirements document contains a mass of information and it is a real challenge to create a good concept map. It is not unusual for seven or eight concept maps to be made before a satisfactory final version is arrived at. The better the understanding of the problem the more lucid and elegant the final concept map will be. Furthermore, creating concept maps based on the high-level responsibilities of the system allows us to split the problem into different use cases or areas of concern. In this case we discover two responsibilities, namely:

(13.1)

- Dispensing of petrol
- Customer payments

Each of the concerns in (13.1) corresponds to a key concept at some level of abstraction. Each one can be studied on its own and they can be integrated at a later stage. Once petrol is dispensed the customer transaction or delivery is closed and the paperwork can be started on to produce receipts and records of what took place.

The full concept map environment is shown in Figure 13.1. The key concept 'Delivery' is a description of the pump assembly concept, the tank concept and the interaction concept 'petrol line' which connects them together.

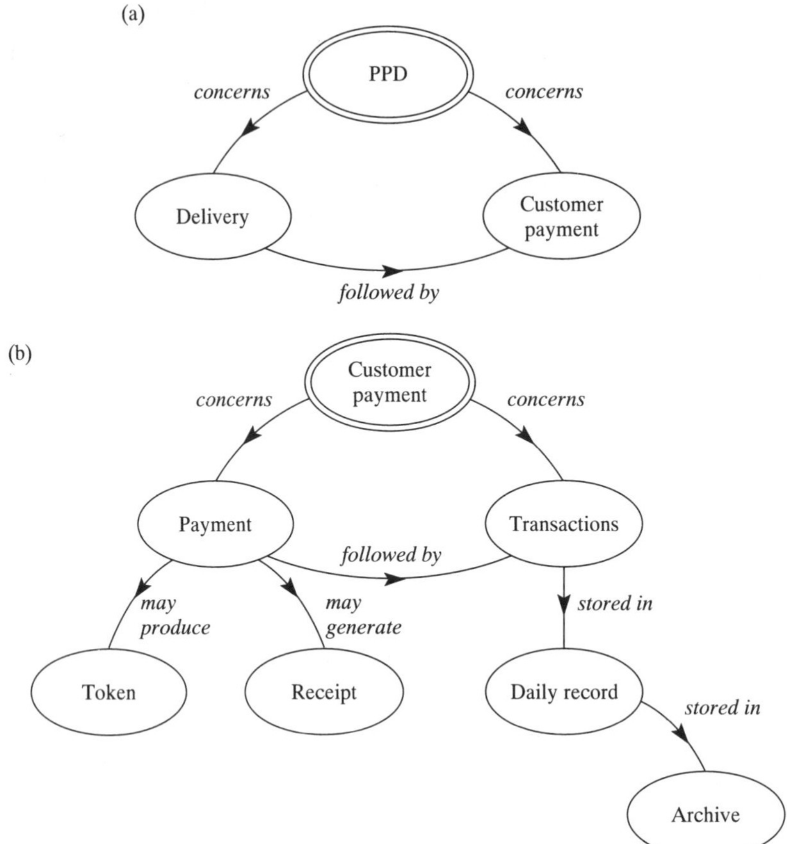

Figure 13.1 Concept maps for the PPD problem.

13.3 Object modelling

This is a relatively easy part of the analysis phase because most of the concepts in Figure 13.1 map directly to object classes. The object diagram for the 'Delivery' concept is shown in Figure 13.2. We model the pump itself as an assembly consisting of all the basic objects which make up the tangible environment in PPD. Most relationships are of the aggregation type here. We have chosen to model the gun–holster assembly as a special aggregation class because it may be useful in later applications, for example if we develop software for pumps with more than one gun in the assembly. The main classes are:

(13.2)

- Pump assembly (high-level client class)
- Pump display
- Pump motor
- Pump clutch
- The pump's gun–holster assembly (composite class)

(c)

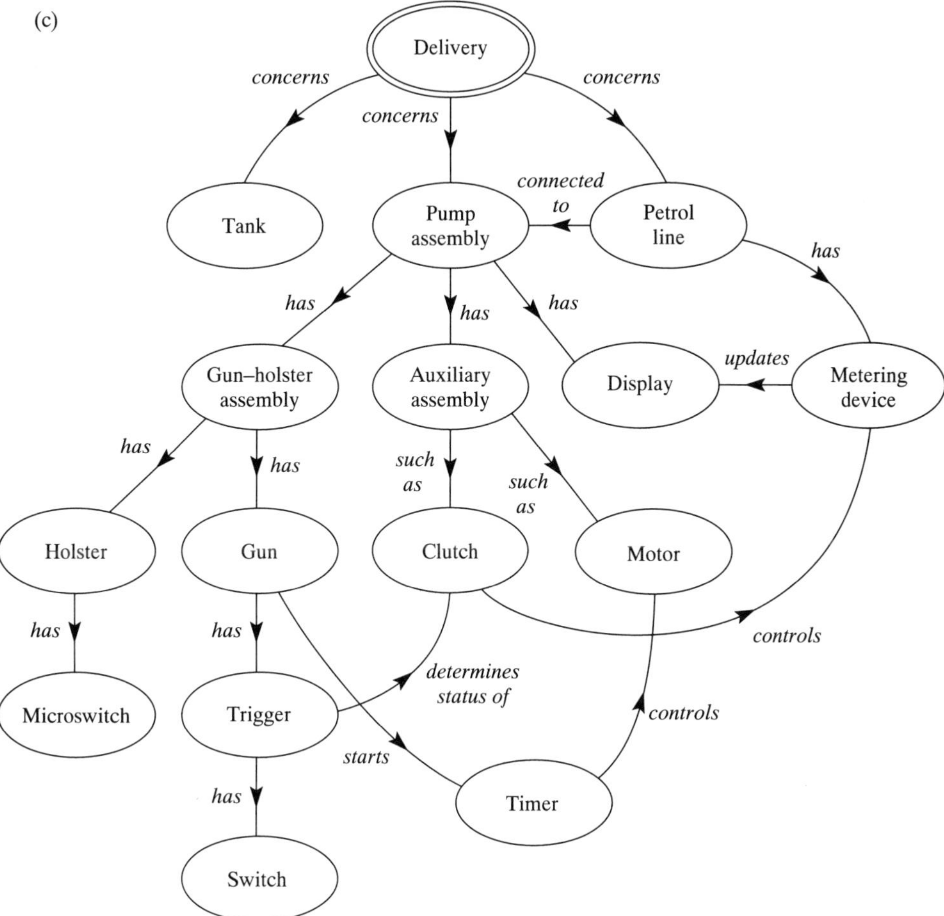

Figure 13.1 *(Continued)*

- The pump timer class, which controls motor status
- The tank class, which contains petrol
- The metering line (an association or interaction object)

The association between pump and tank is many-to-many because any pump can be serviced by a number of tanks (but not simultaneously), while a given tank may dispense petrol to a number of pumps (but not simultaneously).

All of the classes in Figure 13.2 are domain entities (in the Jacobson sense) as they model information about the system which survives for longer periods of time.

The attributes of the classes in Figure 13.2 have not been included for the moment. The behaviour of the classes is much more important at this stage and more attributes will be discovered when we come to dynamic modelling in PPD.

The object diagram corresponding to the concept 'Payment' is shown in Figure 13.3. The classes are:

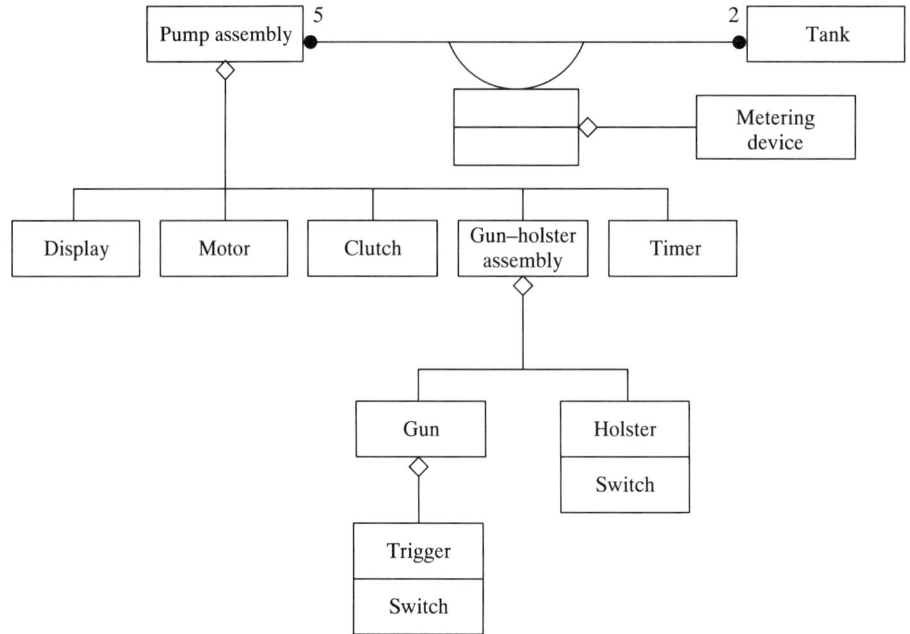

Figure 13.2 Object diagram for the concept 'delivery' in PPD.

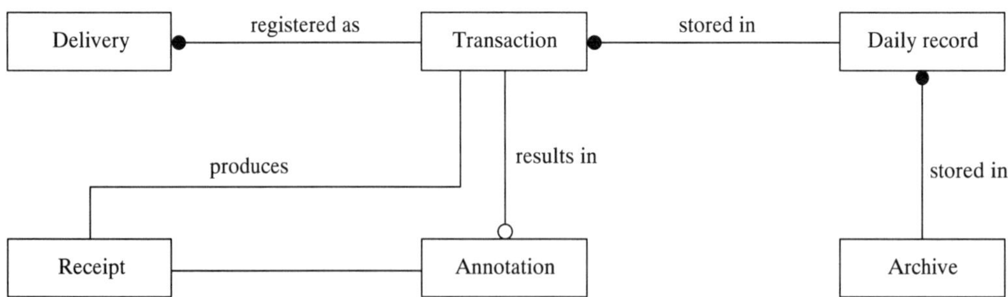

Figure 13.3 Object diagram for the concept 'payment' in PPD.

(13.3)

- The object containing customer transaction information (Delivery)
- Payments, receipts and tokens
- Transactions
- Daily and archive records
- Annotation (in the event that a customer absconds)

Most of the classes in the object diagram are not entity objects (in the Jacobson sense) but are either interface or control objects. The class Delivery is an example of an interface object because it is on the boundary of the system environment of 'Payment'. It plays the role of intermediary between the use case 'Delivery' and the use case 'Payment'. The other classes, such as Payment, Transaction, Annotation, Token and Receipt are control objects since they are neither entity objects nor interface objects. They are more like views of the data which is present in the system in much the same way that views in relational database theory are 'virtual' tables and not 'real' tables. The control objects in PPD contain derivative data.

The classes in Figure 13.3 have very little behaviour. Their attributes are important and they are now listed:

(13.4)

- Delivery: pump#, volume, grade
- Payment: amount of money to be paid by customer
- Transaction: cost, volume, grade, pump#, date, time
- Annotation: car_registration#, remarks
- Receipt: cost, volume, grade, pump#

The behaviour of these control objects is primarily concerned with producing derived attributes which can be used by other client classes.

Some of the candidate classes in (13.4) are either unnecessary or redundant. In fact, we shall show in Section 13.5 that they can be represented as control objects.

13.4 Dynamic modelling

The reason for studying dynamic behaviour in PPD is to find how the state of an object changes over time. The deliverables from this stage will be candidates for the corresponding operations on objects.

13.4.1 Events, responses and constraints

The main events which occur in PPD are now described along with the corresponding responses and constraints. These events correspond to the so-called system operations in the Fusion process (Coleman *et al.* 1994). We see them as visible operations on the pump assembly.

We solve the PPD problem by first considering the 'Delivery' use case and we then discuss the 'Payment' use case. The former case has a strong dynamic behaviour while data transformations are important in the latter case.

The event–response lists for the 'Delivery' use case is given by the following six system operations:

E1: Enable pump // Enables dispensing of petrol
R11: Start pump motor
R12: Free clutch
R13: Clear display counters
C11: Pump not already enabled (do nothing)
C12: Pump is not out of service (do nothing)

E2: Remove gun from holster // Enables gun to pump petrol
R21: Release holster switch

R22: Enable gun

E3: Depress trigger in gun // Start actual delivery of petrol
R31: Close microswitch in trigger
R32: Engage clutch
C31: Pump enabled
C32: Gun enabled

E4: Release trigger in gun // Stop delivery of petrol
R41: Free clutch
R42: Open microswitch in trigger
C31: Pump enabled
C32: Gun enabled

E5: Replace gun in holster // No more petrol can be dispensed
R51: Disable pump
R52: Depress holster switch
R53: Create a delivery object
R54: Send start message to timer object
C51: Pump must be enabled

E6: Disable pump // Pump not in use
R61: Shut down pump motor

From this list we can deduce the following visible operations in the pump assembly abstraction:

(13.5)

```
enable();
disable();
remove_gun();
depress_trigger();
release_trigger();
replace_gun();
```

The C++ class interface for the pump assembly is given as:

```
// pumpass.hxx
//
// Class representing pumps in PPD problem. This is a base
// class for the different types of pump which can arise
// in practice, for example normal pumps and sophisticated.
//
```

```
// This class provides default state and behaviour for
// future pump specializations.
//
// © Datasim BV 1994

#ifndef DS_PUMPASS_HXX
#define DS_PUMPASS_HXX

// The enumerated type represented pump state
enum PumpState {Enabled, Disabled, Out_of_Service};

class DS_PUMPASS
{

private:
  // Attributes
  int pid;            // The pump identification number
  PumpState sta;      // Current state of pump

  // Components which make up the pump assembly
  DS_DISPLAY dis;     // Display
  DS_MOTOR mot;       // Pump motor
  DS_CLUTCH clu;      // The clutch
  DS_GHASS gha;       // Gun-holster assembly

public:
  // Constructors
  DS_PUMPASS(int pump_id);
  DS_PUMPASS(const DS_PUMPASS& pum2);
  virtual ~DS_PUMPASS();

  // Accessing functions
  PumpState state() const;  // Current state of pump

  // Modifier functions
  void enable();            // Enable dispensing of petrol
  void disable();           // Pump unable to dispense
  void remove_gun();        // Enable gun to pump petrol
  void depress_trigger();   // Start delivery of petrol
  void release_trigger();   // Stop delivery of petrol
  void replace_gun();       // Disable gun

  // Operator Overloading
  DS_PUMPASS& operator = (const DS_PUMPASS& pum2);
};
#endif
```

The events in event–response lists have been mapped to member functions in the pump assembly class. The responses to these events are not visible in the class interface but are to be found in the bodies of the member functions. They are given as follows:

```
DS_PUMPASS::DS_PUMPASS(int pump_id)
{ // A pump assembly constructor with a given pump
identification number

  pid = pump_id;
  dis = DS_SDISPLAY();
  mot = DS_MOTOR();
  clu = DS_CLUTCH();
  gha = DS_GHASS();
}

DS_PUMPASS::DS_PUMPASS(const DS_PUMPASS& pum2)
{ // Copy constructor for a pump assembly

  pid = pum2.pid;
  dis = pum2.dis;
  mot = pum2.mot;
  clu = pum2.clu;
  gha = pum2.gha;

}

// Accessing functions
PumpState DS_PUMPASS::state() const
{ // Current state of pump

  return sta;
}

// Modifier functions
void DS_PUMPASS::enable()
{ // Enable dispensing of petrol (event E1)

/*
E1: Enable pump          // Enables dispensing of petrol
R11: Start pump motor
R12: Free clutch
R13: Clear display counters
C11: Pump not already enabled (do nothing)
C12: Pump is not out of service (do nothing)
*/

  // Preconditions
```

```
  if (sta == Out_of_Service || sta == Enabled)
    return;

  // Postconditions
  mot.start();
  clu.free();
  dis.clear();
}

void DS_PUMPASS::disable()
{ // Pump unable to dispense

/*
E6: Disable pump                 // Pump not in use
R61: Shut down pump motor
*/

  mot.shutdown();
}

void DS_PUMPASS::remove_gun()
{ // Enable gun to pump petrol

/*
E2: Remove gun from holster      // Enables gun to pump petrol
R21: Release holster switch
R22: Enable gun
*/

  gha.release_holster_switch();
  gha.enable_gun();
}

void DS_PUMPASS::depress_trigger()
{ // Start delivery of petrol

/*
E3: Depress trigger in gun     // Start actual delivery of
petrol
R31: Close microswitch in trigger
R32: Engage clutch
C31: Pump enabled
C32: Gun enabled
*/

  // Preconditions
  if (sta != Enabled || gha.gun_enabled() == FALSE)
```

```
            return;

      gha.close_microswitch();
      clu.engage();
}

void DS_PUMPASS::release_trigger()
{ // Stop delivery of petrol

/*
E4: Release trigger in gun      // Stop delivery of petrol
R41: Free clutch
R42: Open microswitch in trigger
C31: Pump enabled
C32: Gun enabled
*/

      // Preconditions
      if (sta != Enabled || gha.gun_enabled() == FALSE)
            return;

      clu.free();
      gha.open_microswitch();
}

void DS_PUMPASS::replace_gun()
{ // Disable gun

/*
E5: Replace gun in holster  // No more petrol can be
                            // dispensed
R51: Disable pump
R52: Depress holster switch
R53: Send start message to timer object
C51: Pump must be enabled
*/

      // Preconditions
      if (sta != Enabled)
            return;

      // Postconditions
      disable();
      gha.depress_holster_switch();
      gha.start_timer();
}
```

```
// Operator overloading
DS_PUMPASS DS_PUMPASS::operator = (const DS_PUMPASS& pum2)
{ //
  pid = pum2.pid;
  dis = pum2.dis;
  mot = pum2.mot;
  clu = pum2.clu;
  gha = pum2.gha;

  return *this;

}
```

13.4.2 Exception handling in PPD

Under normal circumstances customers are allowed to dispense petrol. By 'normal', we mean that all components are functioning normally and that there is enough petrol in each of the tanks. However, when a tank reaches the critical level of 4% capacity a message should be sent to the attendant's terminal so that the oil company can be notified to replenish the stock. This situation is a special exception and it is called an 'edge-trigged event' (Rumbaugh *et al.* 1991, p. 103). In some operating systems (such as VAX/VMS) this is called an asynchronous system trap (AST). The software should be able to take care of these exceptional situations.

13.5 Functional modelling

13.5.1 Data flow diagrams

The functional model plays an important role in PPD after a customer has finished a transaction and is ready to pay the bill. Once the customer has replaced the gun in the holster the transaction is deemed to be complete and the delivery information needs to be processed. The delivery contains information about the volume of petrol pumped, its grade and the pump number. The customer is given a receipt after having paid the bill. An example of a receipt is shown in Figure 13.4.

The DCD and top-level DFD for the PPD problem are shown in Figure 13.5. The main source is a Delivery. This is an interface object because it is the output from the use case 'Delivery' and is input for the use case 'Payment'. The sink 'Receipt' is represented as a class but is in fact a view of other data in the system.

We write process descriptions for the processes in the system-level DFD in Figure 13.5. The corresponding OFD is shown in Figure 13.6.

- Process payment

  The purpose of this process is to read delivery data and to produce information on the cost of the transaction.

  Input: grade, volume and pump#

  Output: cost, grade, volume, pump#

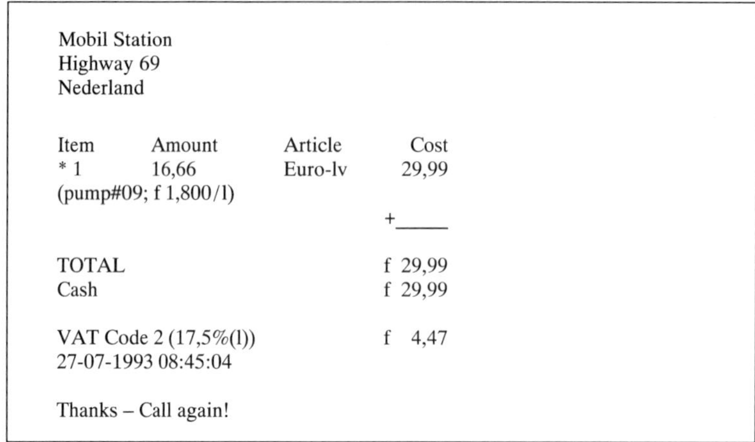

Mobil Station
Highway 69
Nederland

Item	Amount	Article	Cost
* 1	16,66	Euro-lv	29,99
(pump#09; f 1,800/l)			
			+_____

TOTAL	f 29,99
Cash	f 29,99
VAT Code 2 (17,5%(l))	f 4,47

27-07-1993 08:45:04

Thanks – Call again!

Figure 13.4 Receipt issued by a petrol station.

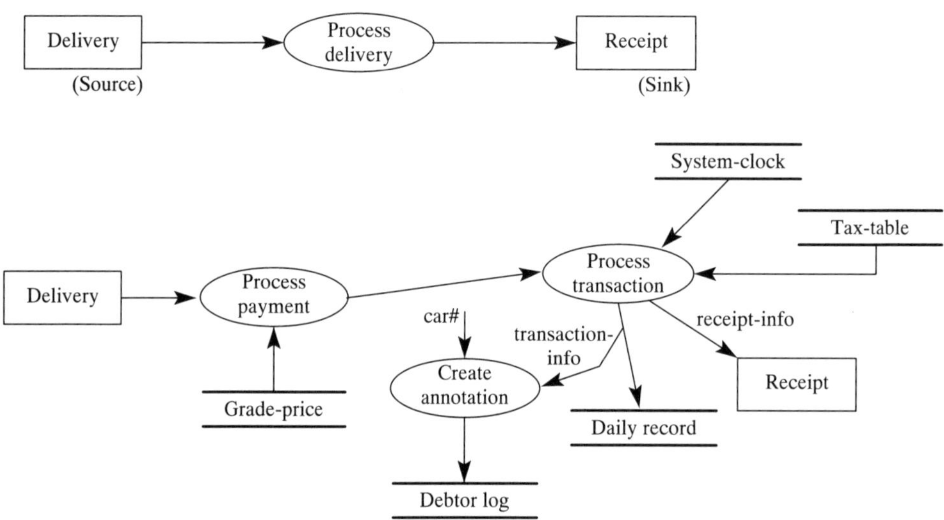

Figure 13.5 DCD and top-level DFD for the PPD problem.

The data store 'grade-price' contains a table for determining the price per litre for each grade of petrol. This table is used together with the volume from the delivery to determine the cost, as follows:

```
cost := price(grade) * volume
```

- Process transaction

  This process produces a receipt and possibly a number of tokens based on the amount spent.

  Input: cost, volume, grade, pump#

  Output: Receipt information, transaction information for daily record log database

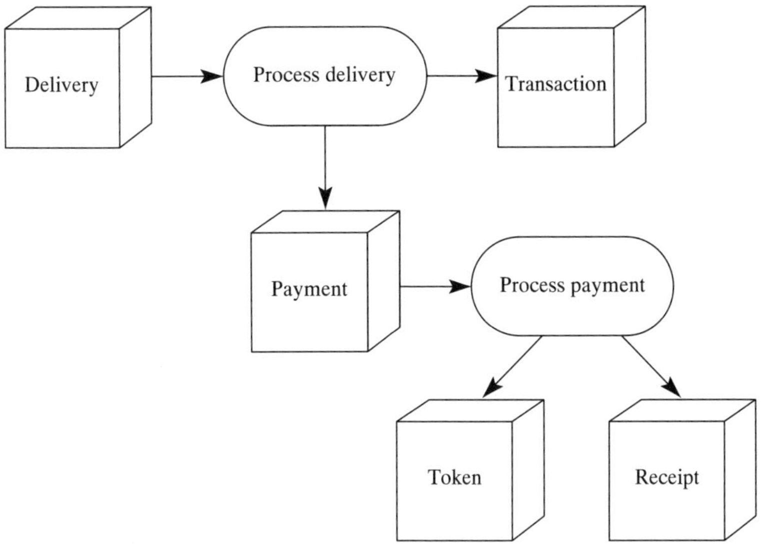

Figure 13.6 Top-level OFD for the payment concept in PPD.

The process description is:

Produce transaction record (TR)

1. Produce receipt

   Read current VAT value from data store 'tax_table'

   Create form as in Figure 13.4

2. Produce daily record

- Create annotation (optional)

  This process merges transaction data with car registration information

  Input: car_reg#, transaction

  Output: An entry in 'debtor_log' data store

The process 'Process transaction' has side effects and it must be decomposed into simpler processes. The problem can be simplified because the processes of making a receipt, daily record and a possible debtor log are three different views of a given transaction object. They are usually implemented as classes. These are control objects in the Jacobson sense, since they are neither entity objects nor interface objects.

13.5.2 Finding operations

The most important class in the 'Payment' use case is concerned with a Transaction. It has the following attributes

- cost
- volume
- grade
- pump#

Class Transaction is a client of class Delivery and it uses a data store in order to determine the price per litre of a particular grade of petrol. The class interface for Transaction in pseudo-C++ is:

```
class Transaction
{

Money cost;
Volume vol;
Integer grade;
Integer pump#;

// Constructor: make a Transaction from a Delivery and a
pricing
// database
Transaction(Delivery d, Price_Db p);

// Producing different views of the transaction
void receipt(TaxTable t);
void daily_record();
void debtor_log(String car_reg#);
};
```

In this case the different views of a transaction are designed as member functions of Transaction. This approach works but it is not the recommended procedure. It is preferable to separate the essential properties of a Transaction from its views by removing the member functions `receipt()`, `daily_record()` and `debtor_log()` from the class interface and implementing them as standalone functions or as classes. This promotes the portability of Transaction. This topic is covered in the general case in Chapter 18.

13.6 Status report

We have succeeded in analysing the PPD problem. In particular, we have found the external behaviour of the pump assembly class by applying event–response lists. Preconditions and postconditions have been determined. The operations obtained in (13.5) are similar to those in Coleman *et al.* (1994), but these results are understandable by both users and designers of the system. Similarly, the problem of producing receipts and transactions has also been solved by 'use cases'.

The products from this phase can now be used as input to system and object design.

13.7 Scalability issues

It is relatively simple to extend PPD. New required functionality corresponds to adding new 'use cases'. These will correspond to concepts which can be analysed using OMT. It may even be possible to reuse classes from previous use cases. For example, it may be necessary to include functionality to monitor the usage of the different pumps in order to ascertain whether there are any customer delays in servicing. The objective of this case is to determine how many new pumps need to be added in order to reduce customer delays. The combination of concept maps, use cases and event–response lists improves the traceability.

A review of the Fusion method is given in Gossain (1994). A number of the points raised there have been solved in this chapter.

Exercises

1. Some really sophisticated pump assemblies are able to handle different grades of petrol. In this case the assembly contains a number of guns from which different grades of petrol can be dispensed. Only one gun can be active at any given time. The new assembly still has one display. Modify the object diagram in Figure 13.2 to reflect this new situation.
2. The 'Receipt' sink in Figure 13.5 is just one view of the results of a transaction. Are there other views which need to be considered in future extensions to the PPD system?
3. Determine the class interface of Tank in PPD. Is this a role object?
4. The petrol line between Pump and Tank is an interaction object. Its contains a metering device which monitors how much petrol has been delivered. Find the attributes and operations of this class.
5. Complete the class interfaces of the minor players (gun, holster, ...) in PPD.

References

D. Coleman *et al.* (1994) *Object-Oriented Development, The Fusion Method*, Prentice-Hall, Englewood Cliffs NJ.

S. Gossain (1994) Object-Oriented Development: The Fusion Method, *Journal of Object-Oriented Programming*, March/April.

J. Rumbaugh, M. Blaha, W. Premerlani, F. Eddy and W. Lorensen (1991) *Object-Oriented Modeling and Design*, Prentice-Hall, Englewood Cliffs NJ.

Part

3

Object-oriented design

Chapter

14

System design

14.1 Introduction and objectives

Once a problem has been analysed it is necessary to decide on how it should be designed. The responsibility of the design phase is to map the products of the analysis phase into constructions which will serve as blueprints for an eventual implementation. The system design stage describes a high-level strategy for solving the problem. The basic architecture of the system is determined in this stage as well as the target hardware and software environments. Object design is the second stage of the design phase and it is concerned with the determination of the full definitions of the classes and associations which will be used in implementation. Furthermore, algorithms which implement operations need to be designed.

This chapter describes the steps that must be carried out during system design.

The approach taken in this chapter is similar to that taken in Rumbaugh *et al.* (1991). However, a number of additions are included here, namely:

- Mapping concepts to potential subsystems
- Integrating exception handling and faults into subsystems
- Criteria for decomposing a systems into smaller modules

The steps in system design are:

- Determining subsystems and partitions
- Choosing functional units to implement subsystems
- Choosing and managing data stores
- Determining system architecture
- Concurrency and control problems
- Making trade-off decisions

14.2 Determining subsystems

Most real-life problems are so complex that it is not possible to solve them as one monolithic system. Some problems may produce as many as a few hundred classes from the analysis phase. For very large problems this number may extend to thousands of classes. The human brain is unable to contain all this information at one given moment. The psychologist Miller (1956) has estimated that humans can hold information on about seven entities simultaneously. An entity can be any type of information, for example object attribute, class name, data flow or event. Miller introduced the idea of a chunk. A chunk may be a high-level or low-level piece of information. Short-term memory cannot retain more than seven chunks of information and the size of a chunk depends on the knowledge that we have in long-term memory. In particular, it is not possible or not even desirable to try to understand a system as one monolithic entity. We decide to split a system into separate subsystems. Subsystems in object-oriented development are groups of related classes and each subsystem is a reasonably self-contained entity having both properties (attributes) and behaviour (operations). Subsystems interact with each other. For example, it is possible for a subsystem to use the services of another subsystem. There is thus a degree of coupling between subsystems. The more coupling there is between a given subsystem and its neighbours the harder it is to design and test the subsystem.

Good system design results in subsystems which have strong internal coupling and weak external coupling with other subsystems.

The OMT method takes a classical approach to system design in the sense that the classes which represent the products of the analysis phase are grouped to form related subsystems. This has its disadvantages, since object diagrams are 'flat' and as such represent all the domain-related entities in a given application. The problem of finding the correct subsystems is made difficult because the analysis phase pays no attention to chunking or clustering related concepts. Some add-ons to OMT have been proposed to allow subsystems to be incorporated into the object model by viewing them as 'superclasses' or ensembles having their own attributes, private and public operations and associations with other subsystems (Gilliam 1994). This is a valid workaround, but the problem should be tackled in the requirements phase. Furthermore, it is not clear how to produce reusable subsystems which can be used in future projects. This book solves such problems because potential subsystems can be discovered at an early stage during the creation of concept maps. The Objectory method (Jacobson *et al.* 1992) does not suffer from this drawback because of its 'use-case' approach; in fact, each use case could be designed as a separate subsystem.

14.2.1 Early determination

The sooner potential subsystems are found the better. The concept mapping technique allows the designer to determine these at an early stage. Good concept maps have a well-defined structure. The key concept will usually correspond to the main system, while the less general concepts will correspond to subsystems. Each less general concept can in turn be analysed as a key concept. This means that it can be decomposed into simpler subsystems and so on. In this way we can split any problem into areas of concern (Jacobson *et al.* 1992). Each concept will then correspond to a potential subsystem. The advantages of this approach are:

- Each potential subsystem can be independently analysed, designed and tested.

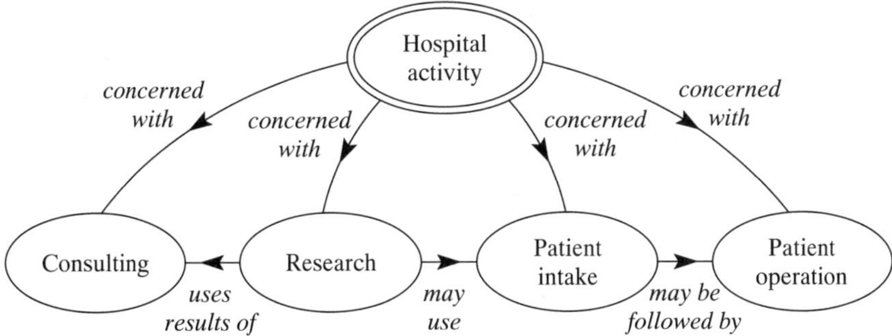

Figure 14.1 Identifying potential subsytems in concept maps.

- The products which result from the analysis and design phases for a given subsystem may be reused in other subsystems if the need arises.
- Interfaces between subsystems can be readily discovered.
- Users understand the scope of potential subsystems.

To take an example, Figure 14.1 shows a concept map representing the activities which take place in a special type of hospital. The key concept is concerned with the high-level activities in the hospital while the level 1 concepts correspond to subactivities within the hospital. The level 1 concepts 'Patient intake' and 'Patient operation' have been expanded as concepts in Chapter 6. Note that all the systems and subsystems in Figure 14.1 have one well-defined responsibility. Furthermore, the different subsystems may be related in some ways.

The subsystems which result from the requirements phase are not the only ones that are used in the design phase. New subsystems which interface with target hardware and software platforms will need to be developed.

It is interesting to note that the Shlaer–Mellor method uses a variation of the above metaphor in which a given system is partitioned in so-called domains in the analysis phase. Domains identify the different aspects of the problem to be analysed and they provide a framework required for managing system size and complexity. Bridges between domains are typically organized as client/server relationships. Examples of domains are:

- Application domains (corresponding to 'canonical' concept maps)
- General service domains (for example, data reporting)
- Architectural domains (the subject matter of design)
- Implementation domains (networks, OS, programming languages)

This is a very clever approach, because each stage of the elaboration process, from analysis through design and implementation, knows about its predecessors, but not the other way around. In this way it is possible to control complexity.

The OMT does not distinguish between such domains; however, the system design phase in OMT takes account of the different architectures which occur in real projects. The Fusion method assumes that abstractions from the problem domain have already been discovered before that we can commence on the object model. For this reason the Fusion method may be unsuitable for beginners because much hand-holding is needed in the early stages rather than a full-blown methodology. Martin and Odell's method does have some provisions for conceptual modelling as a prelude to their OSA (Object Structured Analysis); they treat the different object types that we discussed in Chapter 1 and they pay some attention to the so-called 'realms of interest'. These realms are very similar to domains in the Shlaer–Mellor approach and concepts in the concept mapping technique. It is interesting to note that Martin and Odell give a short mention to concept maps; it is unfortunate that they do not give any examples of how these can be used in conjunction with their method. As far as we know, this book is the first to treat concept maps in any sort of serious way (of course, I acknowledge my source from Umphress in a special article in the *Journal of Object-Oriented Programming* in 1991 which kindled my interest (Umphress and March (1991)).

14.2.2 Late determination

The classical OMT method looks for subsystems once all the classes have been discovered. These classes have no *a priori* relation to one another and a method must be devised to cluster them into groups. This is possible for small-scale problems but the process does not scale very well. This problem has been recognized by a number of authors (Rumbaugh 1994; Gilliam 1994). Most solutions to such shortcomings are solved by using a 'levels of abstraction' or 'uses hierarchies' approach. This is a perfectly valid and tested approach. The major disadvantages, however, are:

- Subsystems do not map very well to groups of classes or concepts which have been found in the analysis phase. This makes reverse engineering and modifications in the design phase more difficult to propagate to object diagrams. We should instead ensure that there is a one-to-one relationship between object diagrams and subsystems.
- Since object diagrams are 'flat' it is difficult to cluster classes to form suitably independent subsystems.
- One of the objectives in object-oriented development is to discover reusable components, in particular reusable subsystems. This is difficult in classical OMT due to the fact that the subsystems have not been discovered at an early stage of the software life-cycle.

14.2.3 Designing subsystems in the face of uncertainty

Software engineers have not been trained to design for change. This is reflected in the fact that most university curricula do not have courses on software engineering or on the design and implementation of reusable software components. Successful software applications need to be modified to suit new needs. Knowing what the possible sources of change are can help in producing software systems which can be quickly adapted to the changing marketplace. It is important to realize that we are not designing a single program but families of programs. These families will have much commonality, but they will also differ in a number of respects, for example:

(14.1)

- They run on different hardware platforms.
- They produce results in different output formats.
- They employ different algorithms depending on the available resources.

A subset of system functionality may be required by less demanding users ('you do not pay for what you do not use').

14.2.4 Problems with extending traditional systems

There is a growing awareness that software should be classified according to the environment in which it is to operate (Giddings 1984). However, many operating systems and software applications have been developed in the last 20 years which are very expensive to change or which cannot be changed without rewriting them. Examples abound in the literature in which seemingly minor changes in functionality have profound effects on the systems. An infamous example is the case of a system which was in use by the US postal department. There was a requirement to extend zip codes from five characters to nine characters. The requirements modification resulted in a multi-million dollar project mainly because the code had a certain fixed length and was distributed in the system. Another example is in the case of operating system versions. Even revisions tend to be reasonably stable while the uneven revisions tend to contain many bugs and errors. The main cause of errors is that small changes in one part of a system have large and unpredictable effects in other places.

There are a number of obstacles which are encountered when extending software systems (Parnas 1979). These are:

(14.2)

- Excessive information distribution
- Data transformation chaining
- Components that perform more than one function
- Loops in the 'uses' hierarchy

Excessive information distribution The US postal example is a good example of how an implementation decision (a zip code is represented as a character string of length five) is advertised and propagated throughout the entire system. In general, a system is difficult to extend if too many programs or software modules assume that a given feature is present or not present.

The software designer should take the sources of uncertainty in (14.1) into account during the system design phase. In this way the designer can anticipate changes in the system and take the necessary action if alterations to the system are needed. The aim should be to design software that is extendible without major surgical changes in the basic architecture.

Data transformation chaining A major problem in software design involves systems which produce output according to a predefined format. Output from one system may be used as input to another system. If the second system is changed so that it needs another input format the first system needs to be modified, or it may have to be completely rewritten.

Components that perform more than one function This is a common situation in software development. There is a tendency to create 'all-singing, all-dancing' programs which perform a number of operations. For example, a common error in C++ is to implement classes which carry out domain-specific activities and which at the same time can write themselves to disk. If we wish to extend the class so that it works with an object-oriented database system we shall probably need to change the source code, relink and test the basic functionality of the class all over again. Furthermore, the task will be impossible if we do not have access to the class's source code. Similarly, systems and subsystems which carry out more than one high-level responsibility can be modified less easily than those systems.

Loops in the 'uses' hierarchy A given subsystem may use the services of another subsystem. However, loops can occur in this uses relationship resulting in a system in which nothing works until everything works. This is a situation which must be avoided at all costs. Management likes to see a prototype or a proof-of-concept of the system that it is sponsoring and it is important for the development team to build the system incrementally so that intermediate results can be demonstrated. In this way management gets the feeling that the project is on course and that money is being well spent.

We now discuss how the problems in (14.2) are avoided by designing subsystems which are built on the following principles:

(14.3)

- Subsystems should carry out one well-defined job.
- It should be possible to use them in different applications.
- They should be based on the levels of abstraction principle.

We should create subsystems for 'virtual' resources, such as hardware, software and application areas.

14.2.5 Creating extendible software

We consider a system as being divided into a set of subsystems with each subsystem having its input and output variables completely defined by an axiomatic specification. Subsystems are built on the 'uses' relationship. We say that a subsystem B uses a subsystem A if correct execution of A is necessary for B to complete the task described in its specification. B is called a client of A because it uses the services of A. A is called a server. The relationship between B and A is called client/server if B is a client of A and A does not use the services of B. The relationship is called peer-to-peer if A is both a client of and server for B and vice versa. Client/server models are easier to design than peer-to-peer models because there is information flow in one direction only. This means that only one set of interfaces needs to be created. The client must be aware of the interface of the server but the server is oblivious of its clients. Changes in the server will demand that clients change also. In the PPD problem we identify two subsystems which partake in a client/server relationship. These are the server subsystem 'Delivery' which registers how much petrol has been dispensed by a customer and the client subsystem 'Payment' which produces the necessary paperwork once petrol delivery has completed.

Peer-to-peer models occur in certain applications, but it is advisable not to use them since they are more difficult than client/server models and it is possible to map them to such models by the 'sandwiching' process (Parnas 1979). Peer-to-peer models introduce unnecessary and complex coupling between systems. Consider the common situation in which system A could benefit from using some of the services in system B while B could also benefit from using A. B is split into two subsystems B1 and B2 such that A is allowed to use B2 while B1 uses A. The resulting layered structure is similar to a sandwich with B (B1 and B2) as the bread and A as the filling. This is shown in Figure 14.2.

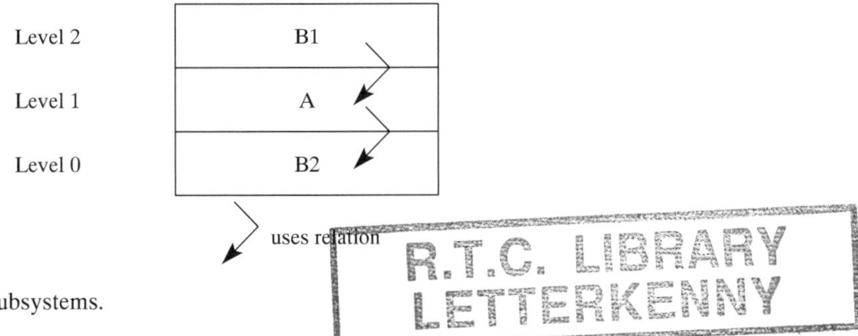

Figure 14.2 Sandwiching in subsystems.

Many applications are built using a layered approach. Figure 14.2 is a simple example in which B1 is a client of A and A is a client of B2. Using a layered approach to system construction ensures that a client/server relationship is maintained. A hierarchy can be constructed in which subsystems at lower levels play the role of server for subsystems at higher levels in the hierarchy.

The rules for developing such hierarchies are:

(14.4)

- Level 0 is the subsystem which uses no other subsystems
- The subsystem at level i (i=1) is the subsystem which use the services of level i–1 and no subsystem at a level higher than i–1

The advantages for software design of the approach in (14.4) are twofold. First, each level offers a usable subset of the system. This means that future projects may be able to use this subset. Secondly, each layer can be tested independently of higher levels. Once a level has been tested it is possible to test the next higher level in the knowledge that all lower levels function according to the specifications.

The concept of using a layered approach is not new and it has been applied in the past to write operating systems. An example is the THE operating system (Dijkstra 1968). This has six layers and consists of the following subsystems:

level 5: user programs

level 4: buffering for input and output devices

level 3: operator-console device driver

level 2: memory management

level 1: CPU scheduling

level 0: hardware

The major difficulty with the layered approach involves defining the layers. Since a layer can only use layers at a lower level, careful planning is needed.

There is a trade-off between creating few layers with more functionality and creating more layers with less functionality. This is an important problem in systems which use object-oriented techniques. Two alternatives are shown in Figure 14.3. The three-layer model produces 'fat' classes which are domain-dependent, while the five-layer model produces flexible subsystems which can be reused in a number of different applications. The System Interface Layer (SIL) in Figure 14.3 provides a consistent interface to a set of fundamental data types

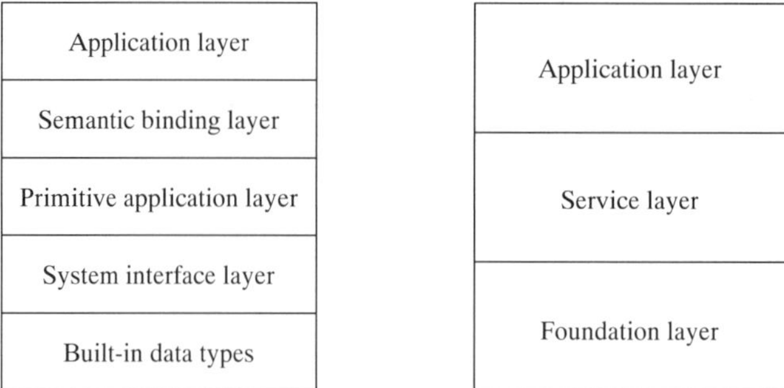

Figure 14.3 Layered systems during object-oriented development.

for use by higher-level classes. The classes in the SIL are constructed using a compiler's built-in data types. The advantage of creating a SIL is that application classes can be isolated or buffered from specific implementation details. Furthermore, porting an application to a new compiler or hardware involves possible changes to SIL but not to classes in the upper levels.

The Object Management Group (OMG) has drawn up a set of standard types which should appear in the SIL. These are:

- 16-bit and 32-bit signed and unsigned integers
- 32-bit and 64-bit IEEE floating point numbers
- ISO Latin-1 characters
- A boolean type taking the values TRUE and FALSE
- 8-bit opaque types which will not undergo any conversions during transfer between systems
- A string type
- Enumerated types consisting of ordered sequences of identifiers

In practice it is usual to implement each of the above types as C++ or Smalltalk classes. For example, string types can be implemented as a user-defined dynamic string class.

The Primitive Application Layer (PAL) uses the services of SIL and it is in this layer that data types are implemented which are used in our applications. Typical classes in this layer are:

- Name, Address
- ComplexNumber, Rational
- Date, Time, TimeStamp, Period, Duration
- Counter, Index
- LinkedList, Set, Bag, Collection
- Point, Circle, Line

The classes in the PAL can be used in different types of applications. They are domain-independent.

The Semantic Binding Layer (SBL) is concerned with assembling classes from PAL to form more interesting application classes. The classes in SBL are domain-dependent but they could be used in different applications within a given domain. This promotes the reusability factor of classes. Typical examples which fit into the SBL are:

- Project, Department
- Pump, MeteringDevice
- Reader, Journal, Issue
- Patient, Nurse
- Option, Asset, PricingModel, AssetModel
- Polyline, FeatureModel
- Insurance policy

The User Application Layer (UAL) is the highest-level layer and this is where an application is assembled from components in SBL. It is in this layer that hard decisions have to be made about the target hardware and software platforms have to be made. However, it is possible to separate the application from the environment in which it is to run by creating so-called 'virtual machines'.

The targets in the application layers are:

- The type of database used to store data (flat files, relational databases, object-oriented databases)
- The type of user interface (character-based, GUI-based)

It is important to construct systems in such a way that they have narrow interfaces with their targets. This is because targets change. For example, many legacy applications use character-based screens as a means of providing user input. If this knowledge is spread throughout applications it may be very difficult to modify the software so that it can work in a modern environment such as Windows NT or Motif. In many cases a complete rewrite of the system is necessary. The most flexible approach is to separate the application from the environment in which it is to function.

14.2.6 Partitions

Subsystems divide a system into horizontal layers. A partition vertically divides a system into a number of independent or weakly coupled subsystems. Each partition provides one kind of service.

14.2.7 Open and closed architectures

Subsystems which are constructed using a client/server model can be designed in a number of ways. The layered architecture comes in two forms, namely closed and open. In a closed architecture, a subsystem at a given level may only use the services of its immediate lower level neighbour. In an open architecture, a subsystem at a given level may use the services of any lower level in the 'uses' hierarchy. There are trade-offs to be considered for each choice. The main ones are:

Closed architecture

- Results in portable and reusable subsystems

- Dependencies between layers are reduced
- Changes in level i impact the classes at level i+1
- Performance could be affected by message passing between layers
- Conforms to the information hiding principle

Open architecture

- Results in non-portable code
- Dependencies between layers are increased
- Less planning design needed than with closed architecture solutions
- Performs well due to limited message passing between layers
- Violates the information hiding principle

14.2.8 Subsystems and exception handling

Under normal conditions subsystems perform their tasks as expected. However, unforeseen events may occur which will cause a subsystem to malfunction or to function in such a way that it compromises the integrity of the application. We say that an exceptional or error situation arises. Subsystems should be constructed in such a way that they can recognize and handle such errors.

Exceptions can arise for a number of reasons. Hardware can break down, resources can become exhausted or users may enter invalid data. Exceptional cases can be included in the design if we view them as just another client/server relationships. There is a contract between clients and servers. Each party involved must fulfil its part of the bargain. A client subsystem requests services from a server subsystem. We speak of a contract between client and server. A common problem in many applications is that a client does not always know when its requests violate the contract. However, it does know what to do once an exception has been raised. The server knows when exceptions occur but it does not know what to do with them. How exception handling is implemented is language- and compiler-dependent, but both Ada and C++ share the same ideas on implementing the concept. Using exception handling in the development of subsystems promotes the robustness of code as it allows systems to continue operating even under abnormal conditions.

The basic philosophy behind exceptions in C++ is simple to understand. We restrict the following description to the case of two C++ classes, one of which is the client of the other. (The same conclusions hold for subsystems if they are considered as being aggregate classes with their own behaviour.) By client we mean that a member function in the client class C uses a member function in a server class S. S should ensure that all its member functions (if need be) check for exceptions. If no error condition is discovered normal processing continues and the server member function returns control to the calling function. If however, an error is discovered a corresponding exception is raised which is then 'thrown' back to the client. The client member function should ensure that it has a 'net' which is able to catch the thrown exception so that it can take remedial action, for example throwing the exception to a higher level client function.

Finding the exception is part of system design and it should be included here and not as an afterthought in the implementation phase. Exceptions should be placed at subsystem boundaries because it is there that things go wrong. In the subsystem itself there should be

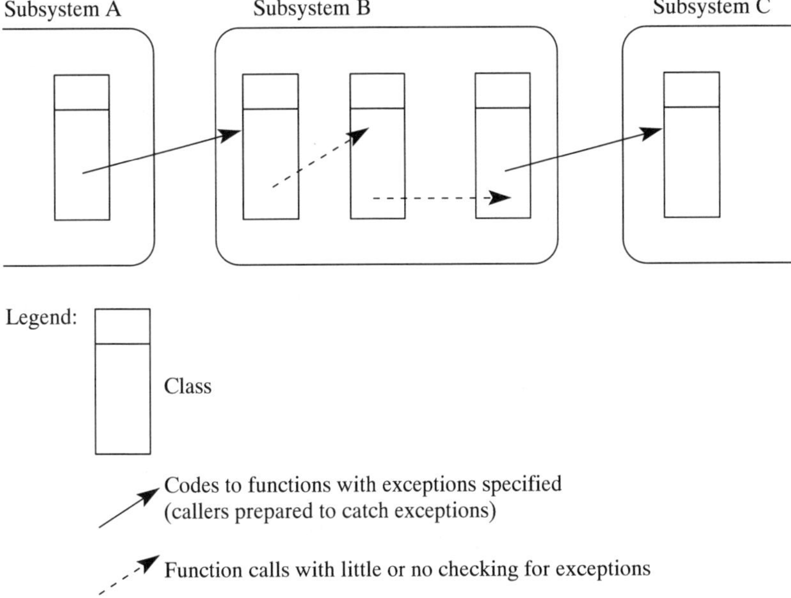

Figure 14.4 Exceptions of subsystem boundaries.

little or no exception handling because the classes making up the subsystem are 'trusted' and hence checking is not necessary (see Figure 14.4).

Firesmith (1993) suggests documenting exceptions as part of the class interface. He uses so-called exceptions abstractions to model error conditions and error handling.

The steps in documenting exceptions for classes and objects are:

(14.5)

1. The exception identifier (its data type)
2. The classification of the exception in terms of:

   Essential versus non-essential

   Class versus object exception

3. The behaviour of the exception:

   Preconditions required to raise the exception

   The exception handling to be performed

   Postconditions ensured by the exception handling

   Invariants which are ensured by the exception handling

   The propagation chains of the exception

   The location of the exception handler

4. Timing criteria, including deadlines and frequency

5. System requirements allocated to the exception, including validating criteria and methods
6. Any analysis and design trade-offs which are made regarding the exception

An essential exception is one which is typically known and understood by the customer or application domain specialist and which is identified during requirements analysis. It is documented either as a required capability or as a design constraint. An example of an essential exception in the PPD problem is when the tank reaches a critical 4% capacity level. In that case the connecting flow line should be disabled and no more petrol dispensed to customers.

A non-essential exception is one which appears in the design or implementation phase and is not visible to the customer. An example of a non-essential exception is when there is not enough memory in the computer to carry out a certain task.

An object exception is one which corresponds to one particular object. A class exception is like a global object and it corresponds to a group of objects in a class. For example, a class exception is raised if we attempt to create a new object when the allowed maximum number of instances has been exceeded.

Objects (including exceptions) may have invariants. An invariant is a condition that must always hold for an object or class. If an invariant is not met the associated exception is raised and further use of the object is erroneous. Examples are:

- A bounded stack becomes full.
- The pressure in a pipeline must not exceed 80 bar.
- The bank account must not have a negative balance.

C++ allows the programmer to create classes implementing error conditions which can implement the conditions in (14.5).

The products from the steps in (14.5) should be placed in the data dictionary for the appropriate class or object.

14.2.9 Example: subsystems for MPC

As an example of finding subsystems the Manpower Control system (MPC) is examined again. The system can be layered into the following subsystems:

- Level 3: Query environment (application layer)
- Level 2: Repository subsystem
- Level 1: Registration and control
- Level 0: Project initialization

This is an example of a closed architecture, since each layer uses only the services of the layer immediately below it. Thus the system satisfies a client/server relationship. We describe each of these subsystems in more detail.

Project initialization subsystem This is the subsystem which is responsible for creating new projects (both internal and external), assigning cost centres for projects and seconding employees to work for departments on projects.

This subsystem is executed only when new projects are developed or when project schedules are modified.

Registration and control subsystem This subsystem is executed once per period when new used resource data is copied from the mainframe. The used resources per employee are registered in the system. Invalid data is checked and written to a log file. Valid data is aggregated for the current period as is the cumulative total until the present period on a departmental basis.

This subsystem also checks with level 0 whether the used resources do not exceed the total budgeted for each project.

Repository subsystem This is similar to the Semantic Binding Layer and it contains periodic and cumulative data for division and project-level data. This layer uses department-based data in order to calculate the used resources.

Query subsystem This is the User Application Layer (UAL) and it provides a framework for senior project planners to view the progress of projects and to produce graphs in the form of histograms, line charts and pie charts. Since the 'essential' application objects are in the Repository subsystem the Query subsystem can be tailored to many different GUIs and database environments due to the fact that the application objects (namely used and scheduled resources) are separate from their representations.

Essential exceptions are few in MPC. The most important event which must take place in MPC is the end-of-period transfer of project data. Usually this occurs as an automatic batch job just before a new period begins. If this does not happen an exception must be raised in the Registration and control subsystem. A possible consequence of this exception occurring is that the MPC will not start up, and system management must be called in to solve the problem, possibly even manually copying the project data to the workstation on which MPC runs.

14.2.10 General criteria for choosing subsystems

Subsystems interact with each other via their interfaces. Each subsystem should have a well-defined interface. Constructing good interfaces is very important in the design phase. It is estimated that 73% of the effort in integration tests for the Apollo space project was due to interface problems, while verification accounted for 50% of the total software development effort. There is thus a need to create stable interfaces which can stand up to changes in requirements. In order to achieve this end the concept of a virtual layer is introduced. A virtual layer is a system in which the output and input variables are completely defined by an axiomatic specification of any given system structure. This specification is equivalent to the services which the system delivers. Changes in the internal representation of the system have no effect on client subsystems. The information hiding principle is thus adhered to. Virtual layers are implemented in languages such as Smalltalk by an application of the so-called model view controller (MVC) paradigm and is concerned mainly with the separation of the essential or non-volatile and volatile parts of an application from each other.

The general criteria which subsystems should satisfy are (Parnas 1972; Parnas *et al.* 1983):

- System software requirements should be unambiguously defined as a black box requirements document before design begins.
- The system should be divided into subsystems using information hiding before writing software begins.
- Each subsystem should have a precise, black box, formal specification.

- Formal methods should be used to give precise documentation.

The concept of virtual layers can be applied to the MPC problem, for example. In this case the essentials of the application consist in ensuring that data for used and scheduled resources per organizational unit (department, division) is accessible at all times. This data has interfaces to the following subsystems:

- The storage area (RDBMS, ODBMS, flat files)
- The type of representation (bar charts, line graphs, textual)

Each of these subsystems represents a view of the data. We should design the problem so that if the storage scheme is changed (for example) the application code does not have to be changed. In practice this is achieved by making sure that 'application' classes have no functionality for reading or writing to permanent storage.

14.3 Mapping subsystems to functional units

Once the subsystems have been found the next step is to allocate each subsystem to a so-called functional unit. A functional unit may be hardware, software or general-purpose processor. Many mainframe applications run on a single functional unit (the mainframe itself), as is the case with many PC applications. Applications in which information is distributed among different locations will be implemented by several functional units. For example, client/server applications use one machine for storing information (the server) while other machines contain subsystems which access this information (the clients). Each client may play a special role in the system.

14.3.1 Mapping the functional units

The steps to be taken in this stage of the design are:

- Estimate performance needs.
- Determine which functional units implement each subsystem.
- Determine the physical connectivity of the resulting functional units.

Choosing a functional unit depends on the application. Some computer graphics programs implement three-dimensional geometrical transformation algorithms in hardware in order to improve performance. Other applications produce a data cache on a local workstation, thus obviating the need to access data on slower permanent storage.

Some applications have stringent performance needs. Such applications may need to access and update critical resources and it is important to choose functional units which solve the given performance constraints. The units should be highly reliable, having a low mean time between failure (MTBF). In some cases it is desirable to create a 'secondary' master unit which is a mirror image of the 'primary' master unit and which can take over the duties of the latter in the event of malfunction. This introduces a certain amount of redundancy into the system, but the main advantage is that resources are always available. Using primary and secondary master units is particularly important in distributed applications. For example, a primary unit could be a database containing host names and their corresponding IP (Internet) addresses in a UNIX network environment. This database is usually situated on a workstation (the so-called primary name server – see Comer (1988)) and other hosts in the network can access the database on this special workstation in order to resolve the IP address of other hosts in the network. If the primary name server crashes this means that hosts cannot communicate with other hosts in the network. This is an unacceptable situation, and for this reason it is necessary to create one or more so-called secondary name servers which contain the same database information as the primary server and which can be queried by client hosts in the event of a crash. This is an example of data redundancy, since definitive database information is distributed among a number of processors.

Functional units may be loosely coupled or tightly coupled. Distributed applications employ one or more loosely coupled units with each unit serving one particular purpose. The units can communicate in a number of ways. The possibilities are:

- Data transfer
- Message passing
- Remote procedure calls (RPCs – Stevens (1990))

Some functional units produce data which is needed by other units. If both units reside on the same processor or if they can both access the data there is no need to transfer the data. In that case the local disk can be queried. In networked environments it is also possible to configure workstations in such a way that applications running on different hosts can access a given disk. This is achieved by Sun Microsystems' Network File System (NFS), which supports file access across a network.

When it is not possible to access data directly it may be necessary to adopt the strategy of copying data from one unit to another one. A popular way of doing this in networked environments is via FTP (File Transfer Protocol) which is a standard for TCP/IP or by its OSI equivalent FTAM (File Transfer, Access and Management).

Performance problems can be encountered when accessing disks across a network or transferring data from one host to another because of network traffic caused by other applications. The network bandwidth is limited to a certain volume of traffic that it can handle, and careful consideration must be given in the design phase to ensure that performance degradation does not occur. It may be necessary to have a dedicated network line installed between the two units which communicate via file transfer mechanisms.

One of the ways in which functional units communicate is via message passing. In particular, it is possible for a process on a local host in a network to invoke a procedure on a remote host. This is the basis of remote procedure calling, or RPC for short. The local host plays the role of client and it calls the remote procedure by a message request. The remote procedure sends a so-called response back to the client.

14.3.2 Example: functional units for MPC

Most of the processing in MPC occurs on one host, usually on a UNIX or VAX/VMS workstation. The used resources are registered and maintained on a mainframe and the project data is copied from the mainframe to the workstation at the end of each period via a file transfer protocol, such as FTAM. Performance is not a major issue since the data can be transferred during non-peak hours. Furthermore, the workstation is powerful enough to execute each subsystem. Finally, the MIS manager can query the MPC database and produce status reports in the form of line charts, histograms and standard reports.

14.4 Choosing and managing data stores

A data store is a passive entity which stores data. Subsystems communicate via interfaces which can be implemented in a number of ways, for example by files, relational database systems (RDBMS) or object-oriented database systems (ODBMS). ODBMSs have the advantage that they support the most important features inherent in the object-oriented paradigm, such as aggregation, inheritance and encapsulation. There is no 'impedance mismatch' between objects and their database representations. An object can be stored on disk without having to know its internal state and it can be retrieved from disk in a likewise transparent fashion. ODBMSs model objects in a natural way and their use is to be advised. However, some subsystems must interface with other subsystems which were written using non-object-oriented languages and database systems. Such subsystems do not understand objects. Their interfaces are usually implemented as flat ASCII files or RDBMS tables.

RDBMSs are widely used and accepted and have been successfully used in solving a range of problems for administrative applications. They are particularly useful for solving problems where the objects have a relatively simple structure and where transactions are short-lived, but they are unsuitable for problems where complex objects need to be created and manipulated. In these cases ODBMSs are better suited and they are beginning to find their way into the following areas:

- Computer-aided design (CAD)
- Financial planning systems, for example risk management
- Office information systems (OIS)
- Computer-aided software engineering (CASE) applications
- Multimedia applications

A number of commercial ODBMSs are available and these are slowly finding their way into mission-critical applications. They should be considered as a serious alternative to RDBMSs, especially if complex data needs to be modelled or if the application is new.

However, it is unwise to neglect RDBMSs, since the user base for applications using relational database technology is so huge.

14.4.1 Example: data stores in MPC

MPC gets its periodic used resource data from the central mainframe database system. The data is copied to the workstation as an ASCII file in CSV (comma-separated variable) format. This is the only data store which should really concern us at this stage. The file consists of records, with each record containing the following information:

```
emp#, proj#, dept#, used_hours, period#
```

It is the responsibility of the Registration and control subsystem in MPC to read the contents of the file and convert the data into the MPC internal data structures. These latter data structures may be C++ objects (transient or persistent) or even relational tables.

14.5 Determining system architecture

There are a number of prototypical architectural frameworks under which most real-life problems fall. Realizing that we are involved with an instance of one of these frameworks may help us in finding reusable components which were developed in previous projects in order to apply them to new situations.

The kinds of systems are:

(14.6)

- Transaction manager
- Batch transformation
- Real-time simulation
- Dynamic simulation
- Interactive interface
- Continuous transformation

A transaction manager is a database system whose main function is to store and access information. It should be able to handle multiple users and concurrency. The Journal Registration Problem (JRP) is an example of such a system. In this case the users are typically readers who access the database, which contains information about the journals and articles in which the readers are interested. Readers may also send requests to the personnel department for copies of articles. Other transactions occur in JRP when new journals and issues arrive for processing or when circulation lists need to be made.

The object model is very important in a transaction manager system. Very little data transformation takes place and hence the functional model will play a relatively minor role. The dynamic model is very important, since transaction managers are inherently distributed.

Batch transformations differentiate themselves by the fact that they do not interact with the outside world. Input to a batch system is transformed to output and this output may itself serve as input to some other process in the system. Batch transformations are a common occurrence in compiler construction, payroll programs and finite element methods (FEM). A typical finite element program reads a file containing the geometrical specifications of two- and three-dimensional objects and calculates properties associated with those objects (such as the strength, heat and fluid flow around or in those objects). The dynamic model is trivial or even non-existent for such problems, whereas the functional model is very important, since it specifies how input is transformed to output. The object model may be important, especially in situations in which complex data structures need to be modelled.

An interactive interface is a system in which interactions between the system and external agents (for example, humans) play an important role. Such an interface may be part of an application. For example, JRP would need to have an interface so that readers can enter data and requests. This interface could be a character-based system or Windows system with keyboard and mouse input.

The dynamic model is very important in an interaction interface. Events, caused by user input, cause responses in the form of code activation or menus being popped up on the screen. The objects in the object model are represented by interaction devices such as scroll bars, buttons, control boxes and pop-up menus. There are numerous commercial packages on the market which implement all these interaction objects as C++ classes. The role of the functional model in an interactive interface is to map user requests into application functions which are then executed.

A real-time system is one which is dominated by time constraints on actions. The dynamic model is of paramount importance, while the object and functional models may or may not be important.

A dynamic simulation system models objects in the real world. Simulations are easy to model since the objects can be based on the tangible objects from the problem domain. Furthermore, the operations may also be deduced from the problem domain. The object model is often complex. The dynamic model is important, while the functional model may also be important. A good example of a dynamic simulation is PPD. The object model is represented by classes for a pump assembly, tank and metering line. The dynamic model describes customer interactions with the system, while the functional model describes processes which take place once a customer has completed a delivery transaction and a receipt needs to be made.

A continuous transformation is a system in which outputs actively depends on changing inputs and must be periodically updated. Whereas batch transformations use a static pipeline (the output is computed only once) continuous transformations operate on an active pipeline in which both input and output are being continuously updated. Part of the PPD problem is a continuous transformation system. This is the case of the pump display which is continuously updated as petrol is pumped. Another example is in financial markets in which stock data, continuously updated as real-time data feeding from organizations such as Reuters, is used in order to compute new share prices.

The object and functional models are important in continuous transformations, while the dynamic model is less important, since most of the interactions in the system are due to the steady flow of data between the different processes and not due to interaction with external agents.

14.5.1 Example: system architecture of MPC

The system architecture for MPC is one of batch transformation type. Input to the subsystem is transformed to output which in its turn is input for a subsystem further down the pipeline. The fact that this is a batch problem can be deduced from the functional modelling phase for MPC.

The user front-end to MPC is an interactive interface written using X11 or Motif.

Exercises

1. The hospital database problem which was analysed using concept mapping techniques delivered the following concepts: patient, private room, ward, nurse, doctor, surgeon, operating theatre, operation. Which of these concepts can be 'reused' in analysing the different level 1 concepts in Figure 14.1?

2. In a flight reservation system the most important use cases are:

   - Check Schedule
   - Acknowledge Flight
   - Confirm Booking

   Discuss how these cases can be mapped to potential subsystems.

3. The main concepts in PPD are 'Delivery' and 'Payments'. These are the potential subsystems. Find the client and server subsystems and the interfaces between them.

4. How far do the subsystems in Figure 14.1 carry out single and well-defined tasks? In which other application areas besides a hospital environment could they be used?

5. Create a simple levels of abstraction hierarchy for the problem of creating portable numeric classes. The following classes should be included:

   - Natural numbers (0, 1, 2, ...)
   - Integers (0, 1, –1, 2, –2, ...)
   - Rational numbers (quotients of two integers)
   - Complex and imaginary numbers

6. Propose closed and open architecture solutions for the classes in Exercise 5. What are the advantages and disadvantages of each solution?

7. Consider the subsystem in an operating system environment which is responsible for printing of files. Identify the exceptions.

8. Find the exceptions which can arise in the class Array which represents an indexed array of objects with elements in the data type T.

9. Identify the essential and non-essential exceptions in the water level monitoring system (WLMS) which was given as an exercise in Chapter 7.

10. Discuss the trade-offs involved when designing the following problems by the use of relational or object-oriented database systems: salary management, reservoir engineering, MPC problem, JRP problem, stock exchange simulations, CAD/CAM applications, computer network control.

References

D. Comer (1988) *Internetworking with TCP/IP: Principles, Protocols and Architecture*, Prentice-Hall, Englewood Cliffs NJ.

E. Dijkstra (1968) The structure of the "THE"-multiprogramming system, *Communications of the ACM*, **11** 341–6.

D. G. Firesmith (1993) *Object-Oriented Requirements Analysis and Logical Design*, John Wiley & Sons, Chichester.

R. V. Giddings (1984) Accommodating uncertainty in software design, *Communications of the ACM*, **27**(5) May.

C. Gilliam (1994) An approach for using OMT in the development of large systems, *Journal of Object-Oriented Programming*, February.

I. Jacobson *et al.* (1992) *Object-Oriented Software Engineering*, Addison-Wesley, Wokingham.

G. Miller (1956) The magical number seven, plus or minus two: some limits on our capacity for processing information, *Psychological Reviews*, **63** 81–97.

D. Parnas (1972) On the criteria to be used in decomposing systems into modules, *Communications of the ACM*, **15**(12) December.

D. Parnas (1979) Designing software for ease of extension and contraction, *IEEE Transactions on Software Engineering*, **SE-5**(2) March.

D. L. Parnas *et al.* (1983) Enhancing reusability with information hiding, in *Software Reusability*, Vol. I (ed. T. J. Biggetstaff), Addison-Wesley, Reading MA.

J. Rumbaugh, M. Blaha, W. Premerlani, F. Eddy and W. Lorensen (1991) *Object-Oriented Modeling and Design*, Prentice-Hall, Englewood Cliffs NJ.

J. Rumbaugh (1994) Virtual worlds: modeling at different levels of abstraction, *Journal of Object-Oriented Programming*, January.

W. R. Stevens (1990) *UNIX Network Programming*, Prentice-Hall, Englewood Cliffs NJ.

D. A. Umphress and S. G. March (1991) Object-Oriented Requirements Analysis, *Journal of Object-Oriented Programming*, Focus on Analysis and Design, pp. 35–40.

R. Wirfs-Brock, B. Wilkerson and L. Wiener (1990) *Designing Object-Oriented Software*, Prentice-Hall, Englewood Cliffs NJ.

Chapter

15

Object design

15.1 Introduction and objectives

The products from the analysis phase of the software life-cycle are a list of classes, their attributes and the associations between them. It is the responsibility of the object design phase to determine the full definitions of these classes and associations. Object design follows from object-oriented analysis, in which a process of elaboration is carried out. In particular, decisions need to be made regarding how operations are to be implemented by algorithms. Attributes are mapped to specific data types. Furthermore, new classes which do not appear in the object model will appear during design. These are the so-called software or internal classes and they play the role of glue between the application and external objects. Internal classes are also needed during optimization in the object design phase. It is likely that these internal classes can be used in many applications.

Object design can be either high-level or low-level. In high-level design we design object classes which are independent of any programming language, such as Smalltalk, C++ or SQL. The advantage of this approach is that several implementations of a given design can be produced. Low-level design assumes that object classes are implemented in some specific language. Since the focus of this book is on C++ applications we shall apply low-level design techniques in this chapter.

Chapter 16 shows how object classes are mapped to relational database tables. This is a special form of low-level design in which the products of the design (namely tables) no longer support the object-oriented paradigm. It is possible to simulate inheritance, associations and classes in this case, but at a cost which is almost unacceptable for the developer of the system.

We adhere to the OMT approach of object design. A number of additions have been included, in particular the inclusion of generic classes (for example, C++ templates), roles and responsibility-driven approaches to class design into the design process.

The steps to be carried out during the object design stage are:

(15.1)

- Expanding the object model to obtain operations on classes

- Choosing and designing algorithms to implement operations
- Using internal and generic classes with application classes
- Rules for designing associations
- Mapping object attributes to specific data types
- Designing role classes
- Refining class hierarchies and discovering polymorphic behaviour
- Optimizing access paths to data
- Discovering reusable components for future applications

15.2 Expanding the object model

The object model is the main edifice around which the design is constructed. The products of the analysis phase serve as input here. In particular, the functional and dynamic models provide the operations, the functional model via processes and the dynamic model via actions and activities. Thus, the first step in object design is to ensure that all operations have been gathered for each class in the system.

15.2.1 Transitions and operations

Some guidelines on finding the operations in the object model are now given. Operations are found from:

- A transition in the state of an object
- An event sent by an object is an operation on another object

In the case of the simple digital watch (SDW) the transition which causes the mode to change from set mode to display mode is represented as an operation. There are other transitions and some are now given in C++ code:

```
void Display();        // Go into display mode
void Hour();           // Go into set hour mode
void Minute();         // Go into set minutes mode
```

Other important transitions in SDW are when the A and B buttons are pressed. They are represented by the following operations:

```
void A();              // Press A button
void B();              // Press B button
```

Thus, knowing what the transitions are for a given problem helps to determine the corresponding operations for each class.

Another way to determine operations is to examine the event–response lists. An event causes a transition and the transition is an operation on some object class. The responses, however, represent operations in other server classes. For example, the event which causes a pump in PPD to be enabled has responses which result in the motor being started, the clutch being freed and the display counters being initialized. We have thus discovered three operation in three classes. The fully qualified names are:

```
Motor::start();        // Start the motor
```

```
Clutch::free();        // Free the clutch
Display::clear();      // Initialize the registers on display
```

15.2.2 Data flow diagrams and operations

An event (action) or activity from the dynamic model may be expanded into an entire DFD. It is interesting to note that this is also the approach taken by Shlaer and Mellor (1988) in which each state of an STD expands into an entire DFD. The expanded processes in the DFD represent the body of operations. Data flows in the DFD represent intermediate values used in operations. The client/server model is of relevance here and each process will be mapped to an operation on a given target class which is the server, and a number of classes will take part specifying the operation, usually as return type or as arguments in the arguments list of the operation. To show how this process works, we consider the case of JRP again. The event in which a new issue of a journal is registered causes a number of responses to take place:

(15.2)

- Add the issue to the issue database.
- Register the articles comprising the issue.
- Find the topics in each article.
- Create circulation lists for special readers.
- Create attention lists of interesting articles for all readers.

The DFD which results from this major event is shown in Figure 15.1. We determine the operations and classes for this case. This is a major source of behaviour. The major classes are:

- Issue
- Reader
- Article
- Topic
- Circulation list (an interaction object)
- Attention list (an interaction list)

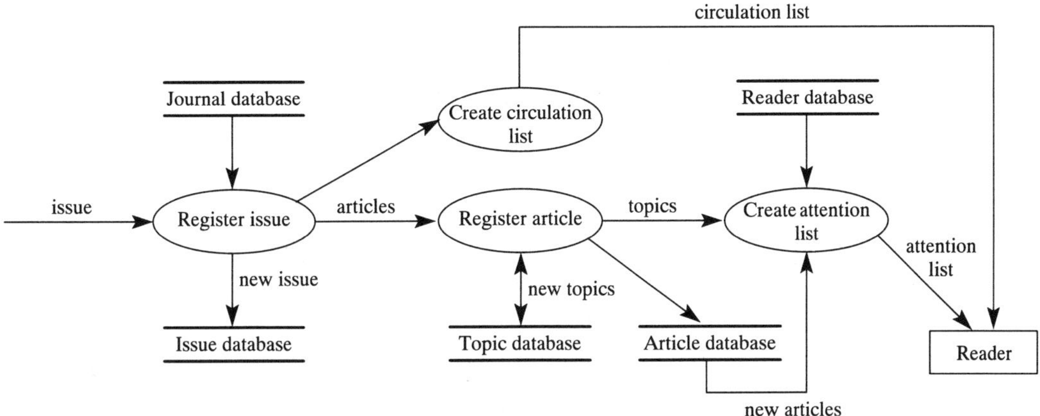

Figure 15.1 DFD resulting from the event 'register issue' in JRP.

For the purposes of this discussion we assume that each data store is implemented as a set in which duplicate entries are not allowed. It is possible to add and remove objects from a set as well as merging sets and finding the intersection of two sets. As will be shown, each of these classes can be implemented as specializations of a generic set class; this is done in C++ as follows:

```
typedef Set<Journal>     JournalDB;
typedef Set<Issue>       IssueDB;
typedef Set<Topic>       TopicsDB;
typedef Set<Article>     ArticleDB
typedef Set<Reader>      ReaderDB;
```

Furthermore, we need to create sets of objects whose contents can vary in JRP; in particular, the following classes are used:

```
typedef Set<Reader>      ReaderSet;
typedef Set<Topic>       TopicSet;
typedef Set<Article>     ArticleSet;
```

It is interesting to note that two new classes are discovered during the functional modelling phase; they are classes which represent circulation lists and attention lists. Jacobson calls these control classes since they are neither entity classes (they do not appear in concept maps) nor interface classes (they do not connect JRP with the outside world). OMT calls them internal classes, although this definition is too general. Control classes are usually specific to an application, while internal classes can be used in many applications. Internal classes will be discussed in Section 15.4.

The control classes in this part of JRP are conveniently called `CirculationList` and `AttentionList`. They represent views of the system. In legacy systems they would have been designed as intermediate work tables. The server classes (or collaborators as they are sometimes called (Wirfs-Brock *et al.* 1990; Coleman *et al.* 1994)) for `CirculationList` are `ReaderSet`, a `Duration` and an instance of `Issue`.

The object diagrams for `CirculationList` and `AttentionList` are given in Figure 15.2. Both `CirculationList` and `AttentionList` use the services of the generic class `Set`, which was discussed in Section 3.6.

The class interface for `CirculationList` is:

```
class CirculationList
{ // Class which produces the circulation list for one issue
```

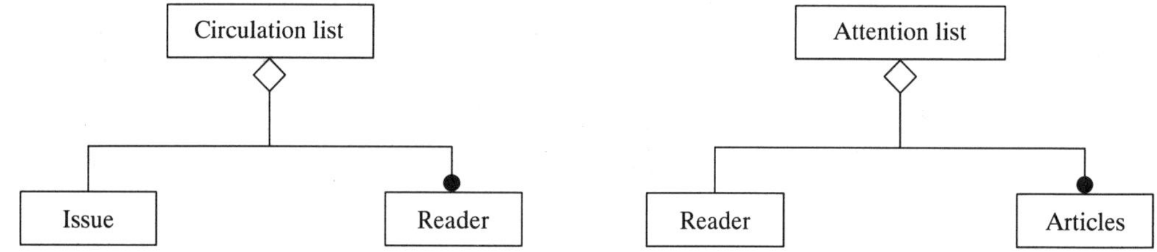

Figure 15.2 Object diagrams for `CirculationList` and `AttentionList`.

```
  private:
    Issue iss;
    ReaderSet rea;

  public:
  // Constructor
  CirculationList(const Issue& issue, const ReaderSet&
        readers);

  // Modifiers
  // Setting default lending periods (global/ per reader)
  void default_lend_period(const Duration& period);
  void default_lend_period(const Reader& r,
        const Duration& p);

  // Selectors
  // Producing the actual circulation list
  Set   <Triple <Reader, Date, Date list>> list() const;
};
```

This class has a constructor for creating a circulation list from a set of readers for a given issue of a journal. It is possible to define a default lending period for all readers in the set or to selectively choose one reader in the set for special treatment. Note that the class `Duration` is abstract and it is possible to use instances of specializations of `Duration` in client code. This promotes the reusability of `CirculationList`, since we are not restricted to one specific implementation. In some cases a duration could represent days, weeks, months or even year intervals.

The most important member function in `CirculationList` is `list()`; this produces a set of triples in which each triple consists of a reader, a start date and end date. This object will usually be printed and pasted onto the issue which is then sent to the first reader on the list. The format is as follows:

Name	Loaned on	Send to next reader before
Daniel	94-4-10	94-4-19
Adriaan	94-4-20	94-5-3
Ilona	94-5-4	94-5-6

`AttentionList` has collaborators `ArticleSet` and `Reader`. Its main responsibility is to produce a list of articles which are of interested to one reader. Its class interface is:

```
class AttentionList
{ // Attention list class for one reader

private:
  Reader r; // The interested reader
  ArticleSet a; // Possible interesting articles

public:
```

```
    // Constructor
    AttentionList(const ArticleSet& aset,
      const ReaderSet& rset);

    // Selectors
    // Creating the attention list
    Set<Pair<Reader, ArticleSet>> list() const;

};
```

The selector operation `list()` in `AttentionList` deserves a few words. The return type is a class representing a set of pairs, the first element of which is a `Reader` instance while the second element in the pair is a set of articles. It is interesting to describe how this is implemented using the class interfaces of `Reader`, `Articles` and `Set`.

The body for `AttentionList::list()` is given by:

```
Set<Pair<Reader, ArticleSet>> AttentionList::list() const
{
    // Loop over all articles in the set of articles; for each
    // article; if the topics it deals with are in the list of
    // topics in which the reader is interested add that
    // article to the result.

    // Use member data r and a in following block of code

    ArticleSet result;
    // What topics is reader interested in?
    TopicSet reader_topics = r.interests();

    // Convert ArticleSet to a list so that we can loop over
    // all articles in the set
    List<Article> art_list = a.list();

    // Help variables
    TopicSet art_topics;   // Topics in current article
    Article current;       // Current article in loop

    // Loop over list of articles
    art_list.first();      // Goto start of list
    while (art_list.end_of_list() == FALSE)
    {
      current = art_list.current();
    art_topics = current.topics();
      if (art_topics.intersect(reader_topics) == TRUE)
      result.add(current);
    art_list.next();  // Process next article
    }
```

```
    // Now create the desired return type
    return Set<r, result>;
}
```

The body of `AttentionList::list()` has been developed based on the functional analysis which was carried out in Section 11.3. This is the classical OMT approach. It is interesting to note that this analysis would become redundant if we had chosen to approach JRP via the use cases approach; both `Attentionlist` and `CirculationList` are concepts and hence classes and it is relatively easy to construct their class interfaces and the corresponding function bodies during the object design phase.

This section concludes with some general steps on finding operations for classes.

(15.3)

- Control classes are found from the functional model as output from processes or as 'use cases'.
- Application classes are found from the object model.
- For each class:
  - find its server classes (collaborators).
  - the operations will arise from the internal events.
- Operation return types and arguments may involve collaborators.

A final remark: new operations and new classes will be discovered during object design. This is a natural process. You will discover new responsibilities as the software life-cycle progresses.

15.3 Designing algorithms for implementing operations

Operations which have been discovered in the analysis phase of the object-oriented life-cycle describe what needs to be done. An algorithm is a recipe or sequence of steps which states in detail how the operation is to be implemented.

Algorithms are responsible for the implementation of the following activities:

- Navigating and searching in object diagrams
- Sorting data
- Performing calculations for special application areas (e.g. clipping in computer graphics)

When implementing an operation using algorithms it is important to weigh the trade-offs between the effort it takes to implement it and the frequency with which it will be used by client code. It is always a good idea to write a quick and easy-to-implement version of the algorithm; then only if and when this version does not satisfy speed requirements is it necessary to design an optimized form of the algorithm. In this way we reduce the risk of not producing a design on time and it may save us writing code that will not be used.

15.4 Internal classes

An internal class is one which does not appear in the analysis model but which does appear during design. There are different types of internal object. The first group consists of those classes which we call control objects. They are application-dependent and are seen as 'glue' objects. Examples of control objects in JRP are `CirculationList` and `AttentionList`. The second group of internal classes consists of those classes which can be used in many applications. There are many commercial packages on the market which deliver functionality for the following internal classes:

Sets	Bags	Lists	Trees
Arrays	Matrices	Dictionaries	

In particular, we are interested in generic versions of these classes. Generic classes only have to be written and tested once, and from them new 'clones' can be created for many different types of applications. This promotes developer productivity. These classes should be bought from a reliable class library vendor so that you can use them in your own application.

15.4.1 Using generic classes

C++ implements generic classes via templates. Chapter 3 gave a short introduction to the template mechanism in C++. We gave some cases in which templates can successfully be used.

We advocate that you use and develop templates for your applications. The advantages for object design are:

- No code duplication: only one template needs to be written.
- Exception handling can and should be included in templates.
- Once a template is tested you can leave it alone.
- Combining inheritance with the template mechanism promotes extendibility and reusability.

You should not get the impression that templates are only useful for mathematical classes such as sets, arrays and lists. They can be used in some cases as an alternative to inheritance in which different classes can be found with similar behaviour (this is called parametric polymorphism which was discusses in Chapter 2).

An example of a template is given. It represents the implementation of an ADT for a fixed array of elements and whose indexing set is of integer type.

Its class interface is:

```
template <class T> class Array
{

private:

  // State not important

public:
  // Constructors and destructor
  Array();
  Array(size_t size, size_t start_index);
  Array(size_t size, const T& t, size_t start_index);
```

```
    Array(const Array& darr2);

    virtual ~Array();

    // Accessing functions
    size_t  size() const;
    BOOLEAN empty() const;
    size_t  min_index() const;
    size_t  max_index() const;

    // Selectors
    BOOLEAN includes(const T& t) const;
    size_t  position(const T& t) const;

    // Modifiers
    void set(size_t j, const T& t);

    // Operator overloading
    T&    operator [] (size_t j);
    T&    operator [] (size_t j) const;
    Array operator = (const Array& darr2);
    Array operator = (const T& t);
    Boolean  operator == (const Array& darr2) const;

};
```

In practice we are interested in creating clones of `Array` which can be used in different application areas. To show the effectiveness of templates we give some specializations and corresponding application areas:

CAD/CAM

- `Array<Point>`(Polyline or line chart)
- `Array<Shape*>`(General drawing)

Finance

- `Array<Pair<Date, Money>>`(a type of cash flow)

Engineering

- `Array<Complex>`(used in digital signal processing)

It is possible to nest classes in order to get new classes for free, for example:

- `Array<Array<T>>`(matrices)
- `List<Array<T>>`(lists of arrays)
- `Array<List<T>>`(arrays of lists)

There is no limit to the uses that templates can be put to. They are becoming part of mainstream C++ and we predict that they will play a major role in software development during the coming years.

Generic classes are supported in the Eiffel language (Meyer 1988), but there is unfortunately no such facility in Smalltalk.

15.5 Designing associations

One of the best kept secrets in the OMT philosophy is that associations can be designed as classes. Beginners tend to have difficulty in grasping the idea that an association may be a separate class. In order to make things a bit more clear, we have devoted Chapter 16 to showing how classes and associations can be designed using relational database tables. In this particular case a binary association is implemented by a so-called 'join' table, a widely used technique which should appeal to those readers who use relational systems. In this section we take the higher ground of designing associations in a more general setting.

15.5.1 Designing binary associations

Associations may be binary or ternary. It is advisable to work exclusively with binary associations since ternary associations are more difficult to deal with. A ternary association can always be decomposed into binary associations with qualifiers or link attributes. An example is shown in Figure 15.3 for the ternary association 'employee works for a department on a project' and its binary equivalents. Conceptually, ternary associations are easier to visualize than binary associations while binary associations are relatively easy to design and implement.

All associations are bidirectional in the analysis phase. This is an idealization. In practice, many associations are uni-directional and the design can be simplified in such cases. For example, in the JRP test case the association '`Reader` is interested in `Topic`' is many-to-many in theory but is one-to-many if we are only interested in finding which topics a given

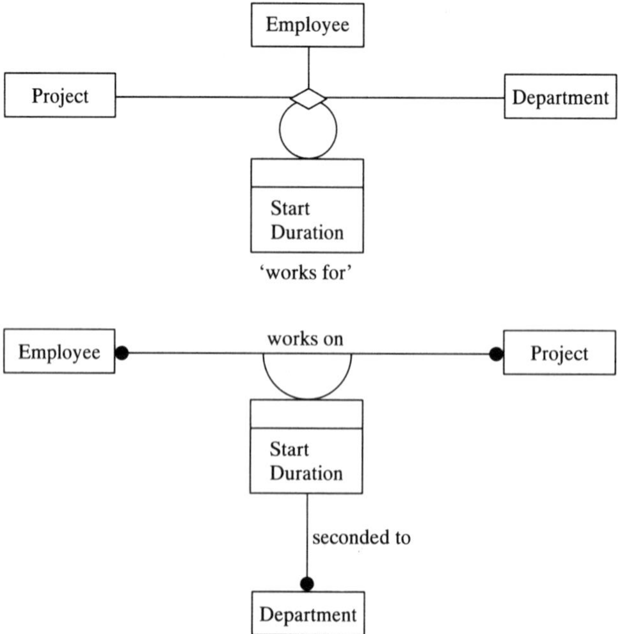

Figure 15.3 Transforming ternary associations to binary associations.

reader is interested in and not in which readers in the organization are interested in a given topic (this latter case would be of interest for a SIG use case, for example). There is only one direction in this case, namely from `Reader` to `Topic`. In this case we can design the class `Reader` by embedding a set of topics in its state as follows:

```
class Reader
{

private:
  String nam;     // Name of reader
  TopicSet topics;  // Topics of interest

public:
  // Constructor
  Reader(const String& name);

  // Accessing functions
  TopicSet interests() const;
  Boolean interested_in(const Topic& topic) const;

  // Modifiers
  void create_new_interest(const Topic& topic);
  void remove_interest(const Topic& topic);

};
```

As already mentioned, `TopicSet` is a synonym for `Set<Topic>`. Class `Set` has been implemented as a sequential linked list. This means that member functions which need to extract information from the topics set will not work very efficiently, especially in the cases in which a reader in interested in many topics. For example, to ascertain whether a reader is interested in a given topic (the function `interested_in()`) the whole set must be scanned to test for membership. If this is a problem it might be an idea to implement `Reader` using other more efficient data structures, such as binary trees or hashing tables. Clients of class `Reader` will not suffer from this change because of the information hiding principle.

Designing two-way associations depends on the frequencies with which the paths between the two classes are traversed. An example of an association where paths could be traversed with equal likelihood is '`Topics` found in `Article`'. We may wish to find all the topics dealt with in a given article and it may also be necessary to find those articles which deal with a given topic. The most general approach is to design the association as a separate association class; this can be a set of pairs of associate objects. In the `Topic_Article` case this is given by the following class interface:

(15.4)

```
class Topic_Article
{
private:

  Set<Pair<Topic, Article>> ta;
```

```
public:

  // ...

};
```

This class does not scale well to large amounts of data because access takes place via linked lists (which access data sequentially). For efficient access an association object can be implemented as two dictionary objects, one for the forward direction and the other for the backwards direction. A dictionary in this context is a collection of key/value pairs. The keys in the dictionary are unique, while the values may be duplicated. The dictionary may be searched by key or by value. Key searching uses hashing for efficiency.

The optimized interface for `Topic_Article` using dictionaries is:

```
class Topic_Article
{
private:

  Dictionary<Topic, Article> topic_key;
  Dictionary<Article, Topic> article_key;

public:

  // ...

};
```

The advantage of this representation is that access is efficient. The disadvantage is that two dictionary instances need to be maintained when topics and articles are added and deleted. Instances of `Topic_Article` take up more space in memory than the less efficient solution proposed in (15.4).

Qualified associations involve two classes and a qualifier attribute. Such associations are implemented as a separate class (as always), but in this case as a set of triples. For example, in JRP the association between `Journal` and `Issue` was a qualified association with the volume number (an integer) of the issue playing the role of qualifier. The association is implemented by the following state:

```
Set<Triple<Journal, Issue, Integer>>;
```

15.5.2 Design of link attributes

Associations having link attributes may be implemented as separate classes. Under certain circumstances it is possible to store the link attributes in one of the classes comprising the association. In particular, we can state the following:

- If the association is 1:1 the link attributes may be stored as attributes of either object.
- If the association is 1:*N* the link attributes may be stored as attributes of the class on the 'many' side of the association.
- If the association is *N*:*M* the association must be implemented as a separate class.

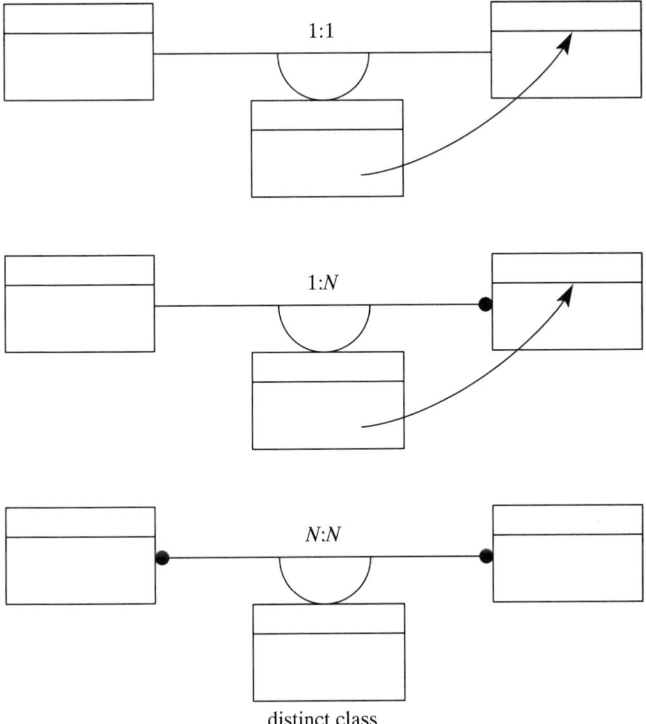

Figure 15.4 Designing associations.

The different cases are shown in Figure 15.4, where the arrow signifies that link attributes may be incorporated into one of the classes in the association.

15.5.3 Adding redundant associations

Each association in the analysis model is necessary if we are not to lose any semantic information in the object model. Furthermore, superfluous or redundant associations are not allowed. They are, however, allowed in the object design phase, where they aid in producing efficient access techniques. Redundant associations do not add any extra semantic information to the model. The questions to be answered are:

- Can the object network be optimized by introducing new associations?
- Can some associations be eliminated?

Consider the case in Figure 15.5 and suppose that we wish to find the set of topics which deal with a given article. A solution to this access problem is to create an association between `Topic` and `Article` which can be searched in constant time (by hashing) in either direction.

Figure 15.5 Chain of associations.

15.6 Discovering roles

Role classes occur in all applications. It is important to discover them since they are specializations of other more fundamental classes which may or may not exist from previous projects. For example, a `Manager` is a role for `Employee` which in its turn is a role for `Person`. Being able to create roles from a repository of already existing classes promotes developer productivity. Furthermore, looking for roles during both the analysis and design phases forces us to look for reusable resources which may have been found in previous problems.

A role class is either a derived class of some other class or it may be a template specialization. Examples are:

- A blood donor is a role for `Patient`.
- An `Employee` is a role for `Person`.
- A `CashFlow` is a role for a template array class.

The question that needs to be asked when determining whether a class is a role is 'Is this class a special case of something more general?', or 'Am I reinventing the wheel (or at least the spokes of the wheel) by defining this new class from first principles?'.

Implementing roles in C++ is easy. We simply create a derived class, as in the following example:

```
class Employee : public Person
{
private:
  // Possible extra state
public:

  // Extra member functions

};
```

Roles can be specializations of template classes. For example, `CashFlow`, `Polyline` and `DigitalSignal` are role classes for `Array`.

15.7 Data-driven and responsibility-driven design

Many novice and even experienced C++ programmers regularly make the mistake of creating classes all of whose member functions directly access the state. This means that any change to the internal representation of a class can have huge knock-on effects. Changes usually entail us having to rewrite blocks of code and then test each member function all over again. The mistake that has been taken is that programmers take a data-driven view to programming C++ classes because they focus too quickly on object implementation. This is called data-driven design. Responsibility-driven design concentrates on what a class should do, and it increases encapsulation by deferring implementation issues until a late stage (Wirfs-Brock and Wilkerson 1989a,b). This is the approach advocated by Bertrand Meyer (1988). Most books and articles on C++ concentrate on syntax and showing how wonderful the language is, while the real concern is to show how C++ can be effectively used in creating correct and robust classes.

The questions that data-driven design answers are:

- What data does a type (class) subsume?
- What are the operations on that type?

For example, a linked list consists of elements belonging to a particular type; each element has a successor and a predecessor in the list and it is possible to navigate in a sequential manner in the list.

Responsibility-driven design asks the following questions:

- What actions is this object responsible for?
- What information does this object share?

Applying the responsibility-driven approach to the linked list example results in the following responsibilities:

- Adding and removing an object from the list
- Scanning all elements in the list (an iterator function)
- Testing whether an element belongs to the list

One consequence of this last approach is that high-level member functions will have no direct contact with the structure of the class; only a small number of primitive or trusted member functions have access to the state. High-level functions use the services of other high-level functions or they may access these trusted functions directly. Changes to the state of an object imply that only the bodies of primitive member functions will have to be changed. As an example, we have implemented a linked list class in C++ using a responsibility-driven approach. The class interface is given by:

```
// gslist.hxx
//
// © Datasim BV, 1994.

#ifndef DSGENSLIST_HXX
#define DSGENSLIST_HXX
#include "constant.hxx"
#include "lelem.cxx"

template <class T> class DSGENSLIST
{
private:
  // Member data
  // Lelem is a help class and is really not important for
  // List's interface
  Lelem<T>  * root;
  Lelem<T>  * cur;

public:
  // Constructors and destructors
  DSGENSLIST();
```

```
    DSGENSLIST(const T &value);
    DSGENSLIST(const DSGENSLIST<T> &ll);
    virtual ~DSGENSLIST();

    // Modifier functions
    void merge(const DSGENSLIST<T>& s);
    void append(const T& value);
    void insert(const T& value);
    void dellist();
    void del();
    void remove(const T& value);

    void remove_all(const T& value);
    void first();
    void end();
    void next();

    // Selector functions
    size_t size() const;
    T current() const;
    BOOLEAN includes(const T& value) const;
    BOOLEAN empty() const;
    BOOLEAN end_of_list() const;
    BOOLEAN front_of_list() const;
};
#endif
```

We give the bodies of several high-level member functions to show how they are protected from `List`'s member data by the use of primitive member functions.

```
template <class T> DSGENSLIST<T>::~DSGENSLIST()
{ // Destructor

  dellist(); // Deletes the entire list

}
template <class T> void
DSGENSLIST<T>::merge(constDSGENSLIST<T>& ll)
{ // Merges a list ll at the end of the list

DSGENSLIST<T> *tmp = new DSGENSLIST<T>(ll);

while(tmp->end_of_list() == FALSE)
{
  append(tmp->current());
  tmp->next();
}
```

```
if (tmp->empty() == FALSE)
    append(tmp->current());
}

template <class T> void
DSGENLIST::append(const T& v)
{ // Appends an element with value v at the end of the list

    end();
    insert(v);
}
```

15.8 Refining class hierarchies and discovering polymorphic behaviour

You never get it right first time, and this is certainly true when discovering inheritance hierarchies during both analysis and design. The following things may happen:

- New classes are found.
- New commonality is found between classes, resulting in a new intermediate class in the hierarchy.

Things to watch out for are:

- Avoid deep hierarchies: you run the risk of producing unmaintainable and tiny classes (Linton and Calder 1987).
- Avoid 'flat' hierarchies: communicating hierarchies are better.
- Avoid the Smalltalk 'cosmic' approach to class hierarchies; build class hierarchies each of which fulfils one major function.
- Do not impose a Smalltalk-type solution when designing classes in C++ ('Smalltalkism').
- Find as many abstract base classes as you can and place them at the top of the hierarchy.

Finally, many beginners make the mistake of using inheritance when it is really delegation that they want. Classic blunders are:

- `Stack` is derived from a `List`.
- A `Circle` is derived from a `Point`.
- An `Issue` is derived from a `Journal` (no, you cannot subscribe to an `Issue`!).
- A `SalesManager` is a `Manager` and a `SalesPerson`.

Several iterations are needed before the inheritance hierarchies begins to stabilize.

Discovering polymorphic behaviour is important during the design and implementation phases of the software life-cycle. In particular, classes which are specializations of abstract base classes and share common behaviour are candidates. In this case the common behaviour will be designed as one or more polymorphic member functions. Examples of polymorphic member functions are:

- Two-dimensional shapes can be drawn on a graphics screen.
- Call options and put options have optimal exercise dates.

- Divisions are involved with internal and external projects.
- Calculate monthly pay for full-time and part-time employees.

We now show how polymorphism is implemented in MPC. In some cases we wish to query the MPC system without having to consider whether a project is an internal project or an external projects. MIS managers, for example, would like answers to the following questions for the current project portfolio:

- What is the status of the project?
- How much resource has a project used?
- How many divisions are involved in a project?

All of these cases correspond to polymorphic behaviour. In C++ we implement polymorphism by using virtual member functions. The following class interfaces show how the functions are implemented:

```
class Project
{
private:
  // ...

public:
  // ...

  Array<Division> divisions() const = 0;
};

class InternalProject: public Project
{
private:
  // ...

public:
  // ...

  Array<Division> divisions() const;
};

class ExternalProject: public Project
{
private:
  // ...

public:
  // ...

  Array<Division> divisions() const;
};
```

The function `Project::divisions()` has no body (it is a pure virtual member function) while `ExternalProject::divisions()` and `InternalProject::divisions()` do have bodies which are implemented in different ways; for `InternalProject` this is easy since each such a project is sponsored by a number of divisions, whereas for `ExternalProject` it is more complicated, since such projects are controlled by different departments, which in their turn belong to divisions.

15.9 Nailing down object attributes

Object state can be implemented in a number of ways. The most elegant solution is to use the closed architecture approach. Open architectures deliver classes which are difficult to maintain and difficult to understand. For example, a `TimeStamp` can be represented as a combination of `Date` and `Time` (closed architecture) or as a very large number (open architecture). In the latter case we lose all of the services that the lower-level classes `Date` and `Time` could deliver.

It is very important to avoid using built-in data types in the state of a class. This is because these types are compiler-dependent, and porting classes from one machine to another may produce unexpected results. It is better to map these built-in types to classes and to place the new classes in the System Interface Layer (SIL).

To take an example, we consider the simple digital watch problem (SDW) again. We choose a closed architecture solution and to this end we use the services of a `Time` class which contains all the functionality needed when working with hours and minutes. The state of the `Watch` class will be:

```
class Watch
{
private:
  HOURS h;            // Displayed hours
  MINUTES m;          // Display minutes
  WatchState sta;     // Current mode of watch

public:
                      // ...
};
```

The classes `Hours` and `Minutes` have the following interfaces:

```
// hours.hxx
//
// © Datasim BV, 1993.

#ifndef HOURS_HXX
#define HOURS_HXX

#include "counter.hxx"

class HOURS : public COUNTER
{ // Hours of the day
```

```
public:
  // Constructors
  HOURS();
  HOURS(int hours);
  HOURS(const HOURS& h);

  // Selector functions
  int value() const;
  void increment(); // Add 1 to current value
  void decrement();

};
#endif    // HOURS_HXX

// minutes.hxx
//
// © Datasim BV, 1993.

#ifndef MINUTES_HXX
#define MINUTES_HXX

#include "counter.hxx"

class MINUTES : public COUNTER
{ // Minutes of the day

public:
  // Constructors
  MINUTES();
  MINUTES(int minutes);
  MINUTES(const MINUTES& min);

  // Selector functions
  int value() const;    // Return the number of minutes

  void increment(); // Add 1 to current value
  void decrement();
};
#endif  // MINUTES_HXX
```

15.10 Object design for risk management problems

Our earlier description of options is repeated below for convenience.

An option is a contract which confers the right but not the obligation to buy or sell an asset on a given date (the so-called exercise or maturity date) at a predefined (exercise) price (Gemmill 1993). Options can be taken out on almost any type of asset, for example, gold, silver, grain, the value of a company and so on. There are options to buy assets. These are known as call options. Put options grant some party the right to sell the assets. Call options are more common than put options and also easier to understand. One buys a call option in the hope that the price of the asset will increase in time. Some options give a buyer an additional right. The option may not only be exercised at the maturity date but also on any date before then. These are known as American options. Options that do not allow such early exercise dates are known as European options. Most options that are traded on exchanges are American but many of the off-exchange ('over-the-counter') deals are for European options.

We shall confine ourselves to studying European options in this example. In particular, we shall design the class `CallOption` and determine its interface. The object diagram for this problem is shown in Figure 15.6. The association between `Asset` and `Option` is one-to-many; an asset may have many options (e.g. call and put), but an option has only one asset. In practice, the association is many-to-many because it is possible for an option to exchange one asset for another asset, involving the simultaneous purchase of one 'leg' and the sale of another. The legs are different assets, for example corporate bonds and government bonds.

Stocks are special assets which are traded on the stock exchange. A dividend is money which is paid to holders of stock at regular intervals. However, we are never sure of the exact date on which a dividend will be paid, but it is very important to be able to predict this date because the value of the stock goes down by an amount which reflects the dividend paid per share. European options pay dividends on a regular basis, while American options do not pay dividends.

The value of an asset varies in time according to some model. A useful approximation is to assume that prices vary according to a Brownian motion regime. This means that prices oscillate around an average value. The presence of dividends affects this motion since just before a dividend is paid out stock prices are at a high, while after the dividend has been paid

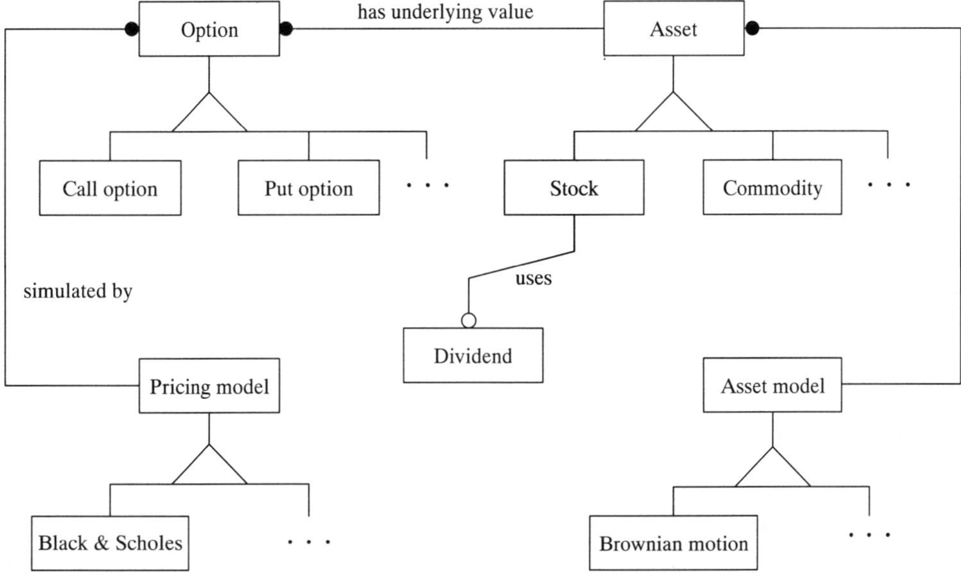

Figure 15.6 Object diagram for the options problem.

out prices drop somewhat. Thus, 'spikes' appear in the graph of stock prices versus time. Similarly, the price of an option is calculated by a `PricingModel`. The most famous model and the one which is used widely in modern finance is due to Black and Scholes (1973).

An option has the following states:

- Its exercise price
- Its time to maturity (the maturity date)
- The asset it corresponds to
- The price model that is used to approximate it

The most interesting questions that are to be answered in relation to an option are its average price and a set of optimal dates and their frequency.

In order to design the class interface for `CallOption` a number of specializations of reusable template classes are created. The optimal pricing data structure is an array of pairs, with each pair consisting of a `Date` instance (the so-called stochastic dividend date) and a `Percentage` instance (which represents the relative frequency of occurrence). We use a synonym class name as follows:

```
typedef DSGENARR<DSGENPAIR<Date, MONEY>> SnapDiv;
```

Another specialization is needed in order to represent arrays of triples, with each triple consisting of a date, an amount and a stock price value. The synonym class is given by:

```
typedef DSGENARR<DSGENTRIPLE<Date, Money, Money>> SnapAsset;
```

The class interface for `CallOption` can now be given:

```
class CallOption
{

private:

  PricingModel  p;
  Asset a;
  Date  x_date;
  Money X;

public:
  // Constructors & destructor
  CallOption();
  CallOption(const PricingModel& pm,
    const Asset& asset,
    const Date& exp_date, double exp_price);
  ~CallOption();

  // Selectors
  SnapDiv optimal_x_date() const;    // Frequencies of optimal
                                     // exercise dates
  Money price() const;               // Average option price
```

```
};
```

Both `PricingModel` and `Asset` are abstract base classes. Their interfaces are given by:

```
class PricingModel
{
private:
  SnapDiv s;          // Array of optimal dates+frequencies
  Interest r;         // Interest-free rate

public:
  // ...

  // The calculated option price
  Money option_price() const = 0;
};
```

The behaviour of class `Asset` is simulated by an instance of `AssetModel`. Each `Asset` instance has a corresponding volatility and this value is the standard deviation of returns. There are a number of ways of calculating the volatility of an asset (for example, based on historical data). A discussion is given in Gemmill (1993). Option prices are extremely sensitive to the level of volatility.

```
class Asset
{
private:

  // Model for simulating asset behaviour
  AssetModel am;

  // Volatility of dividend
  Percentage vol;

public:
  // ...
};
```

The class interface for `AssetModel` is given by:

```
class AssetModel
{
private:
  Percentage vol;   // The stock volatility
public:

  SnapAsset stp() const = 0;     // Stochastic stock prices

};
```

In many cases options are taken out on stocks. The class interface for `Stock` is:

```
class Stock: public Asset
{
private:
  Dividend d;

public:

};
```

A dividend is an amount of money paid to holders of stock shares. The class interface for `Dividend` is:

```
class Dividend
{

private:
  // Array of deterministic dividend information
  Snapdiv default_div;

public:

  // Calculate stochastic dividend information
  Snapdiv stochastic_info() const;
};
```

This example shows how template specializations can be used in combination with domain-specific classes during object design.

Exercises

1. What are the trade-offs between low-level design and high-level design during the object design phase? The criteria are portability, ease of implementation, maintainability and extensibility.

2. Determine the operations in a vending machine environment (Hatley and Pirbhai 1988). The main events are: get customer payment, dispense change, validate payment, get product prices, get valid selection, dispense product. Each operation should be given a name, a return type and a possible list of arguments.

3. Identify control classes for the MPC problem.

4. Extend `AttentionList` by using the `Set` class so that attention lists can be created for arbitrary groups of readers.

5. Consider writing code for the body of `AttentionList::attention_list()` if you did not use the resources of the generic class `Set`. How much extra and duplicate code would be needed when compared with the solution in Section 15.2.2?

6. Find the operations for the classes in (15.3) and provide suitable algorithms for implementing them.

7. Determine the member functions of the class `Topic_Article` and their corresponding algorithms (Section 15.6.1).

8. The class `Topic_Article` is essentially a specialization of the template (generic class) whose interface is:

```
template <class Class1, class Class2> class Two_Way_Assoc
{
private:
  Dictionary<Class1, Class2> forward_link;
  Dictionary<Class2, Class1> backward_link;

public:

  // ???

};
```

   Identify the public member functions of `Two_Way_Assoc`.

9. The header file for a generic qualified association class is given by:

```
template <class Class1, class Class2, class Qual> class
Qassoc
{
private:

  Set<Triple<Class1, Class2, Qual>> assoc;

public:

  // ???

};
```

   Determine the member functions on this class.

10. Find the trusted member functions for the following classes: `Stack`, `Set`.

11. Determine the full class interface of the class in (15.4).

12. Find servant classes, agent classes and master classes (see Chapter 9 for definitions) for the problems MPC and PPD.

References

F. Black and M. Scholes (1973) The pricing of options and corporate liabilities, *Journal of Political Economy*, **81** 637–59.

D. Coleman *et al.* (1994) *Object-Oriented Development, The Fusion Method*, Prentice-Hall, Englewood Cliffs NJ.

G. Gemmill (1993) *Options Pricing*, McGraw-Hill, London.

D. J. Hatley and I. A. Pirbhai (1988) *Strategies for Real-Time System Specification*, Dorset House Publishing, New York.

M. A. Linton and P. J. Calder (1987) The design and implementation of InterViews, *1987 USENIX C++ Conference.*

B. Meyer (1988) *Object-Oriented Software Construction*, Prentice-Hall, Englewood Cliffs NJ.

S. Shlaer and S. J. Mellor (1988) *Object-Oriented Systems Analysis*, Prentice-Hall, Englewood Cliffs NJ.

R. Wirfs-Brock and B. Wilkerson (1989a) Variables limit reusability, *Journal of Object-Oriented Programming*, May/June.

R. Wirfs-Brock and B. Wilkerson (1989b) Object-oriented design: a responsibility-driven approach, *SIGPLAN Notices*, **24**(10).

R. Wirfs-Brock, B. Wilkerson and L. Wiener (1990) *Designing Object-Oriented Software*, Prentice-Hall, Englewood Cliffs NJ.

Chapter

16

Object and relational integration

16.1 Introduction and objectives

Relational database management systems (RDBMSs) are in wide use in many business and industrial applications and have gained wide acceptance because of their rich modelling features, dependability and portability. Furthermore, the data contained in relational databases can be accessed by SQL (Structured Query Language), a non-procedural language which allows data to be updated and modified. SQL is an established standard and it is very unlikely that it will be replaced, even by object-oriented technology. For this reason alone it is important to deal with the integration of object and relational database technologies. In particular, we show how object models can be mapped to relational database tables. We call this 'naive object design', because by doing this we lose support for key object-oriented features in the implementation phase. This is because the relational model has no support for encapsulation or inheritance.

This chapter is useful reading for those designers and programmers who have experience in creating applications using relational database techniques and who wish to see how object-oriented concepts are mapped to tables.

16.2 An overview of relational databases

16.2.1 Theory

Relational database theory is founded on the mathematical notion of a relation. A relation defines a special type of table. Each column is called a domain containing all the values of an attribute and each row is called a tuple. The number of rows or tuples is called the cardinality of the table while the number of columns is called the degree of the table.

The characteristics of a relation are:

(16.1)

- All entries in a domain are of the same kind.

- The ordering of the domains is immaterial.
- Domains are assigned distinct names (attribute names).
- Each tuple is distinct (no duplicate tuples allowed).
- The ordering of tuples is immaterial.

An example of a relation is given below. It has degree 4 and cardinality 3.

(16.2)

```
SUPPLIER (S# Name     Status  City)
S123      Acme        OK      Milan
S635      N&B         NOK     New York
S764      Datasim     OK      Amsterdam
```

Domains can be simple or non-simple. A simple domain contains a single attribute, while a non-simple attribute contains a repeating group (a list of attributes) or a multiple of attributes. We assume that all domains are simple.

A tuple is identified by its key, and this can be constructed from one or more attributes so that no attribute in the key is redundant. A tuple can have more than one possible key. Each such key can uniquely identify the tuple. All these possible keys are called candidate keys. One of these keys is arbitrarily selected to identify the tuple and this is known as the primary key. In the `SUPPLIER` relation (16.2) possible candidate keys are:

- `Name` + `City`
- `S#`

Each of these determines a tuple uniquely, while a possible primary key is `S#`.

If a tuple has attributes whose combination is the primary key in another relation, this key is the called a foreign key. To give an example of a foreign key let us first consider the relation for a product:

(16.3)

```
PRODUCT (P# Name      Color   Weight)
P123     nuts         blue    12.2
P750     bolts        red     23.5
P86      washers      white   0.1
P5632    rivets       red     12.2
P45      nuts         red     34.99
```

The primary key for `PRODUCT` is `P#`. No two tuples in `PRODUCT` may have the same value for this attribute.

We now create a new table which 'joins' `SUPPLIER` and `PRODUCT` and represents which suppliers deliver which products.

(16.4)

```
DELIVERY (S#   P#   delivery_time)
S123      P45  34
S123      P86  10
S764      P750 2
S123      P86  60
```

The relation DELIVERY has primary key (S#, P#). Both S# and P# are called foreign keys in this case.

The normalization process plays an important role in relational database design. A full discussion of normal forms is given in Date (1981). In particular, we assume that all relations are in third normal form. A full discussion of normalization is outside the scope of this book.

Each attribute in a table belongs to a certain data type. Most relational database systems restrict type to a small set of built-in or aggregate types such as:

(16.5)

- Numeric data (INTEGER, SMALLINT, DECIMAL(p,q), FLOAT(p))
- String data (CHARACTER(n), VARCHAR(n), GRAPHIC(n))
- Date/Time data (DATE, TIME, TIMESTAMP) (Date and White 1988)

Modern relational database systems have support for extended objects such as BLOBs (binary large objects) and other data types (see, for example, Oracle (1990)).

To show how data types can be incorporated into relations we consider the following data description language (DDL) commands for creating tables for SUPPLIER, PRODUCT and DELIVERY:

(16.6)

```
CREATE TABLE SUPPLIER
  (S#    CHAR(5) NOT NULL,
  Name   CHAR(20),
  Status     CHAR(3),
  City   CHAR(30),
  PRIMARY KEY (S#))

CREATE TABLE PRODUCT
  (P#    CHAR(5) NOT NULL,
  Name   CHAR(20),
  Color CHAR(4),
  Weight     NUMERIC(10,2),
  PRIMARY KEY (P#))

CREATE TABLE DELIVERY
  (S#    CHAR(5) NOT NULL,
  P#     CHAR(5) NOT NULL,
  Delivery_time SMALLINT,
  PRIMARY KEY(S#, P#),
  FOREIGN KEY (S#) REFERENCES SUPPLIER,
  FOREIGN KEY (P#) REFERENCES PRODUCT)
```

Notice the use of the column constraints for defining primary and foreign keys in these tables.

The commands in (16.6) allow us to create templates for tables. The next step is to populate these tables with data. To this end, we need to take account of the following questions:

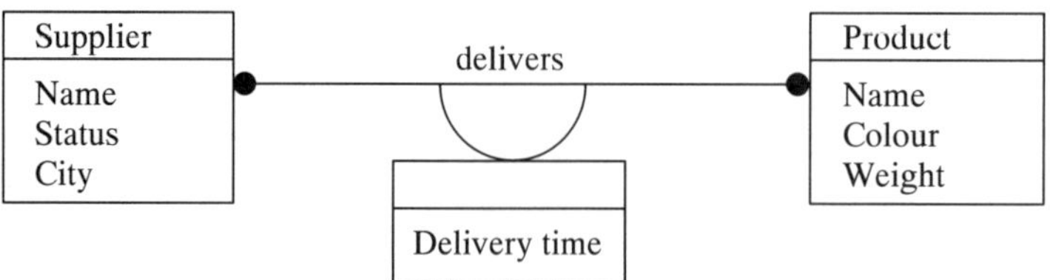

Figure 16.1 Object diagram for supplier–product database problem.

- What is the multiplicity of the DELIVERY relationship?
- How do we preserve the integrity of data?
- Querying and updating the above tables.
- Performance issues (e.g. searching).

The SUPPLIER–PRODUCT–DELIVERY database has been implemented as three tables. The corresponding object diagram is shown in Figure 16.1. We see immediately in this case that the tables SUPPLIER and PRODUCT correspond to classes, while the table DELIVERY corresponds to an 'association class' with link attribute Delivery_time. The mapping from objects to tables is not as easy in general as this example would lead us to believe, but it is nonetheless an interesting test case. The same problem will be implemented in C++ and an object-oriented database system in later chapters so that worthwhile comparisons can be drawn between the different approaches.

16.2.2 The analogy between tables and objects

The statements in (16.6) affect the structure of database objects. In (16.6) the commands create a template structure from which instances (in this case tuples) can be created. The tables in (16.6) are populated using Structured Query Language (SQL). Clients can access the tuples directly and assign values to them. We thus see that relational databases fail to satisfy the information hiding principle; for example, changing tuple data types or names will affect client code.

If tables can be likened to objects we conclude that the DDL code in (16.6) corresponds to the state of the corresponding objects. The next question is: what is the equivalent of object behaviour? The answer is data manipulation language (DML). These are the statements which manipulate data. There are different DML statements. There are DML statements for the following:

(16.7)

- DELETE (delete all or some rows from a table)
- INSERT (add new rows to a table)
- SELECT (perform a query on a table)
- UPDATE (change data in a table)

These commands have their analogues in the object-oriented paradigm. If we assume that a record is the same as an object, then the INSERT command is equivalent to a constructor while the DELETE command is similar to a destructor. The UPDATE command modifies one or more tuples and thus corresponds to a modifier member function on the corresponding object. Finally, the `SELECT` command corresponds to a selector member function.

We take some examples of how the commands in (16.7) are applied in practice.

(16.8)

- Create a new `SUPPLIER` record

```
INSERT INTO SUPPLIER (S#, Name, Status, City)
  VALUES ('S123', 'Acme', 'OK', 'Milan')
```

- Change a value in a tuple for a given record (one object)

```
UPDATE SUPPLIER
  SET City = 'Amsterdam'
  WHERE S# = 'S123'
```

- Remove a record from the table

```
DELETE FROM SUPPLIER
  where S# = 'S123'
```

- View a given `SUPPLIER` record

```
SELECT Name, Status, City
  FROM SUPPLIER
  WHERE S# = 'S123'
```

We now give the equivalent commands in C++. First, the class interfaces for `SUPPLIER`, `PRODUCT` and `DELIVERY` are given. Then a small test program shows how the objects can be manipulated in a manner similar to (16.8).

```
// supplier.hxx
//
// © Datasim BV, 1994.

#ifndef SUPPLIER_HXX
#define SUPPLIER_HXX

#include "contype.hxx"

class SUPPLIER
{

private:

  int LinkCounter;
  char* Name;         // The name of the supplier
  char* Status;       // Its status
  char* City;         // The city where it is located

// Private functions
  void init(char*,char*,char*);   // Initialize data
```

```
public:
  // Constructors and destructor
  SUPPLIER();
  SUPPLIER(const SUPPLIER& supplier);
  SUPPLIER(char* name, char* status, char* city);
  ~SUPPLIER();

  // Selectors
  char* name()      const;      // The name
  char* status()    const;      // The status
  char* city()      const;      // Location

  // Modifiers
  void name(char* newname);           // Change its name
  void status(char* newstatus);       // Change the status
  void city(char* newcity);           // Change the city

  // Only for the non-database version
  SUPPLIER* getp();          // Return a pointer to this
  void forget();             // Forget a reference
  SUPPLIER& operator= (const SUPPLIER& supplier);

  friend ostream& operator<< (ostream& os,
    const SUPPLIER& supplier);

};

#endif

// product.hxx
//
// © Datasim BV, 1994.

#ifndef PRODUCT_HXX
#define PRODUCT_HXX

#include "contype.hxx"

class PRODUCT
{
private:
  int LinkCounter;

  char* Name;        // The name of the product
  char* Color;       // Its color
  double Weight;     // The weight
```

```
// Private functions
  void init(char*,char*,double);    // Initialize data

public:
  // Constructors and destructor
  PRODUCT();
  PRODUCT(const PRODUCT& product);
  PRODUCT(char* name, char* color, double weight);
  ~PRODUCT();

  // Selectors
  char* name()  const;       // The name of the product
  char* color() const;       // The color of the product
  double weight() const;     // The weight of the product

  // Modifiers
  void name(char* newname);          // Set the name
  void color(char* newcolor);        // Set the color
  void weight(double newweight);     // Set the weight

  // Only for the non-database version
  PRODUCT* getp();       // Return pointer to this
  void forget();         // Forget a pointer linkcount

  PRODUCT& operator= (const PRODUCT& product);

  friend ostream& operator<< (ostream& os,
    const PRODUCT& product);

};

#endif

// delivery.hxx
//
// This file contains the header file of a delivery.
// This class is an association between a supplier and a
// product.
//
// © Datasim BV, 1994.

#ifndef DELIVERY_HXX
#define DELIVERY_HXX

#include "supplier.hxx"
#include "product.hxx"
```

```
class DELIVERY
{

private:
  SUPPLIER* Supplier;         // Reference to a supplier
  PRODUCT* Product;           // Reference to a product
  int Deliverytime;           // Time to deliver
  void init(SUPPLIER*,PRODUCT*,int);

public:
  // Constructors and destructor
  DELIVERY();
  DELIVERY(const DELIVERY& delivery);
  DELIVERY(SUPPLIER* supplier, PRODUCT* product, int time);
  ~DELIVERY();

  // Selectors
  SUPPLIER* supplier() const;   // Return supplier
  PRODUCT* product() const;     // Return product
  int deliverytime() const;     // Return delivery time

  // Modifiers
  void supplier(SUPPLIER* supplier);    // Change supplier
  void product(PRODUCT* product);       // Change product
  void deliverytime(int newtime);       // New delivery time

  DELIVERY& operator=(const DELIVERY& delivery);

  friend ostream& operator<< (ostream& os,
    const DELIVERY& delivery);

};

#endif
```

The test program for manipulating suppliers, products and deliveries is now given.

```
// tstall.cxx
//
// Program for testing the product/supplier classes.
//
// © Datasim BV, 1994.

#include "supplier.hxx"
#include "product.hxx"
#include "delivery.hxx"

#include <iostream.h>
```

```
int main()
{
  // Suppliers
  SUPPLIER sup1("Acme","OK","Milan");
  SUPPLIER sup2("N&B","NOK","New York");
  SUPPLIER sup3("Datasim","OK","Amsterdam");

  // Products
  PRODUCT prod1("nuts","blue",12.2);
  PRODUCT prod2("bolts","red",23.5);
  PRODUCT prod3("washers","white",0.1);
  PRODUCT prod4("rivets","red",12.2);
  PRODUCT prod5("nuts","red",34.99);

  // Deliveries
  DELIVERY del1(&sup1,&prod5,34);
  DELIVERY del2(&sup1,&prod3,10);
  DELIVERY del3(&sup3,&prod2,2);
  DELIVERY del4(&sup1,&prod3,60);
  cout << del1 << endl;
  cout << del2 << endl;
  cout << del3 << endl;
  cout << del4 << endl;

}
```

One big difference between C++ objects and relational database tables is that in the latter case we need to define special database keys in order to determine the identity of a record, while this is not necessary with the corresponding C++ objects since this is assured as each object has its own piece of memory reserved for it.

16.3 Mapping object diagrams to tables

Once an object diagram has been made it is in principle possible to start designing the classes and associations which appear in such diagrams. In particular, we can design all these entities by using relational database tables, and some CASE tools (e.g. OMTool) have facilities for generating DDL and DML code from the object diagrams.

It is our aim in this section to show how the transition from object diagrams to relational database tables can be made. This may be necessary or even useful in some cases.

OMT has provisions for allowing tables in object design. A number of chapters in Rumbaugh *et al.* (1991) are devoted to this topic. We repeat the most important conclusions here and we show by a number of examples how the mapping is effected.

16.3.1 Mapping objects to tables

As can be deduced from Section 16.2 we see that a table may correspond to a class in which a record (row) corresponds to instances. This is not always the case. A class maps to one or

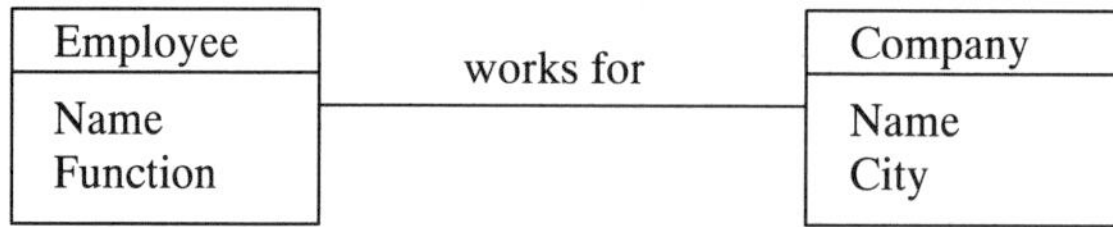

Figure 16.2 One-to-many associations.

more tables in general. A table can correspond to one or more classes. In Section 16.2 the multiplicity between tables and classes was one-to-one.

16.3.2 Mapping associations to tables

We show how binary associations can be mapped to tables. Ternary associations are not treated here because they are complicated and they can always be decomposed into two distinct binary associations.

Binary association can have one-to-one, one-to-many or many-to-many multiplicity. Many-to-many associations map to distinct tables. We have already seen an example of such an association in Section 16.2; a supplier delivers many products while a product may be delivered by many suppliers. The new table which ensures from the association is sometimes called a join table (Figure 16.1).

Indexes may be defined on the join table, which speed up data access time. An index provides direct access to the rows in a table. An example of an index is given in the case of the `DELIVERY` table as follows:

```
CREATE INDEX delivery_index on DELIVERY (S#, P#)
```

Since many-to-many associations may be mapped to distinct tables we note that the same holds for one-to-many and one-to-one associations. However, there are other possibilities. To give an example, consider the one-to-many association in Figure 16.2. A company may employ many people, but an employee is only allowed to work for one company.

The database tables in this case are:

```
COMPANY     (COM#   Name   City)
EMPLOYEE    (EMP#   COM#   Name    Function)
```

In this case the tuple `COM#` in `EMPLOYEE` is a foreign key. The tuples `EMP#` and `COM#` may not be `NULL` in this case.

One-to-one associations are easy to map to tables, either as a distinct table or as a foreign key in the table for either class.

16.3.3 Qualified associations

A qualified association maps to a distinct table with at least three attributes, namely the primary key of each related class and the attribute representing the qualifier. For example, consider the qualified association from JRP as shown in Figure 16.3. This is now a one-to-one association. The table has the following tuples :

```
CREATE TABLE ISSUE
(JOUR#  CHAR(4) NOT NULL,
```

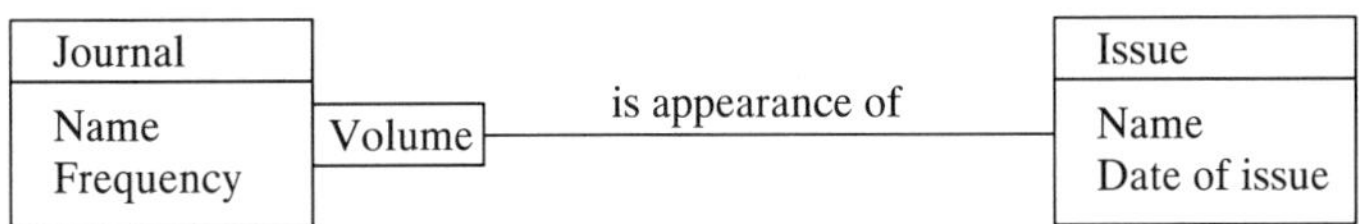

Figure 16.3 Qualified associations.

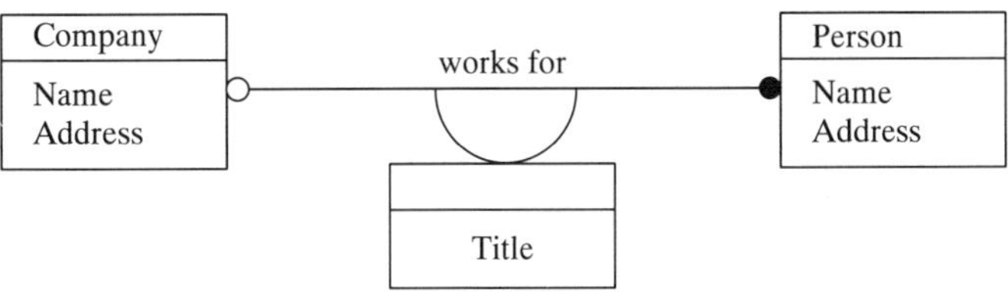

Figure 16.4 Optional associations.

```
ISSUE#   CHAR(4) NOT NULL,
VOLUME   CHAR(10) NOT NULL,
NAME     CHAR(20),
DATE_ISSUE  DATE,
PRIMARY KEY (JOUR#, ISSUE#, VOLUME),
FOREIGN KEY (JOUR#) REFERENCES JOURNAL)
```

16.3.4 Optional associations

Optional associations (for example, the association in Figure 16.4) are mapped to tables in much the same way as for one-to-many associations. The difference in this case is that the foreign key at the optional side of the association may have `NULL` values. In the case of Figure 16.4 the table is:

```
CREATE TABLE EMPLOYEE
(PERSON#     CHAR(4) NOT NULL,
NAME         CHAR(20) NOT NULL,
ADDRESS      CHAR(20),
COM#         CHAR(4),
PRIMARY KEY (PERSON#))
```

16.3.5 Mapping generalizations to tables

We show how single inheritance generalizations (SINGs) are mapped to tables. Multiple inheritance generalization mappings are not discussed.

There are three ways to map SINGs to tables:

(16.9)

A. Both the superclass and subclass map to tables.

B. Elimination of superclasses (no superclass table).

C. Elimination of subclasses (no subclass tables).

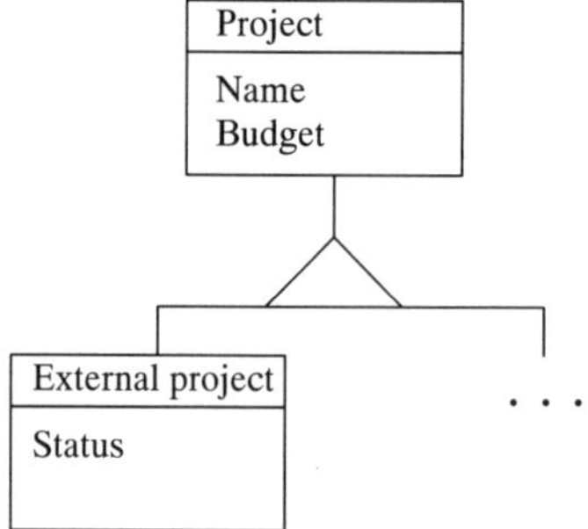

Figure 16.5 Generalization and tables.

The table for the PROJECT superclass is:

```
CREATE TABLE PROJECT
(PROJ#   CHAR(4) NOT NULL,
BUDGET   INTEGER NOT NULL,
PROJECT_TYPE    INTEGER NOT NULL,
PRIMARY KEY (PROJ#))
```

We shall show how each of the scenarios A, B and C is applied to the test case in Figure 16.5.

Option A maps both the superclass and subclass to tables. The identity of an object across a generalization is preserved through the use of a shared ID. This is a clean solution but it involves many tables, and superclass to subclass navigation may be slow.

The table for EXTERNAL_PROJECT in scenario A is:

```
CREATE TABLE EXTERNAL_PROJECT
(PROJ#   CHAR(4) NOT NULL,
STATUS   CHAR(2),
PRIMARY KEY (PROJ#))
```

Navigation using the approach in scenario occurs via the shared ID PROJ#. This is a simple way to simulate inheritance using tables.

In scenario B we eliminate the superclass, and its attributes are replicated in each subclass table. In this case the table for an external project is:

```
CREATE TABLE EXTERNAL_PROJECT
(PROJ#   CHAR(4) NOT NULL,
BUDGET   INTEGER NOT NULL,
STATUS   CHAR(2),
PRIMARY KEY (PROJ#))
```

In scenario C all subclasses are eliminated. One monolithic table is created which contains all the attributes of the subclass tables. In this case table PROJECT would have the following form:

```
CREATE TABLE PROJECT
```

```
(PROJ#   CHAR(4) NOT NULL,
BUDGET   INTEGER NOT NULL,
STATUS   CHAR(2),
TYPE     CHAR(4),
PRIMARY KEY (PROJ#))
```

16.4 Other analogies

We conclude this chapter with a discussion of the problem of combining the relational model with the object model. In particular, we are interested in creating an object model from a relational model. This is a form of reverse engineering in which we wish to map tables to classes, columns to attributes and rows to instances. The starting point for such a migration is based on the following rules of thumb:

- An object corresponds to one or more tables.
- Member data correspond to column values.

These rules are the starting point for defining objects. Tables may be grouped together based on their relationships. A given group is a candidate for an object. If entity relationship (ER diagrams) are available it should be possible to discover the objects from these.

Relational database systems are unable to handle complex data types. Most systems support a limited number of data types which correspond to standard variables used in procedural programming, for example, int, float, double, char, varchar and date. Object systems on the other hand, use the same types but they are encapsulated as classes. Thus, it is preferable to create a class `INTEGER` rather than working with 'raw' int variables because these are not portable across different hardware and software environments. Class `INTEGER` is an example of a foundation class and it is situated in the System Interface Layer (SIL) in the levels of abstraction hierarchy. The classes in this layer serve as a buffer between the relational database system and the object model.

Foreign keys designate relationship between two tables. There are a number of different foreign key relationships. For example, a foreign key can provide the link for a parent–child or supertype–subtype relationship. Foreign keys are also used to denote the fact that a key is part of a set.

Most relational database systems have support for a number of advanced features which can be represented in the object model. These are:

(16.10)

- Default values
- Rules
- Stored procedures
- Views
- Indexes

Defaults are values which are coupled to columns or user-defined types and are used if no other value is given. This functionality can be achieved in C++ by the use of default values in argument lists or by the use of global attributes which are implemented by static member data.

Rules are integrity constraints on specific columns or user-defined types. They can be incorporated into the object model by hard-coding them in member functions.

Stored procedures are precompiled SQL statements. They are represented as member functions of some object.

A view is one way to group data in a number of tables. A view corresponds to how a user sees the data in a relational database system. In the object model, a view could be implemented as a derived class. Views are similar to roles.

Indexes improve database access performance. They provide additional domain-specific information concerning access path. They can be implemented in C++ by dictionaries, hash tables and binary trees.

Exercises

1. Design the following problem using relational database tables:

   A training camp has been set up for the Olympic athletic team.

   The training course lasts two weeks and consists of a number of training sessions where the performances of athletes are registered. Some training sessions are special in that they may have time trials for certain athletes (Figure 16.6).

2. Design the hospital database problem using the relational database approach.

3. What are the disadvantages of applying the approaches in (16.8) in the software development process, especially in the following areas: maintainability, reusability and understandability? When would it be advantageous to design systems using relational database tables?

4. Figure 16.7 shows the entity relationship for a manufacturing firm. Convert it to an object diagram.

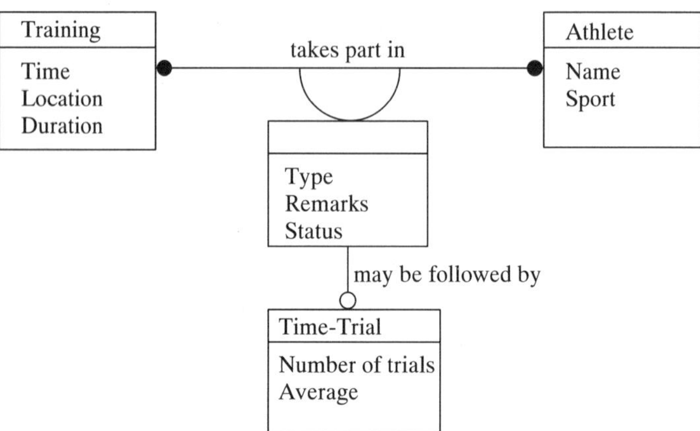

Figure 16.6 Object diagram for training camp.

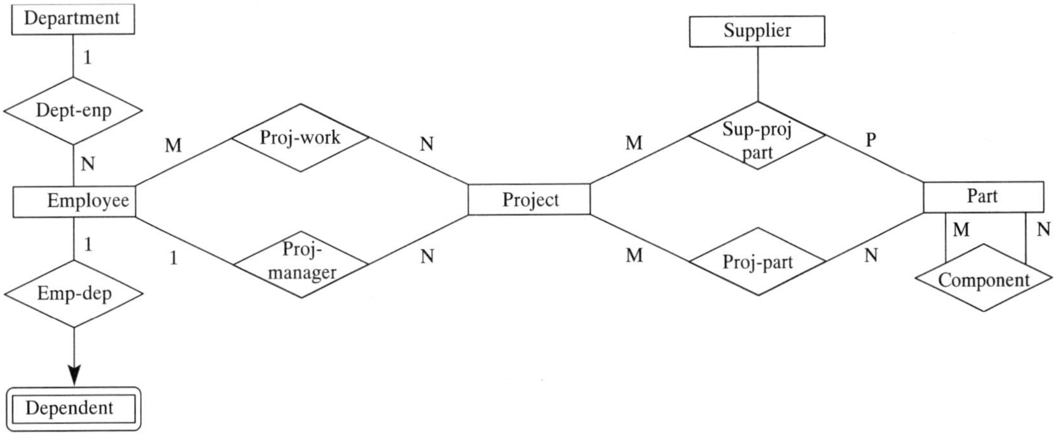

Figure 16.7 ER diagram for a manufacturing firm.

References

C. J. Date (1981) *An Introduction to Database Systems*, Addison-Wesley, Reading MA.

C. J. Date and C. White (1988) *A Guide to DB2*, 2nd edn, Addison-Wesley, Reading MA.

Oracle (1990) *SQL Language Reference Manual, version 6.0*, Oracle Corporation.

J. Rumbaugh, M. Blaha, W. Premerlani, F. Eddy and W. Lorensen (1991) *Object-Oriented Modeling and Design*, Prentice-Hall, Englewood Cliffs NJ.

Chapter

17

Object-oriented database systems

17.1 Introduction and objectives

Chapter 16 was devoted to showing how object-oriented software can be interfaced with relational database systems. In particular, we showed how classes, associations and inheritance relationships are mapped to relational tables. Such mapping results in the classic 'impedance mismatch problem'. This phenomenon refers to the fact that there is no one-to-one mapping between objects and relational database tables. Object-oriented database systems (ODBMSs) do not suffer from such deformation effects because objects can be saved to disk and retrieved from disk in a transparent way. Furthermore, ODBMSs support the object-oriented paradigm, and this means that they can be seamlessly integrated into the software life-cycle without us having to create any unnatural interfaces, as is seen with RDBMSs.

This chapter is an overview of the main concepts underlying ODBMSs. Attention will be paid to what they are, what their advantages are in a software setting and how they can be applied in a software development environment. A number of examples will be given in C++ for two commercially available systems.

ODBMs will compete against RDBMSs in a number of areas in the coming years, especially in applications which use complex data structures. Some of these application areas are discussed in this chapter.

17.2 General database concepts

This section deals with the essential concepts which are needed for an understanding of object-oriented database technology.

17.2.1 Persistence

An object is said to be persistent if it survives the process or thread that created it. Once a persistent object is created it remains accessible until it is explicitly deleted. A transient object in C++ is one which does not survive the block of code in which it is defined. C++ supports transient objects as a default language feature. Many applications demand that objects be saved on disk when the program in which they are defined is exited. One way to achieve this end is to add persistent features to C++. The resulting systems are called persistent extensions to the language. For example, the Poet system (Poet 1994) uses the keyword `persistent` to make a class persistent. This means that all instances of the class will be persistent when used in applications.

An example of a persistent class in Poet is given in the following header file:

```
persistent class Employee
{
private:
  char name[20];
  int   age;
  Address address;

public:
  // ...
};
```

Poet allows instances of `Employee` to write themselves to disk. This is achieved by first creating an object which represent the database itself (via class `PtBase`). Before an object can be stored in the database the database must be connected to and then opened, as shown in the following code:

```
main()
{
  PtBase objbase;
  objbase.Connect("LOCAL"); // Single user environment
  objbase.Open("test"); // Open a database

  // Create an instance of Employee on the heap
  Employee* emp = new Employee(objbase);
  emp->Store(); // Save instance in database

  objbase.Close();   // Close the database
  objbase.DisConnect(); // Disconnect from database

  // Remove instance from heap if no other references to it
  emp -> Forget();   // Remove instance from heap
}
```

For certain applications it may be more viable to create proprietary software for making objects persistent. The main disadvantage of this approach is that the objects may not be interoperable with other object-oriented systems. The situation can be likened to the problem of choosing between flat ASCII files and relational database systems as data stores in applications.

17.2.2 Object identifiers

Each persistent object has a so-called object identifier (OID) associated with it. When an object is created it is assigned a unique OID. When the object is deleted its OID is also removed and is never used again. The OID is what gives objects their identity and it should be of no concern to the programmer. The OID is hidden. It is enough to know that an object is unique and that it will never be confused with other objects in the database.

Implementing object identity in different environments has been discussed in Chapter 2.

17.2.3 Integrity

An ODBMS is responsible for the accuracy of the data contained in it. This is called data integrity. Data integrity guarantees that the data in the database is consistent with both the structural requirements of the DBMS and with the logical constraints specified by the database designer, for example guaranteeing that there are no pointers to non-existent data.

The main integrity issues are:

- Structural integrity
- Logical integrity
- Referential integrity

Structural integrity is concerned with protection against a number of problems. First, the database physical structure should be protected against hardware and software failures. The second source of concern is when a user circumvents the protection built into the system in order to tamper with the data, either inadvertently or by malice.

Logical integrity is concerned with enforcing semantic constraints on the data in a database. Since ODBMSs do not understand the semantics of the data, logical constraints must be supplied by the database designer. RDBMSs implement constraints in such a way that they are always attached to the data and usually implemented by a non-procedural syntax. ODBMSs implement constraints by methods. Each method that updates the database may implement constraints as part of the body of the method. The disadvantage of this approach is that general constraints must be specified in each method. A workaround to this problem is to build a number of primitive update methods which implement constraints and which are always called by 'higher-order' methods which attempt to update the individual data items.

Referential integrity is that property which ensures that an object cannot be deleted if there is a reference to it. An example of referential integrity is given in the test program in Section 17.2.1, where the `Employee` instance is removed from memory by use of the `Forget()` function only if there are no other references to the instance.

17.2.4 Concurrency control

ODBMSs have a concurrency control system which must guarantee that users see a consistent state of the database at all times and which ensures that concurrent transactions move the database from one consistent state to another consistent state.

In traditional database systems all transactions are guaranteed to be serializable, which means that collections of concurrently executing transactions behave as if the transactions are applied to the database in some serial order. Serializability is guaranteed by locking. A transaction will lock a record or object that it reads or writes and keeps it locked until the transaction is committed.

Early object-oriented databases focused on trying to lock each object separately. Object-level locking can in some cases reduce the potential for concurrency conflicts, but at the cost of introducing locking overhead on every object. Present-day ODBMSs (such as ObjectStore

(ObjectDesign 1992) allow locking to be implemented at multiple levels of granularity. Objects can be locked on a segment of the database, on a page or in a user-defined configuration such as an aggregate object. Only a single lock is needed for a segment, page or user-defined configuration, resulting in significant performance gains over object-level locking mechanisms.

Concurrency is implemented in ODBMSs by three main techniques:

(17.1)

- Optimistic concurrency
- Hybrid concurrency
- Versioning

ODBMSs distinguish themselves from RDBMSs in a number of respects. One important difference is in the length of time it takes to commit a transaction. ODBMS applications may have long transactions and objects may be locked for extended periods of time. A large number of locks may need to be maintained while a transaction is in progress. There is a big need to reduce lock overhead, and the techniques in (17.1) are among the most popular.

Optimistic schemes use no locking whatsoever. Objects are retrieved and updated without locks. When the current transaction has committed the reads and writes are checked to see whether they can be serialized with any previously committed transactions.

Conflicts can arise with optimistic concurrency schemes. First, it is possible that two transactions will attempt to update the same object in a conflicting manner ('write–write' conflict). Allowing transactions to operate in parallel violates the serializability constraint. The second type of conflict occurs when one transaction has read a value that a second transaction has written and committed after the first transaction has read the value ('read–write' conflict).

Optimistic concurrency is useful in applications where the probability of concurrency conflicts is low. Locking overhead is eliminated and it provides the user with a consistent view of the database without delays.

Hybrid schemes use optimistic concurrency as the default for all objects. However, locking mechanisms can be defined for those objects for which a concurrency conflict is highly probable. Hybrid schemes are more predictable than their optimistic counterparts and should be employed when the probability of concurrency conflicts is high.

The third approach to concurrency control is to keep all versions of an object on a permanent basis. Versioning effectively disallows updates. The disadvantage is that versions must be merged at a later stage, and this problem is usually left up to the user to decide.

17.2.5 Availability

One of the responsibilities of any database system is to guarantee that information is available when requested. In an ideal world data is always available, but in the real world events can take place which cause a database to become unavailable or leave it in an inconsistent state. Examples are disk and system crashes. ODBMSs should provide utilities which can restore the database to its original state. In particular, good backup and recovery procedures should be provided after a system crash. Database down-time should also be kept to a minimum. This is a weak point with the present generation of ODBMSs.

17.2.6 Transaction management

A database transaction is a sequence of database operations in which either all operations are completed as a single update or none of the changes takes place. A transaction is atomic in the sense that it is seen as one event. A goal of ODBMSs is to guarantee that a user or application sees the database as if that person or application is the only user of the database.

There are two types of transaction, namely conventional transactions and long transactions. A conventional transaction is similar to the type of transaction that takes place in relational database systems, for example updating a bank account record or reading an employee database. Conventional transactions are usually short-lived. Long transactions, on the other hand, take a finite and possibly extended length of time to complete. It is not uncommon for some transactions to take weeks or even months to complete.

17.2.7 Performance

Performance is an important issue with ODBMSs. For certain classes of problems, such as CAD/CAM, office information systems and financial risk management systems, ODBMSs offer better performance than RDBMSs.

Performance can be improved and overhead minimized by the following techniques:

- Locking
- Pointer dereferencing (object traversal)
- Data caching
- Minimal disk access overhead

Locking has already been discussed in Section 17.2.4. Locking is applied at segment or page level. This is locking at large granularity. A number of first-generation OODBMSs used object-level locking mechanisms, but these are very inefficient, especially with composite objects. It is more efficient to lock top-level objects.

ODBMSs are suitable for client/server applications which operate in network environments. A number of so-called client/server locking models have been developed for such cases. A server is a process which runs on a given host and which manages physical data on disks and arbitrates among client processes making requests for the data. A client is a system running an application process which accesses the server across the network. Concurrent access by multiple clients can lead to interference and a number of ODBMSs (see, for example, ObjectDesign (1992)) employ a locking mechanism in which a server keeps track of which objects are in use by which clients. Locking information is usually cached in both the server and the client. This minimizes the need for network communication when the same process performs consecutive transactions on the same data.

A requirement in ODBMS design is that the operation of extracting data from an object should not incur any undue overhead. This operation is called 'pointer dereferencing', and a number of database systems exist for which the cost of dereferencing a persistent object is no more expensive than for a transient object.

Some ODBMSs provide a so-called caching mechanism, whereby previously retrieved objects can be reaccessed without having to refetch or relock those objects. This is a common situation in client/server environments; the client fetches data from the server and this data remains in the client cache until the data dies (via a timeout) or until it is committed to the server database. This approach reduces network traffic, since most of the processing is done in the local client cache.

Database disk access performance can be improved by clustering. This concept refers to storing related objects close together on secondary storage. An application often uses only a portion of a database, and that portion should be stored contiguously in a small section of the database. Access is improved, since contiguous data can be fetched more quickly than randomly accessed data. Clustering is used in RDBMSs where tuples of a relation are stored in the same segment of disk pages on the basis of the values in a column or combination of columns of the relation.

Clustering for ODBMSs is more difficult than for RDBMSs because there are many ways in which sets of related objects may be accessed. There are a number of strategies for clustering data object sets. The different options are:

(17.2)

1. Cluster all objects belonging to the same class.
2. Cluster all objects and their references.
3. Cluster all objects and those objects that they recursively reference.
4. Combine options 2 and 3.

Clustering is optimal for one type of access and suboptimal for other types of access. Determining the most profitable way in which objects should be clustered is part of physical database design (Finkelstein *et al.* 1988; Rullo and Sacca 1988) and decisions should be made on the basis of an analysis of the frequency of access and the cost of different types of access.

ODBMSs usually have a default clustering strategy, while some also have the ability to take clustering hints from users. For example, ObjectStore divides a database into areas called segments. Whenever an application creates a new persistent object it can specify the segment in which that object should be created. ObjectStore supports object-level clustering and this gives the programmer the option of placing objects next to each other on disk pages and to control how many objects are allowed on each page. The advantages of this are that disk I/O is minimized, since objects that are located near each other are retrieved together and that database concurrency hotspots are eliminated so that no performance degradation is experienced with object-based locking.

17.2.8 Data modelling

An object-oriented data model is one which is based on object-oriented concepts such as generalizations, aggregations and associations between objects. ODBMSs which support an object-oriented model should provide high-level primitives to express and manage these concepts. This has the important consequence that ODBMSs can be seamlessly integrated with the products of the object-oriented design (OOD) phase. No interfaces need to be made and no impedance mismatch problems can occur. A number of ODBMSs provide a high-level data manipulation language (DML) which is a set of extensions to C++ and which performs such tasks as querying, iteration, maintaining indexes and managing relationships between objects.

In short, an ODBMS should support most of the object-oriented features which were discussed in Chapter 8.

17.3 ODBMS architecture: general principles

This section discusses some of the issues which determine the physical and logical architecture of ODBMSs. The topics correspond to the tasks that a DBA (database administrator) would perform in a more traditional database environment, but with a number of extensions.

17.3.1 Schema evolution

Typical object-oriented applications change in time. Users may need to change the definition of objects in a database. The process of schema evolution is concerned with managing this kind of change and ensuring that the data in the database remains consistent after changes in object structure have taken place.

Schema evolution involves two special processes:

- Metadata evolution
- Object evolution

Metadata is concerned with describing object structure and behaviour. During metadata evolution it must be possible to modify the database schema information. Typical cases are:

- Adding new classes to the schema.
- Deleting classes from the schema.
- New objects may be created that are subtypes of existing objects.
- Classes may be modified in some way.

There are different ways to modify a class during schema evolution. Typical examples are:

- The inheritance structure of a class may be modified by adding or deleting base classes.
- New member data may be defined for the class or old member data may be deleted.
- Member functions may be added, deleted or have their names and/or signatures changed.

Object evolution is concerned with changes in objects as the database schema changes. Some ODBMSs handle object changes on a default basis.

17.3.2 Schema versioning

Schema versioning allows users to create different versions of one logical schema and to make different views of the database visible to the users under those versions of the schema.

One big advantage of schema versioning is that it allows the evolution of the history of objects to be preserved. This is an important requirement in applications such as computer-aided design (CAD) and geographical information systems (GIS), where it is necessary to have different designs which will be merged at some later stage in the design process.

17.3.3 Indexing and nested attribute versioning

An index is a data structure which is used in a database query to retrieve a small subset of the database. An index can be implemented as an attribute or combination of attributes of a class and is logically maintained as a list of pairs of <key, list_of_identifiers> where the key is a value of the indexed attribute(s) and each identifier in the list is the identifier of an object in which the indexed attribute holds the key value. For example, an index may be maintained on the `Color` attribute in class `Product` which can then be used in order to query `Product` where a search predicate involving `Color` is present.

Most object-oriented applications make use of class hierarchies and aggregation relationships and the conventional indexing techniques become inefficient when applied to these cases. A new type of indexing is needed for each case; the types are:

- Class hierarchy indexing
- Nested attribute indexing

A discussion of these advanced techniques is beyond the scope of this book and we refer the interested reader to the articles in Sigs (1992).

17.3.4 Authorization and access control

Authorization is concerned with users and groups of users acquiring access to database information. RDBMSs have limited support for authorization models. For example, a user may grant a read or write privilege on a relation to another user. The smallest unit of authorization is the relation in this case. ODBMSs extend this model because we are dealing with objects, and they should naturally be the unit of authorization. An authorization is an interaction object (or association in OMT). In general we think of subjects (active agents) being able to access objects (passive objects) in some way. The type of access can vary and is usually a link attribute (Figure 17.1). Authorization problems are common in operating system design and are implemented by so-called access matrices. An access matrix is a two-dimensional grid with subjects representing the rows and objects representing the columns of the matrix. The matrix entries represent the type of access. An example is given in Figure 17.2. Entries with blank values indicate that there is no access between a subject and an object. A number of commercial operating systems, such as VAX/VMS, implement access control in this way.

ODBMSs introduce new levels of authorization when compared with their RDBMS counterparts. Typical examples involves the ability to execute the following commands:

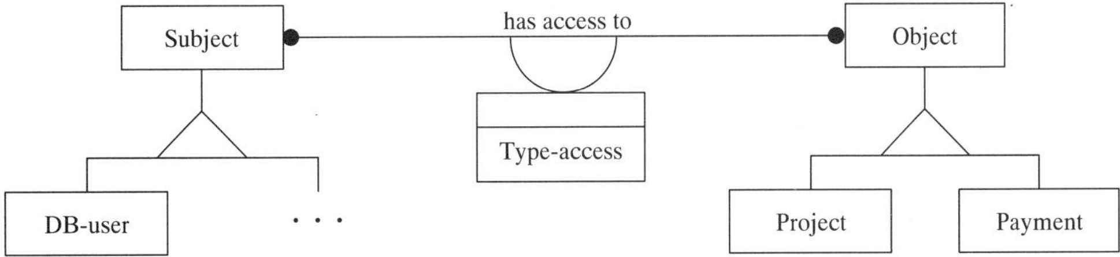

Figure 17.1 Authorization objects.

Subject \ Object	F1	F2	Printer	CD ROM
D1	Read		Print	Read
D2		Execute		
D3	Read write			

Figure 17.2 Access matrix.

- Create a class or a subclass of a base class
- Execute a method
- Change a method

17.4 Using ODBMS with C++; the programmer's viewpoint

ODBMSs may be accessed from high-level programming languages, such as C, C++, FORTRAN and Smalltalk. This section shows in particular how C++ can be seamlessly used with the ODBMS ObjectStore.

In order to get an understanding of how an ODBMS can be used a developer needs to understand how to perform the following tasks:

- Creating a database
- Opening a database
- Starting a transaction
- Creating an entry point (a named object)
- Creating a persistent object
- Managing groups of objects

17.4.1 Creating a database

Objects are stored in databases. Before an object can be stored a database must first be created. ObjectStore has a class 'database' and a number of static member functions, one of which creates a new database object. A typical example is:

```
database* emp = database::create("/datasim/employee", 0666);
```

The first argument is the pathname of the database to be created, while the second argument gives the type of access in a UNIX environment (in this case all users have read and write access to the database).

17.4.2 Opening a database

Before a developer can read or write in the database it must first be opened, as follows:

```
database* emp = database::open("/datasim/employee");
```

17.4.3 Starting a transaction

A transaction is a unit of work whose boundaries are defined by the developer. The process of reading or writing to the database must take place within a so-called transaction boundary. This is achieved in ObjectStore by use of a high-level data manipulation language (DML):

```
do_transaction()
{

  // Place your code here

}
```

17.4.4 Creating a persistent object

Persistence is implemented in ObjectStore by overloading the `new` and `delete` operators. In this way the developer can work with both transient and persistent objects in a transparent manner.

17.4.5 Creating an entry point (a named object)

Persistent objects are retrieved from the database by the use of database roots. The function of the root is to associate an entry point with a name. Once the association has been made the developer can retrieve a pointer to the entry point by using a member function of class `database_root`.

17.4.6 Managing groups of objects

ObjectStore provides tools for managing the following types of object:

- Collections
- Queries
- Relationships

A collection is an object which serves to group other objects. Examples of collections are sets, symbol tables, linked lists and arrays. Consider the problem of writing a class for maintaining information on different types of employee in a company. The base class `Employee` could have specializations for employees who are paid on an hourly basis, weekly basis or monthly basis.

The new class has the following class interface:

```
class Employee_DB
{
private:
  os_Collection<Employee*> &emp;

public:
  // ...
};
```

The class `os_Collection<Employee*>` is a specialization of the template class `os_Collection<T>`. Templates are supported in ObjectStore and this results in high productivity and reusability gains.

17.5 Poet: a persistent extension to C++

The Poet system allows the developer to add persistence to the C++ language. A new keyword, `persistence`, is added to the language and this allows objects to be made persistent. The high-level architecture of Poet is shown in Figure 17.3. The main components are:

- The Poet pre-compiler
- The class dictionary
- Tools environment

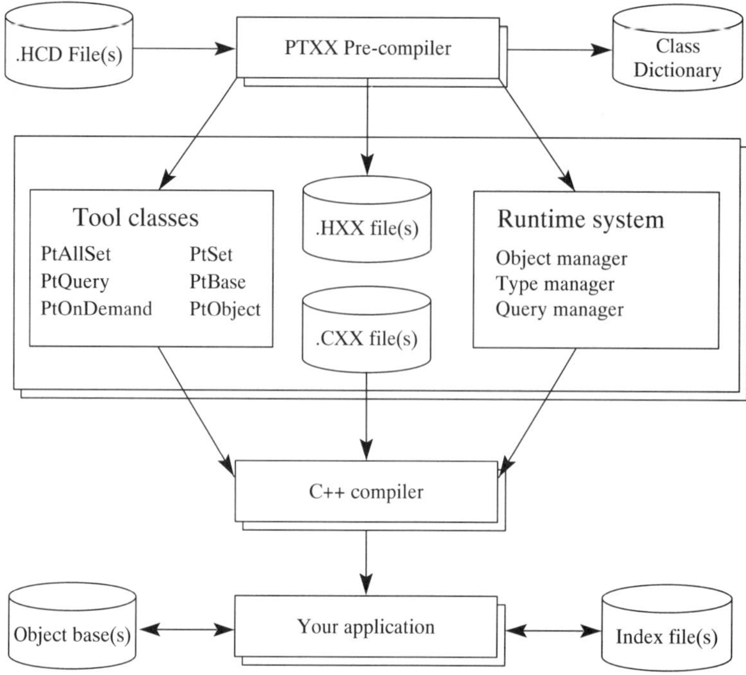

Figure 17.3 Overview of Poet's construction.

- The runtime system

The software process begins in Poet by creating class interfaces and code files. It is mandatory to declare a class as being persistent. This will ensure that objects which are created in an application can be saved on secondary storage. Once a complete class interface has been written it is processed by the Poet pre-compiler. This pre-compiler adds the class schema to the class dictionary and it also produces 'normal' C++ header files as output. The developer may make use of the Tools classes when creating classes and applications. The main tool classes are:

- `PtBase`: a class whose instances represent the database itself. `PtBase` has member functions for creating and opening a database, establishing a link to the server where the database is situated and breaking a link with the server. It is also possible to close and delete a database object.
- `PtOnDemand`: a class which loads objects into memory on a need-by basis. This can be useful in environments where there is not enough memory to hold objects.
- `PtObject`: a base class for all persistent classes which the developer defines in an application. `PtObject` contains member functions for object identity and link counts and for assigning objects to a database. Of course, all derived classes inherit these methods from `PtObject` so that persistence is automatic.

The runtime system contains a number of modules. These are the Object manager, Query manager and Type manager.

The supplier–product database problem was discussed in Chapter 16 and was implemented using relational database tables. This section shows how the corresponding problem is solved in Poet. There are three classes, two of which are roles (product, supplier) and the last one is an association (delivery). The Poet header files which are used as input to the Poet pre-compiler are given by:

```
// supplier.hcd
//
// This file contains the header file of a supplier.
//
// © Datasim BV, 1994.

#ifndef SUPPLIER_HXX
#define SUPPLIER_HXX

#include "contype.hxx"
#include "ptstring.hxx"

persistent class SUPPLIER
{
private:
  // PtString is Poet's string class
  PtString Name;          // The name of the supplier
  PtString Status;        // Its status
  PtString City;          // The city where it is located

// Private functions
  void init(const PtString&,const PtString
        &,constPtString&);       // Initialize data members

public:
  // Constructors and destructors
  SUPPLIER();
  SUPPLIER(const SUPPLIER& supplier);
  SUPPLIER(const PtString& name, const PtString& status,
        const PtString& city);
  ~SUPPLIER();

  // Selectors
  PtString name() const;          // The name
  PtString status() const;        // The status
  PtString city() const;          // City where he is located

  // Modifiers
  void name(const PtString& newname);    // Change its name
  void status(const PtString& newstatus);
  void city(const PtString& newcity);    // Change the city
```

```
  SUPPLIER& operator= (const SUPPLIER& supplier);

friend ostream&  operator<< (ostream& os,
    const SUPPLIER& supplier);

};

#endif

// product.hxx
//
// This file contains the header file of a product.
//
// © Datasim BV 1994.

#ifndef PRODUCT_HXX
#define PRODUCT_HXX

#include "contype.hxx"
#include "ptstring.hxx"

persistent class PRODUCT
{

private:
  PtString Name;          // The name of the product
  PtString Color;         // Its color
  double Weight;          // The weight

// Private functions
  void init(const PtString&,
        const PtString&,double);  // Initialize data members

public:
  // Constructors and destructors
  PRODUCT();
  PRODUCT(const PRODUCT& product);
  PRODUCT(const PtString& name, const PtString& color,
        double weight);
  ~PRODUCT();

  // Selectors
  PtString name() const;          // The name of the product
  PtString color() const;         // The color
  double weight() const;          // The weight

  // Modifiers
```

```
  void name(const PtString& newname);    // Set the name
  void color(const PtString& newcolor); // Set the color
  void weight(double newweight);         // Set the weight
  PRODUCT& operator= (const PRODUCT& product);

friend ostream& operator<< (ostream& os,
    const PRODUCT& product);

};

#endif

// delivery.hxx
//
// This file contains the header file of a delivery.
// This class is the connection between a supplier and a
// product.
//
// © Datasim BV, 1994.

#ifndef DELIVERY_HXX
#define DELIVERY_HXX

#include "supplier.hcd"
#include "product.hcd"

persistent class DELIVERY
{
private:
  SUPPLIER* Supplier;          // Reference to a supplier
  PRODUCT* Product;            // Reference to a product
  int Deliverytime;            // Time of delivery

// private functions
  void init(SUPPLIER*,PRODUCT*,int);     // Initialize
                                         // private members

public:
  // Constructors and destructors
  DELIVERY();
  DELIVERY(const DELIVERY& delivery);
  DELIVERY(SUPPLIER* supplier, PRODUCT* product, int time);
  ~DELIVERY();

  // Selectors
  SUPPLIER* supplier() const;    // Return supplier reference
  PRODUCT* product() const;      // Return product reference
```

```
  int deliverytime() const;     // Return delivery time

  // Modifiers
  void supplier(SUPPLIER* supplier);     // Change supplier
                                         // reference
  void product(PRODUCT* product);        // Change product
                                         // reference
  void deliverytime(int newtime);        // Change the
                                         // delivery time

  DELIVERY& operator=(const DELIVERY& delivery);

friend ostream& operator<< (ostream& os,
    const DELIVERY& delivery);

};

#endif
```

The code file for DELIVERY is now given to show how functionality from Poet can be used.

```
// delivery.cxx
//
// © Datasim BV, 1994.

#include "poet.hxx"
#include "delivery.hxx"
#include "contype.hxx"

// Private functions
void DELIVERY::init(SUPPLIER* supplier, PRODUCT* product,
    int time)
{
  // Objects in POET use reference counting. The Remember()
  // function increments an object's link counter while the
  // Forget() function decrements the counter and deletes
  // the object if there are no more references to it.

  if(supplier == NULL)
    Supplier = NULL;
  else
  {
    Supplier = supplier;
    Supplier->Remember();
  }

  if(product == NULL)
```

```
    Product = NULL;
  else
  {
    Product = product;
    Product->Remember();
  }
  Deliverytime = time;
}

DELIVERY::DELIVERY()
{
  init(NULL,NULL,0);
}

DELIVERY::DELIVERY(const DELIVERY& delivery)
{
  init(delivery.Supplier,delivery.Product,
    delivery.Deliverytime);
}

DELIVERY::DELIVERY(SUPPLIER* supplier, PRODUCT* product,
    int time)
{
  init(supplier,product,time);
}

DELIVERY::~DELIVERY()
{
  Supplier->Forget();
  Product->Forget();
  Deliverytime = 0;
}

SUPPLIER* DELIVERY::supplier() const
{
  Supplier->Remember();
  return Supplier;
}

PRODUCT* DELIVERY::product() const
{
  Product->Remember();
  return Product;
}

int DELIVERY::deliverytime() const
{
```

```
  return Deliverytime;
}

void DELIVERY::supplier(SUPPLIER* supplier)
{
  if(Supplier != NULL)
    Supplier->Forget();

  Supplier = supplier;

  if(Supplier != NULL)
    Supplier->Remember();
}

void DELIVERY::product(PRODUCT* product)
{
  if(Product != NULL)
    Product->Forget();
  Product = product;

  if(Product != NULL)
    Product->Remember();
}

void DELIVERY::deliverytime(int newtime)
{
  Deliverytime = newtime;
}

DELIVERY& DELIVERY::operator=(const DELIVERY& delivery)
{
  if(Supplier != NULL)
    Supplier->Forget();
  if(Product != NULL)
    Product->Forget();

  init(delivery.Supplier,delivery.Product,
    delivery.Deliverytime);

  return *this;
}

ostream& operator<< (ostream& os, const DELIVERY& delivery)
{
  os << "Delivery " << endl;
  os << (*delivery.Supplier);
  os << "Delivery" << endl;
```

```
    os << (*delivery.Product);
    os << "Days for delivery : " << delivery.Deliverytime
          << endl;

    return os;
}
```

Instances of classes `SUPPLIER`, `PRODUCT` and `DELIVERY` can be made persistent in much the same way as in the test program in Section 17.2.1.

17.6 Interoperability

This section deals with the problem of ensuring that ODBMSs can be used in different applications. This is a specific case of the more general problem of writing applications which work in distributed heterogeneous environments. To this end, we outline the efforts which are being taken in this direction.

17.6.1 The OMG CORBA specification

The Object Management Group (OMG) is a body of approximately 300 international companies whose mission is to promote object technology and object interoperability. The high-level architectural structure is shown in Figure 17.4. This is a reference model and it has three intended audiences. The first is for the OMG in order to provide a framework for guiding the process of soliciting and evaluating distributed object oriented technology. The model also serves potential technology providers who wish to position their proposed technology in relation to others. Finally, the model is a reference for application developers

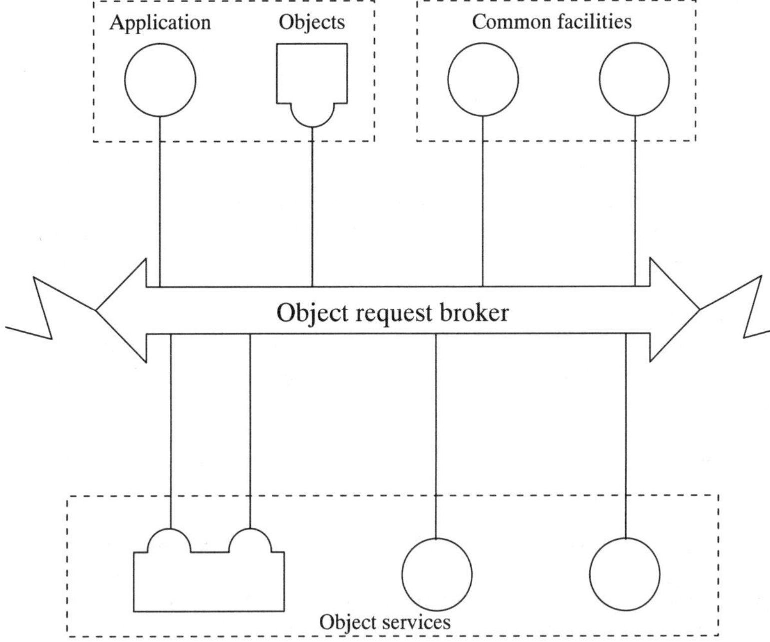

Figure 17.4 Object management architecture overview.

in industry. The reference model articulates OMG's vision for highly interoperable applications and services using object technology.

The reference model identifies and characterizes the components, interfaces and protocols that comprise OMG's object management architecture (OMA). The model specifies in general what the major separable components of OMA are, the functions provided by each component and how components relate to each other and with the operating environments. In particular, the model addresses specific issues, such as how objects receive requests and responses and what the basic operations of each object are, and it describes object interfaces that provide common facilities which can be reused in many different applications.

The OMA consists of the following components (Figure 17.4):

- Object Services (OS)
- Common Facilities (CF)
- Application Objects (AO)

The Object broker (ORB) is the backbone of OMA and it provides the mechanisms by which objects transparently make and receive requests and responses. It is the backbone in the sense that it provides interoperability between applications on different machines in heterogeneous distributed environments and it seamlessly connects multiple object systems.

The ORB addresses the following issues:

- Name service: mapping object names in the naming domain into equivalent names in the domain of the method to be executed. This is similar to creating object location services (see Albitz and Liu (1992) for a special case where a naming system has been constructed from host names in UNIX networks).
- Request dispatch: this determines which method to invoke.
- Parameter encoding: these facilities map the local representation of parameter values into the target environment representation. Industry standards may be used to achieve this encoding, such as ASN.1, OSF/DCE and ONC/NFS/XDR (Comer 1988; Stevens 1990).
- Delivery: this describes how requests and results are delivered to the proper locations. Standard delivery protocols such as TCP/UDP/IP and ISO/Tpn may be employed (Comer 1988; Rose 1990).
- Synchronization: this deals with handling parallelism between objects. Supported paradigms are asynchronous (request with no response), synchronous (request and wait for response) and deferred synchronous (proceed after sending requests and claim a reply later).
- Activation: the housekeeping processing before a method can be activated.
- Exception handling.
- Security mechanisms: determination of higher-level controls and policies.

Object services (OS) is a collection of services with object interfaces which provide basic functions for realizing and maintaining objects. This includes both logical modelling and physical storage of objects. The OS operations are made available through the ORB. It is possible to provide services through non-OMG or proprietary interfaces for higher performance, for example. Object services do not impose a single implementation.

Object services consist of building blocks which can be used in extended functionality in common facilities (CF) such as transaction management that span objects, implementations and machines.

The responsibilities of OS lie in the following areas:

- Class management (as in OMT)
- Instance management (object-level)
- Permanent and transient storage for large and small objects
- Integrity (locking at all levels of granularity)
- Security (defining access control at all levels of granularity)
- Query (navigation with collections of objects)
- Version of objects

Typical examples of subcomponents in OS include ODBMSs, query facilities, transaction managers and directory and file services.

Common facilities (CF) provide facilities that can be used in many applications. However, they are not supported on all platforms. They are optional. The main advantage of CF for application developers is that they save having to write OMA-compliant applications. Some of the functionality provided by CF is contained in the following list:

- Reusable user interfaces
- Communications with ORB
- Catalogues and browsers for classes and objects
- Interfaces to external systems
- Object querying facilities

The Applications objects (AO) represent individual related sets of functionality, such as word processors, spreadsheets and financial planning software. AO and CF are at the same OMA semantic level; however, CF classes offer very general functionality while AO classes are specific to an application or range of applications.

The AO will contain many programs in the future. Among them will be systems in the following application areas:

- Office automation
- Computer-aided design
- CASE tools
- Network management applications

It will take a number of years (maybe even a decade or two!) before these standards become available or are accepted by the software and hardware communities, but it is certainly bound to become a major impetus for creating truly interoperable applications for the 21st century.

Defining an architecture and providing specifications for an OMA-compliant application is described in detail in OMG Group (1993).

17.7 Application areas and ODBMSs

It is unlikely that ODBMSs will replace RDBMSs in the near future as the *de facto* database standard, but they are being used in a number of key application areas and market segments where RDBMS are totally unsuited. The main markets for ODBMS are in the following segments (Chorafas and Steinman 1993):

- Computer-aided design and Manufacturing (CAD/CAM)
- Office automation (OIS)
- Computer-aided software engineering (CASE)
- Cartographical applications (GIS)
- Cross-functional projects (for example, risk management)
- Cross-departmental projects (for example, cost control)

We see that not only technical areas such as CAD use ODBMS but that financial and business applications are beginning to use the technology as an efficient way of storing and retrieving objects with complex structures. RDBMSs are unsuitable for these kinds of application, mainly because they work with the table paradigm while one is interested in more complex structures and queries than they can provide.

References

P. Albitz and C. Liu (1992) *DNS and Bind*, O'Reilly and Associates, Sebastopol CA.

D. N. Chorafas and H. Steinman (1993) *Object-Oriented Databases*, Prentice-Hall, Englewood Cliffs NJ.

D. Comer (1988) *Internetworking with TCP/IP: Principles, Protocols and Architecture*, Prentice-Hall, Englewood Cliffs NJ.

S. Finkelstein, M. Schkolnick and P. Tiberio (1988) Physical Database Design for Relational Databases, *ACM Transactions on Database Systems*, **13**(1) 91–128.

ObjectDesign (1992) *ObjectStore Technical Overview*, Object Design Inc., Burlington MA.

OMG Group (1991) *The Common Object Request Broker: Architecture and Specification*, revision 1.1, Object Management Group Inc., 492 Old Connecticut Path, Framington MA.

OMG Group (1993) *Object Management Architecture Guide*, Object Management Group Inc., 492 Old Connecticut Path, Framington MA.

Poet (1994) *Poet version 2.0 Reference Manual*, Poet Software Company, 4633 Old Ironside Drive, Suite 110, Santa Clara CA.

M. Rose (1990) *The Open Book, A Practical Perspective to OSI*, Prentice-Hall, Englewood Cliffs NJ.

P. Rullo and D. Sacca (1988) An automatic physical designer for network model databases, *IEEE Transactions on Software Engineering*, **14**(9) 1293–306.

Sigs (1992) *Journal of Object-Oriented Programming, Focus on ODBMS*, SIGS Publications, New York.

W. R. Stevens (1990) *Unix Network Programming*, Prentice-Hall, Englewood Cliffs NJ.

Chapter

18

Preventive maintenance of C++ code

Quality software should have the characteristics of being understandable and measurable

(Adrion et al. *1982)*

18.1 Introduction and objectives

This book has assumed that the reader has some knowledge of the C++ language. There are numerous books on C++. Most concentrate on the syntax of the language and very few give the reader insight into how to create good object-oriented software, let alone tell the reader which functionality of the language to use and not to use in different circumstances. Furthermore, there seems to be a chasm between books on OOA and those on C++; the latter group concentrates on showing how to map analysis and design principles to C++, while the former group pays little attention to the design and engineering aspects of the software coding process. Our aim with this chapter is to help the reader make the transition from design to C++ in a way that is consistent with accepted software engineering principles.

For state-of-the art reports on C++ and design issues we recommend the *C++ Report* and the *Journal of Object-Oriented Programming*. For those readers who wish to keep abreast of the very latest developments in software science the journal *IEEE Software* is a must.

This chapter gives a wide-eyed and critical overview of how C++ can be used effectively in applications and it attempts to give a number of warnings on what not to do. The advice given here is to use C++ only when it is appropriate for your particular problems and not to fall into the way of the 'software lemmings' (in the words of Alan Davis), that is those who would lead you to believe that C++ is the answer to all of our software problems.

18.2 Software quality criteria, an overview

The main aim of software engineering is to help produce quality software (Meyer 1988). The question is, what is software quality? A number of quality criteria are in use in the software industry which will be discussed in this chapter. It is interesting to note that many C++ aficionados pay little attention to such issues in books and articles, preferring to concentrate on the language features. Other object-oriented languages (such as Eiffel and Smalltalk) are better in supporting good engineering principles; C++ is a low-level language and it is possible to apply it in a way that is not consistent with the object-oriented way of doing things. Using it in an arbitrary way will eventually lead to maintenance and understandability problems and it is our objective to show how to apply C++ so that pitfalls are avoided. To this end, we discuss several procedures which, when adopted, will help lead to quality improvements. The emphasis is on prevention rather than on correction. In other words, we wish to get it right first time.

A number of the software quality criteria discussed here can be found in Meyer (1988). This book is well worth reading (even if it does deal with non-C++ issues) because of the interesting topics dealt with there. Another good source for finding candidate classes which can be 're-engineered' in C++ is Goldberg and Robson (1983).

The software quality criteria which we discuss are not mutually orthogonal and there is a certain amount of overlap between them. The criteria are:

- Understandability (how easy is it to understand, use and modify C++ code)
- Portability (does the C++ code run without change in different software and hardware environments?)
- Reusability (how easy is it to use and extend classes to new application areas?)
- Robustness (will our classes remain functioning even under abnormal circumstances?)
- Interoperability (can our C++ classes be easily interfaced with other classes and applications?)
- Efficiency (does our code make good use of hardware and other resources?)

The above issues play a vital role in all programming endeavour and are not just limited to object-oriented programming in C++. What is new here is how we apply the quality criteria to producing quality C++ code.

18.3 Understandability

18.3.1 Readability of C++ class interfaces

We need to be able to understand C++ classes for a number of reasons. First, we need to be able to locate a class in a library for possible reuse. This is no trivial problem, as the class that we are looking for needs to be retrieved from a large collection and there are very few commercial software products which allow us to do this. Languages such as Smalltalk have browsers which allows the programmer to search for certain keywords in class collections. Secondly, having found the class that we wish to use there arises the need to be able to apply it quickly and efficiently. In this case the class interface should be properly documented. Note that the interface contains only a description of the class and the declarations of its member functions. No function bodies should be included here, as this confuses those who are trying to understand the responsibility of the class. A properly documented class interface can be used as a so-called specification sheet (Cox 1987) and should be used by both novice and experienced programmers alike. A typical specification sheet contains the following information:

(18.1)

- A description of the responsibility of the class (this is similar to constructing a data dictionary in the object modelling phase of OOA).

- Determine the class's server classes (which classes does it need).
- Grouping member functions in categories (constructors, destructors, selectors and modifiers).
- Document each member function category by so-called strategic comments.
- Document individual member functions by so-called tactical comments.

A strategic comment serves as a header for all member functions which succeed it. It is useful to use such comments as a way of quickly locating groups of related member functions. A tactical comment, on the other hand is a 'one-liner'; its function is to document a single function in a compact and precise way. Finally, it is useful to use good names for member functions; the names should reflect the application area and responsibility of the given class and should be consistent with similar member functions in other classes. Variable names in the parameter list should also be chosen to reflect the role that the variable plays. This is called 'syntactic sugaring', and while not absolutely necessary its use does promote the readability of a class interface.

A number of formal methods exist for specifying classes and requirements. The most popular ones are Z (Stepney *et al.* 1992) and VDM (Jones 1990). Z has a number of object-oriented extensions which make it useful for describing class syntax and semantics, and their use promotes the understandability (and indeed the reliability!) of C++ classes. We describe MooZ, which is of the object-oriented extensions to Z.

A class body in MooZ consists of a sequence of clauses where the order is mandatory and whose presence is optional (we include C++ comments for describing each clause):

```
// The class name.
Class   <Class-Name>

// This clause is present for generic classes,
// absent for 'normal' classes.
givensets <type-names-list>

// Allows single and multiple inheritance.
superclasses <class-references-list>
    <auxiliary-definitions>

// The clauses 'private' and 'public' refer to class
// services.
private <definition-names-list>

or

public  <definition-names-list>

// Define class constants; these play a large role in
// class semantics. The scope of a constant is the entire
// class body.
constants <axiomatic-descriptions-list>
    <auxiliary-definitions>
```

```
// Define the state components here (usually private member
// data)
state <anonymous-schema> or <constraint>

// Define the initial state of the class using
initialization operations.
initialstates <schema> <auxiliary definitions>

// Clause for schemas and class operations (usually public
// member functions)
operations  <definitions>

EndClass <Class-Name>
```

The main advantage (as we see it) of first writing a MooZ specification before writing the actual C++ class code is that it forces us to approach the design of a class in a formal way. Furthermore, the MooZ specification could function as a living document describing the class. finally, it may be a good idea to write a code generator which produces C++ header and code files from such a specification. This reduces syntax errors and speeds up the development process.

A given class should have at most one high-level responsibility. Classes which carry out more than one job tend to be difficult to understand and to use. In particular, they are difficult to program, as the programmer usually has to reconcile potential conflicting demands of the class. Furthermore, a class's member functions should not have more than three or four arguments. If more are needed, try splitting the member function into two less complex ones. In short, the following rough guidelines should be adhered to:

(18.2)

- Keep the number of member functions in a class to a maximum of 40.
- Keep the number of arguments of a member function to at most 4.

It is a good idea to document a class's server classes. This may be important when changes occur in the class when we wish to know what the dependencies are between it and other classes. For example, a `PROJECT`'s server classes are `DATE` and `STRING`. Changes to the interfaces of these last two classes may lead to changes in `PROJECT`.

Understanding C++ code at the interface level is one thing, understanding it so that it can be modified is another matter. Whereas users of a class only need to know about the class interface and how to use it, class maintainers need to have a deeper understanding of the internals of the class member functions.

18.3.2 Maintaining and modifying C++ classes

A C++ class is completely defined by its header and code files. The header file contains the declaration of the class's member data and functions while the code file embodies the code of the member functions. It is always advisable to use separate header and code files; the header file is delivered in source form to customers (they will serve as simple specification sheets) while the code file is delivered only in object or library form.

It will be necessary to modify C++ code for a number of reasons. First, a member function may contain one or more bugs which need to be fixed. Secondly, functionality in the form of new member functions may need to be added to the class.

There is one golden rule for member functions which we adhere to: they may contain no more than five lines of code! This may seem a very strange number, but member functions whose length is more than five lines usually suffer from a number of problems which are symptoms of something more serious. Inspecting the body of such member functions can lead to the following conclusions:

(18.3)

- A number of member functions may contain duplicate code.
- A member function implements code which should be done somewhere else.
- A member function contains many if–else statements, leading to multiple paths from the start to the end of the member function.

Once member functions have been written we notice that a number of member functions contain duplicate code. The main reason for the emergence of such common code is that it was not originally available to the programmer in the form of a member function of the same class or of some other server class. Thus, we should inspect the bodies of member functions for such duplicate code and then promote it to the status of a member function. This makes the code more understandable and it may even add to the functionality and usefulness of the class.

Member functions which contain too many if–else statements are harder to test and understand because we need to create a test function for each possibility. This phenomenon is related to the so-called McCabe Cyclomatic Complexity Metric (McCabe and Butler 1989), which is the most widely used measure of complexity of a program or of a member function. Programs with a metric greater than 10 have been shown to be difficult to test and maintain. C++ member functions usually give a much lower number: a typical value is 3. Since our member functions are never more than five lines long this value can easily be achieved. The McCabe metric gives an indication of the number of paths from the start to the end of a program. As an example, the following function has a metric of 3 because there are three possible paths through the program:

(18.4)

```
void do_something(int i, int j)
{
  if (i < 0)
  {
    if (j <= 0)
    {
        do_something2(i);
        do_something3(j);
    }
    else
    {
        do_something3(j);
        do_something4(i);
    }
```

```
    }
    else
    {
      do_something_completely_different(i, j);
    }
    do_something5();
}
```

We advise a McCabe metric of 2. This can be achieved by splitting the member function into two or more simpler ones. It often happens that member functions with large McCabe values encapsulate semantically important subcases which should really be part of the class interface and not embedded in code.

Inspecting code is a good way of finding defects in software. Applying such techniques to C++ code is in its infancy but it is worth the effort because many defects can be discovered. In traditional programming environments it is estimated that inspection can take up to 15% of a project's schedule (Ackerman *et al.* 1989). A good overview of software inspection techniques is given in Fagan (1976).

Inspection of C++ code is an alternative to testing and it is probably superior in a number of ways. The advantages are:

(18.5)

- It allows us to review all possible paths in a member function.
- Code duplication is discovered.
- Complicated code can be split into simpler member functions.

It is always a good idea to do a code review before testing. This is especially important when apprentices or junior C++ programmers write the code. They tend to write long functions and they sometimes have difficulty in discovering commonality in member functions. In these cases it is important to let an experienced OO designer inspect the code.

18.3.3 Using responsibility-driven programming to enhance maintainability

We have already discussed data-driven and responsibility-driven designs in Section 15.7. Most books and articles on C++ invariably take a data-driven approach to class development, whereas the 'pure' Smalltalk community prefer the responsibility-driven paradigm. So what is the major difference? The data-driven approach to class design takes the viewpoint of first finding the member data of a class and then determining what its member functions are. This approach has the disadvantage that all member functions have knowledge of how the class is implemented (in other words, the member data). Changes in member data demand that all member functions using that data will have to be changed; the corollary is that every member function has to be tested again. It would be better to have a two-tiered structure in which some member functions (the so-called 'primitive' functions) have access to the private member data while other member functions (the so-called client functions) have no access to the private state. Changes to member data only impact the primitive functions. The number of such member functions should be considerably less than normal client functions. Responsibility-driven design ensures that this situation can be achieved. This approach is similar to top-down functional decomposition or levelling in which the highest-level client functions are decomposed into lower-level client functions. At some stage a client function will be coded in terms of possibly simple primitive functions. The down-side of using primitive functions is that our code may become less efficient. This, however, should be an action point during the optimization phase and it certainly should not be considered during initial class design. In this way we can defer implementation details for as long as possible.

The advantages of responsibility-driven design are:

(18.6)

- It allows us to build 'firewalls' between client member functions and the member data.
- The member data do not get published in the class interface (Wirfs-Brock and Wilkerson 1989b).
- Changes in the data only impact the primitive member functions.
- New member functions are discovered at each level of the process.
- We cannot lose sight of what the class's real responsibilities are.

To take an example, we consider the simple case of a generic bounded stack `STACK<T>` with the following responsibilities:

(18.7)

```
void push(const T& t);        // Push t onto top of the stack
T pop();                      // Remove the top (element) of
                              // the stack
void replace(const T& t);     // Replace the top
void dup(const T& t);         // Make a copy of the top
T current() const;            // Non-destructive read of top
```

The functions in (18.7) represent the high-level responsibility of `STACK`. Each one can be levelled into simpler functions. To show how this works, we take the function `replace()`. Its expansion leads to the following:

(18.8)

```
void replace(const T& t)
{ // Replace the top element by t

  // Precondition: The stack is not empty
  if (empty() == TRUE)  // We discover a new function
    return;

  modify_value(t);   // Can be a low-level function
}
```


In `replace()`we discover two new functions: first, `empty()`, which determines whether the stack is empty, and secondly the function `modify_value()`, which performs the actual replacement of the top element. The functions `empty()` and `modify_value()` may or may not be primitive functions.

The code in (18.8) is logically correct and does not use any private member data. These are hidden in `empty()` and `modify_value()`. In the case that we implement the `STACK` as an array:

```
template <class T> class STACK
{
```

```
private:
  ARRAY<T> elements;        // The values on the stack
  int size;                 // Size of stack
  int current;              // The current number of elements
public:
  // ...
};
```

The functions `empty()` and `modify_value()` could now be coded as follows:

```
BOOLEAN empty()
{ // Is the stack empty? (primitive function)
  if (current == 0)
    return TRUE;

  return FALSE;
}

void modify_value(const T& t)
{ // Replace the top element of the stack by t
  // (primitive function)

  // No precondition because this is a 'trusted' function
  // and it is used only with pre-knowledge

  elements[current] = t;      // Using index operator from
                              // class ARRAY

}
```

A good introduction to responsibility-driven programming is given in Wirfs-Brock and Wilkerson (1989a,b), where the technique is applied in a Smalltalk environment.

18.4 Portability

18.4.1 Introduction

Portability is defined as the ease with which software products may be transferred to various hardware and software platforms. It is thus important when creating C++ classes that there are no member functions which have knowledge of the hardware and software platforms in which their instances are to operate. This is because useful classes need to operate in different environments, so that changes will need to be made to member functions to suit the new situation. Thus, it is important to separate the 'essence' of an object from its view or representations in different formats or media. There is a growing realization that software is not homogeneous, but that there is a relationship between software and the environment in which it is to operate. In this case we speak of domain-dependent software (Giddings 1984). We have already dealt with techniques to make systems more portable in Chapter 14. The main techniques are:

(18.9)

- Using levels of abstraction

- Hiding low-level data types by encapsulation
- Using the model–view–controller (MVC) paradigm
- Creating virtual machines

It is important when writing classes to separate concerns. The main ones have to do with storing and manipulating objects, defining their essentials and displaying them in different formats. These concerns are equivalent to the way MVC is set up; the model corresponds to the essential definition of an object, the view corresponds to displaying the object and the controller corresponds to manipulations on the object. The classic example in C++ is the class hierarchies for shapes; the class `SHAPE` is an abstract base class and each of its derived classes has a member function to draw itself. The following code is the incorrect but much publicized way of approaching the problem of drawing graphical objects in different environments:

```
class SHAPE
{
  // ...

  virtual void draw() const = 0;

  // ...
};

  class CIRCLE : public SHAPE
{
  // ...

  void draw() const;

  // ...
};
```

What happens when a customer wishes to draw geometrical objects in a different environment? The solution is to either modify the existing `draw()` or create a new one. The disadvantages of this workaround are:

(18.10)

- Access to source code is necessary.
- Each new draw function implies an increase in code size.
- Not all customers need all features ('you should not have to pay for what you do not use').

There are a number of techniques for separating application objects from their environment, some of which we discuss now.

18.4.2 The MVC paradigm

The model–view–controller paradigm has its roots in the Smalltalk language. In Smalltalk all applications are built to the same plan. In short, each application is built using the following entities:

(18.11)

- Model (the object on which the work is to be done)
- View (the output interface which presents the object to the user)
- Controller (the input interface which allows interaction with the object or one of its views)

Examples of models are numeric and logical data, rules and values in databases. A good example of a view in Windows programming is the visual display of a window. Other views are typically histograms, line charts and pie charts. We note that a view may have one or more subviews. In most cases control is acquired through positioning of the cursor in combination with pressing or clicking the mouse buttons. Controller objects are typically menus, keyboard and mice.

Whenever a model (or subject) is changed, its representations or views must be updated. In order for this to occur automatically some form of dependency must be established between a view and the model that it represents. Furthermore, the view and controller must be aware of one another and they must also know about the model on which they are to work. New MVC applications are invoked in the constructor of the view class of the application. The constructor call results in the creation of the view, display of the model and the passage of control to the controller for the application.

The MVC idea has been applied by the company Microsoft to C++, in particular to an application framework (the so-called Microsoft Foundation Classes (MFC)) for Windows applications. For more information, see Kruglinski (1993).

An interesting article on generalizing the MVC concept can be found in Rumbaugh (1994), in which MVC is subsumed under OMT and guidelines are given on how to design an MVC application. The basic guidelines are as follows:

1. First design the model (or subject) classes without regard to views.
   - this is the OORD/OOA phase of this book
2. Consider the different ways of presenting data to the user (the views).
   - determine how each change in the subject maps to a change in its view
   - make a list of operations on the view if it can be manipulated by the user
   - determine how each view operation maps onto changes in the underlying subject
   - neglect how views affect other views
3. Decide on how view operations will be invoked in terms of external events.
   - take account of events (mouse clicks, menu selections, button pushes etc.)
4. Build a Harel state diagram mapping input events into operations on views.
   - sometimes we can have operations directly on the subject itself
   - the controller is the owner of the state diagram
   - determine the attributes of the controller
   - the controller is responsible for initializing subjects and views

Steps 1–4 above have been implemented in the Microsoft Visual C++ language and it is worth the effort to see how this is done, as it gives many useful insights into how the MVC concept can be implemented in C++.

18.4.3 Creating virtual machines by the use of multiple polymorphism

We show how it is possible in C++ to separate application objects from their interface. The basic technique was suggested to us by Chris Stalenhoef and we thank him for this idea. The answer to the problem is to create two class hierarchies, one for the application objects and the other for their views. To this end, we take the classes in Section 18.4.1. Instead of creating a member function `draw()` in each application class, we choose instead to create a class which knows about all application classes and which has 'drivers' for representing these objects.

Since there are many views we choose to make a base class `CAD_DRIVER` for all of them. This abstract base class knows about all application objects, but all its functions are pure. Its interface is given by:

```
class CAD_DRIVER
{
public:
  virtual operator << (const CIRCLE& c) const = 0;
  virtual operator << (const LINE& l) const = 0;
  // ...

};
```

Derived classes must implement these functions. Suppose that we wish to draw such geometrical objects in a Windows environment. We would create a derived class of `CAD_DRIVER` for this purpose as follows:

```
class CAD_WINDOWS_DRIVER: public CAD_DRIVER
{
public:
  virtual operator << (const CIRCLE& c) const;
  virtual operator << (const LINE& l) const;
};
```

We have deliberately chosen to use the overloaded operator '<<' to make our code look like a generalization of the `cout` mechanism; for example we can display a line under Windows as follows:

```
POINT pt1(100, 100), pt2(200,100);
LINE line(pt1, pt2);
CAD_WINDOWS_DRIVER mydriver;
mydriver << line;
```

This approach is very powerful and it is a simple way to build flexible and portable software for many applications. The main advantages are:

(18.12)

- New application classes can be added; then a new driver needs to be created.
- Customers only get the drivers that they need.
- Customers can create their own drivers by using the public interfaces of the application classes.

We give this technique the name of 'multiple polymorphism', because it uses polymorphic functions and operators in a class hierarchy external to an application class hierarchy.

David Parnas is probably one of the first people who realized the importance of separating an application from its environment; interesting conclusions can be drawn from his articles (Parnas 1972a,b; Parnas *et al.* 1983) by those who wish to write good object-oriented software in C++. We would like to extend this recommendation to anyone who wishes to write yet another book on C++.

18.5 Usability and reusability

There is a subtle difference between the concepts of usability and reusability. The former refers to the ease with which classes can be used in new applications without change. The latter concept refers to the ease with which classes can be used (with possible extensions by the inheritance mechanism) in new situations. If we demand that a class be usable we must then ensure that it be complete in the sense that the class should have all the member functions necessary to model the abstraction that it is trying to simulate. Clients are not interested in customizing such classes because they want to use them in unchanged form in applications. If I buy a new car I am certainly not interested in adding the engine or exhaust pipes myself. Everything should be functioning as expected. On a more serious note, a class for representing stacks, for example, is almost useless if it does not have a member function for popping an element from the top of the stack. In the case of C++ class libraries and components we should demand that they are complete and that very little customization is needed.

There are circumstances in which it is not possible to create classes which solve every imaginable problem. If we did attempt to create classes which tried to be universal we would get monsters. Instead, it is sometimes useful to provide clients with class libraries which deliver default behaviour and which can then be customized to the special needs of different customers. Most articles and books on C++ tell us how to do this by the use of virtual and pure virtual member functions in combination with abstract base classes. This approach is particularly suited to reusable designs (or frameworks). Class libraries for different application areas are a special form of reusable design. A number of C++ libraries (such as the NIH class library (Gorlen *et al.* 1990)) are so-called 'single-tree' libraries because all classes are eventually inherited from one base class. This approach has been inspired by Smalltalk and it leads to a number of major problems, for example:

(18.13)

- The amount of coupling is unduly increased.
- It is necessary for new derived classes to support the protocols which are required by ancestor classes.
- Such hierarchies are difficult to understand.

Applying the Smalltalk philosophy to C++ leads to structures which are difficult to integrate with other class libraries (for example, CommonView). We call this frame of mind 'Smalltalkism', and it alludes to the attempt to map Smalltalk directly into C++. A better approach (in our view) is to create 'forests' of communicating class hierarchies; an example of such an approach is given in Section 18.4.3, where we created two class hierarchies, one for geometric application objects and the other for their representations.

The approach taken in Chapter 14 on building client/server systems using the levels of abstraction approach can be effectively applied to the construction of reusable classes; the System Interface Layer is the only layer which has knowledge of the underlying compiler and machine dependencies, while the other layers contain classes which are impervious to such factors. Classes in the SIL hide the following aspects of hardware and software:

(18.14)

- The number of bits allocated to built-in data types
- Machines with big endian and little endian byte orderings (Stevens 1990)
- Pointers to built-in types
- Hardware interfaces and resources

Building classes in layers allows us to create highly reusable components at each level of abstraction. We thus see from this that inheritance is not the only way to create reusable abstractions! It is our opinion that one of the best ways to promote reusability in C++ is to combine the template and inheritance mechanisms. A good introduction to templates can be found in the series of articles by Michael S. Ball in the *C++ Report* (see, for example, Ball (1993)). Templates are useless unless they are specialized. We saw some examples in Chapter 15 of how and why templates can be specialized to create new abstractions. The general rules when designing templates are:

(18.15)

- They should have minimal functionality.
- They should take care of error-prone things like memory management and exceptional handling.
- They should not make too many demands on the abstract data type on which they are based.

Templates can be constructed for the 'easy' classes such as lists, sets, bags and arrays, but it is more interesting to create templates for domain-dependent abstractions. A simple example is the abstraction for points whose coordinates are to be found in some space. There are many possibilities, such as:

(18.16)

- Cartesian coordinates (double, double, double)
- Cylindrical coordinates (double, Angle, double)
- Spherical coordinates (double, Angle, Angle)
- Colour schemes (short, short, short)
- Windows points (int, int)
- Two-dimensional CAD (double, double)

The preferred solution is to create a template class `POINT` and then derive special cases from its specializations and add new member functions to suit our needs, for example:

```
template <class F, class S, class T> class POINT
{
private:
  F xcoord; // First coordinate
```

```
    S ycoord; // Second coordinate
    T zcoord; // Third coordinate

  public:

    // Universally applicable functions

  };
```

A class representing points in Cartesian space would now be defined as:

```
class CartesianPoint :public POINT<double, double, double>
{
private:

public:

  // Define specific functions here

};
```

This idea can and should be applied in all attempts to create reusable software.

However, discovering and classifying software for reusability is in its infancy, and much work needs to be done (Prieto-Diaz and Freeman 1987; Lanergan and Grasso 1984; Jones 1984; Meyer 1987).

We finish this section with the remark that it is not enough to be on the lookout for reusable code and classes with reusability, but that other artefacts in the software life-cycle need to be examined for reusability, such as:

(18.17)

- Reusable data (e.g. standard interchange formats)
- Reusable architectures
- Reusable designs
- Reusable programs and modules
- Reusable ideas (e.g. during the requirements determination phase)

It was estimated in Jones (1984) that of all of the code written in 1983 probably less than 15% was unique, novel and specific to individual applications. What do you think this percentage is today?

18.6 Correctness

By the term correctness we mean the ability of software to function according to its specifications. However, determining what the correct specifications and requirements are is no easy task, and most methods use informal (usually natural language) techniques. The only OOA/OOD methodology we know of which pays some lip-service to formal methods of determining requirements is the Fusion method (Coleman *et al.* 1994), and even here it is done downstream in the design phase. It would be interesting to apply formal methods such as Z and VDM to proving the correctness of C++ classes, but this has not been done to our knowledge.

Programming in C++ is similar to establishing a contract between two parties; first, there is the supplier code, which is the server, and secondly there is the client or consumer code. There is a so-called agreement between these two parties on how to interface with each other. In particular, a member function in one class may call the member function of another class. Each function has an associated precondition which states the conditions under which the client must operate. If the precondition is satisfied the client will get what is needed; if the precondition is violated the precondition is not satisfied which means that the result cannot be trusted. An exception must be raised in the server code which will hopefully be caught by a so-called exception handler in the given client code or possibly by a higher-level client. Some C++ compilers support exception handling and this feature can be used as a way of creating robust software (see also Section 18.7).

The object-oriented language Eiffel has much functionality to ensure that classes are correctly set up. We recommend that you devote some attention to this language (especially to pre- and postconditions, class invariants and programming by contract) because these ideas can easily be mapped to your C++ classes, thus making them more correct than not applying any methods at all!

The general guidelines for writing correct member functions are given as follows, showing how to use pre- and postconditions:

```
<return_type> <function_name> (<argument-lit>)
{
// Check for preconditions; this is usually a list of
// constraints
if (<constraint_list> == NOT_OK)
  { // OOPS! The naughty customer does not fulfil his part
    // of the bargain

    raise <exception_type>;
    return;
  }

// Everything OK now; postconditions assured
// The customer gets what he wants because he is
// well-mannered and well-behaved

}
```

18.7 Robustness

Robustness is defined as the ability of software to function even in abnormal situations. When the contract between a server function and its client (calling) function is broken an exception must be raised. Exceptions are well supported in languages such as Ada, but it is only very recently that C++ has started to tackle the problem. The exception handling facility is not yet supported in C++ and only some compilers have implemented in any sort of substantial way (the Borland and Watcom compilers have it and Visual C++ has just introduced it). We have treated exceptions in some detail in Chapter 3; in particular we have shown how to integrate them in C++ class code. This section discusses some of the practical issues which necessitate us providing exception handling facilities.

Exceptions can arise for a multitude of reasons. Some of the more important ones for the C++ programmer are:

(18.18)

- Failure to allocate enough memory using the `new` operator (memory error)
- Accessing elements in lists and arrays outside of the allowed range (range error)
- Pushing elements onto full stacks (overflow error)
- File I/O problems (open, read, write, close) (access errors)

and there are many more.

There is a pre-defined function pointer called `_new_handler` which is a built-in exception handler packaged for ease of use. It is used mainly in constructors when the new operator fails to allocate enough memory. The `_new_handler` can be set by users to point to a `user_defined` function. An example is now given in which the function `my_handler()` takes over:

```
void my_handler
{
  cout << "Sorry, not enough memory";
exit(-1);
}
```

It is used as follows:

```
#include <new.h>
set_new_handler(my_handler);
```

Useful discussions of exception handling are given in Booch and Vilot (1993a,b) and Reed (1994).

It is interesting to note that almost no OO methods (with the exception of Firesmith (1993)) deal with exceptions as an essential part of the software life-cycle. The Fusion method pays some lip service to this issue, but it is not convincing. There seems to be a black spot in the literature on this issue. Exceptions and exception objects should be raised to the same semantic level as application objects because they can be part of the problem domain and furthermore they may arise in the design and implementation stages. Firesmith defines an exception as an error condition which is identified and raised by the operations of objects and classes so that they can be properly handled by calling operations, possibly in other objects or classes. An exception abstraction is defined as one which models error conditions and error handling.

We suggest the following documentation techniques to be used when implementing exceptions in C++ classes:

- The specification of objects and classes should include a list of zero or more exceptions.
- An exception handler should document the handling of one or more exceptions in the body of a member function.

More useful information on documenting exceptions can be found in Firesmith (1993, pp. 377–8).

18.8 Interoperability

Interoperability is defined as the ability of software to cooperate with other software. We have spoken of the efforts of the OMG in this area in Chapter 17. We shall not dwell on this difficult and important topic further.

We finish with two simple tips which aid interoperability; first, define class names so that they do not clash with other classes from other applications and class libraries. Secondly, do not define global enumerated types but also 'tie' them in to some class. For example, `DSSTRING` (the `DS` stands for the first two characters of the company I work for) is a much better name than `STRING` as class name. Finally, it is also better to define the boolean enumerated type `DSSTRING::BOOLEAN` rather than its 'global' variant

```
enum BOOLEAN {FALSE, TRUE};
```

It is amazing that many professional software developers forget this simple rule!

18.9 Efficiency

Efficiency is concerned with how C++ code performs in the environment in which it is installed. Many application programmers worry unduly about performance issues in the early stage of class design and implementation. This is a waste of time, because what is efficient in one environment may not be efficient in another. In short, the C++ programmer should first ensure that his or her C++ classes are correct, then worry about performance problems.

There are two issues which need addressing, namely:

(18.19)

- Using C++ efficiently
- Creating efficient data structures in C++

It is important to keep our C++ code as efficient as possible; however, features such as the use of multiple inheritance (whose use we disapprove of anyway), virtual member functions and pointers to members can lead to degradation in performance (Druker 1991). For example, consider the following:

```
class X
{
  virtual void func();
};
```

To implement this virtual function an additional member is added to the storage layout of class `X`. This is in fact a pointer to an array of untyped functions, the so-called `vptr`. This adds to the size of the instances of `X` and its effect can be seen by invoking the `sizeof()` operator. The table that `vptr` points to is called `vtbl` or `vtable` and it is usually held in static storage so that all objects of a given type can share the data. This table has an entry for every virtual function defined in a class hierarchy.

Efficient data structures We finish this section with some tips on efficiency:

(18.20)

- Avoid multiple inheritance and deep class hierarchies.

- Map only 'real' polymorphic operations to virtual functions.
- Use call by value for built-in types.
- Use call by referencing for user-defined types.
- Only use inlining when all else fails.

A good discussion of performance issues in C++ is given in Meyers (1992).

18.10 Are classes enough?

The novice C++ programmer will probably be of the opinion that classes are sufficient in order to ensure reusability. There is a need, however, to have a mechanism for creating, maintaining and using groups of related classes which function as one entity. De Champeaux (1991) has coined the term ensemble: an ensemble has attributes, state transition properties and the ability to interact with objects as well as with other ensembles. An ensemble differs from an object in that it stands for a cluster or bundle of less abstract entities which are either objects or lower level ensembles. Examples of ensembles in the JRP problem would be `CirculationList` and `AttentionList`.

Will the coming years see a shift in thinking from class-based programming to cluster-based programming?

References

A. F. Ackerman *et al.* (1989) Software inspections: an effective verification process, *IEEE Software*, May.

W. R. Adrion *et al.* (1982) Validation, verification and testing computer software, *ACM Computer Services*, **14**(2) 160.

M. S. Ball (1993) What are these things called templates?, *C++ Report*, **5**(2) February.

G. Booch and M. Vilot (1993a) Designing with exceptions, *C++ Report*, **5**(4).

G. Booch and M. Vilot (1993b) Designing with exceptions, *C++ Report*, **5**(6).

D. de Champeaux (1991) Object-oriented analysis and top-down software development, in *ECOOP '91 Proceedings*, Springer, Berlin.

D. Coleman *et al.* (1994) *Object-Oriented Development: The Fusion Method*, Prentice-Hall, Englewood Cliffs NJ.

B. Cox (1987) *Object-Oriented Programming: An Evolutionary Approach*, Addison-Wesley, Reading MA.

S. Druker (1991) What's that compiler doing, anyway? Virtual function overhead, *C++ Report*, **3**(6) June.

M. E. Fagan (1976) Design and code inspections to reduce errors in program development, *IBM Systems Journal*, **15**(3) 182–211.

D. G. Firesmith (1993) *Object-Oriented Requirements Analysis and Logical Design*, John Wiley & Sons, Chichester.

R. V. Giddings (1984) Accommodating uncertainty in software design, *Communications of the ACM*, **27**(25) May.

A. Goldberg and D. Robson (1983) *Smalltalk-80, The Language and its Implementation*, Addison-Wesley, Reading MA.

K. S. Gorlen, S. Orlow and P. Plexico (1990) *Data Abstractions and Object-Oriented Programming in C++*, John Wiley & Sons, Chichester.

T. C. Jones (1984) Reusability in programming: a survey of the state of the art, *IEEE Transactions on Software Engineering*, **SE-10**(5) September.

C. B. Jones (1990) *Systematic Software Development using VDM*, Prentice-Hall, Hemel Hempstead.

D. J. Kruglinski (1993) *Inside Visual C++*, Microsoft Press, Redmond WA.

R. G. Lanergan and C. A. Grasso (1984) Software engineering with reusable designs, *IEEE Transactions on Software Engineering*, **SE-10**(5) September.

T. McCabe and C. Butler (1989) Design complexity measurement and testing, *Communications of the ACM*, **32**(12) 1415–25.

B. Meyer (1987) Reusability: the case for object-oriented design, *IEEE Software*, **4**.

B. Meyer (1988) *Object-Oriented Software Construction*, Prentice-Hall, Englewood Cliffs NJ.

S. Meyers (1992) *Effective C++: 50 Specific Ways to Improve Your Programs and Designs*, Addison-Wesley, Reading MA.

D. Parnas (1972a) A technique for software module specification with examples, *Communications of the ACM*, **15**(5) May.

D. Parnas (1972b) On the criteria to be used in decomposing systems into modules, *Communications of the ACM*, **15**(12) December.

D. Parnas, P. C. Clements and D. M. Weiss (1983) Enhancing reusability with information hiding, in *ITT Proceedings of the Workshop in Programming*, Newport RI.

R. Prieto-Diaz and P. Freeman (1987) Classifying Software for Reusability, *IEEE Software*, January.

D. R. Reed (1994) Using C++ exceptions, *C++ Report*, **6**(5).

J. Rumbaugh (1994) Modelling models and viewing views: a look at the model–view–controller framework, *Journal of Object-Oriented Programming*, **7**(2) May.

S. Stepney *et al.* (eds) (1992) *Object Orientation in Z*, Springer, London.

W. R. Stevens (1990) *UNIX Networking Programming*, Prentice-Hall, Englewood Cliffs NJ.

R. Wirfs-Brock and B. Wilkerson (1989a) Object-oriented design: a responsibility-driven approach, *Sigplan Notices*, **2**(10).

R. Wirfs-Brock and B. Wilkerson (1989b) Variables limit reusability, *Journal of Object-Oriented Programming*, **2**(1).

Appendix

The software process

If you have a guy who's good in a crisis, get rid of him, or you'll always have one
(Fenton 1979)

A.1 Introduction and objectives

The main objective of this appendix is to put the results of the previous 18 chapters into perspective. The steps which we develop in this appendix will serve as a working document for the busy engineer who wishes to get his or her application up and running. It is possible to take different approaches depending on the time and budget, whether the application is mission critical or if we only wish to write a prototype which will be demonstrated to customers.

It is our feeling that the main object-oriented development methods suffer from a number of drawbacks. In all fairness we should not be too harsh because most methods have only been around for a few years (with the possible exception of Objectory) but it is important to mention some of the things that we would like to see included in future versions:

- More emphasis on requirements engineering before OOA and better traceability between phases.
- Fewer diagrams (the Fusion and Booch methods suffer from this problem). Software development is more than just drawing pretty pictures.
- Discovering potential subsystems during requirements determination rather than during the system design phase.
- Better support for both relational and object-oriented database systems.
- Support for systems which do not adhere to the OO way of thinking (e.g. rule-based programming, constraint hierarchies, Cobol!).
- The ability to create rapid prototypes ('quick and dirty').
- Mechanisms for discovering reusable ideas, systems and classes.
- The user should be involved during the software process.

There is a lot that needs to be done before OO methods get to the stage that their undoubted advantages can reach their full potential. Projects fail not for technological reasons but because the necessary infrastructure is not available. People and not CASE tools determine success. Just because an application which was written using object-oriented techniques fails does not mean that such techniques are incorrect or unsuitable; it is more a reflection on those who were involved on the project. In my experience the most successful projects were those in which I worked with users to build an initial prototype of the system which after some time went into production after all desired functionality was found. This was in the pre-OO era, and it is interesting to note that many methodologists are rediscovering this!

Alan Davis (1994) has made a number of useful comments on the way that software is developed and written at the moment. He wishes to get away from the 'Software Lemmingeering' mentality. His main thesis is that most IT professionals follow one of a half-dozen or so well-trod 'lemming paths'. Some paths may lead to glory, but nobody really knows what the results will be. He advocates a number of techniques which lead to low-risk, low-cost applications. Most are so obvious and common-sensical that they have eluded many people! These are:

- Talk to your customers (Gause and Weinberg 1990).
- Build prototypes (Andriole 1993).
- Do trade-off analyses on software architectures (Garland and Shaw 1993).
- Play with formal methods (Davis 1993).
- Review, walkthrough and inspect (Gilb and Graham 1993).
- Salvage previously used requirements, designs, test code and documentation (Tracz 1990).

We discuss how you can apply the results of this book to your own particular environment.

A.2 The ideal software life-cycle

We present the ideal plan for writing systems using object-oriented techniques when applying the principles which are expounded in this book. There are more ways than one to 'skin a goat', and we do not claim that there is one unique solution. There is, however, a solution which is best for your particular needs, budget and time frame.

The following steps should be followed.

A.2.1 Learn the fundamentals

You should be thoroughly familiar with the concepts, mechanisms and techniques which OO has to offer, because these are used in almost every stage of the software life-cycle. In particular, the first four chapters of this book could be read in order to bring you up to the desired level.

Remember that OO should be used to solve practical problems and it should not become an objective in itself. Adopt an engineering attitude to software development: don't let the scientists or computer theorists take over or you are doomed. Talk to customers about their work.

A.2.2 OO development is iterative

The typical object-oriented software life-cycle is iterative, with different phases overlapping each other. For example, it is possible that different versions of the same 'product' exist at the same time, with one team working on analysis, while other teams may be designing, implementing and maintaining other versions.

It is important to realize that this way of working will be the norm rather than the exception in real-life applications, and you had better get your team organized to cope with this.

A.2.3 Requirements determination

This is the phase in which we determine what the system must do. It is also the phase that gets skipped or is incorrectly applied. The mistakes made here will be very costly to fix if they are allowed to slip into the phases downstream in the software process. The steps are:

1. Develop concept maps (the steps are described in Sections 6.5.1 and 6.5.2).

   Concept maps should be made for both the abstractions in the problem domain and for the different 'use cases' in the problem. Each use case is in fact a conceptual subsystem which is designed during the system design phase of OMT. An example of a use case concept map is given in Figures 6.13 and 6.14. Another advantage of this approach is that we can examine architectural alternatives in this early stage of the life-cycle. This approach is similar to the Shlaer–Mellor domain concept.

   The products of the concept mapping phase are a list of concepts (classes), links between them (associations) and a concept map for all the use cases in the system (Section 6.6).

   Concept maps can be mapped directly onto OMT object diagrams.

2. Develop event–response lists and storyboards

   These are treated in Chapter 7. Events correspond to external stimuli and are eventually implemented as operations on classes. Responses, on the other hand, correspond to processes in the functional modelling phase and they can be 'levelled' in much the same way as in done in many textbooks. We advise against using too many DFDs, as they are inferior (in our opinion) to expanding the processes using pseudocode or structured English; each subprocess corresponds to an operation on a given class (this is similar to the Wirfs-Brock approach).

We recommend that you try using the scenario- and inquiry-based techniques, which were discussed in Section 7.5. These processes involve users as part of the discovery and decision processes; these are the people you are making the system for in the first place.

The steps in finding events, control and scenarios are:

- Enumerate all event–response lists in the system (only external events should be considered).
- Enumerate all necessary use cases for the system.
- Make a storyboard for each use case in the system.

The products from this stage are:

- The major external events in the system
- The control in the system
- Storyboards, which can be used for acceptance tests and documentation purposes

We can discover states of objects by mapping events and responses into their equivalent postcondition statements (see answers to Chapter 13 where this is done for PPD problem).

The inputs for OMT will be:

- Events here are mapped into OMT-defined events.
- The states discovered here will play a major role when creating Harel statecharts.
- Responses map to processes during functional modelling.

The states that are needed for the Harel statecharts can easily be found by reformulating the external events in terms of their equivalent postconditions. These postconditions correspond directly to the states of the respective objects. We show how to do this by taking an example from PPD. The pump assembly object is taken as a good case. It has the following operations:

```
enable()
disable()
remove_gun()
depress_trigger()
release_trigger()
replace_gun()
```

The corresponding states of the pump assembly object are:

```
Enabled
Disabled
GunRemoved
TriggerDepressed
TriggerReleased
GunReplaced
```

This technique can and should be applied to all subsequent problems.

We recommend that you invest in buying some animation software which will allow you to represent storyboards in a GUI environment. In this way you can communicate your prototype solution to the customer in terms that are easily understood. Not many users are interested in the niceties of ER diagrams or OMT charts (at least, if I was a user I would not want to see them). They just want you to solve the problem!

The products of this phase are the classes, operations and their interactions from the problem domain. We can now move on to the analysis. For those in a hurry or those wishing to make a prototype you could even start implementing at this stage! For example, the software product OMTool from the Advanced Concepts Center of Martin Marietta allows you to generate C++ code from object diagrams. This improves programmer productivity.

A.2.4 Object-oriented analysis

This phase is concerned with the determination of the object model, dynamic model and functional model for the given problem. The steps in the object modelling phase are described in Section 8.7 and of course in Rumbaugh *et al.* (1991). The advantage of the approach taken in our book is that most of the hard work in finding the long-term structural relationships has already been done (together with the customer!) during the concept mapping phase. We would hope that our book would be complementary to the classical OMT approach. If we succeed in this endeavour we shall be satisfied.

The deliverables from the object modelling phase are:

- The classes from the problem domain and their attributes
- The relationships between classes
- The classification scheme for classes

It is important not to spend an inordinate amount of time on this phase; beware of 'analysis paralysis'. Get it more or less right and move on to dynamic modelling (remember, the object model is static, so you won't be able to answer many interesting questions about its behaviour at this stage).

The steps in dynamic modelling in OMT are very similar to what we did in Chapter 7. An important part of this phase lies in the construction of Harel statecharts with which we can validate the control flows in the system. They are an important mechanism in ensuring that the dynamic model is correct.

The precise steps to be executed during dynamic modelling are:

- Assemble the scenarios/storyboards from the requirements model.
- Assemble the external events found.
  - Concentrate on normal events, then abnormal ones.
  - Parametrize events.
  - Find the sender and receiver of each event.
- Build a statechart for each active class.
- Draw an event flow diagram for system.
  - Events generated by each class.
  - Each event should have a receiver and sender.

The products of this phase will be used during object design, in particular:

- Parametrized events map to operations on 'receiver' objects. These events are 'called' from the 'sender' object.

We are not a great supporter of using DFDs for functional modelling on OMT (I believe that Jim Rumbaugh is working on some new changes in this area, some of which can be read about in recent issues of the *Journal of Object-Oriented Programming*). We prefer to level processes and 'assign' them to operations on classes in much the same way that Fusion and Wirfs-Brock do, but without diagrams, as we think that they tend to overburden the designer with too much detail. This levelling is done using structured English, for example, and results in a much tighter coupling between classes and processes than is possible with DFDs.

The steps in functional modelling are:

```
For each response from the requirements model, do:
{
  1. Determine the signature of the process
  2. Level the process into simpler sub-process
  3. Use the object diagrams for navigation purposes (see
     answers in Chapter 11)
  4. When all sub-processes can be mapped to object operations
```

```
        stop; otherwise go to step 2 and repeat the steps
}
```

A.2.5 System design

This phase is concerned with system architecture, subsystems and their mapping to hardware and software units. The steps in system design are worked out in Section 14.1. The process is very similar to system design in OMT except that we effectively know the subsystems before we embark (look at the concept map for PPD in which each supporting concept is in fact a subsystem; this was no accident).

More work needs to be done in general on determining the optimal combination of hardware and software when mapping subsystems to functional units. This has not been treated in this book.

A.2.6 Object design

The function of this phase is to elaborate the object model. In particular, the events from the dynamic model and the processes from the functional model can be mapped directly into operations on classes. The steps are described in Section 15.1.

Some tips:

- Try to use software rather than writing it yourself.
- Use generic classes (templates in C++).
- Think hard about whether to use relational databases rather than object-oriented databases (see Chapters 16 and 17).

A.3 And finally, implementing all this stuff

It looks as if C++ will be the standard object-oriented programming language for the coming years and well into the next century. A major reason for its popularity is that it is in principle compatible with C; all the C code which has ever been written can be integrated with new applications written in C; if James Joyce was alive today he might say that 'C++ has a great future behind it' (Joyce 1969). However, C++ is not the correct solution in many cases. For example, it is inferior to Smalltalk for building prototypes because it is difficult to learn and one must compile and debug code. With Smalltalk you can type in code and run it! Beware of those who advocate one language against the other, however. Object-oriented technology is just one paradigm which is useful for solving a (possibly large – we just have to wait) class of problems. I have taken to writing user interfaces for Windows applications in Visual Basic (a predecessor of which I learned some 22 years ago!) because it is possible to write such interfaces in a fraction of the time that is possible in C++. Visual Basic is not object-oriented, although it supports operating overloading to a certain extent. The purists would probably frown on such a language because of its humble roots.

The bottom-line is what counts: can you get the product out on time and within budget? And finally, is the customer happy with the product?

References

S. Andriole (1993) *Rapid Application Prototyping*, QED, Wellesley MA.

A. M. Davis (1993) *Software Requirements: Objects, Functions and States*, Prentice-Hall, Englewood Cliffs NJ.

A. M. Davis (1994) Rewards of taking the path less traveled, *IEEE Software*, special issue on Measurement-Based Process Improvement, July.

J. Fenton (1979) *The A–Z of Sales Management*, Pan Business Management, London.

D. Garland and M. Shaw (1993) An introduction to software architecture, *Advances in Software Engineering and Knowledge Engineering*.

D. Gause and G. Weinberg (1990) *Are Your Lights On?*, Dorset House Publishing, New York.

T. Gilb and D. Graham (1993) *Software Inspections*, Addison-Wesley, Reading MA.

J. Joyce (1969) *Ulysses*, Penguin, London.

J. Rumbaugh, M. Blaha, W. Premerlani, F. Eddy and W. Lorensen (1991) *Object-Oriented Modeling and Design*, Prentice-Hall, Englewood Cliffs NJ.

W. Tracz (1990) Tutorial: Software Reuse, IEEE CS Press, Los Alamitos CA.

Appendix

B

Answers to exercises

Chapter 1

1. A journal has a name, first publication date, frequency of publication and language in which it is written. An issue is an appearance of a journal; it has a name, contains articles and a certain publication date, volume and number. A division consists of a number of departments and has a main activity. A circulation list consists of a list of readers who have access to an issue of a journal. For example, issue instances react to the following messages:

   - List all articles in the issue.
   - What is the name?

   The proposition 'allow a reader access to a journal' is not a message which can be sent to either reader or journal. Such examples are treated in Chapters 6 (links between concepts) and 8 (object associations).

   The JRP (Journal Registration Problem) system is a special case of a library management system. Such systems are concerned with maintaining information on circulation, acquisition, indexes, series information and location. Library systems differ from ordinary record-based systems because the items being retrieved actually 'circulate' and are expected back; users often have very poor navigation skills; physical location is extremely important; and circulation and access control are the most critical elements.

   Possible use cases in such systems are:

   Document acquisition

   Document payments (e.g. journals)

   Shipment details

   Cataloguing documents

   Borrower information

   Circulation information

Overdue material

Before a document can be acquired it must first be ordered, the purchase must be approved and funds must be transferred. The roles that arise here are librarian, publisher, requester, borrower and user.

2. The collection {1, 3, 8, –9, 10} can be viewed as a set or an array but not as a sorted array. The collection {1-1-1994, 2-7-1995, 5-8-1996} can be viewed as a set of dates or as an array of integers (where '-' is interpreted as subtraction).

3. `EMPLOYEE` member functions: (a) constructor, (b) selector, (c) modifier, (d) modifier (can be), (e) selector, (f) department (we have assumed that an employee works for only one department).

4. A point in 3D space can be represented by *x*, *y* and *z* coordinates or in cylindrical or spherical coordinate systems. A line segment can be represented by two points; a circle can be represented by three points on its circumference or alternatively by a centre point and a radius. An arc is a piece of a circle determined by a start and an end angle. A polyline is an ordered array of point instances. The class interfaces for these classes correspond to the usual mathematical/geometrical operations which are needed for computer graphics and computer-aided design (CAD).

   For other types of applications we may need a completely different class interface description.

   Line segments are clients of points; circles are clients of points and lines; arcs are clients of circles; polylines are clients of line segments and points.

5. Creating classes which represent data in graphical format is in fact an application framework. The following classes play a role in such a framework: `Graph`, `LineGraph`, `ScatterGraph`, `BarChart`, `PieChart`, `Axis`, `Legend`, `Polyline`, `PolyMark`. The role that the `Polyline` plays in this problem is different from its role in Exercise 4.

6. The question of whether a class is a server or a client is highly context-sensitive. An issue is a client of journal, an article is a client of an issue, a reader and topic are independent classes. The class `Date` is a client of `Day`, `Month`, `Year`; `Time` is a client of `Hours`, `Minutes`, `Seconds` and `Milliseconds`; `Timestamp` is a client of `Date` and `Time`; `Duration` (an interval of time) is a client of `Timestamp`.

7. A `Date` can be represented as three built-in integer types or as `Day`, `Month` and `Year` objects.

8. The answers are context-sensitive.

   Tangibles: rectangle, petrol tank

   Incidents: visit, flight (viewed by a flight controller), accident, delivery, enrolment

   Interactions: visit, flight (viewed by a passenger), account, location, transaction, enrolment, circulation list, project, licence

   Specifications: catalogue, architectural drawing

   Roles: position (role for point), student, reader, project (it's just a job!)

   Intangibles (will probably never get the status of class): velocity (it is a number), temperature, direction (maybe, I'm not sure), petrol tank (possibly).

9. The owner of the car is interested in whether the car is functioning properly; the taxman is interested in how much money he can get on it; the garage is also interested in making money by replacing faulty (and possibly non-faulty!) components in the car; the insurance company wishes to insure the car based on its age, the age of the owner and the number of passengers and kilometres driven per year. Each perspective gives rise to a rich set of messages for this class.

10. This problem is part of HDB (Hospital Database) which is discussed later in the book.

Chapter 2

1. The solution is taken from Guttag and Horning (1978); the same case is examined in Meyer (1988) where it is implemented in the Eiffel language. The axioms for `Stack` are:

   ```
   empty(new)     == TRUE
   empty(push(t))     == FALSE
   pop(new)  == ERROR
   pop(push(t))  == return t
   ```

   The preconditions for the functions are:

   ```
   push(); none (infinite memory)
   pop(); stack is not empty
   top(); stack is not empty
   ```

   A bounded stack has a new member function `full()` which tells us whether the stack is full. The function `push()` will need to be redefined since its precondition is that the stack is not full.

   We could define a bounded stack type as a subtype of the unbounded stack type.

2. We recommend Sengupta and Korobkin (1994).

3. We give the pseudo-C++ class interfaces for `PERSON`.

   ```
   class PERSON
   { // Open architecture solution in state
   private:
     char* nam;        // Name
     char* add;        // Address
     int nday;         // The date of birth of person
     public:
     // Constructors
     PERSON(char* name, char* address, DATE date_of_birth);
     virtual ~PERSON();

     // Modifiers
     void address(char* new_address);

     // Selectors
     char* name() const;
   ```

```
  char* address() const;
  DATE date_of_birth() const;
};
```

The closed architecture solution is given by:

```
class PERSON
  { // Closed architecture solution in state
  private:
  STRING nam;       // Name
  STRING add;       // Address
  DATE nday;        // The date of birth of person
public:
  // Constructors
  PERSON(STRING name, STRING address, DATE date_of_birth);
  virtual ~PERSON();

  // Modifiers
  void address(STRING new_address);

  // Selectors
  STRING name() const;
  STRING address() const;
  DATE date_of_birth() const;
};
```

4. Employee is a role for `Person`; postal worker and hourly employee are roles for `Employee`. Roles are usually implemented as derived or subclasses in object-oriented languages.

5. Employee numbers change. This means that all applications and databases using this information need to be modified if and when such numbers are modified. This is not trivial to do in practice because the numbers may be on secondary storage.

6. The most general matrix class is called `MATRIX`. This is an abstract class and its subclasses are `FMATRIX` (general rectangular matrices) and `SMATRIX` (sparse matrices, that is matrices with many zeros). Matrices for geometrical transformations in three and two dimensions are represented by 4×4 and 4×3 matrix subclasses of `FMATRIX`, respectively.

7. Left to the student.

8. The class `PASSENGER` is derived from `PERSON` and has the following extended interface:

```
class PASSENGER: public PERSON
{ // Knows about this next journey
private:
  DATE next;  // The date of next journey
  CITY dest;  // Destination
```

```
    public:
    // ...

    // Modifier
    void plan(DATE next_j, CITY destination);

    // Selectors
    DATE next_journey() const;
    CITY next_destination() const;

};
```

9. Variable, variable, recursive, fixed, fixed.

10. These are examples of the mistakes that beginners make. A circle is not a special point, it is a client of a point. The `Sales_Manager` uses multiple inheritance, which is suspect in our opinion. A stack is not a list but it uses the functions of a list when necessary; for example, we can implement `STACK` as a list as follows:

```
class STACK<T>
{
private:
  LIST<T> elements;
public:
  // ...
};
```

11. Left to the student.

12. Engineering company: project leader, draughtsman, piping engineer. Petrol pump station: customer, attendant, service personnel. Hospital: nurse, doctor, surgeon, security, patient, cleaning staff.

13. Petrol pump is a client of pump motor and a server for customer. Display is a server for petrol pump. Petrol line has servers pump, tank and metering device.

14. Left to the student.

Chapter 3

C++ pseudocode

1.

```
void STACK::push(const T& t)
{ // Push an element onto the stack

  // Precondition: stack is not full
  if (full() == TRUE)
      raise OVERFLOW_ERROR;

  // O.K.
  elements.append(t); // Delegate to list
```

```
}

T STACK::pop()
{ // Destructive read of top elements of stack;
  // conceptually the same as dequeueing the last
  // element of the list

  // Precondition: stack is not empty
  if (empty() == TRUE)
      raise UNDERFLOW_ERROR;

  // O.K. now
  return elements.dequeue();

}
```

2. Probably the best way is to start from scratch. Using inheritance gives major problems when we try to understand the code.

3. Choice 1: A circle is a special ellipse. This means that we first create ellipse and its member functions, which is more difficult than circles.

   Choice 2: Create class `Circle` (we know a lot about it), then create the class `Ellipse` as a projection of `Circle` onto a new axis. In this case `Ellipse` delegates to `Circle`.

   Beginners tend to apply inheritance based on class structure rather than on class behaviour. This is the reason that there are so many incorrect class hierarchies out there.

4.
```
FMATRIX:
(1)    double* marr;         // The elements of the matrix
       size_t nrow;          // Number of rows
       size_t ncol;          // Number of columns
(2)    ARRAY<double>* arr;  // Array of arrays
       size_t nrow;          // Number of rows
(3)    // High-level nested arrays
       ARRAY<ARRAY<double> > mat;
```

The final choice will depend on how efficient the code will be and on how easy it is to maintain the class code if the implementation changes.

```
HISTOGRAM:
  ARRAY<POINT> dat;    // The data to be presented
  STRING title;
  STRING Xtitle;
  STRING YTitle;

PURCHASE:
  CUSTOMER* cus;   // The counterparty
  SUPPLIER* s;     // The vendor
  PRODUCT p;       // The product to be sold/bought
```

```
int q;       // The quantity handled
```

The solutions for `SMATRIX` and `DEPARTMENT` are left to the student.

5. `PROJECT`:

   How much budget

   Time to completion

   When started

   `PUMP`

   Number of grades possible (at least one)

   Clear the display data

   The solution for `MATRIX` is left to the student.

6.
```
template <class T> class CircularQueue<T>: public
Queue<T>
{
public:

  // ...

  void feed(const T& t);  // Feed information into list
  T remove(); // Remove and process info

  BOOLEAN overflow() const;    // Ring buffer full?
  INTEGER free_slots() const; // Buffer filling up?

};
```

   The solution for `Stack` is left to the student.

7. Smalltalk implements integer types by using inheritance (inclusion polymorphism). However, it is interesting to see how these classes could be implemented by using templates (parametric polymorphism). We create a generic numeric class and clone special integer classes from it; for example:

```
class NUMERIC <T>
{
private:
  T value;

public:

  // Numeric operations

};

class SmallInteger : public NUMERIC<short>
{
```

```
public:

  // Possible extensions and redefinitions

}
```

Similarly, we could define other integer-based classes.

8. Static member data play the role of the global objects for classes.

```
Full_time employee
  Company-wide normal working week
```

The solutions for file access and allocation of disk space are left to the student.

9. Keep it simple (always)!
Small is beautiful
Document what you are doing
Keep class declaration and definition separate

Chapter 5

Left as student research projects.

Chapter 6

1. Left to the student.

2. Left to the student.

3. This could function as a team project. This problem is discussed in Rumbaugh *et al.* (1991) and it could be interesting to see how concept mapping techniques simplify the analysis. Wirfs-Brock and Wilkerson (1989) also solve this problem by other techniques.
   Concentrate on the static, long-term relationships between the concept from the problem domain; this is called the canonical concept map. Furthermore, it is desirable to create concept maps for each of the 'use cases':

   Deposit

   Withdraw

   Transfer

   Query

   (More information on use cases and scenarios is given in Chapter 7.)

4. We extract the relevant offending pieces of text from the requirements document:

   Noise: 'Thus, the input can be viewed as sequence of words separated by breaks, with possibly leading and trailing breaks, and ending with ET', 'one ET character in each input stream'.

   Contradiction: 'line' and 'sequence of words' contradict each other.

   Ambiguity: 'on each line', 'up to the point of error'.

Overspecification: 'whose end is signalled with a special end-of-text character ET. There is exactly one ET character in each input stream', 'variable, Alarm', 'the value TRUE', 'and ending with ET'.

5. These are solved throughout this book. It is however, a good idea to discover them yourself!

6. This is part of the student project.

Chapter 7

1. The ATM problem could serve as the basis for a term project. It has been solved in Rumbaugh *et al.* (1991) and also in the book of Wirfs-Brock and Wilkerson (1989). You could solve this problem using concept maps, event-response lists and scenarios.

   We enumerate some events and their responses:

   E1: Customer inserts card
   R11: Customer asked to give card number

   E2: Customer gives card number
   R21: Card number validated

   E3: Customer gives amount to be withdrawn
   R31: Money withdrawn
   C31: There must be enough money in account

2. The event 'end-of-month' occurring causes data to be transferred to the host machine on which MPC runs and it causes the task which registers and validates data to be started.

   The response 'aggregate data to division and project level' cannot be fired unless the monthly data has been validated and corrected.

   A response (a sort of internal or output event) can be seen as an event. These have constraints. The external event 'read in monthly data' has the following constraints:

   It *must* be the end of the month
   Monthly data cannot be read in twice during the same period
   Monthly data cannot be read in zero times during the same period

   Thus, we could view MPC as a problem in which timing constraints (albeit, on a macro scale) play an important role.

3. The main scenarios are:

   Alarm Control
   Get Display Data
   Get Water Level
   Update Stored Data
   Pump Environment

Check WatchDog Timer

Pump Control

4. This problem is discussed in the answers section of Chapter 11. The main scenarios are:

   Register personnel information and work schedules

   Register patient

   Checkout of patient

   - To operation theatre
   - Let patient go home

   Operate on patient

   Checkin of patient from theatre back to ward

5. MPC

   - Initialize/modify project information
   - Read in monthly data
     - validate data
     - correct data
   - Update monthly data
     - aggregate to division level
     - aggregate to project level

   PPD

   - Customer delivery
     - normal delivery
     - abnormal (customer absconds)
   - Customer payment
   - Tank level monitoring

6. Left to the student.

7. The full problem specification is taken from Williams (1994). The tank abstraction has been worked out for problem PPD (see answers for Chapter 13). This problem forms the basis for a student project.

   As in Williams (1994), we concentrate on pump control. The modes of operation can be found from event-response lists (see the technique in the answers for Chapter 13):

   Operating: normal WLMS operation

   Shutdown: Water level is outside established safe limits

   Standby: WLMS is shutdown but ready to operate pending user action (default entry state)

   Test: WLMS is shutdown and presenting test date to the user

   We identify the superstate 'Shutdown' which has subordinate state 'Standby' which in its turn has subordinate state 'Test'.

Allowable failure modes are:

AllOK: all devices are operating OK

BadLevDev: The device monitoring the water level has failed

HardFail: The WLMS itself has failed

The pumps must shut down whenever the system enters the states Standby and AllOK or Test and AllOK modes or when the failure mode is BadLevDev or HardFail in any operating (no constraints). Thus, we see shutdown as a response to multiple events. The event-response lists are:

E1: WLMS fails
R11: Shutdown

E2: Monitor device fails
R21: Shutdown

E3: WLMS enters Standby mode
R31: Shutdown
C31: All devices working OK (AllOK mode)

E3: WLMS enters Test mode
R31: Shutdown
C31: All devices working OK (AllOK mode)

If the operating mode is Shutdown and the failure mode is AllOK no event will change the pump status. If the operator presses the reset button and the operating mode is Operating and the failure mode is AllOK the status of the pumps remains unchanged until the button is released, at which point they are turned on.

8. Left to the student. (*Hints*: `Issue` is a client of `Journal` and a server for `Article`.)
9. Solved in Chapter 9.
10. Student project.
11. Entity objects are `Article`, `Journal` etc. Interface objects are difficult to find because this is a simple problem. Control objects are `CirculationList` and `Attention-List`.

Chapter 8

1. The most general situation is many-to-many. We recommend that you do not lose too much sleep about multiplicity in the analysis phase and to make all relationships many-to-many. These can always be specialized to one-to-many or even one-to-one in the design phase.

   Guidelines are:

Make everything many-to-many (at least initially)

Consider the one-to-many and one-to-one cases

Document your decisions! (these are assumptions)

We take one example to show what we mean, namely

'An issue is an appearance of a journal'

The relationship is many-to-many when an issue may appear in many journals and a journal has many appearances. Special cases are when an issue appears in one journal, in which case the association is one-to-many.

The other examples are left as a student exercise.

2. The ternary association 'An employee works on a project for a department' can be decomposed into the binary associations

   Employee works on project

   Employee is seconded to a department

   The other examples are left as a student exercise. In some cases a qualifier is needed.

   Examples of converting ternary associations to binary associations are given in Rumbaugh *et al.* (1991).

3. Programmer
   How many lines of code per month

   Years of experience

   Profit centre
   Annual profit/loss

   The other examples are left as a student exercise.

4. Roles are trader, senior trader, market maker, counterparty (could be a customer or a bank), buyer and fool. Risk management applications use a variety of so-called derivative products.

   A swap is an agreement between two parties and it can be seen as a role for a general association between two classes. There are different kinds of swap, namely interest rate swaps, currency swaps, amortizing swaps and forward start swaps. These correspond to specializations of basic swaps and each has its own peculiar behaviour.

   A bond is a debt instrument requiring the issuer (the so-called debtor or borrower) to repay the lender/investor the amount borrowed plus interest over some predefined period of time. There are numerous types of bonds; for a discussion, see Fabozzi (1993).

   Some examples of this type of application are given in Section 15.10.

5. We can view table, bridge and road as roles for arch. Can you think of behaviour for these roles? (*Hint:* a table has space for a number of guests, a certain amount of leg room etc.; a bridge has a certain span and can take a certain load.)

6. Issue: Issue volume and number

   Article: Title

   Reader: topic(s)

Department: department number

7. Journal: Title

   Issue: Title + volume + number

   Title + month + year

   Article: Issue + title of article

   Reader: Company number

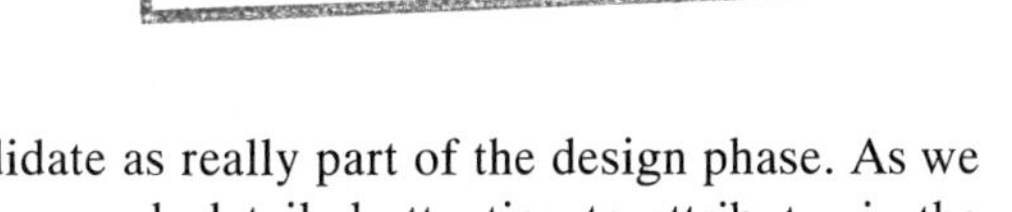

We see the use of qualifiers and candidate as really part of the design phase. As we have already said, we should not pay too much detailed attention to attributes in the analysis phase; behaviour, control and processes are much more important.

8. Circulation list

   Attributes

   The duration that a reader may have access to the journal (there will be a default global attributes for all readers and journals)

   Start date that a reader may have access

   Validated (Y/N) (permission from management)

   Reason for being on circulation list

9. Student exercise. This is fairly easy since the exact requirements are described in Section 6.5.3. Use the concept maps in Figures 6.9 and 6.10.

Chapter 9

1. This is a problem which is of vital importance in distributed computing and object-oriented database technology (e.g. ObjectStore) in network environments.

   The main objective of this exercise is to get an idea of how objects communicate with each other in a distributed environment.

   E1: Client contacts server

   R11: Server responds

   R12: Data is transferred to client

   R13: Connection is broken

   E2: Client locks remote object

   E3: Server becomes aware of its client

   R31: Client added to server's acquaintance list

   E4: Server contacts a client about availability of services (callback)

   Events E2, E3 and E4 have corresponding responses. Can you think of any?
   Some typical scenarios are:

   Client successfully contacts primary server

   Secondary server takes over from primary server

Client successfully locks object

Most of the above events and scenarios can be deduced from the text in Section 9.3.1.

Creating event classes is tantamount to determining how the above events can be parametrized to include arguments for the networks locations of clients and servers, type of data transferred and whether an operation was successful. For example, a client may wish to send a string to a remote server; the syntax is

```
send (Node client, Node server, String info);
```

The class `Node` represents a host in a computer network, for example, TCP/IP, DECnet or SNA. TCP/IP hosts use a 32-bit addressing scheme, while DECnet uses a 16-bit scheme for uniquely addressing hosts in a local or wide area network.

2. This is fairly simple as it involves introducing a third button C which when pressed increments seconds in the watch. (See also Harel (1988); Harel *et al.* (1987, 1988), where even more complicated examples of watches are given.)

3. This is an interesting extension to SDW. Such an extension is needed for lazy people who wish to set their watch in 'either direction'; for example, if the current time is 11:00 hours and we wish to set the time to 10:59 it would be very useful to have buttons to allow us to decrement the hour and minute values.

4. Left to the student.

5. This is a chain reaction of length 3 since the event n triggers the response f, which in its turn triggers g. Chain reactions can be discovered from event–response lists.

6. Figure 9.15 is a simplified version of a statechart for problem PPD. The states for pump are `Enabled`, `Disabled` and `Pumping`. The states for `Motor` are `On`, `Off` and `StandbyMode`. The states for the gun–holster assembly are `Active` and `NonActive`. The states for `Clutch` are `Free` and `Engaged`. Discovering object states for PPD and in the general case is fully discussed in the answers for Chapter 13.

   The correct set of states for the pump assembly object is:

   ```
   Enabled
   Disabled
   GunRemoved
   TriggerDepressed
   TriggerReleased
   GunReplaced
   ```

   Finding states is discussed in the answers to Chapter 13.

7. This is a special case of a problem which is in essence quite general in nature. We could apply the results in this exercise to a variety of real-world applications, such as:

   Bug fixing and software enhancements in a development group

   Registering and solving complaints in a bank

   Applications in which information is transferred between different groups using a message-passing metaphor

   A subsystem in a customer database system (CDB)

Looking at this problem in an abstract way enables us to discover the following concepts:

Problem initiator (e.g. customer group, dealer, developer)

Problem (e.g. call, complaint, bug fix)

Solver (e.g. help desk, system support, bank manager)

The use case concepts correspond to the following subsystems:

Problem registration

Problem allocation

Query subsystem

Problem closure (solving the problem)

Historical database (e.g. for capacity planning)

One or more events may cause the above subsystems to 'trigger'. The major event–response lists are:

E1: Signal a new problem

R11: Register problem

R12: Assign problem to specialist group

E2: Close problem

R21: Notify all interested parties

R22: Log problem data for future post-mortems

E3: Problem has not been solved within a certain period

R31: Start escalation procedure

The possible states for a problem are `{OPENED, PENDING, WARNINGZONE, OVERDUEZONE, CLOSED}`. Notice that these states are very closely related to the events E1, E2 and E3.

Some possible scenarios are:

A problem is opened and solved within the given period

A problem goes into a warning zone

A customer is informed about the status of a problem

The marketing department wishes to know about the types of problems

The training department may wish to know whether customers need special training (e.g. in the use of a word processor)

The level 1 concepts in this problem are `CustomerGroup`, `Call` and `ServiceGroup`. Lower level concepts are needed which correspond to queues of pending calls, expertise database, users and specialists. Furthermore, the system should have knowledge about the workload of the different support groups.

There is considerable role playing and hence opportunity for reusability.

Chapter 10

1. Normal scenarios
   - Motor running normally

   Exceptional scenarios
   - Motor is reset
   - Motor powers up via 'on assertion'

   Abnormal scenarios
   - Motor overheats

2. Left to the student. `Motor`, `OtSensor` and `StartingRelay` are servers for the aggregate object `MotorControl`. Actors and external events send messages to `MotorControl`, which in turn sends messages to its components.

3. This has been partly solved; the exercise is to finish it off.

Chapter 11

General remarks and hints on functional modelling We give an account of the steps to be taken in determining the products of the functional modelling process:

1. Determine which functionality is needed; each piece of functionality is a high level process and can usually be identified as a 'use case' concept map.
2. Do a levelling for each high level process (this is similar to how OMT does it, except that we map subprocesses to object operations at each step instead of mapping processes to object operations in the object design phase, as is done in OMT).
3. Use object diagrams to help in the identification of where to place responsibility for each operation. This is a client/server problem and distribution of responsibilities needs to be determined in this stage.
4. Stop when all subprocesses have been mapped to operations on the correct objects.

   The steps 1–4 can also be used to verify the complete analysis process; in particular, the following shortcomings may arise:

   - It is not possible to associate certain processes with objects; this may occur because we are missing vital abstractions. If this occurs, go back to the requirements phase. Some concepts may be missing.
   - It may not be possible to navigate in the object diagram; this may be due to certain data being unteachable or the multiplicity being incorrect. For example, the association 'interested in' between `Reader` and `Topic` in Figure 8.17 (JRP problem) should be many-to-many, because some processes may need to know which readers are interested in a given topic (we assume that there is more than one!).

Example Expand the process in SDW for setting the time to a given value; for example, we wish to set the time to 17:10 hours. The only way to do this is to use the 'A' and 'B' buttons. The parametrized process make use of a TIME server class which has a class interface for incrementing hours and minutes:

```
void set_time (TIME new_time)
{ // Set the time in watch to a given 'new_time'.
  // The return type 'void' means nothing is returned but
  // that the state of Watch is changed.

  // Go into display mode (this depends on where we are)
  if (mode == Minutes)
  {
    press_A();
    press_A();
  }

  if (mode == Display)
  {
    press_A();
  }

  // Postcondition: we are now in set Hour mode. We assume
  // we can ask what the current hour and minute values are
  // for the watch. The watch has the member functions
  //
  // current_hour()     give the current hour value
  // current_minute()   give the current minutes value
  //
  while (current_hour() != new_time.hour())
  {
    press_B();
  }

  // Set minutes
  press_A();
  while (current_minute() != new_time.minute())
  {
    press_B();
  }

}
```

We see in this simple example that new operations `Watch::current_hour()` and `Watch::current_minute()` need to be created if we are to be able to create this process.

An alternative to the above process would be to define it in terms of its constituent components for hours and minutes using the classes HOURS and MINUTES in Chapter 15 (see Section 15.9). The pseudocode is given by:

```
set_time(HOURS new_hour, MINUTES new_min)
```

```
{
  // Go into display mode (this depends on where we are)
  if (mode == Minutes)
  {
    press_A();
    press_A();
  }

  if (mode == Display)
  {
    press_A();
  }

  // Use the class interfaces of HOURS and MINUTES
  // In this case we assume that we have two functions in
  // watch for giving hours and minutes as integers
  while (current_hour_value() != new_hour.value())
  {
    press_B();
  }

  // Set minutes
  press_A();
  while (current_minute.value() != new_min.value())
  {
    press_B();
  }

}
```

Which function to choose in practice depends on our priorities; these are discussed in Section 15.9. This problem is related to the concepts of closed and open architectures, which are discussed in Section 14.2.7.

And now for the answers to the Exercises in Chapter 11.

1.
```
Register(Issue issue)
{ // Register an issue in JRP. This process must take
  // place when a new issue arrives in the personnel
  // department
     add(issue); // Add issue to knowledge base

     // Make the list of readers for dissemination
     create_circulation_list(issue);

     // Others interested in certain articles
     create_attention_list(issue);

}
```

One possible implementation of `create_attention_list()` is given in Section 15.2.2.

2. Apply steps 1–4 above. The main objective of SIG ('birds-of-feather') is to create groups of readers who are interested in a certain topic.

3. The main top-level processes are:

   A: Register personnel

   B: Checkin of patient

   C: Operate on patient

   Notice that two of these processes are related to each level 1 concept in the concept map in Figure 6.9. The third one was missed out during the requirements phase and it would be a good idea to look at the concept map again so that more loosely coupled subsystems can be created which correspond better with the desired functionality. It will certainly mean modifications to the concept maps in Figure 6.10.

   Process C can be broken into the following sequence of subprocesses:

   Determine the necessary resources

   Carry out operation

   Bring patient back to ward (or private room)

   We see that the subsystems B and C satisfy a peer-to-peer relationship. B needs to know which patients being operated on at the moment come back to the ward and C needs to know which patients are bound to have an operation at some time in the future. Each one knows about the existence of the other. We prefer to convert these to a client/server case (this is discussed in Section 14.2.5). We split the process 'Operate on patient' into the two simpler processes

   C1: Operations taking place now

   C2: Operations planned in the future

   In this case we shall have B as a client of C1 and C2 as a client of B. This process is called 'sandwiching'.

Chapter 12

1. Left to the student.

2. Constraints:

   It is not possible to aggregate data if not all monthly project data has been validated

   It is not possible to read in monthly data more than once in a given period

3. MPC is a simple planning project, but it has no idea of activities and the relationships which hold between them. In CPM, PERT and GERT applications an activity has the following attributes and properties:

   What are its critical activities?

   Earliest start date

Earliest finish date

Latest start date

Latest finish date

The amount of extra time (FLOAT)

We can introduce dependencies between activities. These are concerned with when one activity may or may not start as compared with another one. Examples are:

Activity 2 can start after completion of activity 1

Activity 2 cannot start before a certain date

Activity 2 cannot start until a number of other activities have been completed

Activity 2 can finish some time after activity 1 has completed

Activities 2 and 3 can start upon completion of activity 1

A typical project consists of a number of activities, and we wish to compute total time and identify the critical path.

Critical path methods (CPM) assume that a single value estimate of the time required for each activity is obtained. PERT (Program Evaluation and Review Technique), on the other hand, has facilities for determining several measures of performance. These are the most optimistic, most pessimistic and most likely completion times of a project.

4. Left to the student.

Chapter 13

General remarks and hints The petrol pump problem is special because it exhibits most of the things that we are interested in, for object aggregation structures (pump assembly), associations (the petrol line), real-time behaviour (events such as `enable_pump()` and so on) and it has a functional component as exemplified in the 'Customer Payment' concept map.

The concept map 'Delivery' is really a merged concept because it deals with both pump assemblies and the distribution of benzine to the pump from the tank via the petrol line and monitored by the metering device. It might be better to create a new level concept called 'Monitor' which consists of the tank, petrol line and metering device and whose function it is to monitor the benzine supply and check that the critical value of 4% capacity is discovered as soon as it arises.

The new 'subsystems' obey a client/server concept as follows:

`Customer_Payment` is a client of `Delivery`

`Monitor` is a client of `Delivery`

The interfaces between these subsystems are very narrow; `Monitor` needs to know about pump activities in `Delivery`, while `Customer_Payment` needs a delivery record (volume, grade and pump number) from `Delivery`.

Exceptions can be raised in the different subsystems (they could be called 'asynchronous system traps' (ASTs)), for example:

`Delivery`

A component breaks down or fails to respond

The gun has not been replaced in the holster within a given period of time

`Customer_Payment`

A transaction has not been paid within a certain time (if the customer absconds)

`Monitor`

A tank reaches critical level (this is an edge-triggered event)

From the object diagram in Figure 13.2 we see that the class 'Pump assembly' is an aggregate. We decide that this class is the receiver of all external events from the attendant or customer. It then delegates to its components later as it sees fit. For example, this class is the receiver of the event 'remove gun from holster'. Having received this event it then tells the class `Ghass` (gun–holster assembly) to do the actual execution. How this is done is the responsibility of the class `Ghass`.

There are other possibilities for assigning responsibility among the different objects in a distributed system; we have chosen this particular approach because we found it to be workable. This part of the process always involves applying the client/server paradigm to classes. In this case we can identify the following types (Section 2.9):

- The association formed between the pump, tank and petrol line is a master.
- `Display`, `Trigger`, `Clutch`, `Timer`, `Holster` and metering device are servants.
- `Motor` is possibly an agent (it may contain more than what we show in Figure 13.2).
- `Ghass` is an agent(it is a server of the pump and a client of `Gun` and `Holster`).

The relationships follow a closed architecture paradigm because the pump cannot directly access `Gun` or `Holster` but it must 'communicate' with these indirectly via `Ghass`. We could have chosen a flatter structure in which `Ghass` was absent and whereby `Gun` and `Holster` were placed directly under the pump class.

In order to create Harel charts for objects and classes it is necessary to have some way of discovering what their states are. These can be found from ER lists, in particular from the constraints and by reformulating events and responses in their passive forms (the postconditions). For example, the postconditions resulting from the following ER lists are:

E1: Enable pump
R11: Start pump motor
R12: Free clutch
R13: Clear display counters

They are rewritten in 'postcondition form' in order to discover the states, as follows:

E1_post: `Pump` is enabled (`PUMP_ENABLED`)
R11_post: `Motor` started (`MOTOR_STARTED`)
R12_post: `Clutch` freed (`CLUTCH_FREE`)
R13_post: `Display` cleared (`DISPLAY_CLEARED`)

Continuing in this way allows us to find all states for the classes in PPD. For example, the following states can be found:

1. `Pump`

   `(ENABLED, DISABLED, PUMPING)`

   We discovered the state `PUMPING` because we forgot to add the response R33 (an activity) defined as follows:

   R33: Pump petrol

   The petrol will be pumped for as long as the customer keeps the trigger depressed.

2. `Motor`

   `(ON, OFF, SHUTDOWN_MODE)`

3. `Ghass`

   `(ENABLED, DISABLED)`

4. `Clutch`

   `(FREE, ENGAGED)`

These modes determine new attributes for each class. For example, class `Motor` will have an attribute which we call `MotorState` and is defined in pseudo-C++ as an enumerated type as follows:

```
enum MotorState {ON, OFF, SHUTDOWN_MODE};
```

Possibilities for scenarios are:

Customer tanks for a certain volume of benzine

Customer tanks without paying

The tank levels reach critical level

A pump is put out of action

And now the answers to the exercises in Chapter 13.

1. In this case the multiplicity of `Ghass` in Figure 13.2 is not one-to-one with respect to the pump but is now many-to-one with the qualification that there is at least one `Ghass` instance in the aggregation.

2. We may need to be able to store all information about a transaction to include the type of payment, whether the customer bought items in the shop (oil, ice cream, magazines) and other relevant information for possible future marketing pitches and direct mailings (now you know how people can get your address!).

3. A `Tank` is a role for a `Vessel` (this is similar to the roles in the WLMS problem (see Exercise 7 in Chapter 7). This is a candidate for reusability.
   The interface for `Tank` is:

   ```
   class Tank
   {
   ```

```
private:
  Volume vol;                      // How much can it hold?
  Volume current;                  // How much is there now?
  // may be more ...

public:
  // Constructor
  Tank(Volume capacity);

  // Modifier
  void replenish();                // Fill until full
  void replenish(Volume vol);      // Fill

  // Selector
  Volume capacity() const;         // Total capacity
  Percentage level() const;        // Current volume
  Volume stock() const;            // Current volume

};
```

Class `Tank` has server classes `Volume` and `Percentage`.

4. This is a complicated association. It has an association with a single metering device, but there may be more at some later stage, which is the reason why we use an association instead of an embedded attribute.

   The link attributes of interest in this case could be:

   Total number of pulses sent after initialization

   Diameter of line

   Length of line

   It may be necessary to add more attributes if we demand more reliability in the system, for example sensor data.

5. Left to the student. The interfaces will be determined by their responsibilities in the current problem and by what they must do for the aggregate class 'Pump assembly'.

Chapter 14

1. The concept patient is reused in `Consulting`, `Intake` and `Operation`. Thus, discovering a class in one use case means that it can be reused in new ones. This is also the Jacobson idea.

2. Student project. Particular attention should be paid to reliability and good response time.

3. `Payment` is a client of `Delivery` since it uses the delivery information from that subsystem (volume, grade and pump number).

4. We think that we are solving very general problems, but the hospital problem is in fact a role for something. Discovering the 'something' is difficult and is a process of discovery. The hospital database system is an example of a resource allocation problem.

5. The class levels are:

   `Natural`, `Integer`

   `Rational`

   `Complex`

   `Imaginary` (a special type of complex number)

   There are two ways to implement `Imaginary`, first as s derived class of `Complex` (real part=0) or by using delegation by ensuring that each imaginary number is suitably massaged into its complex equivalent, as the following C++ code shows for creating instances:

```
class Imaginary
{
private:
  Complex c;

public:
  Imaginary(double im_part)
       { c = Complex(0.0, im_part);}
};
```

6. Closed architecture:

```
class RATIONAL
{
private:
  INTEGER num;      // Numerator
  INTEGER den;      // Denominator
};
```

   An even more clever implementation, which is due to John Carolan, is the 'Cheshire Cat' approach:

```
class RATIONAL
{
private:
  INTEGER* num;     // Numerator
  INTEGER* den;     // Denominator
};
```

   Class `RATIONAL` has no knowledge about the static properties of `INTEGER`; this means that the implementation of `INTEGER` can be changed without recompiling `RATIONAL`. A useful consequence is that you do not need to deliver the source code of `RATIONAL` to your customers (it contains your intellectual property). You can give them the source code of `INTEGER`, thereby letting them customize your products to their environment. This technique in used in CommonView, a portable GUI application.

Open architecture:

```
class RATIONAL
{
private:
  long num;    // Numerator
  long den;    // Denominator
};
```

7. The main objective of a print subsystem is to print files that enter the subsystem via some type of priority queue. A print subsystem consists of a print server and a number of specific types of printer, for example dot matrix or laser printers. Possible exceptions are:

   Paper needs to be loaded (notify operator)

   Printer has failed; impossible to print

   Contents of a file are corrupted; file is partially printed

   Print subsystem resources exceeded

   A good treatment of a print subsystem is given in Wirfs-Brock *et al.* (1990).

8. Array exceptions

   Unable to allocate memory

   Indexing error (range error)

9. Left to the student. Use the definitions in Section 14.2.8.

   Essential exceptions could be called external exceptions while non-essential exceptions could be called internal exceptions.

10. The following problems could be successfully solved by relational database technology: MPC and JRP. The other applications use complex data structures and have complicated behaviour, and object-oriented database systems may be more useful.

Chapter 15

1. High-level design allows us to implement the solution in different languages, such as Smalltalk, C++ and relational database systems. Low-level design usually focuses on one language and its idiosyncrasies.

2. Left to the student. See Hatley and Pirbhai (1988).

3. These are mainly the help classes/tables for aggregating data.

4. Student project.

5. Student project.

6. Student project.

7. Student project.

8. The class interface for `Dictionary` is:

```
// gdict.hxx
//
// Class which represents a dictionary.
//
// The following operations are applicable to
// dictionaries:
//
//    - Add a new name to the dictionary
//    - Add a new group of names to the dictionary
//    - Determine whether a given name is in the dictionary
//    - Access the information associated with a given name
//    - Add new information for a given name
//    - Delete a name or group of names from the dictionary
//
// Assumptions about the data types 'Key' and 'Value'.
//
//    - Key names are unique
//    - Several instances may occur of a single value
//
// © Datasim BV 1994

#ifndef DSGDICTIONARY_HXX
#define DSGDICTIONARY_HXX

#include "gset.cxx"

template <class Key, class Value> class DSGDICTIONARY
{  // Key == key, Value == value

private:
  // ... Implementation not important at this stage

public:
  // Constructors
  DSGDICTIONARY();
  DSGDICTIONARY(const DSGDICTIONARY& syt2);
  DSGDICTIONARY(const DSGSET<Key>& kwl);
  DSGDICTIONARY(const DSGSET<Key>& kwl,const Value& val);

  // Modifiers
  // Interactions with elements

  void add(const Key& element);
  // Add a Key element

  void add(const Key& element, const Value& val);
  // Add a Key element plus its information value
```

```
  void remove(const Key& element);
  // Remove an element from the dictionary

  void replace(const Key& t1, const Key& t2);
  // Replace t1 by t2 in the dictionary

  void modify(const Value& val);
  // All keys have corresponding value val
  // Get and set a value in the dictionary by using
  // references

  Value& value(const Key& name);
  // Give the value corresponding to a certain name
  // keyword

  Value& value(const Key& name) const;
  // Const value function

  // Special functions for adding and modifying info field
  void modify(const Key& name, const Value& val);
  // The key 'name' now assumes the value 'val'

  // Selectors
  DSBOOLEAN empty() const;
  // Is the dictionary empty?

  DSGSET<Key> keywords() const;
  // Return the corresponding keyword set

  DSGBAG<Value> values() const;
  // Return the array of information items

  DSGSET<Key> keys(const Value& v) const;
  // Give the keys having the value 'v'

  size_t size() const;
  // The number of entries

  DSBOOLEAN includes(const Key& name);
  // Is the key in the dictionary

  // Operator overloading
  DSGDICTIONARY<Key, Value>& operator =
      (const DSGDICTIONARY<Key, Value>& sym2);
  // The assignment operator
};
```

```
#endif
```

The class interface for the general association object is:

```
// gassobj.hxx
//
// A class representing association objects between
// generic objects. Only binary associations (that is,
// between pairs of objects). This is implemented
// using dictionaries for quick access.
//
// This class typically represents many-to-many
// associations.
//
// The responsibilities of this class are:
//
//    1. Manage relationships between pairs of objects
//    2. Ensure the integrity of the associations (for
//       example, referential integrity constraints)
//    3. It models associations in OMT (Object Modelling
//       Technique)
//    4. It is possible to make derived specializations of
//       it for particular types of applications.
//
// © Datasim BV 1994

#ifndef DSGASSOCOBJECT_HXX
#define DSGASSOCOBJECT_HXX

#include "gconst.hxx"x
#include "gdict.cxx"
#include "gset.cxx"

template <class L, class R> class DSGASSOCOBJECT
{

private:
    DSGDICTIONARY<L, DSGSORTEDLIST<R> > fl; // Forward link
    DSGDICTIONARY<R, DSGSORTEDLIST<L> > bl; // Backward link

    size_t sz;

    // Implement as two dictionaries for efficiency

  public:
    // Constructors
    DSGASSOCOBJECT();
    // Default Constructor
```

```
    DSGASSOCOBJECT(const DSGASSOCOBJECT<L,R>& g2);
    // Copy Constructor

    // Destructor
    ~DSGASSOCOBJECT();

    // Accessing and selector functions
    size_t size() const;
    // Number of entries on association

    DSGSET<R>& forward_list(const L& left);
    // The list of objects associated with 'left' object

    DSGSET<L>& backward_list(const R& right);
    // The list of objects associated with 'right' object

    // Boolean functions
    DSBOOLEAN hasLmember(const L& left)const;
    // Does left play a role in the association?

    DSBOOLEAN hasRmember(const L& right)const;
    // Does right play a role in the association?

    DSBOOLEAN link(const L& left,const R&  right);
    // Is there a link between left and right

    // Modifier functions
    void add(const L& left, const R& right);
    // Add a new association object

    void removel(const L& left);
    // Remove all occurrences of left

    void remover(const R& right);
    // Remove all occurrences of right

    // Operator overloading
    DSGASSOCOBJECT<L,R>& operator =
        (const DSGASSOCOBJECT<L,R>& g2);
    // The assignment operator

};

#endif
```

9. Left to the student. (*Hint*: use Exercise 8.)

10. Left to the student.

11. Left to the student. This should be found by using scenarios.

12. These roles for PPD can be found in the answers for Chapter 13. For MPC we can give some clues:

    `Project` is a master

    `Department` is a client of `Division`

Chapter 16

1. Left to the student.

2.
```
Surgeon(name, address, phone)
Consultant(name, speciality)
Patient(number, ward#, name, address, phone,
date_of_birth, sex, blood_group)
PrivatePatient(number, name, room)
Nurse(staff#, name, address, phone, sex, grade)
Theatre(number, theatre-type)
Operation(op#, name, theatre#, patient#, op-type, date,
time)
Supervises(surgeon-name, consultant-name)
Assists(op#, name, role)
WardAssign(staff#, ward#, date-assigned)
Theatre(staff#, theatre#, date-assigned)
```

3. Left to the student.

4. Left to the student.

References

F. J. Fabozzi (1993) *Bond Markets: Analysis and Strategies*, Prentice-Hall, Englewood Cliffs NJ.

J. V. Guttag and J. J. Horning (1978) The algebraic specifications of abstract data types, *Acta Informatica*, **10** 27–52.

D. Harel (1988) On visual formalisms, *Communications of the ACM*, **31**(5) May.

D. Harel *et al.* (1987) On the formal semantics of statecharts, *Proceedings of Symposium on Logic in Computer Science.*

D. Harel *et al.* (1988) STATEMATE: a working environment for the development of complex reactive systems, *10th International Conference on Software Engineering.*

D. J. Hatley and I. A. Pirbhai (1988) *Strategies for Real-Time System Specification*, Dorset House Publishing, New York.

B. Meyer (1988) *Object-Oriented Software Construction*, Prentice-Hall, Englewood Cliffs NJ.

J. Rumbaugh, M. Blaha, W. Premerlani, F. Eddy and W. Lorensen (1991) *Object-Oriented Modeling and Design*, Prentice-Hall, Englewood Cliffs NJ.

S. Sengupta and C. P. Korobkin (1994) *C++ Object-Oriented Datastructures*, Springer, Berlin.

D. K. Smith (1982) *Network Optimization Practice, A Computational Guide*, Ellis Horwood, Chichester.

L. G. Williams (1994) Assessment of safety-critical specifications, *IEEE Software*, January (Special Issue on Safety-Critical Systems).

R. Wirfs-Brock and B. Wilkerson (1989) Object-oriented design: a responsibility-driven approach, *Sigplan Notices*, **2**(10).

R. Wirfs-Brock, B. Wilkerson and L. Wiener (1990) *Designing Object-Oriented Software*, Prentice-Hall, Englewood Cliffs NJ.

Index